LUST
ON TRIAL

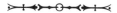

CENSORSHIP
AND THE RISE OF
AMERICAN OBSCENITY
IN THE AGE OF
ANTHONY COMSTOCK

AMY WERBEL

COLUMBIA
UNIVERSITY
PRESS
NEW YORK

Columbia University Press
Publishers Since 1893
New York   Chichester, West Sussex
cup.columbia.edu
Copyright © 2018 Columbia University Press
All rights reserved

Library of Congress Cataloging-in-Publication Data
Names: Werbel, Amy Beth, author.
Title: Lust on trial : censorship and the rise of American obscenity in the age of
Anthony Comstock / Amy Werbel.
Description: New York : Columbia University Press, 2018. | Includes bibliographical
references and index.
Identifiers: LCCN 2017042441 (print) | LCCN 2017049977 (e-book) |
ISBN 9780231547031 (e-book) | ISBN 9780231175227 (cloth: alk paper)
Subjects: LCSH: Comstock, Anthony, 1844-1915. | New York Society for the
Suppression of Vice. | Censorship—United States—History. | Obscenity (Law)—
United States—History. | United States—Moral conditions.
Classification: LCC HV6705 (e-book) | LCC HV6705 W47 2018 (print) |
DDC 306.77/1097309034—dc23
LC record available at https://lccn.loc.gov/2017042441

Columbia University Press books are printed on permanent
and durable acid-free paper.
Printed in the United States of America

Cover design: Philip Pascuzzo
Cover image: *Bernarr Macfadden's Women's Physical Culture Competition*, 1903.
Photograph. H. J. Lutcher Stark Center for Physical Culture & Sport.
The University of Texas, Austin.

For the Defense

CONTENTS

....

ILLUSTRATIONS

....

FIGURES

PLATES

LUST ON TRIAL

INTRODUCTION

....

I n 1888, a great scandal burst onto the front page of New York
newspapers. A young man named La Grange Brown had taken
photographs of nude young women in his parents' posh home at
100 Hicks Street in Brooklyn Heights. The Heights was prized then as
now not only for its stately homes and elegant churches, but also especially for its spectacular views of Manhattan, just across the East River.
News coverage of the story was profuse. The *New York World* reported that
police had taken Brown into custody, along with 239 negatives and 520
pictures that "are the counterfeit presentment of women and young girls
in the giddy garb of Nature, and it is whispered that some of the females
who have had their charms focused by young Brown are the daughters of
highly respectable families."[1]

The discovery of Brown's enterprise was not the result of intrepid
police work but instead stemmed from a tip from Anthony Comstock,
Inspector for the United States Post Office Department and Secretary
of the New York Society for the Suppression of Vice (NYSSV). A few
days before the raid, a gentleman visited Comstock's office and told him
that "while he was waiting for a 'prescription' at the saloon of Valentine
Schmitt in Brooklyn the evening before, a young man had exhibited to

a throng of people there obscene pictures of nude females." When Comstock and two police officers went to find Brown, they discovered him drunk in Schmitt's saloon. Upon being apprehended, Brown warned Comstock and the officers that he had wired his studio to electrocute any attempted interlopers. Undoubtedly skeptical of Brown's drunken boast, the three men carried him back to his house, where they unfortunately discovered that he had not lied.

When a detective opened the door to the "laboratory," he received a shock from a "current of electricity." Inside the secretive lair, Brown was found to have "all the latest appliances," including "instruments used by microscopists," and plates and photographs "from life, and several were evidently taken by a flash light, instantaneous process worked with an electrical or clock-work appliance, for the subject of them was Brown himself with a nude or partly nude female on his knee. Some of the women had modesty enough that they hid their faces with their hands or arms, and others turned their faces away from the camera." When Comstock grilled Brown as to the subjects of the pictures, he backed off his claim that they were respectable local women and instead insisted that they were "naturally women of loose morals; the majority of them women who have passed beyond the pale of society."[2] The case ended on a dramatic note when Brown forfeited his $1,000 bail and ran away to Canada, where he died of unknown causes the following year, "off among strangers."[3]

The evidence we have today of what actually happened in Brooklyn Heights is scant, but the episode nevertheless is illuminating about the state of production, distribution, and suppression of photographs of nudes at the height of Anthony Comstock's career as a professional censor. First, we may note that Brown's paranoia about the possibility of arrest was extreme but not unwarranted. By 1888, New Yorkers were well aware that the penalties for breaking obscenity laws were harsh. They also knew Anthony Comstock's name and the address of the NYSSV, where they could report items they found offensive, such as Brown's photographs. Witness fees, set at a percentage of the penalties assessed, served as incentive for individuals to come forward.

As in most of the legal proceedings in which Comstock was involved, the Brown case raised important issues of class and social standing. Were they already "loose," or had Brown damaged the good reputations of "respectable" women? All of this seemed to make a big difference in how the story was told and its meaning. Reporters of course were fascinated by the idea of girls in "the giddy garb of Nature." They also enthusiastically reported on all the new technologies in Brown's home, including his amateur electrified security system, "flash" lighting, and "microscopists" equipment. This was an age filled with innovations, and a constantly changing array of visual culture. Brown limited the display and sale of his photographs to the homosocial setting of a saloon and only to other men, which was typical of the manner in which "photographs from life" circulated in the nineteenth century. But unlike in previous decades, now even respectable newspapers covered this type of story, thus making it available to any reader, male or female and young or old.

The simple economic reality was that the exploits of Anthony Comstock sold newspapers. He was America's go-to man for obscenity, and a lightning rod for controversy that made good copy. If Comstock wasn't physically in your hometown during his career between 1873 and 1915, he was there in your hometown newspaper, fighting the purveyors of vice on the streets and in court, weighing in as a critic of art, theater, and literature, suffering editorial and physical attacks from his many enemies, being defended by ministers and moralists, and lampooned as a Puritanical knucklehead. Comstock dramatically changed American law and culture in ways that still resonate with us today. More than any other American in history, Comstock made vice, and vice suppression, into industries of monumental proportions, mutually bound in an ongoing cycle of production and suppression.[4]

Comstock's biographers have been remarkably consistent in framing their subject over the course of more than a century. Charles Gallaudet Trumbull titled his authorized hagiography *Anthony Comstock, Fighter* in 1913. Heywood Broun and Margaret Leech chose *Anthony Comstock: Roundsman of the Lord* in 1927, and Anna Louise Bates used one of Comstock's own favorite monikers, *Weeder in the Garden of the Lord*, in 1995.

These bellicose designations, "fighter," "roundsman," and "weeder," are in no way misleading. From childhood, Comstock framed the narrative of his life along the lines of one of the most popular hymns of his era: to be a "follower" of Christ meant being a "Soldier of the Cross."[5]

Lust on Trial contributes a wealth of new archival information to our understanding of Comstock's life, via research in public and private libraries, archives, museums, and historic newspaper databases.[6] These materials allow a new view of the trials Comstock faced during his arduous life, and the spiritual and intellectual filters through which he understood the world and his place in it. Seen through a clearer lens, Anthony Comstock is not a typically heroic biographical subject whose deeds outweighed his flaws. Nonetheless, his story is important because his life affected not only so many individuals during his own time, but also the course of American intellectual, cultural, sexual, and legal history.

In addition to these biographies, in the last two decades a wide variety of scholars have written about Anthony Comstock as relevant to the histories of law, literature, sociology, sexuality, journalism, publishing, and politics. Of these, my work relies most heavily on Helen Lefkowitz Horowitz's *Rereading Sex: Battles Over Sexual Knowledge and Suppression in Nineteenth-Century America* (2003), Donna Dennis's *Licentious Gotham: Erotic Publishing and Its Prosecution in Nineteenth-Century New York* (2009), and Geoffrey R. Stone's *Sex and the Constitution: Sex, Religion, and Law from America's Origins to the Twenty-First Century* (2017). In *Rereading Sex*, Horowitz explores the multiple dynamic, distinct, and conflicting conversations about sexuality evident in American literature and culture before 1883. Dennis's work demonstrates the many unintended consequences of Comstock's early suppression efforts, especially in spreading the trade to more sites of production across the country. Following on these examples with analysis of an expanded range of years and individual cases, *Lust on Trial* draws a broader picture of the evolution of American desires and fantasies, the means used to satisfy them, and American regulatory mechanisms to curtail them as they evolved before World War I. This effort complements Geoffrey Stone's much more ambitious survey, by focusing on the efforts of one especially potent religious zealot as he attempted to make America a more Christian nation by policing its sexual habits.[7]

In chapter 1, I look closely at Comstock's childhood in Connecticut, including his family's genealogy, economic, political, and social contexts, and especially the beliefs about religion, visual culture, and sexuality that provided the foundation for his intellectual and spiritual development. As a child in New Canaan, Comstock experienced a seamless theocratic power structure in which the same ideologies and individuals governed home, church, school, and municipality. His early exposure to erotic prints is typical of the surfeit of this material even in rural areas in the middle of the nineteenth century. Chapter 1 ends with a recounting of Comstock's actions and experiences as a soldier in the Civil War, his employment as a clerk in Manhattan in the late 1860s, and then his marriage and purchase of a home in Brooklyn in 1871. During these early years, Comstock developed his very particular obsession with the prevention of lust through censorship. It was in Connecticut that Comstock formed his view of America as a Christian nation, governed by God's laws.

Chapter 2 charts Comstock's early vigilante efforts to suppress liquor and pornography sales and then his fortuitous meeting in 1872 with leaders of the Young Men's Christian Association (YMCA), who had already been active in combatting similar vices. In Comstock they found an agent willing to wage war against offenders, and they used their combined wealth and political power to form a new organization, the NYSSV, to support his efforts. In its early years, the NYSSV was enormously successful at passing sweeping new state and federal anti-obscenity laws. Comstock's position was unique; as an agent of the Post Office Department, he had the power to act as a federally appointed censor of mailed material. Comstock broadly interpreted his position as empowering him to enforce specifically Christian ideology among the masses.

From defendants such as the notorious Victoria Woodhull, Comstock quickly learned how to use publicity to make his name a household word. Through trial and error in these years as well, Comstock learned how best to investigate and indict those who trafficked in arousing materials. He also learned to use the same materials he confiscated as effective show-and-tell presentations to build support for his cause among wealthy men. Under Comstock's guidance, the NYSSV focused its efforts on crushing women who preached sexual liberation, or even simply advocated recognition of female desire.

Chapters 3 through 5, the bulk of the book, are framed by the very literal boundaries of the three volumes of "Records of Arrests" in which Comstock chronicled the efforts he made to defeat Satan in America. In chapter 3, we see Comstock gradually evolve from utter frustration at the unwillingness of courts to convict his defendants in 1872 to vastly increased powers and success by the end of Volume I in 1884. Materials he managed to destroy or suppress in these years include illustrated books, pamphlets, newspapers, sexually explicit photographs, "articles to aid seduction," contraceptives, burlesque and brothel performances, and "classical" art and literature. By the end of this volume, Comstock's effectiveness was greatly enhanced by judicial implementation of the expansive *Hicklin* test of obscenity, adopted during trials of Free Thought advocate D. M. Bennett in 1879 and art dealer Edmund Bonaventure in 1883.

Chapter 4 covers arrests chronicled in Volume II between 1884 and 1895, years during which Comstock reached the peak of his powers and then began a bitter and unhappy descent in the public eye, fueled by brutal opposition from criminal defendants and an increasing number of attorneys determined to thwart censorship and expand civil liberties. American art dealers and artists, including Edmund Knoedler, Napoleon Sarony, Thomas Eakins, and members of the Society of American Artists, vigorously protested against the idea that photographs of nude models and paintings and sculptures of nudes should be deemed "obscenities."

Attempts to suppress images most community members accepted as art provoked an uprising of artists, who rebelled in part by representing nudes with increasingly graphic specificity. Comstock, in many cases, effectively publicized images he condemned rather than successfully suppressing them. Pictures of females wearing tights or cross-dressing as men became extremely popular as theatrical entertainments, then as souvenirs on the streets, and soon spread through the rapidly expanding industries of photography and commercial advertising. Opportunists even created new and profitable private anti-vice societies during the last years of the nineteenth century. Some of these, such as Charles Parkhurst's Society for the Prevention of Crime, were legitimate, but others served as little more than façades for blackmail. In both cases, competition for prosecutorial targets diluted the efforts of the NYSSV at the same time that Progressive Era social reformers began insisting that civil servants and police, rather than private societies, take responsibility for law enforcement.

Comstock's efforts to remove erotic visual culture from homosocial spheres such as saloons (both low and high) contributed to his increasing personal and professional difficulties in sustaining friendships and political support. Despite his many seizures, "obscenities" flourished, not merely in New York City but in far-flung corners of the country as well, as faster transportation networks enabled the flow of commerce. Speech about pornography in the public sphere also vastly increased during these years, as stories about Comstock's raids and targets were reprinted across the country. Americans responded to this new information, and the new sense of threat posed by Comstock, in extraordinarily diverse ways, ranging from self-censorship to even more loudly broadcasting their diverse sexual expressions.

Finally, chapter 5 follows Comstock's descent from 1895 to his death in 1915. Volume III begins with the 1893 World's Columbian Exposition, in which viewers were both shocked and thrilled to see a level of public exposure of nudity never before exhibited in America, in statuary, paintings, photography, and live performances. Artists including Augustus Saint-Gaudens and Frederick MacMonnies used the opportunity to vastly expand the size and specificity of details in their nude statuary. On the controversial "Midway" in Chicago, performers presented stereotypical views of scantily clad belly dancers and Dahomean villagers. This influential exhibition set a new standard for public display of the nude that thwarted Comstock's best efforts to use censorship to shape a less sexualized public discourse.

In these same years, the original members of the NYSSV gradually died, depleting the organization's funds. Comstock's personal difficulties also contributed to his diminishing well of support. The Woman's Christian Temperance Union (WCTU) organized committees in the 1890s to support purity efforts, and particularly to suppress the display of the body in tights in *tableaux vivants*, also known as Living Pictures exhibitions. Comstock should have collaborated with these natural allies, but instead fought over petty matters in order to preserve his own smug stature as the chief if not sole arbiter of obscenity in the country. Undermining his efforts to preserve power, a new generation of writers, artists, and lawyers took direct aim, caricaturing the aging censor mercilessly with visual and textual barbs, and even physical assaults. Comstock's decline was matched by a concomitant rise of lawyers devoted to supporting the rights of defendants in obscenity trials. Their efforts, and organizations they formed such as the Free Speech League and National Defense Association, laid the foundation for the remarkable expansion of First, Fourth, and Fifth Amendment protections in landmark cases of the twentieth century.

While legal arguments proceeded, outside the courtroom technology experienced remarkable growth and innovation that changed the conversation. Volume III describes dirty songs on wax cells for phonographs, peep-show machines with early films of raunchy subjects, and vast numbers of photographic postcards illustrating sexual jokes. When Comstock raided the Art Students League in New York in 1906, artists including John Sloan, George Bellows, and Robert Henri rebelled, painting nudes often inspired by these new technologies for erotic display and vigorously supporting Comstock's famous defendants, including the anarchist and feminist Emma Goldman. Just as Comstock's career began with the prosecution of a powerful woman, Victoria Woodhull, it ended with another "rebel," Margaret Sanger. Comstock died during the trial of her husband William for circulating her pamphlet describing birth control techniques.

Several terms and concepts are useful to consider at the outset of this text. The word "censor" derives from the Roman concept of an assessor, someone in power to review and regulate the conduct of others. While the concept of censorship may originally have been based on the idea of a singular person exerting control over others, it has since evolved into a far more complex array of actions and reactions. Comstock most typically engaged in "direct censorship" when he seized and destroyed materials to prevent their public circulation.[8] Direct censorship in any society, no matter how repressive, is just one means through which discourse is limited. Concern about the possibility of censorship in many cases results in an unwillingness of artists and writers to risk producing potentially indictable work, resulting in self-censorship. As individuals respond to perceived limits in this manner, a new "canon" is formed, shaping the perception of what speech is considered to be normal or transgressive. This process of "social censorship" typically serves to amplify the voices of those who already hold power and to reduce, marginalize, and silence the expressions of those who are vulnerable.[9]

"Regulatory censorship" alternatively functions to effect silencing by making speech simply too expensive or time-consuming to produce. Instead of threatening criminal prosecution (when such proceedings would have been too lengthy or difficult), Comstock sometimes used municipal ordinances, such as theater licensing, as an effective means of shutting down performances of which he disapproved. In light of these several meanings, I use the terms "censorship" and "cultural regulation" interchangeably, to signify all actions and processes that limit, curtail, and therefore "regulate" expression.[10]

Censorship has other complicated aspects as well. As many theorists have noted, censorship does not just result in limitations; it can also, conversely, be productive and constitutive. In Comstock's case, those seeking attention and profits frequently baited him. His stamp of disapproval was highly valuable in the marketplace, inspiring many artists, writers, and producers to fashion new and more highly sexualized work. In other words, even in the face of official oppression, cultural producers respond in a variety of ways, sometimes even profitably. I have attempted to tell the very particular stories of Comstock's prosecutions from the perspective of defendants, using newspaper accounts, court records, case files, and other forms of research. In agreement with Richard Meyer, censored work is reproduced as a "means to frustrate, the avowed mission of censorship, the mission of making these images disappear."[11]

These goals also have informed my approach to choosing which stories to tell. Some cases were so important in Comstock's career—those of Victoria Woodhull and D. M. Bennett, for example—that I have summarized the prodigious work of others on their trials while attempting to add some new detail. For the most part, however, I present the stories of individuals like La Grange Brown that have never been analyzed in scholarship before. I have also selected cases that are representative of the full array of gender and sexual expressions represented in Comstock's blotters. The limited inclusion of African Americans in this text is a function of their rare appearance in Comstock's arrest records.

My approach to the history of sexuality seeks to stay specific to individual experience. Catherine Cocks offers a thought-provoking "rethinking" of sexuality in the Progressive Era: "Although evidence of prescription and punishment is relatively abundant in the historical record, evidence of emotions, practices, and self-conceptions is scarce and difficult to interpret."[12] I would argue that material and visual culture can help fill this gap, showing us what people consumed, rather than what they said, as they experienced, understood, and performed gender, sexuality, racial, ethnic, and class statuses.

Another term worth defining at the outset is "pornography." Etymologically, this word, which first became common in the mid-nineteenth century, derives from Greek roots, translating roughly as "writing about prostitutes." I use the term in a less narrow and more socially constructed manner to describe sexually themed materials that were produced, distributed, and consumed in a manner indicating fear of criminal prosecution. It is important to point out that pornography is not a legal term. In court, evidence deemed to be criminally liable becomes "obscenity."

Finally, it is important to take seriously the term "evangelical." Understanding Comstock's faith, and his implicit belief in the inseparability of church and state, is essential to comprehending what happened in American law and culture during his lifetime. The word once again derives from a Greek root (*euangelion*, meaning "good news"). During the Protestant Great Awakenings of the late eighteenth and nineteenth centuries, evangelicalism became associated with commitment to Christian scripture, belief in acceptance of Jesus as the only means to salvation, and therefore a devotion to converting others to the faith. In chapter 1, I explore much more deeply the tenets of the faith Comstock absorbed during his childhood. In later years, he migrated from the Congregational Church to a Presbyterian congregation, but always he was deeply evangelical in his belief that blatant sinners, and even those who simply did not share his Christian commitment, were destined to burn in hell. On the basis of these religious beliefs, he viewed his own work as a great humanitarian cause, even when it caused grave immediate harm.

Comparison with a profoundly dissimilar figure on the American stage during many of the same years is instructive. From 1871 to 1883, Anthony Comstock lived in Clinton Hill, the same Brooklyn neighborhood near the Navy Yard in which Walt Whitman had resided while drafting his first versions of *Leaves of Grass* in the 1850s.[13] Unlike Comstock, whose Congregationalist faith was instilled from birth, Whitman's childhood influences were diverse, and at an early age he "developed a liberated openness to all kinds of religious discourse."[14] As a journalist and bard, Whitman took a similarly ecumenical approach to culture. He attended and wrote about entertainments high and low, often spending as much time critiquing audiences as performers. Both men disdained pornography, but for different reasons. For Comstock, pornography produced a lifelong inducement to sin. For Whitman, this material was simply dishonest. He "was puzzled that some inferred from his poetry that he would take an interest in what he called 'all the literature of rape, all the pornograph of vile minds. . . . No one would more rigidly keep in mind the difference between the simply erotic, the merely lascivious, and what is frank, free, modern, in sexual behavior, than I would: no one.'"[15] Whitman trusted that honest discussion of sexuality would liberate Americans; Comstock believed it would condemn them to hell.

While Whitman observed, chronicled, illuminated, and often celebrated America's vibrant and pluralistic cultural expression, Comstock witnessed the same rowdy American scene and endeavored instead to use law and police powers to reduce it as much as possible to a singular mold. These competing visions of cultural expression and repression offered profoundly different visions for the project of democratic government, which was especially fragile in the years following the Civil War. As the federal government and American bourgeois capitalists first began to amass vast power, the relative clout and civil liberties of ordinary citizens were weakened. Whitman observed and worried about this as well.

Between 1867 and 1871, Whitman penned his most forthright prescription for American democracy, in a series of essays published as *Democratic Vistas*. Here, the nation's most influential poet expressed his concern about the corrupt condition of American government, but also his optimistic hope that "the fruition of democracy, on aught like a grand scale, resides altogether in the future." As David S. Reynolds summarizes, "the most crucial element to be cultivated to save American democracy was a 'primary moral element,' a 'penetrating Religiousness.' For Whitman, the deist, this phrase referred to a personal cultivation of morality, informed and improved by honest and vibrant literature, and exercised in concert with fellow citizens to produce "a more perfect union."[16]

The liturgy and hymns Comstock internalized each Sunday offered a frankly different, and diminished, message about the power held by citizens. Geoffrey Stone notes, "It is no accident that unlike the Fundamental Orders of Connecticut, the United States Constitution cited as its ultimate source of authority not 'the word of God,' but 'We the People.'"[17] It is precisely during the reign of Anthony Comstock that an epic battle between these two paradigms first played out, pitting the deist vision of the founders brought forward by Walt Whitman and vigilant attorneys for the defense against those who favored the ideal of a Christian nation policed by "Soldiers of the Cross." For forty-two years, Anthony Comstock vigorously asserted his power to serve as a Christian censor of morals within a supposedly secular government position. This mission was not easy, and his adversaries did not cede their liberties without a vigorous fight. The contours of this battle still shape our national politics.

If nothing else, Comstock's story should prove the fundamentally unwinnable nature of his cause in this battle. Despite his energy and dedication, Comstock could not stop the profound and inexorable cultural and technological changes that were taking place in a nation growing ever more pluralistic, progressive, and innovative. Change, driving and unstoppable, proved a crucial obstacle to his life's work. His efforts should serve today primarily as a cautionary tale. While Comstock celebrated that La Grange Brown died an early death "off among strangers," removed for all time from American streets, there were legions more who followed him, in ever more obscene succession.

Emerging from this study of a battle against vice lasting forty-three years is a portrait of the "bright line" boundary between free and suppressed culture, and the critical importance of "We the People" in determining its place. This delineation shifts through time and place, influenced by power dynamics related to class status, sex, sexual orientation, gender, ethnicity, and race. Observing the movement of this boundary during the course of the government's most intense exertions to shape public morals through censorship allows us a new perspective on the effects and efficacy of such efforts. We see the choices publishers, artists, photographers, writers, merchants, theatrical producers, pornographers, and consumers made in response to threats of censorship. We also see the expanding legal craft practiced by defense attorneys in representing their clients, and the shifting values and assumptions judges and juries brought to bear on their decisions. We see what censorship actually accomplished, as compared with its stated goals. Undoing Comstock's censorship by examining surviving examples of censored visual and material culture offers us the opportunity to viscerally engage with realities he tried his best to erase both from his contemporaneous scene and from the historical record.

Throughout this book, I have tried in every instance possible to tell the stories of individuals who made choices amongst the options available to them in difficult moments of personal conflict and legal risk.

In their particular human dramas, we see how vast changes happen as the result of a tangled web no one person can control. Comstock brought fierce energy to his campaign to force Americans to practice his version of Christian virtue. Every win in this attempt, however, was accompanied by uncontrollable contradictory results. In pushing back against censorship, Americans developed a much more muscular view of civil liberties. And despite Comstock's best efforts, American lust did not diminish.

1

ANTHONY COMSTOCK

....

From Canaan to Gotham

NEW CANAAN

In 1863, Anthony Comstock acknowledged in his diary with great disappointment, "I debased myself in my own eyes today by my own weakness and sinfulness, was strongly tempted today, and oh! I yealded [*sic*] instead of fleeing to the 'fountain' of all my strength. What sufferings I have undergone since, no one knows. Attended pr. Meeting yet I found no relief; instead each prayer or Hymn seemed to add to my misery."[1] Given the seriousness of his repentant grief, the fact that Comstock was nineteen at the time, and his lifelong obsession with preventing others from this same solitary offense, it is reasonable to assume that he had succumbed to natural urges and masturbated.

Thanks to his early education and home life in New Canaan, Connecticut, Comstock had no doubt that this was a terrible sin. Genesis 38:8–10 was quite clear that God had slain Onan for the sin of spilling his seed on the ground, even though he chose to do so rather than impregnate his brother's wife.[2] Nonetheless, conception was God's call, not Onan's, and every evangelical Christian knew that masturbating and "spilling" were interpreted as the same thing, and that both were unlawful in God's dominion. Seeing both interior and external worlds through the lens of biblical parables and paradigms came naturally to most of the women and men reared in New Canaan, Connecticut, in the first half of the nineteenth century.

Twenty years later, Comstock affirmed that the biblical worldview he had embraced resolutely during his early years in Connecticut had endured as the foundation of his life. In 1883, he returned to his hometown to speak at the 150th anniversary of the organization of the Congregational Church of New Canaan. During his speech, Comstock proudly boasted that the "eternal truth" he had internalized during his youth, with all its arduous moral imperatives, had continued to guide him through the many "trials and perplexities" he encountered attempting to "put into practice the doctrines" he learned in New Canaan.[3] Anthony Comstock's life, like the lives of his ancestors before him, was predicated on ideas and assumptions relatively unaffected by the significant shifts in politics, economics, and social structures experienced by the rest of the nation during the first 150 years of the New Canaan Congregational Church. Independence, immigration, industrialization, the Civil War, and Reconstruction, all had barely changed the worldview of the church's parishioners.

The chairman of the Celebration Committee, Mr. A. B. Davenport, opened the event by reminding his "*Christian Brothers and Friends*" that "the *past* and the *present* are so closely interwoven, in the flow of human events, that it is almost impossible, in the nature of history, to separate them . . . The contour of this site bears no small resemblance to that where stood the Temple of Solomon."[4] This was God's Canaan and their Canaan, and gazing upon its verdant spring landscape, congregants had little difficulty visualizing a heavenly homeland both present and American and "inseparably" ancient and Christian. Church and state were wed inextricably and unquestioningly.

Anthony Comstock undoubtedly spoke with an exuberance of pride and ownership on that June day as a returning local hero, then just shy of his fortieth birthday. Comstocks were among the first English women and men to settle in this hilly terrain and construct a Solomonic meetinghouse for the nascent community.[5] Once their petition to form a parish was

approved in 1733, these new Canaanites were responsible not only for providing support for a minister and meetinghouse but also for appointing a
"Tything man," who was empowered by state law to enforce attendance and
good behavior during church meetings, as well as "strict observance of the
Sabbath."[6] Tything men, constables, and grand jurors were all appointed
by Congregational Church officials, thus constituting a seamless theocratic power structure that Comstock descendants and their neighbors
enforced for more than 150 years after Americans were ostensibly freed
from laws promoting the "establishment of religion."[7]

In 1836, one of those descendants, Thomas Anthony Comstock, married
his neighbor Polly Ann Lockwood. The union extended the continuity of
the family's New Canaan roots, as well as its prominence within the power
structure of the local Congregational Church. Thomas Comstock grew up
on Smith Ridge in New Canaan and worked in farming and millwork as
a young man. Neither occupation, however, generated sufficient income
to support a family. Presumably contemplating his marriage the following
year, in 1835 he accepted the position of teacher in the Fourth District's
winter school.[8] Thomas's tenure as a schoolteacher was remembered by
students, but not fondly: even at the age of twenty-three, "his was a regime
of strict rules and perfect order, in a school opened each morning with
prayer."[9] Thomas Comstock's career as a teacher did not last long.

One year after Thomas married Polly, his new father-in-law seems
to have helped the young couple acquire land and a sawmill on nearby
Canaan Ridge.[10] Chester was their first son, born in 1838, followed by
Samuel in 1842. Their third son, Anthony, who would become the most
famous man ever to emerge from New Canaan, came into the world on
March 7, 1844. Four younger sons and daughters followed.[11]

During Polly's life, the Comstock home seems to have been a strict
but orderly environment in which the children were taught the importance of work and prayer. Anthony recounted memories of his childhood
home with ascetic reverie. The farmhouse was "unpainted," and members
of the family were required to pray early every morning and in the evening under Thomas's supervision. The dozens of hired men who helped
the family cultivate 160 acres and operate two sawmills were also required

to be present for prayers. The family spent the Sabbath in church, with morning services followed by Sunday school and then often by an evening service, after which the family might indulge in "pie and milk."[12] Although no images or further narrative descriptions of the Comstock farm survive, a comprehensive probate inventory was prepared in 1849, when Anthony was five years old.

Assessor's records confirm that the interior of the farmhouse was not much more decorated than its unpainted exterior. Besides land and farm equipment, little was recorded that was very valuable. The probate inventory included one clock, eight "cane set" chairs, one "China Tea Sett," one feather bed bolster and pillows, and one looking glass.[13] Given the relative affluence of the estate overall, these sparse amenities speak to an austere environment within the home inspired more by choice than by necessity.[14]

The austerity of the Comstock home as described both by Trumbull and in probate records is matched by the recollections of other neighbors as well. Remembering her girlhood in New Canaan in the 1850s, Mrs. C. H. Demeritt recalled that "duty and obedience were the slogans of the day. If one did not live up to them, there was someone to see that he did. In the Church was the disciplining by the officials; in the schoolhouse was the rod. Riding for pleasure on Sunday was considered almost a 'mortal sin.'"[15] The "official" chiefly responsible for enforcing this austere and punitive atmosphere during Mrs. Demeritt's and Anthony Comstock's youth was Theophilus Smith. When Comstock referred to "doctrines" he learned as a child, and which served as the foundation for his life, he was referring specifically to those delivered by Smith.

Like most Congregational pastors in nineteenth-century Connecticut, Theophilus Smith honed his academic talents as an undergraduate at Yale.[16] During his pastorate, which began in 1831, Smith was particularly remembered for his "carefully formulated *Confession of Faith*" and his *Instruction in Righteousness*, which provided for "the unquestioning correctness of doctrine which has kept the members of this church, and their scattered descendants, satisfied to let alone the shifting charms of speculation." To enforce and evangelize his "correct" and strictly doctrinal brand of Congregational faith, Smith "instituted neighborhood prayer meetings," after which parishioners would preach from door to door.[17]

The centrality of fervent religious devotion evident in Comstock's boyhood experiences in home and church was reinforced by his education in New Canaan's nominally secular public schools. In this, as in most aspects of social life, Connecticut again was slow to change. Beginning in the 1830s, New England states in general oversaw a vast expansion of subjects taught in their public common schools. There was one exception: Connecticut.[18] Given the realities of gubernatorial and legislative indifference, the residents of New Canaan funded and controlled the district on their own. As a result, although the schools Comstock attended as a small child technically were secular, the reality was quite the opposite.

For a few brief years after 1839, Connecticut did attempt some statewide educational improvements; in 1841, for instance, New Canaan leaders were forced to choose an "inspector" who would report on local schools to State officials. Not surprisingly, they selected Reverend Theophilus Smith. Under Smith's tenure, no book in the school district's list came anywhere close to the New Testament in terms of its ubiquity and centrality within the program of study.[19] Smith had little doubt about the usefulness of the Bible for teaching almost any subject. With genealogy, history, and even "practical truths" emanating from scripture, the common school curriculum Anthony Comstock experienced as a child was largely an extension of catechism.[20]

This chiefly religious curricular focus of Comstock's common school experience is unlikely to have been tempered during his brief attendance at the "Academy Junior" beginning in 1857. This small private school, "in which were educated many of the men and women of whom New Canaan in its later years was most proud," was run by the new pastor of the New Canaan Congregational Church, Reverend J. C. Wyckoff."[21] The centrality of scripture here was presumably no less pronounced than it had been at home, in church, and in the district school. Nothing in the curriculum, pedagogy, or structure of New Canaan's municipal, religious, or educational institutions caused Anthony Comstock to doubt the doctrines and dominion of the Congregational Church, nor to entertain any "charms of speculation."

GRACE, WRATH, AND LUST

In the same year that Anthony Comstock bemoaned his lack of disci-pline in "yealding" [*sic*] to his own youthful "weakness," he also penned another evocative entry in his diary: "One of the sweetest days of my life, so near to Jesus. The grave seemed but a dark receptical [*sic*] for rubbish where to through [*sic*] this worthless frame or body at death, while above it was radiant with purest light. Were it not for the Loved ones of earth mourning and were I sure they would all meet me Home, I would with joy welcome the tomb."[22]

By the mid-nineteenth century, the Congregational Church had shed all vestiges of Calvin's idea that God elected the saved before birth through predestination. By the time Anthony Comstock was old enough to paraphrase Romans 5:5 in his diary, the sermons, hymns, and commen-taries he venerated all promised that a heaven "radiant with purest light" was possible through deeds on earth.[23] Salvation now was to be earned, rather than discerned.

As his diary entry reveals, at the age of nineteen Comstock was fairly certain of his own salvation; however, he was not so sure that all his "loved ones" would be coming with him. Throughout his life, Anthony Comstock pointedly said little about his father, in contrast with his glowing accounts of Polly, who had died when he was only ten. From this omission and the documentary record, we may at least entertain the possibility that it was Thomas's soul that his son worried about.

Although the verdant hills of New Canaan swelled with fragrant fruits and flowers in temperate months, the soil underneath was rocky, winters were barren, and the parish was by no means an easy place to feed a large family. Anthony Comstock's father was a typical New Canaanite in this regard. Following his initial acquisition of land in 1836, state records docu-ment a series of Thomas's land purchases and sales, mostly between family members.[24] The lurching enhancements and reversals of fortune suggested by these purchases and sales were by no means uncommon at the time, as the Panic of 1837 and subsequent economic turbulence placed many families in difficulty.[25]

Thomas followed this unhappy path in 1849, the year that probate records list him as an Insolvent Debtor. As such, he was forced to attest that he was "somewhat embarrassed in my circumstances and desirous that my creditors may be paid out of my property in full." Thomas and Polly were both thirty-seven at the time of his bankruptcy.[26] Five years later, much worse tragedy struck when Polly died, leaving her seven children in the care of their dour father.[27] This situation lasted only five years. In 1859, Thomas obtained a passport and left America for England, changing his status in public records to "farmer and mill owner up to about 1860, and thereafter a promoter."[28]

In England, Thomas Comstock started a new family, marrying a London woman nearly thirty years younger named Bertha Edith Giles, with whom he fathered three additional sons.[29] Evidence is scant as to what happened to Thomas's and Polly's children in the years immediately following her death and his departure, but whatever the exact disposition of the scattered family in the years between 1859 and 1863, the Comstock children must have found it profoundly unsettling to be abandoned by their father following their mother's death, with no clear expectation of a reunion. This may well have contributed to Anthony's concern for his father's soul.

During the difficult years following his mother's death, Anthony Comstock's diary attests that his greatest source of comfort was prayer. Fortunately, by 1854 the New Canaan Congregational Church was a better facility in which to seek solace than ever before. Although Reverend Hoyt's tribute to Theophilus Smith emphasized his doctrinal orthodoxy, the romantic language he used also hints at a new "Culture of Sentiment" that accompanied passionate religious revivalism during the mature phase of the Second Great Awakening in the 1830s and 1840s.[30]

Although Yale-educated ministers like Theophilus Smith were generally averse to religious experimentation, these "New Divinity" pastors responded to the shift away from predestination by emphasizing the personal responsibility of each congregant to live up to God's moral laws and thus *earn* salvation. This new emphasis on free will aligned well with the political rhetoric of democracy in the antebellum republic, but it also placed a greater burden on pastors to inspire the "affections" of their flock.[31] Most obviously, Smith appealed to his congregation's affections by supervising the construction of an ethereal new and modern church, completed in 1843, and by making an "effort to improve the choir."[32] For the rest of his life, Anthony Comstock would find his greatest source of joy in the soaring spaces and melodious hymns of America's evangelical churches.

Like its churches and choirs, Connecticut's visual culture emphasized the goal of winning hearts and minds for Jesus. Although Congregational-ists generally were averse to hanging paintings or prints in their churches, they did purchase uplifting works for their homes. Frugal and austere families like the Comstocks rarely would have purchased an expensive oil painting. However, it is possible that they might have invested in a more cost-effective version of this type of visual Christian lesson through the medium of lithographs by the state's best-known and most successful purveyors.

In 1849, a *Hartford Daily Courant* journalist visited the Kellogg Broth-ers Lithography Company in Hartford and noted, "Scarcely a cottage or hamlet can be found, however obscure or isolated, but what displays upon its walls . . . specimens of this art, pleasing the eye, enlivening the solitude, informing the mind, and cultivating . . . that taste for the fine arts which everywhere tends to refine and ennoble humanity."[33] Among the Kellogg Brothers' popular designs were two images of trees representing *Grace* and *Wrath* (figures 1.1 and 1.2 / plates 1 and 2), which perfectly reflect New Divinity Congregationalist theology.

Grace, or *The Good Tree or Hieroglyphics of a Christian*, illustrates Psalm 1:3: "And he shall be like a tree planted by the rivers of water, that bringeth forth his fruit in his season." The passage highlights the blessings extended to those God deems to be righteous; a tree with a good supply of water bears fruits of both material and spiritual sustenance. In the background, the depicted landscape resembles the Connecticut River valley, with its low and gently sloped hills and calm water. At right in the scene, an angel waters the *Good Tree*, whose trunk is Hope and Love, growing from roots of Faith and Repentance. Looming above all at the apex of the print is

FIGURE I.I Kelloggs & Thayer, *The Good Tree or Hieroglyphics of a Christian*, 1846–1847. Hand-colored lithograph, 32.4 × 23.8 cm. The Connecticut Historical Society. See also color plate I.

the simple word GRACE, emphasizing the mercy of an overseeing God. The absolute power of the Lord and promise of Heaven depicted here all reiterate the messages of the most popular evangelical hymns of the era. A land of eternal life beckoned those who could keep the devil at bay. [34]

Beyond its overt Christian message, this large, portrait-size print carries less elevating meanings as well. The devil is depicted with tight curly hair and in this version is hand-tinted a dark shade of brown, in contrast to the angels, whose skin is left untinted on the light paper and whose hair is depicted as straight blond or brunette. These formal choices reflect pervasive and insidious comparisons between "uncivilized" and unsaved African descendants and Christians of European ancestry. *The Good Tree* is an excellent reminder not only of Connecticut's stubborn adherence to older evangelical paradigms, but also of its deep-seated prejudices. In contrast to its neighboring New England states, Connecticut abolished slavery so slowly that there were legally enslaved people in the state until 1848— among them Onesimus Comstock, held in bondage by one of Anthony Comstock's New Canaan relatives. [35]

In contrast to *The Good Tree*, which optimistically promised the possibility of grace, *An Evil Tree or the Natural Heart* depicted the bitter landscape of wrath, with a dark cloud blowing this word into the scene at upper left. *An Evil Tree* paraphrases Matthew 7:18: "A Corrupt tree cannot bring forth good fruit. / Cut it down why cumbreth it the ground." The *Evil Tree* withers within a barren scene, with shades of yellow mixed into the grass to suggest drought. The river behind is similarly sickened, with mud brown tones laid on thickly to suggest not only pollution but also stagnation. At lower left, a tree stump shows no hope of bearing new life, and at lower right, a bush burns, though with no humans present to take instruction. The roots of this disaster, according to the print, are labeled as Unbelief, which provides the foundation for a trunk of Pride, Self Will, and then three main branches: Lust of the Eye, Pride of Life, and Lust of the Flesh. The use of the word "Lust" to describe two of the main three branches of the evil tree is a good reminder that the most direct path to hell was through "sensuous appetite or desire," which tempted the pure to sin and thus fall from grace. [36]

FIGURE 1.2 D. W. Kellogg & Co., *An Evil Tree, or the Natural Heart*, ca. 1830–1840. Hand-colored lithograph, 32.9 × 25.4 cm. The Connecticut Historical Society. See also color plate 2.

Although the Kellogg Brothers specifically referenced *Matthew* and *Psalms* in their lithographs, the presence of the serpent at the heart of the tree makes clear that they were alluding to mankind's original fall from grace as well. In Genesis 3, as New Canaan Congregationalists well knew, the difference between the states of grace and wrath was the fruit of the tree of knowledge.[37] The serpent entices Adam and Eve to eat the fruit God has forbidden by promising "that in the day ye eat thereof, then your eyes shall be opened, and ye shall be as gods, knowing good and evil." The result of their "Disbelieving the Word" in this case does not render them gods, but does result in a very particular transformation: "And the eyes of them both were opened, and they knew that they *were* naked; and they sewed fig leaves together, and made themselves aprons" (Genesis 3:7). The specific fashioning of "aprons" covering their genitals makes clear that the fear and shame of nakedness was specifically located in the display of reproductive and sexual anatomy.[38]

With nakedness and sexuality equated so clearly with man's fall, observant Christians in nineteenth-century Connecticut generally dressed in a manner that covered much of the body. As Augustus Washington's daguerreotype of *Lydia Smith Morgan Bulkeley* of 1850 (figure 1.3) demonstrates, dresses for public display revealed little skin, with high necks and long hems. By the mid-nineteenth century, as Lourdes Font points out, some relaxation of these strictures was already common. The sleeves and collar of this dress were removable, for instance, during the latter parts of the day when a respectable woman moved into more private spheres.[39] Washington, a successful African American photographer in the 1840s and early 1850s in Hartford, would have been well aware of this convention, and made a photograph of Mrs. Bulkeley in her most public presentation.

Like Washington, most Connecticut artists of the era similarly avoided showing any bare flesh that might cause concern. The Kellogg Brothers, for example, even avoided showing bare flesh when they took up the popular, usually sexy and titillating theme of *Ladies Bathing* (figure 1.4). Reading the image from left to right, we see one woman immersed in water up to her armpits. If she is unclothed, we can't tell (although it is doubtful, given the women bathing in gowns). As the figures progress toward the right, they finish bathing, put on more formal attire, put up their hair,

FIGURE 1.3 Augustus Washington, *Lydia Smith Morgan Bulkeley*, ca. 1850. Daguerreotype on silvered copper plate in leather case with gilt mat and embossed red velvet pad, image 3 ½ × 2 ¾ in. (8.9 × 7 cm.). The Connecticut Historical Society. (1960.138.1)

FIGURE 1.4 Kellogg & Comstock, *Ladies Bathing*, 1850. Hand-colored lithograph, 20.5 × 31.3 cm. The Connecticut Historical Society.

and prepare themselves for mixed company. The addition of color further serves to detract from, rather than highlight, the small amount of flesh that is apparent in the lithograph. While the lush fertile forest is emphasized with additions of green watercolor, the women themselves have no shading or decorative watercolor flourishes at all, rendering their bodies closer therefore to the cool aesthetics of classical sculptures. Only the slightest indication of buttocks is visible in the standing figure at right.

In rendering bathing nudes with their own versions of fig leaf aprons through composition and formal elements, the Kellogg Brothers were not only responding to the sensibilities of their local Connecticut customers but also subscribing to conventions American artists generally adopted in the antebellum period. In 1851, a writer in the *Bulletin of the American Art-Union* proudly boasted, "it should be a pride with us that American Art, thus far, has preserved itself unpolluted. While we have observed in French papers complaints at a tendency which has characterized their late exhibitions to violate the laws of decency . . . there is nothing in American exhibitions or publications, generally speaking, that can justly wound the most fastidious delicacy."[40] Later in the article, the author defended the ability of "fastidious" American artists even to depict and sculpt the nude in a manner that would not violate the laws of decency.

Members of the Art-Union were all well aware of the recent success of Hiram Powers's *Greek Slave* and other glistening white marble nudes that quickly followed from the studios of American artists. Nonetheless, this was still very careful business, given the evangelical ethos and aesthetics that dominated public discourse. Lust still was the clearest path to wrath and ruin. Letting down one's guard by viewing the naked body, appearing in public in scant clothing, straying from scripture, or even jesting with a "light heart"—all were akin to taking the first steps toward Satan's fiery abyss. The terrifying possibilities of personal, communal, and even national damnation were not an abstraction for children brought up in strict Congregationalist churches in nineteenth-century Connecticut.[41] These dark messages and worries would never have been far from Anthony Comstock's mind as he came of age in New Canaan and grappled with the inevitable desires of his own "natural heart" and body.

INSIDIOUS EVILS

Charles Gallaudet Trumbull's 1913 biography *Anthony Comstock, Fighter* chiefly struck a hagiographic tone, driven in large part by the subject's own view of himself, carefully conveyed to the author in lengthy interviews. Comstock did, however, exhibit some small humility in admitting to momentary and youthful lapses from Grace, albeit stemming from exposure to "vicious characters" rather than from any personal deficiency. Trumbull noted, for example, "certain things that were brought into his life in those boyhood days started memories and lines of temptation that are harder for him to overcome than anything that ever came into his life in later years. . . . Once gaining entry into a life, through book or story or picture, it stays . . . to be called up freely and used at will by the Devil."[42] Comstock's personal diary seems to record several instances in which he gave in to the "lines of temptation" stimulated by viewing books or pictures as Trumbull describes.

The seriousness of Comstock's agony in these passages reflects his own deep faith, as well as a general anxiety about masturbation common in America in the nineteenth century. Self-declared health experts like Sylvester Graham, inventor of the cracker that still carries his name, published tomes describing an extraordinary list of ailments that could be caused by "self-pollution," including heart attack, cancer, and eventually death. In keeping with the theories of the day, it was best for boys to be kept from any stimulation that could arouse the senses. Hard beds, cold baths, and "farinaceous" food were all advised.[43] Boys were constantly warned against this evil in the antebellum era, and even Walt Whitman's sensual poems invoked "reformers' remonstrative language."[44]

In the formation of Comstock's faith and worldview, what he did not read or publicly discuss was at least as important as the material he read or might have read as a child. As he came of age, fear of inciting lust prevented conversation about numerous issues that typically are of concern to boys, including sexual impulses. Catharine Beecher, in her ubiquitous tome *Treatise on Domestic Economy* penned in 1845, expressed well the Congregationalist point of view on sexual education, which amounted to a policy of "see no evil, hear no evil": "Disclosing the details of vice, in order to awaken dread of its penalties, is a most dangerous experiment, and often leads to the very evils feared. . . . The safest course, is, to cultivate habits of modesty and delicacy, and to teach, that all impure thoughts, words, and actions, are forbidden by God, and are often visited by the most dreadful punishment."[45] Beecher's strongly worded recommendation of silence regarding the "mysteries" of the body would prove to be foundational for Comstock in the future. Literature that even mentioned sexuality was a "dangerous experiment." All that could be done to counter children's propensity toward solitary evils was to hint at the "dreadful punishment" associated with sexuality in general terms, and restrict access to any stimulation that might provoke "impure thoughts and actions."

Although Connecticut's conservative Congregationalists clearly made an effort to avoid any exposure of their children to culture that stimulated "Lust of the Eye or Flesh," and with it such harmful practices as masturbation, Comstock's own recollections to Trumbull reveal that even the strictest families were unable to completely succeed in this effort. It never was possible even for New Canaan to be as morally pure as Beecher advised. This was especially true because the "poison of impurity" was so easily available through the mail.

A *Private Circular, for Gentlemen Only* in the collection of the American Antiquarian Society is typical of an enormous number of solicitations in the mid-nineteenth century that advertised popular erotic materials that could be "sent either by *Mail or Express*, with perfect safety and done in a manner as to defy detection."[46] Although most of the books advertised in these illicit circulars are now lost, or at least not catalogued in public collections, the most prominent title, *Fanny Hill*, survives in numerous editions, having been continuously in print since its initial publication in 1748.

John Cleland's novel, often known by its formal title, *Memoirs of a Woman of Pleasure*, tells the story of a young woman's introduction to prostitution and then her happy pursuit of this profession. The text of the novel, like its illustrations, "is repetitive and episodic. . . . What it contains is a narrative designed for repeated male sexual arousal."[47]

At the beginning of the story, Fanny is a shy virgin, forced into prostitution by the death of her parents and exploited by those who seemingly would help her. After a violent and frightening introduction to sex, the other women in the brothel educate her in their craft; the bulk of the text is devoted to describing her mostly satisfying sexual encounters with graphic specificity. At the end of the story, which is told in the form of an epistolary, Fanny leaves the profession, inherits a fortune from marriage to a short-lived man of wealth, and embarks on a life of "virtue" with her childhood sweetheart. The novel was by far the most popular erotic book sold in Europe and America in the nineteenth century. Helen Lefkowitz Horowitz describes *Fanny Hill* as "the *ur*-text, at least for erotic writing available to Americans."[48]

Although the storyline of *Fanny Hill* technically involves a moralizing narrative arc, beginning and ending in "virtue" as Cleland ironically constructs it, clearly the novel was meant to be sexually stimulating above all else. Illustrators entirely grasped this primary function. In stark contrast to the Kellogg Brothers' artist, who depicted ladies bathing with a clear objective of inciting as little temptation to lust as possible, illustrators producing plates for *Fanny Hill* left little to the imagination, using compositional and stylistic elements to accentuate the arousing nature of the story. A hand-painted wood engraving (figure 1.5 / plate 3) seized by police in New York in 1850 demonstrates many of the techniques artists used to facilitate arousal. Most important was choosing a scene in which the participants themselves are aroused. The artist in this unusually large and sumptuous print illustrates one of the more dramatic scenes in *Fanny Hill*, in which Fanny satisfies the "cruel taste" and "ardent desire" of a wealthy man named Mr. Barville, who likes to take turns being "unmercifully whipped" and then whipping others.

To highlight the playful nature of the scene, the artist shows an enthusiastic and smiling Fanny administering "ten lashes with much goodwill and the utmost nerve and vigour of arm that I could put to them, so as make those fleshy orbs quiver again under them." Fanny's rose pink gown, in a Renaissance Revival style popular at that time, with demi-gigot sleeves fashionable in the 1820s and 1830s, is pulled down below her own

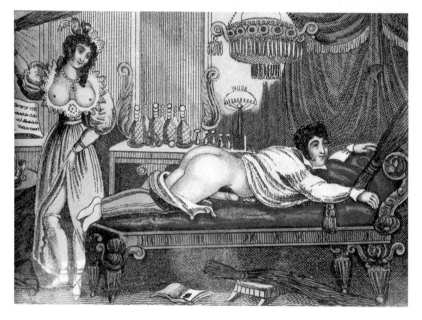

FIGURE 1.5 *Fanny Whipping Mr. Barville*, scene from *"Memoirs of a Woman of Pleasure,"* ca. 1850. Engraving with hand-painted color. Included in: *Deposition of Officer Augustus Furnald against John Sweeney, with five pornographic images.* Courtesy, American Antiquarian Society. See also color plate 3.

"fleshy orbs."[49] The neckline lowered below the breasts to highlight the erotic display is mirrored by the exhibition of rolled down stockings and naked thighs below, as Fanny lifts her gown delicately. The binding of her feet and ankles may hint at her own turn yet to come.

Mr. Barville's face similarly wears a happy smile, as he gazes upon a fresh birch rod while awaiting his next thwack from Fanny.[50] The happy mood of the scene is enhanced by the wealth and comfort on display in the busy room surrounding the protagonists, particularly in the heavy carved daybed with its plush upholstery and the crystal chandelier and elaborate gold swag of drapery above. Throughout, phallic forms are emphasized, in the stout legs of the elaborately carved daybed, the liquor bottles standing on the table in the background, and the lamp that rises above Barville's back. A touch of pink paint on the head of his penis directs the viewer's attention to his arousal. Through these inventive choices, the artist combines fantasies of both wealth and sexual satisfaction. Whether or not a purchaser ever read the story, the thoroughly explicit display of aroused reproductive anatomy offered in illustrations like this clearly fit the type of visual material Trumbull described as "lasting poison . . . that could be called up freely and used at will by the Devil."[51]

At the same time that America's antebellum schools and libraries happily circulated narratives promoting Christian tenets, pornographic books like *Fanny Hill* flourished within an abundant underground economy only occasionally interrupted by prosecutorial efforts. As Donna Dennis recounts, America's pornography trade was initially centered in lower Manhattan, which "housed a dark, congested warren of bookstores, print shops, second-hand and antiquarian book dealers, engravers, lithographers, stationers, job printers, newspaper offices, and small and midsize publishing firms."[52] In the years of Comstock's youth, printers commonly reproduced erotic European texts as part of their output, using engraved plates they imported from England or France; bookstore owners likewise directly imported and sold texts like *Fanny Hill* along with pornographic prints in large numbers.

Enterprising American publishers began to generate their own content beginning in the 1840s, including "Flash" newspapers, such as *The Rake* and *The Libertine*, which offered "a titillating brew of gossip about prostitutes, theatrical denizens, and sports contests . . . [that] offered guidance to men young and old intent on navigating the new world of unrestricted pleasure and commercialized leisure in the city."[53] District attorneys prosecuted these publishers using the concept of "obscene libel" initially established in the English case of *Rex v. Curll* (1727), which made it a crime to inflict damage "against civil society or the public at large." In the abrupt transition following the Revolution, former English colonies, now American states, largely continued their use of English common law, with provisions that new legislatures would subsequently revise and write their own statutes.[54]

Although the defendants in New York's early obscenity prosecutions rarely faced significant prison terms or fines, any publications deemed obscene were seized and destroyed, rendering the initial format of Flash newspapers too risky to be profitable. The Tariff Act of 1842 similarly had a short-lived dampening effect on the circulation of erotic works in this era.[55]

None of the defendants in these cases made any effort to invoke the protections of the First Amendment of the U.S. Constitution. The free speech clause of the First Amendment did not apply to state legal proceedings until 1925, when the Supreme Court ruled in *Gitlow v. New York* that the First Amendment is incorporated into the Fourteenth Amendment's "due process" language. Instead, "few participants in the obscene print trade challenged the legitimacy of moral censorship in any direct way" in any state or federal proceedings.[56]

Rather than foreswear a profitable business in the face of potential seizures and prosecution, printers ceased their vulnerable storefront retail sales and turned instead to the U.S. mails, using newspaper advertisements and circulars to lure consumers, like the "vicious characters" who presumably introduced Anthony Comstock to pornography in his early years in rural Connecticut. Newspaper editors capitalized on the profitability of the Flash papers' "rich and racy" subjects by "repackaging" their "salacious, titillating, voyeuristic" material into new formats that thrived "for decades to come."[57] These printers also shifted their methods of production, authoring their own erotic texts and images rather than trying to import them.

As Comstock's diary entries and childhood reminiscences suggest, despite the best efforts of ministers, educators, and parents, even the most observant boys could not entirely avoid illicit materials, or the biological urges that made them tempting. The realities of human sexuality, including "insidious evils," all persisted and coexisted in New Canaan during Comstock's youth, despite strenuous attempts by Theophilus Smith and others to create a pure flock. In spite of his brief lapses in purity, Comstock nevertheless felt worthy enough to "come into" the Congregational Church of South Norwalk. He avowed his Confession of Faith in a ceremony presided over by Reverend Homer Dunning sometime around 1860.[58]

Standing publicly before the congregation, Comstock affirmed declarations including:

Art. IV. You believe, that all men, since the fall, are, by nature, entirely corrupt; having no conformity of heart to God, and being destitute of all moral excellence.

and

> Art. XI. You believe that the righteous, at the general judgment, will be approved of God, and received to life everlasting; and that wicked angels, and wicked men, will be condemned of God, and cast down to endless punishment, where the worm dieth not, and the fire is not quenched. . . . Thus you believe in your heart, and thus you confess before men.[59]

Having come into the Congregational Church through baptism as an adult, Comstock was now fully responsible for the fate of his soul through the performance of moral purity and good deeds. It was here, in South Norwalk, that Comstock began his unique and self-made career as the Lord's nineteenth-century "Soldier of the Cross."

SOLDIER OF THE CROSS

Although Polly Comstock died when Anthony was just ten, his recollections of her were vivid and glowing. In particular, he fondly recalled that on Sunday nights, "she would gather the children round her, close up, and tell them stories. These stories were often from the Bible, sometimes from other sources; but always they were stories of moral heroism."[60] Although we cannot be entirely sure which nonbiblical stories Polly included in her Sunday evening readings, the frugal Comstocks would not have needed to buy their own collection.

New Canaan's first library was formed in 1811, for the purpose of "the improvement of the mind in important knowledge." To safeguard the community, the original constitution of the organization stipulated that the pastor of the Congregational Church would serve as moderator. Predictably, the first books purchased included a large number of doctrinal treatises, including *Smith on the Prophecies* and *Edwards on the Affections*.[61] But if Polly Comstock in fact did borrow volumes from this small Young People's Library of New Canaan to read to her children, there fortunately were more engaging works of popular fiction as well.[62]

The most famous novel on offer in the Young People's Library, John Bunyan's *The Pilgrim's Progress*, was extremely effective in illustrating the "road to salvation" in the format of engaging and action-packed narrative fiction. Bunyan's protagonist, unimaginatively named Christian Pilgrim, consistently confronts sin and turns from the path of temptation on his route to the City of Zion. Although the "repetitive and episodic" structure of the book is equally as predictable as *Fanny Hill*, its purpose of course was vastly different. As Alan Trachtenberg summarizes, "From its publication late in the seventeenth century until the Civil War, *The Pilgrim's Progress* ranked with the Bible as the best-read book in America, a standard catechism and mode . . . of instruction."[63]

Particularly in the antebellum era, *The Pilgrim's Progress* served as an influential prototype for Christian authors, especially for those hoping to emphasize that personal choice, rather than fate, determined salvation or condemnation. The recurring tropes of paths, choices, and consequences, along with the arc and atmosphere of these narratives, were undeniably influential in shaping Comstock's voice as a prolific author in future years. Throughout his adult life, he wrote copiously in a personal diary and authored a steady stream of magazine articles, pamphlets, books, and richly annotated arrest blotters. Comstock acknowledged the importance of childhood stories in his remarks to Trumbull: "'I do enjoy the story of any man or woman, boy or girl, who sacrifices self for principle.'"[64] A great example of this type of literature that was available in the New Canaan Library from its earliest days is *The History of Sandford and Merton*. This widespread Christian favorite demonstrates clear kinship with Comstock's own framing of his life, and voice as an author, in future years.

The History of Sandford and Merton tells the story of a rich boy, Tommy Merton, who has been spoiled and rendered unlikable and hapless by his upbringing on a plantation in Jamaica, where "he had several black servants to wait upon him, who were forbidden to contradict him upon any account."[65] Fortunately for Tommy, his family moves back to England when he is six years old. There, he meets Harry Sandford, a virtuous, compassionate, and poor young farm boy. The story of their friendship begins when Tommy is walking through a field and a snake coils itself around his leg. Paralyzed with fear and unable to defend himself, Tommy is saved by Harry, who, "though young, was a boy of a most courageous spirit . . . instantly seizing the snake by the neck with as much dexterity as resolution" and throwing him "a great distance."

Later in the story, the two friends are out walking when they come upon a troop of performers hosting a "bull-baiting," with vicious dogs that rile up the "noble animal." When the bull escapes and charges at Tommy, his death seems certain, "had not Harry, with a courage and presence of mind above his years, suddenly seized a prong . . . and at the very moment when the bull was stooping to gore his defenceless [sic] friend, advanced and wounded him in the flank."[66] Comstock's recollections of his early years include a remarkably similar narrative of extraordinary boyhood courage and morality in facing down a vicious animal.

Charles Gallaudet Trumbull titled his chapter on Comstock's childhood "In Training for the Fight." Like Harry Sandford, Anthony Comstock is presented as a boy of extraordinary virtuosity. The opening scene for the biography is set in 1862, when Comstock is working as a "country-boy clerk" in Winnipauk. News has arrived of a rabid dog prowling the town, terrifying residents. Everyone else is too afraid to try to kill the beast, but Comstock "went to his room and prayed to God for courage, and for success in killing the animal." His prayers, of course, are answered, and just like Harry, Comstock acts swiftly to save the day: "There was just time to jump down and back, and get his gun up, as the dog reached the edge of the wall. He fired, hitting the beast between the shoulders, full in the breast. The dog rolled over, and a bullet through his brain, from the pistol, finished the business." What Comstock learned, according to Trumbull, is that "a man who will throw himself and all that he has into an effort to protect others will be protected by his heavenly Father."[67] For the rest of his life, Comstock presented himself to the world as though he were Harry Sandford or Christian Pilgrim, ready to kill to save others. This narrative was already fully formed in his mind when America's treacherous and tragic Civil War began.

Having earlier come into the church in South Norwalk through his sworn Confessions of Faith, Comstock presumably was in the pews in 1861 when his minister Homer Dunning delivered his eloquent sermon on the "awful chasm of separation" that had consumed the nation: "The volcano of slavery, which has been so long seething and muttering with dangerous elements has at length burst forth in a fiery eruption to consume and destroy the nation; and the earthquake of rebellion has rent asunder the Union with an awful chasm of separation, and with a shock whose echoes have sounded over the world."[68] Dunning's passionate rhetoric reflected the high emotions that naturally accompanied this traumatic time.

The early years of the war were undoubtedly difficult for Anthony Comstock. His older brother Samuel was one of the first to enlist in New Canaan's H Company of the Seventeenth Connecticut regiment on July 23, 1862. Fairfield County, with its high percentage of Christian abolitionists, rallied to the cause in large numbers.[69] When the Seventeenth departed for the South, the community formed a crowd in Bridgeport to cheer them, presumably with Anthony and his younger siblings in attendance: "They showered Godspeeds and blessings on their sons, and braced their hearts to the parting by pledges to keep all right and bright at the firesides of the county."[70] Unfortunately, the Seventeenth Connecticut regiment quickly found itself at the epicenter of the terrible "earthquake of rebellion."

At both Chancellorsville and Gettysburg, the Seventeenth Connecticut suffered devastating losses, including Sergeant Samuel Comstock, who died of his injuries in an army field hospital at Gettysburg after wasting painfully for two months, eventually weighing less than one hundred pounds at his demise.[71] A comrade reported to the Comstocks that with his last breath, Samuel Comstock quoted Isaac Watts's hymn "Why Should We Start, and Fear to Die?": "Jesus can make a dying bed feel as soft as downy pillows are."[72]

In the meantime, the home fires were not burning bright. Trumbull writes: "The old homestead at New Canaan was in the hands of the sons when the war broke out. . . . The farm was mortgaged, and the mortgage was held by certain local sympathizers with the South who threatened to foreclose the mortgage if the boys entered the Northern army. This did not stop the boys' enlisting. The threat was carried out;

the mortgage was foreclosed, and the farm was lost."[73] Faced with the opportunity to provide "entirely for the little ones at home" through receipt of his bounty, along with the stirring last words of his brother and the sermons of his minister urging young men to take up the great fight, Anthony Comstock mustered into Company H as a replacement for his brother on December 30, 1863.[74] Fortunately, Gettysburg was the last of the company's heated battles.

On February 7, 1864, an excited New Canaan boy, Justus Silliman, wrote to his mother from South Carolina: "I had for some time been expecting Anthony by every boat and when possible have been on the wharf when mail boats arrive. I was there last night when the 'Alice Price' came in with mail and passengers, before the boat was made fast I heard my name called. I looked up and rested my eyes on Anthony . . . I was *very* glad to see him."[75] The company arrived in Jacksonville, Florida, a few weeks later, meeting with "but slight resistance," and in mid-April was sent seventy-five miles up the St. John's River to Volusia County.

Even in the absence of any battles, Silliman was fascinated by the experiences of Company H during the latter half of the war, as recorded in his thoughtful and descriptive letters home. During the fourteen months of their service in Florida, the men of Company H confronted a steady stream of Confederate deserters "seeking employment under the government" and others who presented themselves as lifelong abolitionists who now wanted only to protect their homes from the destruction and confiscation raids companies like the Seventeenth routinely engaged in.[76]

On September 8, 1864, Silliman wrote to his cousin Mary Silliman from Jacksonville of an extraordinary meeting he had been privileged to attend:

> The colored soldiers & citizens of this place had a meeting a short time since for the purpose of expressing their sentiments through a delegate, to the colored convention soon to be held in New York. The Church was crowded with excited darkees, some of whom made some smart stirring speeches, in favor of being allowed to vote, & of electing some of their own color to office in our National government. They instructed their

delegate to resist to the utmost all efforts that might be proposed for their emigration or colonization. They seemed to think that they could not be satisfied with anything less than living with us, associating with us as equals in every particular, & taking part in the government of all our institutions. They exhibited some envy & prejudice against the whites & were very excited in their feelings. This is but the commencement of what will soon follow, & we will soon have a very difficult & perplexing [situation] to settle in regard to them.[77]

Silliman continued to report on the "perplexing" circumstances soldiers found themselves engrossed in while attempting to manage a city filled with hungry, desperate, confused, and scared Floridians. The truce they managed with local residents was tense, especially after Lincoln's assassination, when "deep threats [we]re heard on every side from our soldiers, many of whom have expressed a desire to be led against the enemy under the black flag and carry out a war of extermination, but I trust that, as heretofore, we may not be influenced by such motives, but that we may be incited by our desire to perpetuate our institutions of justice & liberty & to put down wrong & oppression."[78]

After his first letters mentioning Anthony Comstock, Silliman never mentioned his fellow Company H comrade again, except for his last preserved letter home on June 25, 1865, asking his brother to direct correspondence "in care of Anthony Comstock Asst. Insp. Generals Office D.S. Hilton Head S.C."[79] Comstock had been promoted, but not for long. The entire regiment "was mustered out at Hilton Head the following month, on the 19th of July, 1865."[80]

While Justus Silliman spent his years of Civil War service trying to make sense of the inscrutable complexities of the American South during and immediately after the Civil War, Comstock in contrast almost single-mindedly focused on battling vice. Although his letters do not survive, we know his thoughts about this period of time from his copious diary entries, quoted by Heywood Broun and Margaret Leech in their 1927 biography *Roundsman of the Lord*. Broun and Leech are the last people known to have seen Comstock's diaries, which have remained lost since that time.

The diary entries Broun and Leech recount suggest that Comstock suffered a pained and miserable existence during the war. On the occasion of his first entry into camp on January 8, 1864, Comstock wrote: "as we entered the Barracks a feeling of sadness came over me & it seems as though I should sink when I heard the air resounding with the oaths of wicked men." He later referred to his barracks as a "Den of cursing and Blasphemy."[81] In response to the sin he confronted, Comstock evangelized almost constantly. He organized prayer meetings for his company, which lacked its own clergy member. Scouting everywhere for pastors, it was probably here that he was first introduced to the sermons of pastors from other Christian denominations, including an Episcopalian chaplain who delivered a "delightful meeting, good sermon."[82] His efforts to elevate his comrades failed to make him any more popular. On December, 2, 1864, he recorded in his diary: "Seems to be a feeling of hatred by some of the boys, constantly falsifying, persecuting, and trying to do me harm. Can I sacrifice Principle and conscience for Praise of Man? *Never*."[83]

Comstock also undoubtedly came into contact with the same type of visual "poison" that had plagued him in Connecticut. Administrative reports document that large quantities of pornographic books, prints, and photographs were mailed to soldiers during the Civil War, including "Pictures for Bachelors," "Bedroom Photographs for Gentlemen Only," and a standard assortment of illustrated titles including *Fanny Hill*, *The Lustful Turk*, etc.[84] As Judith Giesberg chronicles, soldiers and officers alike circulated large quantities of pornography and also engaged in sex with prostitutes when they were unoccupied by military duties; violence and salacious voyeurism went hand in hand during the war.[85] Comstock again recorded giving into the same vices that plagued him in New Canaan. Broun and Leech describe the diary as "filled with confessions of guilt and outbursts of bitter remorse" during these years.[86]

Back in Connecticut following the war, Anthony struggled through another battle—this time against boredom. Although he had secured a position in New Haven as a clerk and bookkeeper in a grocery store, he seems to have felt that his work was mundane and impoverishing. For several months, he tried his hand as superintendent of a government hospital at Lookout Mountain in Tennessee. But neither situation suited him.[87] Whether driven by temperament, repressed desire, economic desperation, or simply curiosity, sometime before 1868 Anthony Comstock left the land of Canaan forever and moved to a place far more resonant of John Bunyan's Land of Destruction and Town of Carnal-Policy.

For a man who worried so much about the poisons of alcohol and pornography, and his own "weakness," we can only wonder why Comstock chose to move to a place so opposite from Bunyan's City of Zion in every way imaginable. New York City in the post–Civil War era was not just a dense, crowded urban environment; it was infamous for pervasive and shocking levels of sin. If we accept Comstock on his own terms and consider his origins, we can understand this decision best in the light of the Kellogg Brothers' rendering of the *Evil Tree* of *Wrath*: *"A Corrupt tree cannot bring forth good fruit."* / *"Cut it down why cumbreth it the ground."* What better place was there to cut down the trees that nourished the most evil vices of the world?

Comstock probably had little fear. He left Connecticut armed not only with unshakable self-confidence and the narrative of a conquering Christian hero, but also with an ingrained belief in the superiority of his sex, religion, race, aesthetics, sexual orientation, physical capability, and brand of morality. All of this would be demonstrated in years ahead by his fierce courage in seeking out and facing down insidious evils, matched by a vigorous public performance of restraint from the many temptations of Lust he encountered nearly on a daily basis. For almost fifty years following his audacious move to New York City, Anthony Comstock tried to pluck and burn the corrupt fruits of the Evil Tree, deep-rooted in Gotham. The city, however, proved to be a much denser forest than he could have imagined.

THE GREAT CITY

Accounts of Anthony Comstock's arrival in New York City in 1867 differ in some small details. Charles Gallaudet Trumbull recorded in 1913 that the future censor disembarked from the train "with three dollars and forty-five cents in his pocket," but Comstock himself had told a reporter several years earlier that the amount was thirty-four dollars.[88] In either case, such scant fortune put him at a severe disadvantage in the city's post–Civil War housing market, in which a flood of recent migrants had resulted in rent prices nearly doubling "within a year after Appomatox."[89]

With no connections, and a first job as a porter in a dry goods store, Comstock's initial "cheap lodging house in Pearl Street, near the City Hall" likely suffered from deprivations similar to those described by Edward Winslow Martin (pseudonym of James D. McCabe) in *The Secrets of the Great City*: "apartments may be indifferently ventilated by half-windows, and attics constructed so that standing erect within them is only practicable in one spot. . . . notice the mortal remains of mosquitoes (not to mention more odoriferous and objectionable insects) ornamenting ceilings and walls, where they have encountered Destiny in the shape of slippers or boot-soles of former occupants."[90]

Even at inflated prices, lodgers rarely enjoyed comfortable or even safe accommodations. In 1867, a committee of the New York State Assembly determined that more than half of Manhattan's tenements were a serious threat to the health and even the lives of occupants.[91] The situation on the streets outside these treacherous residences was scarcely any safer. The frontispiece of Martin's book (figure 1.6) illustrates his cautionary message with a visual narration of a common tragedy. We follow our protagonist in farmer's dress from upper left, where two women and a loving dog bid him farewell as he departs for the city, to a saloon at upper right, where four "waiter girls" in low-cut dresses and a man sporting a top hat drink with him. At center, the women are seen walking away, and several men watch as he downs yet another glass of liquor. Finally, he is roughed up and robbed at night in a dark scene on a dock, and his body is "Found by the Harbor Police."

In the hundreds of pages of text that follow this cautionary montage, Martin lists myriad types of frauds, shams, and ruses to avoid, including bummers, bogus stock salesmen, pickpockets, deceptive marriage brokers, pocket-book droppers, mock auctions, and foreign, hotel, and female swindlers.[92] All of these dangers were readily available on the streets surrounding Comstock's first New York City residence.

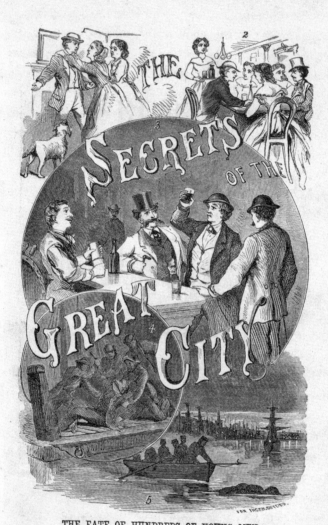

FIGURE 1.6 James D. McCabe [a.k.a. Edward Winslow Martin], *Frontispiece: The Secrets of the Great City: A Work Descriptive of the Virtues and the Vices, the Mysteries, Miseries and Crimes of New York City* (Philadelphia, Cincinnati, Chicago, St. Louis and Atlanta: Jones, Brothers & Co., 1868), frontispiece. From the New York Public Library.

In 1867, Pearl Street at the intersection of City Hall Place was densely packed with narrow residential buildings, many with first-floor retail shops filled with a full array of the city's "vices, miseries, and crimes." Several guidebooks affirm Martin's report that neighborhoods within a half mile of Comstock's lodging offered brothels of various types, "assignation houses" where one easily could bring a liaison, saloons, dance houses, gambling dens, rat and dog fights, fortune tellers proffering "love charms," and "quack doctors." As Timothy Gilfoyle notes, "hordes of streetwalkers plied their trade in the hotels and lodging houses stretching from the Brooklyn Bridge to Chatham Square at the foot of the Bowery, and along Chambers Street behind City Hall Park."[93] Although Martin certainly would have warned Comstock about the dark streets surrounding his first lodging house, he was in a perfect place to take in not only the lows but also the highs of the "Great City."

Adjacent to New York's political epicenter at City Hall, America's foremost publishing industry nestled into the maze of streets east of the park, framed by Broadway, John Street, Frankfort Street, and Franklin Square. From here, the nation's newspapers of record—including *The Sun*, *The New York Herald*, *The Evening Telegram*, *The New York Times*, *The New-York Tribune*, and *The New York World*—not only printed hundreds of thousands of copies daily, but also cast their stories far afield through an immense network of telegraph wires. Most of the nation's influential weekly and monthly magazines were also housed in this area, including *Harper's*, *Frank Leslie's*, *The Nation*, *The Mercury*, *The Days' Doings*, *The New-York Evangelist*, and an astonishing array of foreign language publications catering to the country's new immigrants and evangelicals.[94] Across Broadway from the garishly ornate courthouse at the south end of City Hall Park, the nation's retail epicenter sprawled northward, anchored by the enormous warehouse of the famed A. T. Stewart department store. Comstock told a reporter in 1906 that his initial efforts in New York were directed at becoming "a second A. T. Stewart."[95]

Not surprisingly, no records or diary entries survive that would reveal whether Comstock ever let his curiosity, sense of adventure, or even lust entice him to partake in any of the dark and disreputable entertainments available to him during his bachelor years in New York. Given all that he accomplished in those three years, however, it seems highly unlikely that he would have had much time to do so. Trumbull writes that by the end of Comstock's first week in Manhattan, he had secured work at the dry goods firm of Amidon, Lane & Co. as a porter. This first job was located at 37 Warren Street, just a stroll through the park and a handful of blocks away from his lodging house. Due to his assiduous efforts, he was soon promoted to the post of shipping clerk. Two years later, he moved to a better job as stock clerk and salesman at J. B. Spellman and Sons, a short distance farther down Warren Street.[96]

Comstock's final position in the dry goods business, and the last leg of his aborted mission to become "the second A. T. Stewart," drew him into a significantly more upscale corner of the city. In 1871, Comstock accepted a job as salesman at the much larger and more prestigious establishment of Cochran, McLean, and Co.[97] His workplace literally had moved up, to the impressive intersection of Broadway and Grand, where neighboring businesses included Brooks Brothers and Lord and Taylor.

Comstock's rapid ascent in the dry goods world is a fairly clear indication that he was focused on nobler pursuits than New York's many "mysteries" and "dark secrets." Additional support for this conclusion lies in the annual reports of the YMCA, in which Anthony Comstock is listed as an "active member" from the year of his arrival in 1867. Comstock's eager membership in the organization is hardly surprising. He had already participated in the YMCA's sister organization, the Christian Commission, during the Civil War by distributing donated Bibles and arranging prayer meetings. In fact, the New York YMCA's central mission since its founding in 1852 was precisely to protect young men like Comstock from the dangers so graphically catalogued by Martin and others.

An article in the *Evening Post* in 1866 titled "The Clerks of New York" described the aims of the YMCA's Gotham chapter on the eve of Comstock's arrival: to provide "improving associations and harmless amusements" for young men, with a library, lectures, "social, musical and literary meetings," and "religious instruction and help." The article went on to tell tragic cautionary tales of unfortunate young clerks who had not found their way to the YMCA. To save more men, the article asserted, bold action was needed in the form of a magnificent new building that would supplant the inadequate smaller rented spaces that rendered the association "but little known." Donations were eagerly solicited.[98]

The building that resulted from these calls for action was an extraordinarily grand French Second Empire palace on Twenty-Third Street designed by James Renwick. *Harper's Weekly* termed the new building the nation's first "Christian Clubhouse."[99] The *New York Times* gushed as well, with special admiration for the lecture hall with galleries on each side. The massive organ in the hall offered "great advantages over any organ in the country," with "more mechanical appliances than any organ in the world."[100] New York was no longer just the center of the nation's business, publishing, and vice industries. Just as Anthony Comstock arrived, it asserted its preeminence also as the most exciting place in America to be a Christian.

As a member of the YMCA, and especially after the opening of the new building in 1869, Comstock was able to escape the environs of his cheap and lonely lodging and associate with like-minded Christians in a much better neighborhood. He could have used the modern gymnasium and enjoyed lectures on subjects including travels to foreign lands, Christian principles, and literature. Still, however, most of Comstock's time was spent in pursuit of his mercantile aims in the loudly beating heart of New York's retail sector.

Martin described the neighborhood surrounding Cochran, McLean & Co. as the busiest part of the city, with hundreds of horse-drawn omnibuses in the street and sidewalks that were thronged "with every class and shade and character. . . . High and low, rich and poor, pass along these side-walks at a speed particular to New York, and positively bewildering to a stranger. No one seems to think of any person but himself, and each one jostles by him with an indifference amusing to behold."[101] Following in the footsteps of many New Yorkers before and after him, in 1871 Comstock used his hard-earned savings to leave the congestion, noise, and filth of the city behind. He set his sights on Brooklyn.

In 1871, the city of Brooklyn was a serene antidote to Manhattan, a still semirural municipality that appealed to those willing to commute back and forth across the mile-wide East River on ferries. Brooklyn's relative isolation would be short-lived; the opening of the Brooklyn Bridge in 1883 launched an era of rapid population growth. Nevertheless, at the time Comstock chose Brooklyn as the place to buy his first home, it truly was a world apart from its noisier neighbor across the water. *Miller's New York As It Is* guidebook, published in 1872, described Brooklyn in a manner that undoubtedly would have appealed to a young man who always remained nostalgic about his childhood home: "It is a favorite place of residence by the New Yorkers, from its pure air, as well as its numerous trees, which line most of its streets, and impart to it a rural aspect."[102]

Comstock was especially lucky in his choice of the Clinton Hill neighborhood in Brooklyn in 1871. Just three years after Comstock purchased his home, businessman Charles Pratt chose to build his own residence on Clinton Avenue just a few blocks away. As director of John D. Rockefeller's Standard Oil Trust, Pratt had amassed a fortune, and he spent a significant part of it building mansions in the neighborhood for himself and his children (several of these homes still survive today). He also went on to found the Pratt Institute, located on an enormous campus just a few blocks from Comstock's home.[103]

Although Clinton Hill's beautiful mansions and churches were undoubtedly enjoyable to look at and certainly would have raised his property value, Comstock may also have felt envious or even resentful as he eyed his new neighbors' elaborate Italianate facades, beautifully manicured gardens, and in particular, their massive domestic spaces. Grand Avenue, contrary to its name, was not especially grand; instead it offered "rows of modest houses built for workers."[104] The house Comstock bought at 354 Grand Avenue no longer survives, but it appears in a detailed Brooklyn map of 1898 as a brick residence measuring just eleven feet wide, probably with just two floors of living space; as such, it was one of the smallest houses in Clinton Hill.[105]

Nevertheless, as a photograph from around this time reveals, Anthony Comstock was now a respectable salesman and homeowner, sporting a

FIGURE 1.7 Photograph of Anthony Comstock, ca. 1871. Illustration included in: Heywood Broun and Margaret Leech, *Anthony Comstock: Roundsman of the Lord* (New York: A. & C. Boni, 1927).

carefully knotted silk bow tie, formidable woolen overcoat, and bushy mutton chop whiskers (figure 1.7). Moreover, he had taken one further step toward respectable adulthood. The house at 354 Grand undoubtedly felt crowded soon after his purchase, for he did not arrive alone: on January 25, 1871, Anthony Comstock married.

Margaret Hamilton Comstock, known as Maggie, left little documentation behind that reveals her thoughts about marriage, or indeed any other aspect of her life. The scant available evidence, consisting mostly of small asides enmeshed within stories about her husband, suggests that after 1871 she lived a quiet life in his growing shadow. The couple started their lives together on a cold winter day and shortly after their ceremony in Brooklyn, left for a patriotic tour of Philadelphia and Washington, D.C. Anthony and Maggie spent time at Independence Hall, the Capitol Building, and the beautiful U.S. Post Office and Patent Buildings. Although Comstock's diary was filled with wonder and joy, he described his wife frequently as tired, preferring "the quiet evenings in the hotel to rambunctious expeditions through the raw, snow-filled streets." Comstock visited the White House without her.[106]

This pairing of fierce energy with retiring inertia seems to have marked the Comstock marriage through all of its forty-four years. Maggie Hamilton was ten years older than her new husband and arrived on Grand Avenue with her father, a struggling shopkeeper, and her sister Jennie, who "was to pass long years in their home as a bed-ridden invalid." Comstock's diary reveals that he initially thought of the marriage as a special joy because it was also a charitable act that aided a family in difficult straits. On the day of their wedding, he wrote in his diary "my darling is at last free from her long years of cares."[107] The charitable aspect of the union allowed the Hamilton family finally to quit their failing and exhausting efforts to survive in trade and never again to worry about how or where they would live. Whatever might have been the imperfections of his family or his marriage, Comstock would never again be alone. He soon set in motion a series of events that assured he never would be on his own in his professional life and evangelical mission as well.

2

ONWARD CHRISTIAN SOLDIERS

....

Creating the Industry and Infrastructure of
American Vice Suppression

FROM SOLDIER TO ARMY

Anthony Comstock wasted no time in setting down roots after purchasing a home in Brooklyn and marrying his wife, Maggie, in 1871. Among
other things, this included promptly joining the nearby Clinton Avenue
Congregational Church, a short walk from his home on Grand Avenue.
Comstock was fortunate in his proximity to the lovely brick Romanesque
church at the corner of Clinton and Lafayette Avenues, especially because
it was filled with fellow Connecticut men, including his new pastor
William Ives Budington, whose emphasis on audience participation in
singing hymns and chanting psalms undoubtedly made services more
enjoyable.[1] In addition to regularly attending services, Comstock taught
Sunday school to boys in a mission and held prayer meetings in the wom-
en's ward of a jail.[2]

Despite his many occupations during his early years in New York,
including career, home, family, and church, Comstock's diary entries reveal
that he was "restless and dissatisfied . . . eaten by a longing to live nobly, to
do his duty."[3] Since childhood, Comstock had seen himself as a "Soldier of
the Cross," as the popular hymn jubilantly proclaimed, and in New York

there was more Satanic vice surrounding him than ever before, against which to wage war. Comstock's first foray into cleaning up the city's gargantuan vice industry occurred as early as 1868, less than a year after his arrival in Gotham.

In discussing the beginnings of his vigilante efforts in New York, Comstock always cited as his first motivation the death of a fellow clerk who "had been led astray and corrupted and diseased" following exposure to pornography.[4] He was determined to save other young men from the dangerous desires provoked by sexually arousing materials. During his time as a clerk in a dry goods business on Warren Street in lower Manhattan in 1868, Comstock became aware that one of the city's largest publishers of sexually explicit literature was located just a block away from his workplace. Comstock took it upon himself to investigate Charles Conroy's basement lair and later returned with a police officer.[5] For the next four years, Comstock continued making these types of raids, turning down bribes and facing death threats, but always refusing to relent. Offenders near his home in Brooklyn especially caused irritation. When Comstock unsuccessfully tried to shut down saloons in Clinton Hill operating on Sundays in flagrant violation of the law, he found himself utterly frustrated, and railed in his diary against "the actions of corrupt officials in our city. This is a murderous age. Crime stalketh abroad by daylight and Public officers wink at it. Money can buy our judges and corrupt our juries."[6]

Despite his lack of success in jailing offenders, Comstock all the while was studying the vice trade and making progress in strategizing how best to achieve his desired results. Comstock described the case of William and Mary Haines with detailed interest: "About 35 years ago he was a prominent Physician in [the] Old Country [Ireland]. Married noblemans [sic] daughter. Lechered another. Forced to leave Country. Came to America & married Mary S. present wife." The couple had been producing obscene books in New York for 30 years, with a complex operation in which the printing was done in Brooklyn, the binding in Manhattan, and the stock "stored in Atlantic Hotel Room 10 Jersey City." According to Comstock's notes, the couple regularly paid blackmail money to police, including once the enormous sum of $750 to an officer named Dusenberg, in order to avoid seizure of their stock.[7]

In addition to learning about the various specializations within the industry and its physical and financial exigencies, Comstock also began to understand that New York was the manufacturing hub for a vast national trade in illicit materials. Books produced in Warren Street and stored in New Jersey were sold not only by boys hawking wares on city streets, but also by dealers across the country who used newspapers and circulars to advertise products that then were delivered through the U.S. mails. The magnitude of the materials produced and consumed was simply enormous, matched by an immense flow of illicit payments to police officers. Clearly, Comstock needed help. He never would be able to succeed alone as a Soldier of the Cross—he needed an army. Thankfully, sympathetic troops had already been amassing.

Across the East River from Comstock's home in Brooklyn, the gentlemen leaders of the New York YMCA likewise were eager to reduce the city's many inducements to evil that might cause young men to abandon their Christian principles. Since 1852, YMCA leaders had been providing resources that encouraged young men to choose paths of virtue. Now they embarked on a new project: using legislation to punish those who impeded their efforts. In addition to serving as Angels of Mercy, the YMCA now also sought to act as Soldiers of the Cross.

In contrast to Comstock, who acted alone with passion, courage, and typically in haste, the YMCA's leaders proceeded with methodical and deliberate collaboration by forming and tasking committees, generating reports, and making, amending, and approving motions for even the smallest of actions. These diligent and officious methods reflected well the professional skills of the YMCA's directors, who came from the ranks of the city's wealthiest evangelical lawyers, bankers, merchants, and industrialists. As Sven Beckert notes, in the post–Civil War years, this rapidly rising class of bourgeoisie "focused ever more narrowly on the guarding of their own elevated social position."[8] Ridding New York's streets of pornography and pornographers not only would achieve their evangelical aims, but also would raise their own property values. Keeping pornography out of the hands of their children was imperative to preserving the social capital of their families.[9]

Another impetus was politics. Heywood Broun and Margaret Leech, Progressive-era libertarians, placed the new laws these men advocated for in the context of post–Civil War expansion of the federal government, when "the Jeffersonian theory of the autonomy of the State was lost in the submergence of the Democratic party in the years following the Civil War."[10] Members of the YMCA's board of directors uniformly were Republicans. Neatly organized minutes of their meetings, special committee reports, and correspondence all clearly illustrate the path they took between 1865 and 1873 to invent a new governmental and private American occupation: vice suppression.[11]

To begin their efforts, leaders first commissioned an exhaustive study in 1865 of the city's most outrageous vices, incorporating an innovative combination of comprehensive cataloguing and impressive statistical analysis. The report then was sent to 1,000 "persons of high standing and influence" as part of a lobbying effort to pass a comprehensive law in the New York State Assembly that would outlaw the city's vast trade in "Obscene Literature, Illustrations, Advertisements and Articles of Indecent or Immoral Use."[12] This first post–Civil War foray into fighting immorality set a pattern that would be repeated in later years, consisting of data collection, reporting, drafting legislation, and lobbying for new laws and enforcement.

Most of the directors' meetings in the years following 1865 were consumed with the planning and fundraising necessary to complete their grand new YMCA building on Twenty-Third Street. Nonetheless, the directors still found time to return to their legislative agenda on a regular basis. At the board's May meeting in 1867, Cephas Brainerd, an attorney and member of the YMCA executive committee, reported that the bill they had authored on obscene literature had been passed in New York's State Senate, but stalled in the House. "When upon being again called up for action, it was discovered that the Bill had been stolen from the Clerk's desk, and so was defeated."[13]

The directors, however, were unfazed and persistent. Secretary Robert McBurney recorded on April 1, 1868, that an appropriation of $500 had been approved "to aid in the passage through the Legislature of this State a bill against Obscene Literature now 'held' in that body." With this added grease and a flurry of amendments, the bill finally passed in Albany. The minutes do not specify what types of persuasions were purchased with the $500, but regardless, the investment had paid off in a substantial victory. The language of the new bill prohibited for the first time "articles of indecent and immoral use" and the advertisements that facilitated their sale. Contraceptives, abortifacients, and advertisements that recommended them now all were fair game for police and prosecutors in New York.[14]

Finally armed with a comprehensive state law, the board of directors moved forward with their plans to suppress obscene publications. In 1869, board members raised funds and hired detectives, but the results of their efforts were discouraging. Corrupt police and district attorneys, and disinterested judges and juries, all were resistant to upholding the new law. The YMCA directors desperately needed a foot soldier to do the ungentlemanly work of actually rounding up the producers and their wares.[15] Cephas Brainerd, who became committee chair in 1872, wrote a lengthy reminiscence of these years in 1901, in which he recounted the fateful moment when the gentlemen of the YMCA first met the effective roundsman who would catalyze their efforts.[16]

As Brainerd recalled, Comstock wrote a letter to Robert McBurney, after he "had made some complaints and had been unsuccessful in some of them and . . . some Police officer at the Tombs who had taken an interest in his work, had recommended him to go to the Association, saying that they had been able to secure convictions."[17] At that moment, Morris Ketchum Jesup, chair of the YMCA board, entered the scene, thus changing the course of Comstock's life, and American law and culture, for the next century. Jesup's biographer writes that Comstock's letter sat on McBurney's desk "so indistinctly written that he returned it to the writer to be recopied. But before it left his hands he showed it to Mr. Jesup, and the latter was so much impressed by what he read that he determined to visit the writer in person, in order to hear his story for himself."[18]

Comstock was greatly surprised when Jesup showed up at his workplace at Cochran, McLean, & Co., but also thrilled that after the interview "Mr. Jesup invited me to meet Mr. McBurney and himself at his home on Madison Avenue. At that meeting, I disclosed the facts that I had discovered. I said I thought if I had a little money I could get at the stock of the publishers." The next morning, Jesup's check was in the mail.[19] Clearly, he suspected that the directors finally had found the "competent person" they had been hoping for, an individual who could effectively lead the fight to suppress the city's obscenity industry.

Comstock must have been wonderfully excited by Jesup's visit to his office, and by the invitation to meet at his home. Morris Ketchum Jesup today is most famous for his role as a founder and president of the American Museum of Natural History, a position he held for more than twenty-five years. He also cofounded the YMCA of New York, led the Christian Commission during the Civil War, and maintained leadership roles in the New York City Mission and Tract Society, the Audubon Society, the Union Theological Seminary, and the American Society for the Prevention of Cruelty to Animals.

In some small ways, Comstock and Jesup were very much alike. Jesup was also from Connecticut and the descendent of families that had arrived there in the mid-seventeenth century. The two men shared a childhood spent in impoverished circumstances. After his father's death, Jesup left school at the age of twelve "to help his mother, whose fortune had been swept away in the Panic of 1837."[20] Both men were deeply conservative, going so far as to favor side-whiskers long after they were out of fashion, a hirsute signal of their preference for conservative values. Despite these similarities, however, the two men lived in vastly different worlds.

Unlike Comstock, Jesup was enormously wealthy. He had formed a partnership in 1857 that acted "as middlemen between the manufacturers and the railroads" and soon "drifted into a banking business" and several other profitable ventures.[21] The home Jesup shared with his wife, Maria Van Antwerp, was a brick building with a stone façade, measuring 25 feet wide by 100 feet deep, with four stories.[22] The mansion was located in the city's fashionable Murray Hill neighborhood on Madison Avenue, which was wide and sunny and lined with stately single-family brownstones—a far cry from the narrow and somewhat dark confines of Comstock's home at 354 Grand Avenue in Brooklyn.

When Comstock was welcomed into Jesup's sumptuous parlor, he surely understood that he was making an important alliance. Comstock had begun his life on a sparse farm and moved on to even sparser army barracks, cheap lodging houses, and most recently to a tiny, crowded house in Brooklyn. In all of his lifetime experiences, he had never been invited into the inner circle of the wealthy and powerful. And yet, at this moment, he dealt with a rich man not as a clerk or salesman but as a valued ally and expert. Jesup would remain one of his most stalwart supporters until his retirement from public life in 1898.[23] As Comstock's diary entries reveal, as a young man he was plagued by normal bouts of youthful self-doubt and sometimes confusion about what the Lord wanted him to do. He never would suffer those painful emotions again. He had found an army of like-minded Soldiers of the Cross, equipped with an arsenal of money and political clout. They wasted no time in amassing troops.

HOT HASTE

Following Morris Jesup's initial meeting with Anthony Comstock in April 1872, the "warfare against obscene books" moved extremely quickly. A few weeks later, on May 9th, Jesup organized a meeting at his home for the entire YMCA Committee for the Suppression of Obscene Literature, other prominent New Yorkers, and members of the press. A *New York Times* article published the following day termed the event an "important private meeting" of "select company." This principally was Comstock's show, and he not only detailed his efforts and frustrations with perpetrators, police, juries, and judges but also "made startling exposures of persons high in official position and honored in the Church, who have made fortunes by backing men who manufactured and sold these things."[24]

Comstock had more than mere gossip to share. After he told his stories, he "exhibited plates and books which he seized, aided by the Police."[25] This undoubtedly was one of the most rousing YMCA committee meetings anyone had ever attended. At the end of the meeting, the "company united in pledging MR. COMSTOCK both influence and money to carry on the work which he had prosecuted so successfully."[26] Liberal contributions followed swiftly, in amounts sufficient to pay Comstock a robust salary of $3,000 per year plus expenses. Thanks to the YMCA's largesse, Comstock was able to quit his job as a clerk and take up the work of fighting vice on a full-time basis.[27] While Jesup, McBurney, and Brainerd solicited donations and began to draft language and lobby for even more stringent legislation, Comstock continued to seek out obscenities for zealous prosecution under the strengthened New York State statute.

In the months following the May meeting, Comstock added an effective new strategy to his previous efforts. Using a variety of aliases and addresses, he ordered goods advertised in popular lowbrow newspapers such as the *Sunday Mercury*, *Days' Doings*, *New Varieties*, and *National Police Gazette*. With the evidence in his possession, Comstock then worked with postmasters to prove the identity of the persons who had mailed them, at which point he could easily obtain a bench warrant for their arrest. Comstock termed the resulting haul of materials a "hydra-headed monster" of obscenity.[28]

The haul was so dramatic that in December 1872, YMCA leaders commissioned Comstock to describe his seizures in a "Private and Confidential" report that was circulated to raise awareness, generate political support, and solicit more funds for the cause. Comstock wasted no time in setting an apocalyptic tone for his subject: the cover of the report bears an ominous warning that each copy is "numbered, and the name of each person who receives one from the Secretary is preserved with the number of the pamphlet."[29] Inside, Comstock detailed the "baldest facts" he had uncovered.

The report began by describing "the extent of the traffic" with a list of seizures, typically made by police after Comstock's investigative work.

These included seven tons of books, 187,600 pictures and photographs, 625 negative photographic plates, 350 engraved plates, five tons of stereotype plates, 5,500 playing cards, 10,000 advertising circulars and catalogues, letters showing orders from 10,000 customers, and account books detailing the names of more than 6,000 dealers across the country.

Certainly, if they so chose, readers of the report could have used it as an educational guide to learn how to locate vice rather than suppress it. Comstock included detailed descriptions of specific items for sale and their usual cost. "Preventives of conception," readers were assured, "are a license to illicit intercourse between persons nominally respectable, by defeating results otherwise likely to follow, while they throw open the doors of brothels by almost ensuring against infection from diseased women." Expensive books such as those by Paul de Kock ranged from one to six dollars, while cheaper versions could be had for twenty-five or fifty cents. Ironically, Comstock's explicit and frank language made the report itself a possible candidate for seizure under the 1868 New York State anti-obscenity law. Nevertheless, no mention of the report ever was made in the press, and only a single copy survives today.[30]

From the start of his career as a full-time vice fighter in the summer of 1872, Comstock's energy was nearly boundless; he vigorously pursued prosecutorial targets, extensively documented and wrote about his efforts, and actively courted influential and wealthy supporters. He was learning at a furious pace about the intricacies of both criminal investigations and court procedures. At the same time, Comstock was also gaining insight into the power of the press, or more specifically, of publicity.

Between March and August 1872, the *New-York Evangelist* and *New York Times* mentioned Comstock's name in several brief stories on court actions involving his prosecutions. Although these stories were buried deep within the papers, still it must have been gratifying to Comstock when the *Evangelist* described him as "zealous in this good work."[31] His relative anonymity lasted only a short time, however. In November 1872, Comstock burst onto front pages thanks to his prosecution of a woman who herself had mastered the art of using publicity in spectacular fashion to become "one of the modern world's first celebrities."[32]

Victoria Woodhull has been studied by numerous historians, including most notably Amanda Frisken, who have employed a variety of delightful adjectives to describe her career: improbable, unlikely, astounding, extraordinary, surprising, and incredible, all are words that aptly apply. Born and raised in Ohio, Victoria Claflin married Canning Woodhull at fourteen to escape a difficult home life as the daughter of a con man and a mother who channeled the voices of the dead to earn money through the popular practice of spiritualism. The marriage was disastrous, and Woodhull soon divorced her abusive and alcoholic husband. At the age of twenty-eight she married again, this time to Colonel James Harvey Blood, a Civil War veteran and doctor. Woodhull kept her first husband's name, along with the assumption of her right to pursue her professional ambitions rather than any domestic responsibilities. She believed in the perfect equality of the sexes, universal suffrage, and the ideal of free love, which sought to eliminate state involvement in marriage, and sex in general, in favor of individual choice and freedom.[33]

The improbable part of her story is not that Woodhull held these radical beliefs, but rather her boldness in acting upon them. After moving to New York City in 1868, Victoria and her sister Tennessee Claflin became acquainted with Cornelius Vanderbilt, who utilized Woodhull as a spiritualist adviser and purportedly had an affair with the beautiful "Tennie." In 1869, with Vanderbilt's assistance, the two sisters became the first women to own a brokerage firm trading on the New York Stock Exchange: Woodhull, Claflin & Company.

Thanks to Vanderbilt's financial support, Woodhull and Claflin quickly made enough money to lease a stately home just three blocks from Morris Jesup on Murray Hill in 1870. From there, Woodhull launched a new career as a spokesperson for spiritualism, suffrage, and what she called "social freedom." The most prominent venue for her views was a newspaper, *Woodhull and Claflin's Weekly*, which she, Tennie, and Colonel Blood founded and edited beginning in May 1870. The sisters frequently appeared on the front pages of other sensational newspapers as well, such as the *Days' Doings* and *The National Police Gazette*, and soon even the mainstream press regularly covered the sisters' novel lifestyle and radical ideas.

In January 1871, Woodhull took her show to an even bigger stage. With the support of Massachusetts Congressman Benjamin Butler, she addressed the House Judiciary Committee to advocate for women's right to vote. Flanked by Susan B. Anthony and Elizabeth Cady Stanton, Woodhull electrified the room by eloquently and fiercely arguing that the language of the Fourteenth Amendment granted suffrage to women, and all that was needed was a declarative act from Congress to affirm that right. Although the committee quickly and almost unanimously tabled the motion, nonetheless Woodhull made her mark in history as the first female speaker to address the most powerful men's club in America. Victoria Woodhull was now a bona fide national celebrity.

Throughout the course of 1871, Woodhull grew increasingly bold, taking on new causes such as socialism and communism. *Woodhull and Claflin's Weekly* became the first American newspaper to publish Karl Marx's *Manifesto* in English translation; as a result, Woodhull's lecture circuit expanded to include trade unions. At the end of the year, on November 21, 1871, Woodhull gave a speech to "one of the largest audiences ever collected together . . . in this City" at Steinway Hall in New York. The *New York Times* reported that the text of her speech, "The Principle of Social Freedom, Involving Free Love, Marriage, Divorce, &c.," "was directed chiefly to an attack on the marriage system, as at present constituted, as an outrage on individual freedom and happiness." On this matter, "as in all others which affected private life, the Government should not be permitted to interfere."

The assembled crowd mostly booed and hissed, and Woodhull was even interrupted by jeers from a third sister, Mrs. Utica "Utie" Brooker, but eventually she did finish her lecture. Assisting her in holding the floor was the writer Theodore Tilton, who had introduced her to the stage with a speech assuring the audience that "notwithstanding all insinuations to the contrary, she was a virtuous woman, and he could vouch for it."[34]

The unlikely story of a poorly educated woman rising to become the first woman to run a brokerage firm on the New York Stock Exchange and testify in Congress took another surprising turn toward sheer circus the following year. Notwithstanding the reaction to her controversial speech in Steinway Hall, Woodhull still enjoyed some support for her controversial views. The tiny Equal Rights Party nominated her in May 1872 as the first female candidate in history for president of the United States. Most of her former supporters, however, began to disavow her as too radical. Susan B. Anthony did not think the suffrage movement benefited from an association with free love, and Cornelius Vanderbilt also withdrew his support following her rabid pronouncements against capitalism.[35]

By the end of August of that year, the *New York Times* reported that Woodhull and Claflin were "not worth a single dollar."[36] Woodhull was desperate, and bitter at what she felt was the utter hypocrisy of her enemies. Instinctively turning to press publicity to engineer her rise again, she decided to use *Woodhull and Clafin's Weekly* to prove that the "social freedom" and free love for which she advocated were already practiced by many of the most prominent men and women in the city.

Woodhull could not have chosen a more sensational target for the launch of her campaign against the city's social hypocrisy. Henry Ward Beecher was a Protestant superstar—a gifted orator, son of the famed minister Lyman Beecher, and brother of the best-selling authors Catharine Beecher and Harriet Beecher Stowe. From his desk as the leader of the Plymouth Congregational Church in Brooklyn Heights, Beecher supported some of the same radical causes and beliefs as Woodhull, including women's suffrage and Darwin's theory of evolution. As forward-thinking as he was, however, Beecher still maintained the value of the traditional family, and disavowed free love.[37] Woodhull was incensed by his hypocrisy. For more than two years, she had heard rumors and kept secret the very credible allegations that Beecher had been carrying on an affair with Theodore Tilton's wife Elizabeth, and had even fathered her child.

Facing bankruptcy in the fall of 1872, Woodhull gambled that she could gain sympathy for her social views by outing Beecher's story. She first spoke out about the affair at a conference of spiritualists in September 1872, and then prepared a lengthy article detailing Beecher's acts and hypocrisy in *Woodhull and Claflin's Weekly*. Tennessee added an article to the issue that accused a wealthy Wall Street speculator named Luther Challis of debauching young women. The *Weekly* "was immediately controversial, and demand was so high that copies sold for as much as $40 each."[38]

While Woodhull and Claflin's scandalous allegations were even more profitable than they had hoped, they also resulted in an unforeseen consequence: criminal prosecution by New York's newest vice suppressor. Anthony Comstock was incensed by the attack by radical women on Beecher's good name. He first tried to obtain a bench warrant for the arrest of Woodhull and Claflin under New York State's new anti-obscenity law, but was turned down. Then he applied his newest investigative trick. Comstock ordered a copy of the paper by mail from Greenwich, Connecticut, using a fictitious name. When it arrived, he presented it as evidence to obtain a warrant in federal court for the arrest of Woodhull, Claflin, and Blood on charges of using the U.S. mails to distribute obscenity.

Federal marshals promptly arrested Claflin and Woodhull in their carriage on the way to the post office, with 3,000 copies of the *Weekly* ready to mail. Under Comstock's direction, the papers were seized and the sisters were deposited in the Ludlow Street jail. Bail was set at the then outrageous and staggering sum of $10,000, and the three offenders sat in jail while federal prosecutors readied their case and Challis's lawyers filed a separate civil lawsuit against them alleging libel. Comstock's name now began to appear frequently in newspaper coverage of the trials.[39]

In the course of these events, Comstock learned a valuable lesson about the power of the media: targeting high-profile defendants implicated in spicy crimes was the quickest way to build his name as America's preeminent vice suppressor. Comstock continued to seek out defendants who were already in the news, and frequently brought press with him on raids. For many of his cases in 1872, Comstock even listed himself and "Robert Griffith N.Y. Tribune" as witnesses.[40] As the criminal and civil proceedings against the three editors in the instructive case of *Woodhull and Claflin's Weekly* moved slowly through the courts, Comstock's notoriety grew, along with his powers of advocacy. He now made rapid progress in efforts to pass an expanded anti-obscenity law in Congress that would set the stage for the arrests of more newspaper editors and entrepreneurs sending sexually explicit stories, advertisements, images, and objects through the

U.S. mail. In December 1872, just one year after his honeymoon in the nation's capital, Comstock once again was on the train for Washington, D.C., this time carrying suitcases filled with examples of obscenity rather than the trousseau of his bride.

That cold winter session was far from an obvious moment to push through new law. The Forty-Second Congress was embroiled in a scandal of epic proportions involving kickbacks to representatives and senators from investment in a scam organization known as the Crédit Mobilier of America, a corporation that had contracted to build railroads with federal dollars. The Crédit Mobilier scandal has been described as providing motivation for legislators to appear virtuous by passing new censorship legislation. Comstock certainly did not see things that way. In his diary, he instead complained that the scandal was "the chock before the wheels of legislation. The exebitions [*sic*] of today in the Halls of legislation has been one that outrages all decency. Men assailing one another while legislation goes begging. Malice fills the air. Party bitterness and venom. Loud talk of constitution, law, justice. It seems a burlesque on our Forefathers." Throughout January, he complained in his diary about delays.[41]

Presumably seeking the same momentum he had gained from exhibiting seized materials in Jesup's parlors, in January Comstock returned to Washington and began to display his traveling road show of obscenities around the capital. On January 31st, the *New York Times* reported that "the enormity of the traffic in obscene literature has been made so apparent lately, that many of [the representatives] express a willingness to vote for any measure that will put a stop to it, even to the stretching of a constitutional point, if necessary."[42] On February 24th, the *New York Herald* reported more details of the exhibitions:

> A fellow named Comstock . . . came here a few weeks ago with a budget of indecent engravings and immoral articles, which he professed to have obtained in response to letters which he sent, enclosing money, to parties who advertised them for sale. His first exhibition was at the house of that statesman, Sub. [Samuel Clarke] Pomeroy, and the leading lights of the Young Men's Christian Association were invited by printed circulars to

go there and gaze upon this collection. Then they were displayed in the room of [Vice President Schuyler] Colfax at the Capitol, and Comstock eloquently decanted on the necessity for a law not only to prevent the sale of dirty trash, but to suppress all advertisements which did not meet his approval.

Despite carping from the press about Comstock's "decanting," the exhibitions in the capital clearly energized their audiences.[43]

Although the gentlemen who attended these events certainly would not have had time to read the lengthy narratives in the confiscated books to discern the full dimensions of the situation, it was hardly necessary for them to do so. As Comstock no doubt anticipated, the shocking illustrations, photographs, and "immoral" objects he displayed rapidly conveyed the "enormity'" of the problem.[44] Following his exhibitions, a bill that soon became known as the "Comstock Act" moved out of committee and through the Senate at an extraordinarily rapid pace. First introduced by Senator William Windom (R-MN) on February 11, 1873, it was adopted on February 21st and sent to the House for its concurrence.

On March 1st, the Speaker of the House, James Blaine, introduced the Senate's bill on the House floor. Its formal title was S. 1572, *A bill for the suppression of trade in, and circulation of, obscene literature and articles of immoral use*. Hon. Clinton Merriam of New York spoke first, making a motion to suspend normal House rules and vote on the bill straightaway, without referral to a House committee or even floor debate.

Several representatives disagreed with the speedy process, including Michael Kerr, a leader among House Democrats opposed to expansion of federal powers in the Reconstruction era. His brief objection is chronicled in the *Congressional Record*:

MR. KERR. I move its reference to the Committee on the Judiciary. Its provisions are extremely important, and they ought not to be passed in such hot haste.

MR. COX. Is debate in order?

THE SPEAKER. It is not.

MR. MERRIAM. I move to suspend the rules and pass the bill with
my amendment.

MR. KERR. Is my motion in order?

THE SPEAKER. Not under that motion.[45]

Kerr was stymied. After Merriam insisted that "tellers" record the individual votes of the representatives on the matter of suspending the rules, the "ayes" won out, and Merriam's motion passed. The House then approved the legislation by a two-thirds majority, and President Ulysses S. Grant signed the bill into law on March 3rd. In his diary, Comstock recorded his ecstatic response: "O how can I express the joy of my Soul or speak of the mercy of God."[46] The army Comstock and the gentlemen of the YMCA together had created indeed had proved to be a mighty force.

THE WORD IN THE LAW

Throughout the winter of late 1872 and early 1873, Anthony Comstock was fortunate to experience an extraordinary education in the American legislative process. From his teenage years, he had fought vice through ardent prayer, conspicuous example, and occasional use of force. Now he firmly understood the legal process through which the might of a government could be steered in the direction of a great Christian cause. Among the many lessons Comstock learned in this early phase of his career, perhaps the most important was that in the sphere of law, words meant everything.

The supreme power of The Word was by no means unfamiliar to a Christian evangelical. Protestants from the outset had distinguished themselves from Catholics through their faithfulness to the text of the Bible rather than to images and icons. This devout adherence to Scripture only increased over time, as the Evangelical belief that the Bible was the inerrant Word of God "solidified in the nineteenth century in response to the challenges of European biblical-historical criticism and

American romanticism." As Candy Gunther Brown notes, faced with writings that treated the Bible either as a type of literature, or merely as symbolic, evangelicals doubled down on their insistence that "the Scriptures not only contain but ARE THE WORD OF GOD."[47]

Not surprisingly, evangelical brethren in Washington assisted the gentlemen of the New York City YMCA in drafting and passing the specific language of the Comstock Act. William Strong, Associate Justice of the U.S. Supreme Court stood chief among these. Strong was the son of a minister from the small town of Somers, Connecticut who helped Brainerd and Comstock to revise and strengthen the language of the new bill. From 1868 to 1873, in the same years he sat on the nation's highest court, Strong also was the president of the National Reform Association, which "sought to add a sixteenth amendment to the Constitution to include reference to God and Jesus in the preamble of that document."[48] Just three days before Congress passed the Comstock Act, Strong presided over the Association's annual convention held in New York City's Cooper Union Hall, at which a resolution was passed affirming: "legal presumptions may be created in favor of Christian morality, Christian usages, and Christian institutions."[49]

Strong's effort to codify the dominion of God and Jesus in the U.S. Constitution ultimately failed, but he must have been gratified that some progress was made on his goal of living in an officially Christian nation when the Comstock Act was signed into law.[50] This new legislation was vastly stronger than the federal anti-obscenity legislation that preceded it, which had been adopted in 1865 in an attempt to regulate the enormous quantity of erotic materials shipped to Civil War soldiers. That law had prohibited the Post Office Department from transporting any "obscene book, pamphlet, print, or other publication of a vulgar or indecent character," but this was a limited list, and included no mechanism for enforcement.[51]

The new language Comstock shaped with Brainerd, Strong, and several Senators incorporated the structure and language of the expanded New York state statute adopted in 1868, but went even further. The revised New York law banned "any obscene and indecent book, pamphlet, paper drawing, painting, lithograph, engraving, daguerreotype, photograph, stereoscopic picture, model, cast, instrument or article of indecent use, or articles or medicines for the prevention of conception or procuring of abortion." The 1873 federal legislation listed all of these, and added several new categories of banned items based on Comstock's seizures in 1872, including paper, writing, advertisements, circular, "drawing or other representation," figure, and "image on or of paper or other material." The broad additions of "paper," and "writing" stemmed from Comstock's particular venom for news outlets such as *Woodhull and Claflin's Weekly*. These additions also reflected the growing diversity of erotic materials in the 1870s, which included new formats and processes for photography, as well as an explosion of cheaply printed erotic fiction.

Although the addition of such broad categories as "paper" and "writing" made the Comstock Act vastly more restrictive than previous legislation, arguably the most significant additions to the list of materials newly-banned under federal law were contraceptives and abortifacients. Comstock justified their inclusion by emphasizing the inseparability of these articles from arousing images, texts, and objects. In Merriam's speech to Congress, he quoted Comstock's frequent talking point: "For be it known that wherever these books go, or catalogues of these books, there you will ever find, as almost indispensable, a complete list of rubber articles for masturbation or for the professed prevention of conception."[52] In other words, articles that provoked lustful arousal outside of marriage or prevented the consequences of immoral liaisons were "indispensable" aids to the crime of satisfying that arousal.[53]

This point of view was based both on ideology and on personal observation. By 1873, Comstock had already seen firsthand the use of an abortion to cover up disgraceful extramarital sex. During a raid intended to seize obscene matter from a "doctor" named George Selden, he "caught Selden in [the] act of operating upon Barbara Voss of Jersey City who had just been brought there by Thomas Savage." Savage, her employer, was a married man fifty-five years old, who had impregnated Voss, then just seventeen. She ended up in jail, but Comstock was disgusted when both Selden and Savage had their cases "fixed" in the district attorney's office.[54]

Comstock clearly hoped that making abortifacients illegal would make it more difficult for men to cover up their evil deeds.

Comstock's proposed additions to the federal law also undoubtedly were a response to some of the many "conjugal" catalogues that specifically marketed contraceptives to married women. Moralists were horrified as they observed purveyors use marriage announcements to identify likely customers, and then again as they watched the birth rate among the well-heeled drop dramatically after the Civil War.[55] A rare surviving example of one of these circulars is *Mme. Simmons Price Catalogue of Conjugal Goods.* "Mme. Simmons" was not especially coy. She began first by recommending her free pamphlet "Fifteen Minute Conversation with Married Ladies." She then went on to list a variety of types of condoms at differing prices, including examples made of "goat skin and bladder," $3.75 per dozen, and "India rubber condoms," at $3.50 per dozen. To spice things up, women also could order "tickler rings," "surprises," and "Aphrodiasic Powders, to excite the sexual desire in either sex, $2. a package. Sold only to the married." The entire second side of the circular was devoted to a catalogue of pictures, thus proving Comstock's complaint that erotic materials and contraceptives went hand in hand.

Mme. Simmons divided her picture collection into "secret and only for Gents" and "for Ladies." The titles were not much different. Ladies were recommended to buy pictures with titles similar to those for men, including "Bathers Surprised," "Did You Ring, Sir?" "It's No Use Knocking at the Door," "Sinking the 290," and "After the Matrimonial Sorrows."[56] The evangelical lens through which Comstock viewed these materials made them especially dangerous in his mind, as they were aimed at humanity's "weaker" sex. As Helen Lefkowitz Horowitz writes, "it was Eve who had tempted Adam. Although woman was not seen as more passionate than man, she was perceived as more wanton, for she was less under the control of reason."[57] We will never know if Comstock blamed Barbara Voss, rather than her boss Thomas Savage, for the "wantonness" that led to her abortion. Comstock made no mention of Voss's fate in his arrest blotter except to report that she was "very sick" when he deposited her in the House of Detention. Nonetheless, as his words and actions made clear, Comstock always believed that efforts to limit conception contradicted the "laws of heaven" and created conditions that encouraged unsanctioned sexual activity. The fate of women like Barbara Voss was never his concern.

Instead, in addition to vastly expanding the categories of illegal materials between the language of the 1868 New York State law and its 1873 federal counterpart, Comstock's new law made it possible for many more individuals to be deposited in prisons, like Voss. Whereas the 1868 state law specified prosecution of any person who "shall sell, or offer to sell, or shall give away, or have in his or her possession with intent to sell or give away" specified contraband, the 1873 bill went further by making it a federal crime to "lend, in any manner exhibit, publish, offer to publish, have in possession for any such purpose or purposes, and take or cause to be taken from the mail hereinbefore mentioned articles." In proposing this new language, Comstock was again responding directly to several cases recorded in his arrest blotter for 1872. These included the cases of William Simpson, who "used to loan the vilest Books, to young boys & girls," and Thomas Allen, who had books by Paul de Kock "publicly displayed, on his stand, for sale."[58]

The 1873 federal legislation enlarged on the 1868 New York statute in another important respect as well, through the introduction of expanded mandatory minimum and maximum sentences. The fine for an obscenity offense in New York, then a misdemeanor, had been set in 1868 at "not more than one year in a county jail or $1000." Congress took a harder line in 1873, adopting penalties for conviction of "not less than $100 or more than $1,000 and imprisonment at hard labor not less than one year or more than ten."[59]

Finally, Congress followed the model of the New York statute by providing a "clear method of enforcement" under federal law. Now, any complainant with evidence and a story to tell could petition a judge or magistrate in a U.S. district court or circuit court to issue a bench warrant, which a marshal would then serve. Seized materials were to be kept under seal until a conviction was obtained, and then destroyed. The non -postal provisions of the bill only applied in Washington, D.C., and the

U.S. territories, over which Congress had sole jurisdiction; nonetheless, they were important in setting the precedent for new bills that soon were introduced in state capitols across the country.

Little contemporary debate is recorded regarding the potential benefits and dangers of all this legislation. On the floor of the House, Congressman Merriam proclaimed, without any debate, that obscene materials were a dire moral and social hazard. Even the verbose 1872 private and confidential report justified suppression of vice almost as an afterthought on its final page: "No language can exaggerate the widespread and terrible effect of this traffic."[60] The "thoughtful citizen" reader of the pamphlet presumably could fill in the void left by so few words with his own understanding of the dread effects of wanton lust.

Despite the confidence exhibited in their presumptions, the Christian gentlemen who advocated these new laws did not take for granted that their noble cause was unassailable. Many of them also were smart jurists and lawyers, and while they knew that "no language" was necessary when persuading other like-minded Christians, the power of the law literally rested on the words they conscripted to their cause. Any law, no matter how obviously righteous, would eventually need to survive the crucible of cross-examination.

Brainerd, Comstock, Strong, and others never recorded any reservations about their attempts to codify such vague terms into law. Nevertheless, they worked tirelessly to expand state and federal anti-obscenity statutes, in the fervent hope that each added noun, verb, and adjective would buttress the law's judicial force. To this end, Comstock's arrest blotters provided ample documentation of newly available materials (nouns) and means of producing, using, and distributing them (verbs). Adjectives were a trickier problem.

The precise meaning of "obscene" never was at issue because the term served simply to categorize anything found to be criminally liable by a judge or jury. Much more problematic was how to articulate the qualities that would condemn images, text, and "articles" to the category of obscenity. The terms written into the 1868 and 1873 laws are a case in point. The 1868 New York law used only the adjectives "indecent" and "immoral" to express the qualities of obscenity. In 1867, Noah Webster defined these as follows: "IN-DĒÇENT, *a.* Not decent; unfit to be seen or heard. SYN. Unbecoming; indecorous; indelicate; unseemly; immodest; gross; shameful; impure; unchaste; obscene" and "IM-MŎR'AL, *a.* Inconsistent with rectitude; contrary to conscience or the divine law."[61] The principles these adjectives signified suggested that judges and juries should consider whether work was fit for public consumption in the case of indecency, and/or contrary to conscience or "divine law" in the case of immorality. Both needed to be true to justify a determination of obscenity.

Perhaps because these terms in the 1868 law were impossible to define precisely, having more of them seemed prudent. The 1873 federal law contained two more potent adjectives that speak to a shift in the concept of obscenity that was rapidly evolving: "LEWD 1. Eager for sexual indulgence. 2. Proceeding from unlawful lust. SYN. Lustful; libidinous; licentious; profligate; dissolute; sensual; unchaste; lascivious; lecherous" and "LAS-ÇĬV'IOŬS, *a.* 1. Loose; lewd; lustful. 2. Tending to produce lewd emotions."[62]

The new terms *lewd* and *lascivious* helped clarify that the concept of "obscenity" principally described work that inspired lust. This was a shift away from previous American legal concepts deriving from English common law, which considered obscenity to constitute blasphemy against religion, libel against a person, or a clear threat to public morals.[63]

Obscenity under the new law did not require proof of public endangerment, or even of individual physical, mental, or emotional harm; now, lust inducement itself was a violation of law. This new definition perfectly expressed a very particular blend of Christian "divine law" and secular administration that derived not from the moral wellsprings of New York State or the District of Columbia, but rather from the theocratic culture of antebellum Connecticut, in which Comstock, Jesup, and Strong had all been raised. Fittingly, William A. Buckingham, a Republican from Connecticut, brought the bill to the Senate floor.[64] In 1873, these men accomplished what Theophilus Smith could only have dreamed of: legally sanctioned jurisdiction to enforce evangelical Protestant doctrine regarding sexuality. Anyone who facilitated the arousal of lust and sexual gratification other than for procreative purposes within marriage could now technically be prosecuted under federal law. These like-minded sons of Connecticut all were elated when the Comstock Act passed, but as they soon were to learn, enforcing the Word in the law would not be as simple as "stretching a Constitutional point" in congressional legislation.

Just as evangelicals had many disagreements over the exact meaning of the supposedly inerrant Word of God inscribed in the Bible, so too did lawyers, judges, juries, and defendants have difficulty reaching agreement on the working definitions of the adjectives inscribed in the anti-obscenity laws passed in 1868 and 1873, and in other revisions and amendments that followed in the decades to come. Even before the ink had dried on the codification of S. 1572, smart attorneys were already contriving sophisticated defense arguments and "windy oratory" on behalf of Comstock's defendants.

On January 15, 1873, the *New York Herald* printed a long description of the most famous federal obscenity trial ongoing as Congress deliberated. In the proceedings against Woodhull, Claflin, and Blood, "Messrs. Howe & Hummel, Jourdan and McKinley appeared for the accused. Judge Dowling seemed to enjoy the fun immensely, and the frown which usually clouds his classic brow in his own court gave way to half concealed smiles as the learned counsel quoted spicy extracts from 'Hudibras' and Aristophanes' Greek plays. The Judge seemed to know all about it."[65] Jourdan's "spicy" readings from Samuel Butler's *Hudibras* and Aristophanes' plays made a strong argument that determining the boundaries between moral and immoral was an impossible task. Was the judge willing to allow that sexually explicit works accepted as masterpieces within the Western canon of literature also could be criminally liable? Certainly, plays like Aristophanes' *Lysistrata* conveyed mature ideas about lust and sex in language that was "indelicate" and "sensual." If *Lysistrata* was illegal, what next?

After recess, William F. Howe, counsel for the defense, "submitted the following points":

First—That the prosecution infringed upon the freedom of the press, there being nothing obscene in the paper.

Second—That if a decision were given against the prisoners the Holy
Bible, Byron, Smollett &c. were indictable matter as a whole.

Third—That Comstock should be arrested if the Commissioner's
decision were adverse to the prisoners, on the ground that he was
the cause of having obscene matter transmitted through the United
States mail, having paid for it.[66]

Although no specific mention was made of the First Amendment (at least
in the newspaper account), clearly that language was implied in invoking
"the freedom of the press."

Howe's further attempt to assert that Comstock had induced his client
to commit a crime, therefore making the censor complicit rather than his
client, stood on less firm legal ground. Entrapment as a defense had no
basis in either English common law or U.S. statutes and "did not achieve
general acceptance until well into the twentieth century," although it was
"given early impetus in several influential pre-twentieth century state
cases that attacked the propriety of governmental involvement in crime."[67]
The frequent use of the entrapment defense by attorneys battling Comstock, beginning with the Woodhull case, suggests that his tactics may
have played a role in stimulating the "impetus" that led to codification of
this defense strategy.

In the Woodhull case, ultimately none of Howe's learned arguments
was considered to trump a more basic problem. The *New-York Tribune*
titled its coverage of the final verdict: "WOODHULL AND CLAFLIN
ACQUITTED: A Technicality Under the Old Law." In his charge to
the jury, District Court Judge (and future member of the U.S. Circuit
and Supreme Courts) Samuel Blatchford asserted: "'It is very clear to my
mind that the alleged obscene publication is not covered by the words of
the act . . . it certainly is not a book, a pamphlet, or a print.' . . . The jury,
without leaving their seats, found a verdict of 'not guilty.'" Even though
Blatchford confirmed that the 1873 law by that time had fixed the "technicality" problem by adding "paper" to the list of media that could be
restricted, still he ruled that in this case, the timing of the arrest meant
that the older federal statute applied.[68] This was the end of an era.

After 1873, federal law was more squarely on Comstock's side, and he was much harder to ignore or treat with diffidence. In future years, Blatchford became a significant staunch defender of the NYSSV in cases under his jurisdiction, as precedent and legislation advanced. Another factor was equally important to the rise of Comstock's powers. In 1873, not only had S. 1572 passed and been signed into law, but the postmaster general was so impressed with Comstock and his advocacy that he appointed him a special agent of the Post Office Department. Of the many innovative changes legislated in that year, Comstock's odd appointment as a special agent for a government department stands out.

As a special agent, Comstock reported directly to the Office of Mail Depredations under the aegis of the postmaster general. In that capacity, he joined a fairly substantial group of agents throughout the country, who previously had only investigated crimes such as stagecoach robberies, pilfered mail, and forged stamps. In some ways, Comstock was no different than these other postal agents. He investigated cases involving illegal use of the mails and received an annual commission that he was able to show to train conductors in order to travel for free throughout the country. Beginning in 1874, Comstock also began dutifully to submit reports to Washington, sometimes including samples of the evidence in his cases. Eventually, a few other agents specializing in obscenity cases joined him in this work, most notably the St. Louis–based Robert W. McAfee, who worked for the Post Office Department and the Western Society for the Suppression of Vice.[69]

In other important ways, however, Comstock's position was thoroughly unique and incongruous. Although technically he worked for the U.S. Government, Comstock refused a salary. The decision not to be paid was made on the advice of YMCA members who realized the danger of turning the position into a ripe plum for a political appointment.[70] The 1874 report of the YMCA's (now-renamed) Committee for the Suppression of Vice further specified that in the matter of state cases, "To avoid all semblance of pecuniary interest in the result of a trial, the Committee, under whom Mr. Comstock has acted, has heartily approved his refusal to accept in a single instance that share in the fines imposed, which the law permits him to receive."[71] As a result of these unusual arrangements, Comstock technically worked for the federal government and served as an informant in state cases in which he legally had the right to collect a share of the fines imposed. However, he received a salary only from a private, nonprofit, faith-based organization. So for whom did he really work? On that question, Comstock himself was quite clear.

In one of his earliest surviving reports to Charles Cochran, Jr., chief of the Division of Mail Depredations of the United States Post Office Department, Comstock began his lengthy report of eight arrests made in August 1875 with a dramatic greeting: "I have the pleasure of reporting that notwithstanding the best efforts of the Enemy to the contrary, I still live." He probably did not need to elaborate for Cochran on the several attempts to murder him that had already been carried out, including an attack by the abortionist George Selden and another by the book distributor Charles Conroy—these had been covered extensively in newspapers. Comstock's report went on to summarize the numerous new threats against him, as well as the arrests he had recently made of eight men charged with selling obscene pictures.

Although these were not postal cases, Comstock was eager to demonstrate that he "had not been idle." Finally, he concluded his long note with a stirring farewell: "If die I must, I want to die with the harness on, fighting the enemy of the youth of our beloved land. The only comfort for me is in My Maker . . . And if, in the Providence of God, I never see you again bear witness that I have always endeavored to do my duty, and nothing but my duty, and that with a pure motive, I have tried to please my Master. To him belongeth the glory of my success."[72] This was not a typical report from a postal inspector. Comstock here was acknowledging that his "master" was Jesus, not the United States Post Office Department.

Between 1868 and 1873, Comstock had been able to empower himself through smart and strategic alliances, and fierce passion. There was much, though, that would remain out of his control as he pursued his dream of national purification. Despite the many nouns, verbs, and adjectives he now was empowered to define, Comstock would soon learn that human sexuality was beyond moral or intellectual suasion. It would prove much more difficult to remove lust from America than to insert the Word into American law.

HOME FIRES

How exactly did a law that was as sweeping as the Comstock Act pass through a dysfunctional federal legislature in such "hot haste"? There were two primary reasons: legislators' concerns about feisty women like Victoria Woodhull, and the content of Comstock's obscenity exhibitions in 1873. In his impassioned speech to Congress before moving to suspend the rules and vote on the law without debate, Clinton Merriam quoted Comstock's melodramatic testimony as to the discomfort involved in doing his due diligence to research the problem the bill sought to remedy. Going "willingly down into the gutters of human depravity," as illustrated by Comstock's show-and-tell exhibitions in the nation's capital, clearly had a forceful impact.[73]

No contemporaneous checklist survives to document the specific items Comstock brought to Congress in the winter of 1872–1873. However, several sources make it possible to surmise the contents of the suitcases he carried on the train from New York. The "hydra-headed" monstrosities he showed to the "select company" of gentlemen in Jesup's parlors in March 1872 and the halls of Congress in January and February 1873 were samples of the enormous haul of materials he had collected within the past year. Although the perpetrators had largely escaped punishment, the materials they produced had all been confiscated and tallied in Comstock's arrest blotters, and in his 1872 "Private and Confidential Report." One of the items sure to have most aroused the anxieties of the lawmakers, and energized their efforts, was an item Comstock described in detail in his Report, presumably because he did not think they would be familiar with it: the "dildoe."

Comstock seized dildos in large numbers as part of 30,000 "articles made of rubber for indecent purposes." The object was neither novel nor rare. Comstock had confiscated twelve different molds from one man alone, "whose principal business was the manufacture of the articles for self-pollution, for use by females." The dutiful agent went on to describe the object as best he could: " 'dildoes' (that being the trade name), made of stout rubber, and in the form of the male organ of generation, for self-pollution."[74]

Unlike its wooden or ivory predecessors, the rubber version of this object was a relatively new American creation. Charles Goodyear's invention of "vulcanized" rubber in 1844 led to a proliferation of American-produced inventions using the new material in following years. The first operative rubber condom appeared in the United States in 1869, followed by other types of rubber contraceptives including "caps, diaphragms, and IUDs."[75] The new material also stimulated another burgeoning American industry: sex toys. Comstock was utterly confounded. Toward the end of his confidential report, he wondered: "The extent to which articles for self-pollution are proved to be manufactured suggests a phase of depravity heretofore little suspected. Prostitutes do not use them; the married do not. Their cost, being about six dollars, would seem to preclude their use by the poor and the low. One concern was engaged almost wholly in this manufacture. Who were its customers?"[76] Six dollars was in fact an enormous sum of money for a toy; nevertheless, this question was rhetorical only to a person entirely unable to fathom that an unmarried woman of means might want to take pleasure from masturbation using an artificial penis.

Even further from Comstock's imagination was the possibility that a brothel patron, a married woman or couple, or men or women engaging in same-sex play might enjoy using such a device. A surviving example of an early dildo in the shape of a mermaid (figure 2.1) demonstrates that the producers who created a variety of types were, in contrast, not at all confused about their function. The testicular flippers clearly were designed to add clitoral to vaginal stimulation.

Comstock's limited understanding of the variety of human sexual feelings and behaviors in 1872 is not surprising; his assumption of respectable female "passionlessness" was a normal element of evangelical discourse in the middle of the nineteenth century.[77] In publicly available literature, American readers across a wide spectrum were presented with polite female characters interested only in "holy and pure" love, in contrast with immoral women who succumbed to seduction and from there fell into prostitution. Both types of narratives "preserved predominant beliefs about the dependency of female desire on male impetus."[78] Comstock's confusion about dildos proves this point: if respectable women were presumed

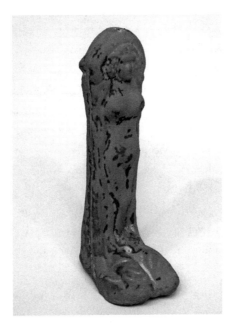

FIGURE 2.1 Mermaid-shaped dildo, n.d. Rubber. Courtesy, The Kinsey Institute. (ISR 79.2)

to experience desire either not at all or only as the result of seduction by a male actor, then what possible purpose could a dildo serve for the type of woman who could afford it?

Comstock's obliviousness on this subject would not last long, given the turn his career path was taking. In future years, Comstock included a large number of quasi-medical texts in his seizures that discussed sexuality, often with illustrations. These ranged from "quack" pamphlets that hawked special powders and tonics to serious works by physicians that aimed to explain and provide cures for problematic diseases. After 1870, an increasing number of these works rejected the idea of female passionlessness and embraced a view of female desire and orgasm as necessary to good health.[79]

One of the most common diseases serious doctors diagnosed among women in the mid-nineteenth century was "female hysteria," which overlapped with other vaguely defined syndromes such as "chlorosis" and "neurasthenia."[80] European and American doctors were conflicted in their diagnoses and proposed treatments for this broad category of ailments. Many, however, recommended curing the problem with induced orgasms, either produced by physicians who massaged the vulva by hand, often on a weekly basis, or hydrotheraphy that directed a strong stream of water onto the clitoris. In the early twentieth century, doctors involved in the time-consuming labor of manually facilitating female orgasm were instrumental in inventing the electric vibrator as a labor-saving device.[81] The expense of a visiting gynecologist helps explain why six dollars was a small amount of money to pay for a dildo.

The *Grand Fancy Bijou Catalogue of the Sporting Man's Emporium* demonstrated in its advertisement for dildos in 1870 that the intended market for the product indeed was not "the poor and the low":

The Dildoe [*sic*]: or, Artificial Penis.

The instrument is manufactured of white rubber, and is a wonderful facsimile of the natural penis of man. For reserved females it is a happy and harmless substitute for the natural "Champion of Woman's Rights." Price $6[82]

The meaning of the term "natural 'Champion of Woman's Rights' " is somewhat unclear. Whatever the intimation of that phrase, however, the description of the potential beneficiaries of the product—"reserved females"—is clear: the dildo was a masturbatory aid that could provide "happy and harmless" fun for women of some means who wished to masturbate. Nowhere in the *Grand Fancy Bijou Catalogue* is a concern about "passionlessness" in evidence.

Like the dildo, many of the erotic texts, images, and objects listed in circulars like the *Grand Fancy Bijou Catalogue* and subsequently seized by Comstock and recorded in his arrest blotters similarly prove precisely the opposite of female passionlessness. One of the most common texts seized by Comstock was *The Roue's Pocket Companion*, a compilation of plates and short stories that had been produced for George Ackerman's larger series *Venus' Miscellany*.[83] Ackerman was Comstock's fourth recorded prosecutorial target. The seizure of his stock from a basement on Ann Street was enormous, including 6,000 cards, 4,000 pictures, and 244 printing plates made of steel, copper, and wood.[84] A surviving copy of the original *Venus' Miscellany* demonstrates its inclusion of illustrated stories about women who were both nominally respectable and uncontrollably lusty.

In the tale of Lola Montes, for instance, Lola is the young bride of a navy lieutenant named Thomas James who has quickly become a tiresome lover. Lola echoes the tracts of free love advocates by proclaiming that she is not one of those wives to "cool down in time, and become a regular domestic Joan! . . . If I do not love and am not loved ardently, I must go elsewhere." On her transatlantic honeymoon voyage, Lola eyes a handsome sailor named Israel Stanhope who is "young and beautiful, he is my *beau ideal* of all that is attractive and bewitching in the other sex." Rather than repressing her lust and saving herself for the "pure and holy" love of her sanctified marriage, Lola acts.

The artist of *Lola and the Young Stanhope in the Cable Tier* (figure 2.2) illustrates the scene that follows: "She whispered him to take her to some private place under the deck where they could converse far from observation. He led Lola quietly down into the cable tier encountering no obstacle on the way. As soon as they had reached that secure place, Lola threw her arms around the young sailor, pressed him ardently to her bosom and gave way to the voluptuous fervor which he had inspired in her burning bosom." Although Lola initiates the fun, eventually Stanhope loses his restraint and with his "blood on fire" he tears off their clothes and lovemaking ensues. The scene ends, as one might expect, with Lola "choking with sobs," and Stanhope in "the most heavenly raptures." The story dramatized the supposed adventures of a courtesan and actress named Lola Montez, who began her life in Ireland as Eliza Gilbert, and became popular as the embodiment of romanticized and eroticized ideas about Spanish culture.[85]

In one of the book's illustrations, the artist shows us precisely the moment when Stanhope takes over the action, liberates Lola's breast from her dark gown, and fondles her exposed nipple. Although she is not the primary actor in that moment, Lola embraces Stanhope fully with her arms surrounding his shoulders, and her parted legs also convey

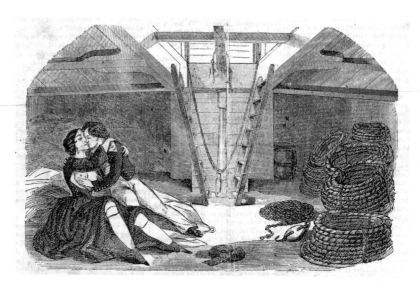

FIGURE 2.2 *Lola and young Stanhope in the cable tier* in *Venus' Miscellany* (June 20, 1857), 1. Rare Book Division, Department of Rare Books and Special Collections, Princeton University Library.

FIGURE 2.3 *Mary Ann's Liaison Discovered*, Illus. in Charles Paul De Kock, *Mary Ann Temple* (New York, n.d.), 85. Courtesy, American Antiquarian Society.

the clear message that she is a very willing participant in the *denouement*. To heighten the eroticism of the scene, the artist also incorporated a series of suggestive orifices as background for the couple, including the V-shaped staircase at center, and the neatly wound hemp anchor cables at right. Like Fanny Hill, Lola is a forceful actor in fulfilling her own desire.

Another printer on Ann Street named Frederick Brady also produced cheap illustrated fiction recounting the bawdy fun of lustful young women.[86] *Mary Ann Temple* tells the story of an "amorous" young woman "born of respectable parents" from Boston whom a friend introduces to a "book of a peculiar character." In the privacy of her bedroom, Mary Ann "must confess, what many young ladies in my place would also confess, if obliged to tell the truth, that my eyes were riveted to its pages till. . . . I had devoured all its contents and examined the pictures thoroughly; . . . at night my dreams were of transport and joys that I had so far tasted only in my imagination." Sold for twenty-five cents and printed on cheap paper, *Mary Ann Temple* offered few illustrations, but among them yet again was an image illustrating a scene in which the young woman is an eager actor in satisfying her own desire (figure 2.3).

Now living in the home of an elderly widow at the age of nineteen, Mary Ann is bored until she meets a young and handsome neighbor of high standing named Armington. One afternoon he calls on the widow, but finds only Mary Ann at home:

It grew dark. The chandelier was lighted; and still no progress had been made. Every moment I feared that Armington would rise up and retire. Determined to venture all by one bold stroke, I suddenly sprang up, and exclaiming,

"Your mouth is so handsome that I must kiss it," I threw my arms around his neck and inflicted a warm kiss upon his red, luxurious lips. He was astonished, but did not long hesitate. I had waked up a more dangerous passenger than I suspected. He was consuming with the flame of desire; but needed downright encouragement before he would put forth his powers. He clasped me in his arms—I felt his heart beat violently— his face flushed, his eyes flamed. He kissed my lips, neck, and bosom.

His embrace became more and more fervent till I felt my strength give way. I was in his power, and he made use of it!

That evening I lost my virgin innocence.

As in the story of Lola Montes, the illustrator here depicts the moment when our heroine's chosen suitor accepts her invitation and places his hand on her breast.

Mary Ann angles her body toward him, parts her legs, and lifts her lips to his in clear and eager participation, while undulating drapery at right echoes the curving tresses of her unfastened hair. The drama of the scene is heightened by the presence of a maid named Betty at left who, undetected, observes the scene entirely and reports the next day on "all of our proceedings, not even omitting the words, the sighs, the expressions of rapture that I uttered while in the act of coition with the ardent youth."[87] For both women, a hand lies on the breast, bringing attention to the sensuality of the scene. As in the story of Lola, Mary Ann's own sexual pleasure is also expressed with strongly affirming text and visual display.

The common depiction of women as lustful agents in fulfilling their own sexual pleasure within Comstock's seizures was by no means limited to illustrations in books and periodicals. A stereograph showing a woman in an armchair with an album of pornography (figure 2.4), for instance, vividly demonstrates that the depiction of self-actualized and aroused women in erotic visual culture of the mid-nineteenth century extended to photography as well. In this stereograph card, a woman reclines on an armchair covered with a delicate crocheted pattern. Her *au courant* large charm necklace, dangling earrings, and upswept hair suggest that she is a fashionable woman of the early 1870s. Although this woman clearly has styled her hair and accessories for public display, we see her in an act of great intimacy. With her petticoats pulled up high above her waist, she strokes herself while gazing intently at an open photographic album.

Clearly visible in the album, the two oval scenes above show tightly cropped views of women's pubic regions, shaved to exhibit just a small vertical stripe of hair at center. The stereograph card below shows us a similarly fashionable woman, attired with an enormous bonnet on her head. Her legs are splayed, and she is inserting a dildo into her

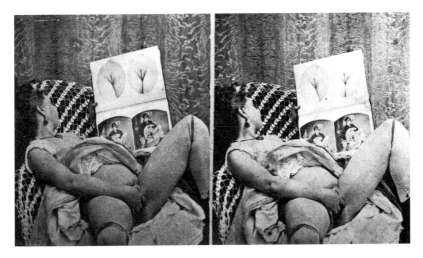

FIGURE 2.4 Stereograph of a woman in an armchair with an album of pornography, ca. 1872. Stereograph card. Courtesy, the Kinsey Institute. (kidc67502)

vagina. Nothing we see in any of these vignettes suggests the presence of a male partner. The assumed viewer of the work, whether male or female, is expected to take pleasure in the sight of a woman satisfying her own self-motivated sexual desire. Given his confusion about the expense of dildos and their intended customers, Comstock might similarly have questioned why so many texts and images were printed that showed women enjoying sex without any reference to men's pleasure or the biological possibility of procreation.

The popular medium of stereoscopic views for pornography must have been a further surprise to Comstock. The stereoscope was a prominent feature of parlors and libraries in every respectable household, through which scenes of foreign capitals, wars, national heroes, and popular entertainers were viewed in a spectacular three-dimensional display. In 1859, Oliver Wendell Holmes had kicked off the American craze for stereographs, remarking that they were already "common enough to be in the hands of many of our readers." Essayists wrote in hyperbolic terms of the miraculous verisimilitude of stereoscopic views, most famously Holmes: "The first effect of looking at a good photograph through the stereoscope is such as no painting ever produced. . . . The elbow of a figure stands forth so as to make us almost uncomfortable."[88]

Despite the undisputed value of stereoscopes in educating and inspiring Americans, the medium was also quickly put into service as a mechanism for the display of sexually explicit pictures. In 1872 alone, Comstock recorded seizure of 350 "negative plates for printing Ob. Photos and stereoscopic pictures" and 500 "stereoscopic views." Clearly, given the volume in which they were produced, erotic stereographs also were being inserted into this awe-inspiring and thoroughly respectable device. We might especially apply Comstock's query regarding dildos to stereographs like the one depicting a woman in an armchair: "Who were its customers?"

Lacking a comforting answer to that question, the gentlemen of the YMCA and members of Congress in the winter of 1873 responded with an intense level of fear and anxiety, and worked in "hot haste," with little debate, to codify a vast expansion of federal prosecutorial powers. Clinton Merriam introduced his speech on the House floor in personal terms, by warning that "recent revelations have convinced us that no home, however carefully guarded, no school however select, has been safe from these corrupting influences. The purity and beauty of womanhood has been no protection from the insults of this trade." He concluded his remarks by urging that "the good men of this country who regard their homes as their sanctuaries, warned by this exposure, will act with determined energy to protect what they hold most precious in life—the holiness and purity of their firesides."[89] With Victoria Woodhull threatening the privacy and authority of respectable men, and examples of "amorous" women run amok flooding even wealthy homes, these men needed to act, and fast, lest the "dildoe's" purchaser be their own daughters or wives. The threat from women seeking political and sexual empowerment was simply too terrible to ignore.

FROM ARMY TO INDUSTRY

Despite the enormous success of the YMCA's Committee for the Suppression of Vice in passing the Comstock Act in Washington, not everyone at the parent organization in New York City was impressed.

Indeed, many YMCA members were no longer willing to be associated with the "unpleasant" work of the committee and, even further, attached great "odium" to its controversial agent, Anthony Comstock. After seven years of nurturing and supporting the battle against vice, the New York City branch of the YMCA refused to further sponsor the work of the committee.[90] This turn of events was distressing for men like Morris Jesup who were entirely devoted to the work, but in retrospect they should hardly have been surprised, given the bleak historical record of such efforts in America.

Seventy years earlier, in 1803, Connecticut's most renowned Congregationalist minister, Lyman Beecher, preached the first of dozens of sermons across the northeastern United States urging evangelical congregations to organize societies for the promotion of "good morals." In his sermon, Beecher referenced earlier American efforts to organize for this purpose, in Maryland in 1760, and in Massachusetts and Pennsylvania in 1798. Unfortunately, none of these had taken hold to serve as thriving examples for the new nation.[91] Beecher instead was inspired to begin his campaign for church-sponsored cultural regulation by the example of the London Society for the Suppression of Vice (LSSV), founded in 1802.

In its first annual report, the London Society gave an account of its foundation and advertised some small successes in its initial year. The organization divided itself into three subcommittees: the first devoted to "cases of profanation of the Lord's day, and of profane swearing"; the second attending to " blasphemous, licentious, and obscene books and prints; and false weights and measures"; and the third directing "its attention to disorderly publick [*sic*] houses, brothels, gaming-houses, procurers, lotteries, breaches of the peace, and cruelty to animals." On the charge of "blasphemous, licentious, and obscene books and prints," the society favored suppression not only of sexually explicit works, but also of "grammars and other elementary productions . . . which either suggest doubts respecting the truth of Revelation, or infuse principles unfavorable to virtue." Despite its lengthy vitriol on this subject, the society claimed credit only for the successful prosecutions of three men and one woman in this category in its first year.[92]

Beecher's efforts to stimulate American versions of the LSSV were initially quite successful, resulting in the establishment of associations including the Connecticut Society for the Promotion of Good Morals (1813), the Trenton Moral Society of Utica, New York (1815), the Moral Society of Albany, New York (1815), the Exeter Society for the Reformation of Morals in Exeter, New Hampshire (1815), the Bath Society for Discountenancing and Suppressing Public Vices in Bath, Maine (1815), and the Committee of the Society in Portland for Suppressing Vice and Immorality in Portland, Maine (1816). None of these, however, seems to have survived for very long.[93]

The difficulty of sustaining the work of censorship in these first private societies likely stemmed from two major problems. The first was wariness against intrusion upon private liberty, which was especially prominent in America before the Civil War. Whereas the LSSV boasted of the validity of its work as sanctioned by "the King's Proclamation Against Vice and Immorality," Beecher had to legitimate his proposed watchdog work in a nation passionate about its newly won freedoms from such monarchical dictate. On this point, Beecher trod carefully, noting, "At present we are highly distinguished: We enjoy a freer constitution, and milder laws than any nation under Heaven: and, let it never be forgotten that it is by our habits of Religion, and our moral habits which grow out of our religion, that we have attained the happy eminence on which we stand."[94] "Milder laws" brought both benefits and dangers, from an evangelical perspective. A publication of the American Tract Society dating to the antebellum era listed libertarian "scepticism" [sic] as chief among the insidious temptations facing the new United States: "We exult in that liberty with which God has blessed us above other nations; and swayed by ingratitude and pride, suppose that, as we are free from the oppressive domination of man, so we are free from the law and government of God."[95]

Conscious of libertarian American sentiments in the wider community, Beecher chose to focus on the "promotion of morals" in his early advocacy. He suggested only that society members meet regularly and discuss three basic questions: "1. What evils of a moral nature, are now existing in this community? 2. What is the probable cause of those evils?

3. In what manner can they, with the most probable success, be remedied?"[96] Beecher's influential daughter Catharine advocated for a similarly non-prosecutorial form of censorship, suggesting in 1845 that each community needed "editors, clergymen, and teachers" who would serve as "guardians of the public weal."[97] This choice of professionals was distinctly different from the legislators, police officers, and magistrates involved in the London example.

In the late spring of 1873, in contrast, concerns for libertarian principles were little in evidence among the members of the YMCA's Committee for the Suppression of Vice, who were determined to serve as "guardians of the public weal." Instead, they turned once again to government allies, this time in Albany. Just two months after passage of the federal Comstock Act, on May 16, 1873, the New York State Assembly formally incorporated the New York Society for the Suppression of Vice (NYSSV).

An act of incorporation is typically a standard and relatively inconsequential bit of legislation. In this case, however, the new organization was granted unusual powers for a nongovernmental body, most particularly those in section 5: "The Police force of the city of New York, as well as of all other places where police organizations exist, shall, as occasion may require, aid this corporation, its members or agents, in the enforcement of all laws which now exist or which may hereafter be enacted for the suppression of the acts and offences specified in section three of this act." In addition to compelling the police to make arrests at the society's request, the act of incorporation also directed, in section 7: "One-half the fines collected through the instrumentality of this society, or of its agents, for the violations of the laws in this act specified, shall accrue to its benefit."[98] Mandated assistance from the police and funding, combined with much more stringent laws to enforce, created a dramatically new landscape of vice suppression in New York and the United States after 1873.

On January 28, 1874, the YMCA committee issued its final secret report, which provided an overview of its work during seven years of existence, once again requesting that the "Private and Confidential" pamphlet be "destroyed when read." This report particularly credited Comstock for his role in seizing and destroying 134,000 pounds of books, 194,000 "bad pictures and photographs," 6,250 microscopic pictures, and 60,300 "articles made of rubber for immoral purposes, and used by both sexes." Also counted among the haul were 4,750 newspapers, 130,275 advertising circulars, and 20,000 letters. A total of 106 persons had been arrested, including eighty-nine in the State of New York, ten in Massachusetts, one in New Hampshire, and two in Connecticut. The report was mailed to all those who had contributed money to the YMCA's special committee between 1872 and 1874, with a listing of the donations that had been made during that time.[99] This list was subsequently used in fundraising for the committee's successor organization, the NYSSV. The torch had been passed.[100]

Although it was endowed with substantially heftier powers than the YMCA committee, the new NYSSV initially was quite modest in scale. In 1874, the society paid $400 for a "Safe, Office Furniture, etc." in a small workplace in the American Tract Society building at 150 Nassau Street.[101] The location was ideal: The NYSSV was a tenant of a Christian organization devoted to disseminating Bibles and other religious literature, but at the same time operated in the heart of the city's vice-publishing industry. The society was also a relatively short walk from the Fulton ferry dock, which facilitated a swift commute for its first (and, for a time, its only) employee, secretary and agent Anthony Comstock.

In early 1875, the NYSSV issued its first annual report, which set the tone for more than seventy editions to follow, including tables of the number of arrests made; years of imprisonment and fines imposed; the type, count, and weight of materials seized; donations and fees received; and expenses paid. Despite its small size, the NYSSV was able to report much success destroying pornography and contraceptives right away.[102] The goal of convicting offenders, however, was decidedly less successful, as the libertarian sentiments of lawyers, judges, and juries had not abated much since Lyman Beecher's day. The city's pervasive corruption made the situation even worse. In its *Annual Report* for 1878, the society lamented: "in the absence of a healthy public sentiment to sustain the law, a fair trial is too often prevented; or, if the prisoner is convicted, he fails to receive the sentence he deserves."[103] To change this situation, it was necessary to win hearts and minds for the cause. Ultimately, the gains the society's members hoped to achieve would require a broad shift in American attitudes, one that that would compel district attorneys, judges, and juries to indict and convict defendants in their cases. Changing public sentiment was an especially difficult task becuause it was hard to find language to describe the problem that was not in itself offensive.

While the Christian reformers of the NYSSV clearly disagreed with the libertarian sentiments that prevented imposition of harsher fines and punishments on those convicted of obscenity offenses, the problem of how to draw attention to the cause provoked more immediate consternation. The primary reason the YMCA had discharged its Committee for the Suppression of Vice was the "feeling among many persons who sympathized with Comstock's objects that the matters with which he had to deal were too unpleasant to be touched by persons of sensitive feeling, and that more harm was done by stirring up the pool than by letting it lie."[104]

Lyman Beecher first acknowledged this problem in 1804, complaining that "no one is willing to incur the displeasure of the offender, or to risque [sic] the difficulty and censure, that may be connected with the attempt."[105] In 1845, Catharine Beecher added her warning that "guardians of the public weal" risked "much danger . . . that men will seek the excitement of the imagination, for the mere pleasure it affords, under the plea of preparing to serve the public, when this is neither the aim nor the result."[106] Fashioning a career that required looking at sexually explicit materials inevitably raised suspicions about motives, to say the least.

Anthony Comstock accepted this mantle of disdain with some relish, reasoning through this new phase of his life in his diary: "I am called 'obscene man.' Well, what matters. . . . Sometimes we serve the Master as well by '*bearing patiently*' as any other way."[107] Thanks to a blend of wealth, political power, and social standing, the executive members of the new NYSSV were in a different position than their agent. Morris K. Jesup was a wealthy and prominent philanthropist, Alfred S. Barnes and Birdseye Blakeman were prosperous publishers, and William E. Dodge,

Jr., John M. Cornell, and Kiliaen Van Renssalaer all were "scions of prominent families."[108] Few were willing to sacrifice their reputations as nobly as Comstock for the sake of the cause. They had to be careful, lest they be sullied by the splatter from Comstock's splashing about in the "gutters of human depravity."

In their 1878 *Annual Report*, NYSSV leaders complained: "From the nature of the work in which the Society is engaged, of necessity repugnant to every refined taste and sensibility, it becomes impracticable to present facts as we find them, in their hideous enormity. Even with the guarded language and bated breath in coming before the public, our agents, while presenting facts in their simplest form, are often suspected of dealing in exaggeration, if not in statements utterly beyond belief. Hence the difficulty of arousing public sentiment to a true conception of the evil."[109] After five years of practiced euphemism, the Society's "guarded language" indeed had evolved to an astonishing level of metaphor likely to engender the "suspicion of exaggeration." In 1879, for example, the NYSSV's *Annual Report* described obscenity as an "uncouth ogre which sits over one of the fountains in Berne, in Switzerland, crunching in his mouth little children, whilst the limbs of others are dangling from the side-pockets of his clothes."[110]

The only place the members of the NYSSV did not have to worry about such euphemisms in discussing obscenity was within the sphere of their own necessarily exclusive company. Although few men were willing to serve on the society's board, many were willing to attend meetings in which the problem of obscenity was discussed. In 1875, the *Brooklyn Daily Eagle* reported on one of the society's first large gatherings, held in Brooklyn, which served as a model for annual meetings in the future. Invitations had been extended privately to "about four hundred of Brooklyn's most respectable moral and financially solid citizens." The reporter took pains to note that the press had not been invited, "nor was it expected by the promoters of the meeting that any of them would be present, the circular in fact stating that on its presentation alone could one be admitted." As was his now usual method, Comstock "illustrated his remarks by exhibiting to his audience a large number of hideous implements of vice. . . .

Subscriptions were then called for, and twenty gentlemen came forward, and subscribed $50. each."[111]

The tactic of reaching out via "private call" to "moral and financially solid citizens" was effective; subscriptions to the NYSSV in its first five years grew from fifty donors in 1874 to 212 individuals and organizations in 1878, and these new donors included some of New York's "most respectable" citizens, with even Theodore Roosevelt and J. Pierpont Morgan appearing briefly in the list of donors in the society's annual reports for 1876 and 1877.[112] As members of the NYSSV, donors were entitled to receive its annual reports, filled with titillating stories about scrappy publishers, base criminals, new types of contraceptives and sex toys, and erotica of every possible medium. Members also earned a ticket to the exclusive meetings at which they could see the fruits of Comstock's efforts and express their disgust. Although women were permitted to contribute to the society, they were entirely excluded from its meetings.[113] This rule made it at least arguably defensible that members viewed and discussed materials they described not only as "repugnant" but also as an "infectious" threat akin to a child-munching ogre. White, wealthy, evangelical Protestant men, presumably, were uniquely equipped to withstand the harm.

Whether or not NYSSV members' scrupulous exclusion of women truly legitimized their viewing "obscenities" en masse, the NYSSV still constituted an extremely unusual club, in which gentlemen read about, looked at, and discussed pornography and other illegal materials in the name of Jesus. The meetings of the society, held in a variety of venues, soon fell into a repeating pattern of prayer, the perusal of obscenities, expression of communal disgust, and more prayer. As Nicola Beisel amply demonstrates, the need to protect youth was by far the most powerful and common justification members of the NYSSV offered for their lurid occupation.[114]

At the NYSSV's 1880 annual meeting, Reverend Dr. Horatio Potter reminded the gentlemen present of the necessity for the work: "I remember very well the meeting which we held some years ago . . . when Mr. Comstock made a much less cautious statement in regard to the publication of obscene pictures and articles, some of which he exhibited. . . .

In the midst of this exhibition there arose in the audience a minister who, with flushed cheek and indignant eye, protested against such an exhibition even in such a company." In response to the minister's complaint, a young father called out that he had two daughters who had been ruined by the same "infamies" Comstock exhibited. Potter continued: "I venture to think that there was not a man in the house that evening, who did not listen to the utterances of that heart-broken father, and recognize in that appeal the call to a new crusade."[115]

Like Potter's speech, the insignia of the NYSSV (figure 2.5), which made its first appearance in 1877, was also designed to demonstrate that the purpose of the organization was the destruction rather than the perusal of obscenity. On the right-hand side, flames and smoke rise up from a large pile of books as a representative of the society feeds the fire with additional seized volumes; he sports a well-tailored vest and suit jacket, tight-fitting trousers, bowtie, and top hat, all affirming that his natural habitat is a world of professional offices and respectable parlors rather than saloons or prisons. His spine is straight, and he stares without flinching at the cleansing fire, unafraid of taint.

FIGURE 2.5 Insignia of the New York Society for the Suppression of Vice. Collection of the author.

To the left, a convict is seen in profile, with a sorrowful expression. In contrast to the virtuous individual on the right, the prisoner wears no hat and only a workingman's plain shirt and pants. A sturdy police officer sternly pushes him by the scruff of his neck into a subterranean cell undoubtedly modeled on New York's infamous "Tombs" prison. The bifurcated design of the insignia emphasizes that there is no gray area between the poor, convicted, and entombed perpetrator at left and the gentleman who acts with knowledge, conviction, and moral rectitude on the right. These visual cues embody the unerring faith of NYSSV leaders that its members had the proper religion, education, taste, and class status to distinguish between materials that were edifying and those that should be condemned to burn. No one had firmer belief in his own moral rectitude than the society's secretary and chief enforcer.

When Anthony Comstock turned thirty in 1874, he surely must have felt great satisfaction in contemplating his accomplishments. He was employed, well paid, and in command of his own "pure" home and fireside in Brooklyn. Nevertheless, as his critics loved to point out, in future years Comstock would become the best informed man in America regarding the dazzling array of visual and sexual predilections, desires, and fantasies enjoyed by his fellow citizens. Although many men were willing to attend the NYSSV's meetings and contribute to its coffers in the 1870s and the years following, a far larger number still operated as though "they were free from the law and government of God."[116]

In brothels, saloons, barbershops, theaters, bookstores, art galleries, respectable homes, and on city streets, women and men conducted themselves in a manner quite opposite to the pious hopes of the wealthy evangelical Christians who established the NYSSV. The arrest blotters Comstock assiduously compiled on behalf of that organization serve as a road map to the many "uncouth ogres" of obscenity Americans enjoyed. What Comstock could not have known or even guessed in 1873, as he began his efforts in earnest and with incorporated support, was that they would be more than matched by the celebrations of laughter, licentiousness, liberty, and invention he would encounter across the nation from that year until his death in 1915.

3

TAMING AMERICA'S "RICH"
AND "RACY" UNDERBELLY

. . . .

(Volume I: 1871–1884)

THE LAY OF THE LAND

Surviving accounts do not specify who purchased the enormous bound volume in which Anthony Comstock began recording his life's work in 1872. Nonetheless, the nearly 300-page tome, bound in leather and lined with Venetian paper, speaks to the substantial expectations of its purchaser. A label identifies the manufacturer as "Wilbur and Hastings, Blank Book Manufacturer." This volume, however, was never entirely blank. Instead, the thick paper within was printed with columns headed by labels that clearly articulated the work to be done, including: Date of Arrest, Name and Residence of Prisoner, Warrant Issued By, Offence, Disposition of Case, Bailed, Examination, Indicted, Case Tried or Adjourned, Officer by Whom Arrested, Name and Residence of Witness, Inventory of Stock Seized, and Sentence.

For the next forty-three years, Comstock's small and tight cursive handwriting meticulously recorded facts in each case for which he took credit, as well as information about the "social condition" of every defendant he targeted: Age, Aliases, Nationality, Religion, Marital Status, Number of Children, Education, and Occupation. In the last column, Remarks,

Comstock provided wonderfully florid opinions about the defendants, their alleged crimes, and the outcome of the proceedings. This volume, and two others that followed in later years, provide a "rich" and "racy" chronicle of the lay of America's legal, sexual, visual, and cultural landscape between 1871 and 1915.[1]

In his first thirty-six pages of entries under the aegis of the YMCA's Committee for the Suppression of Vice, Comstock recorded a web of printers, binders, bookstore owners, and deliverymen in New York and New Jersey, many of whom were elderly members of a dying generation. Erotic book publisher William Haynes, for example, who had been in the business for thirty years, died in March 1872, and George Ackerman, who sold his stock from a basement store in Brooklyn, also died later that year. Together, they had produced vast quantities of books offering a liberated sexual counter-narrative to more public proscriptions for behavior, as demonstrated by characters such as Mary Ann Temple and Lola Montes.[2]

Younger defendants died too, including Patrick Bannon, an Irish Catholic bookstore owner, at forty-five. Comstock was incensed when the presiding judge subsequently refused to punish Bannon's eleven-year old son, who clerked at the store on Saturdays.[3] In his early years on the job, much of Comstock's literary venom was directed at the many police officers, district attorneys, judges, and juries who declined to imprison his defendants. Indeed, during Comstock's earliest years on the job, most of the "punishment" suffered by defendants was a premature demise, brought on by the stress of indictment. Official leniency occurred at every level of the legal system. In the society's first *Annual Report*, Chairman J. M. Stevenson blamed several pardons by President Ulysses S. Grant for causing "the prosecuting attorneys and the courts to treat this class of offenders with indifference or unwonted leniency."[4]

Whether or not Grant personally was to blame, Stevenson did not exaggerate the unwillingness of many law enforcement officials to uphold the new laws the YMCA and NYSSV had fought so hard to pass. In the case of Charles Conroy, for instance, Comstock wrote on April 1, 1872, that he had seized 500 circulars and pamphlets, but also added: "Through mismanagement of Police, & ignorance of law he was discharged. I arrested this man in 1868 & he was convicted in Special Sessions & sentence suspended."[5] The suspension meant that Conroy was set free to continue circulating his "Rich, rare, & Racy books, Pictures, &c." through the mails. It also meant that Comstock stayed on his case, arresting him in 1872, and then again in 1874. At the time of this third arrest, Comstock listed twenty aliases for the thirty-eight-year-old "Smut-dealer." This time, when Comstock was just about to deliver Conroy to a prison in Newark, the defendant stabbed him twice in the head, "the last stab cutting a gash from the temple to the chin, laying open the flesh to the bone."[6] Only then did Comstock get a conviction and sentence—two years at hard labor for assault. A sentence on the obscenity charge was considered to run concurrently.[7] The attack left Comstock with a quite visible facial scar for the rest of his life.

Although he had very little luck in securing punishment in most of his early obscenity cases, Comstock still must have been quite gratified that he was never prevented from destroying the vast quantities of evidence he seized. In the case of the newspaper publisher Robert E. McDermott of Jersey City, Comstock wrote, "Finding it impossible to get case tried, I got an order from Recorder Hackett to destroy stock." The stock he referred to consisted of approximately 11,900 pamphlets entitled *The Little Red Lounge or Beecher's Fix*. Although Comstock recorded that only 100 of the pamphlets already had been sold, two versions survive today, one of which is illustrated. As Comstock correctly complained, the satirical publication consisted of a witty "plagiarism on [Alexander] Pope, with Beecher's name dragged in."[8]

The illustrated version in Harvard's Houghton Library (figure 3.1) shows the Reverend Henry Ward Beecher and his parishioner Elizabeth Tilton holding a nest beside the "Little Red Lounge" on which they allegedly conducted their illicit affair.[9] "Nest-hiding" was known as Tilton's euphemism for their sexual liaison. Despite Tilton's amorous gaze and Beecher's lascivious grin, all the figures in *The Little Red Lounge* are clothed and the language is euphemistic throughout, much more suggestive than actively salacious. Still, Comstock was given permission to destroy the stock. His was the

FIGURE 3.1 *My weapons were love, untiring generosity, and nest hiding* in *The Little Red Lounge or Beecher's Fix*, (Boston: Parisian Novelty Co., 1875). Houghton Library, Harvard University. (pamphlet AC85.B3918.Z875s)

only judgment that mattered in the determination of obscenity, and this presumption continued throughout most of the cases recorded in Volume I of the NYSSV's arrest records. Even when Comstock confessed in his blotter that he acted as his own "arresting agent" with "no warrant," nobody in the justice system seemed terribly concerned when he seized and destroyed property that had never been seen by a judge or jury.[10]

With his license to destroy unquestioned, Comstock sent to pulp mills and metal works a staggering weight of materials by the end of 1876, including more than 21,000 pounds of books and 14,000 pounds of stereotype plates for printing books.[11] While these seizures from publishers were publicized at the time and have been written about since, Comstock also seized and destroyed several less-studied categories of items.

After books and circulars, the largest number of seized items in Comstock's records fell into the category of "pictures and photographs." By the end of 1876, he had destroyed more than 202,000 of these, some by well-established professionals.[12] On June 10, 1875, for example, Comstock

FIGURE 3.2 Peter F. Weil, *White Fawn*, 1868. Stereograph, albumen silver print. The J. Paul Getty Museum, Gift of Weston J. and Mary M. Naef.

arrested Peter F. Weil, who owned a photograph gallery at 685 Broadway, from which he produced stereoscopic city views, interior scenes, and actress cards showing female performers in scanty garb, which were highly popular souvenirs of theatrical entertainments and undoubtedly the source of Comstock's ire. A surviving example titled *White Fawn* (figure 3.2) foregrounds a young actress clad in a form-fitting corset and baring nearly an entire leg. Comstock wrote in his arrest notes that Weil "seemed to think he could do about as he liked. . . . The more he swore & talked the more we searched his place & seized his stock."

The judge in the case postponed the trial for several years and then in 1879 acquitted Weil, informing Comstock that "he was opposed to trying these cases after so long a time had elapsed."[13] Weil's lenient treatment in the courts suggests that he probably had not crossed the line into producing sexually explicit scenes. Comstock's arrest records demonstrate that, in contrast, some other professional studios were definitely involved in the overt pornography trade.

In 1876, Comstock reported to Chief Special Agent Patrick Henry Woodward at the Post Office Department that a defendant, James A. McIntire, was employed at the very reputable photography studio of

Suddards & Fennimore at 820 Arch Street in Philadelphia. After hours, McIntire printed pornographic pictures and then distributed them to "smaller dealers."[14] One of these, William O. Benkerts, ran a barbershop at Twentieth and Nicholas Streets in Philadelphia near Girard College, which was "thronged with young men. He had a stereoscope through which he exhibited & sold different pictures."

Comstock wrote a lengthy and gritty description of Benkerts's arrest in his report to Woodward on the case: "If total depravity exists at all, I have seen it today, or the results of it. He said to a fellow whom he asked to come and run his shop for him while he was away, 'You can sleep with the old lady tonight, as I shan't be able to get bail.' . . . The judge, before whom he will be tried, said the other day, when he was shown specimen of the pictures 'the person who would sell such stuff as that ought to be hung.'" Given that Comstock and the judge identified these pictures as "the worst kind," they probably included graphic images of sexual acts. Despite Comstock's outrage at the level of obscenity in the photos Benkerts displayed, and the judge's harsh words, the jury does not seem to have been as horrified. Like McIntire, Benkerts received a sentence of only two weeks' imprisonment.[15]

Examples of surviving erotic photographs in the Kinsey Institute include a diverse yet highly predictable range of sexual practices that almost certainly qualified as "the worst kind" for Comstock and judges. These scenes show nudity, fondling, licking, penetration, etc., involving two or more partners. Many surviving examples of late-nineteenth- and early-twentieth-century pornography appear to have derived from negatives created in brothels.[16]

Comstock frequently seized albums of photographs in brothels, which served a dual purpose. Customers aroused by sexual images made for quicker and more profitable transactions. Photographs also simplified the process of negotiating services and prices, especially in cases where the participants did not speak the same language. McIntire certainly could have produced or procured his negatives in brothels and then printed copies at Suddards & Fenimore's after hours.

FIGURE 3.3 Photograph of a semi-nude figure, Photograph, n.d. Courtesy, The Kinsey Institute. (kipc28)

Alternatively, McIntire might have made his negatives at Suddards & Fenimore's using the props and equipment available there. A surviving photograph of a semi-nude figure (figure 3.3), for example, shows an ornate upholstered chair and painted backdrop, standard accouterments in professional studios. Wherever the initial negatives were made, the examples of McIntire and Benkerts confirm Donna Dennis's point that the suppression of large-scale erotic publishers in the early 1870s did not lessen the trade. Rather, their demise made way for "men at lower levels of the book and novelty trade, such as job printers, bookstand operators, photographers, and second hand book dealers, to move into writing, manufacturing, and distributing pornography."[17] The production of fodder for Comstock to bring to pulp mills seems to have shifted, rather than decreased, over the course of his career.

ARTICLES TO AID SEDUCTION

Another category of Comstock's seizures in the 1870s is even less well studied, but perhaps even more telling about the social context for illicit materials at that time. The NYSSV's second *Annual Report* referred to these types of items as "charms, all designed and cunningly calculated to inflame the passions and lead the victims from one step of vice to another, ending in utmost lust."[18] Descriptions of these goods and surviving examples provide us with a glimpse of a vibrant industry devoted to sexual pleasure and humor in equal measure.

One of Comstock's first defendants, "Dr. Manches," was typical of many merchants in the 1870s who aggregated a variety of "charms" that served as aids to seduction. "Dr." Charles E. Manches kept a shop at 735 Broadway not far from Washington Square Park, where he prescribed cures for sexual problems and also sold and mailed a variety of contraceptives and sexual aids. Although Manches's circular does not survive, a dutiful district attorney copied its entire text for the court record in 1872. After listing several types of skin and rubber "French patent male safes," Manches also advertised: "No. 7—French segars, each containing a condom—to hand to a friend as a joke" and "No. 8—Nuts and Fruits, each containing a fine condom for a joke on the ladies—by cracking a nut, or candy, the joke comes in."[19] The "segars" clearly were meant for a male "friend" presumably enjoying tobacco in a homosocial setting, while the nuts and fruits "for a joke on the ladies" suggest a witty proposition that could be made in a domestic setting. In either case, the joke presumably would serve to initiate a moment of intimate laughter as prelude to "ending in utmost lust."[20]

Before and even after passage of the Comstock laws, many similar circulars were filled with descriptions of small objects that were advertised as conversation starters with potential sexual partners. For example, the *Grand Fancy Bijou Catalogue of the Sporting Man's Emporium* in 1870 advertised "Emblematic Sleeve Buttons," which had "on their surface a series of emblems consisting of a 'can,' an 'eye,' and a 'screw,' all enclosed in the letter 'U,' and can easily be construed into asking a very *pointed* question."

The copy of the *Grand Fancy Bijou Catalogue* held by the American Antiquarian Society does not list the name of its business owner. However, its 1870 date and Philadelphia origin strongly suggest that this was the product of Thomas Scroggy, whom Comstock relentlessly pursued between 1874 and 1884. In a long letter to his supervisor at the Office of Mail Depredations in 1874, Comstock complained, "Of the 19 tons seized in the past 2 years I have seen much nastiness and filth: but sir for down-right nastiness, or as I have heard it sometimes put, 'pure devilishness' this man excels."[21]

In his circular, after listing several pages of books, songs, rubber goods, and items to assist with sexual problems, not least of which was "that feeling of lassitude and exhaustion caused by the low hanging of the testicles," Scroggy turned to a variety of flirtatious "charms." The most numerous items in this category were "microscopic goods," which referred to the tiny photographs known also as Stanhopes. These were the brainchild of a French inventor named Rene Prudent Patrice Dagron, who first patented the Stanhope optical device in 1859. Soon after, "the hidden erotic novelties, or 'peeps' as others called them, were the 19th century's dirty little secret."[22] Although they were referred to as "microscopic," Stanhopes could be seen without any optical aid once someone was made aware of their existence. The trick was to know where to look, since the tiny photographs were affixed to glass cylinders just 1/8 inch in diameter and ¼ inch in length. As such, like the "nuts and fruits," they provided a humorous surprise when the secret was shared in an intimate exchange.

Scroggy's promise of "fancy views" with two or more figures probably did not include any views of sexual acts. Most surviving Stanhope erotic subjects are relatively tame by contemporary standards, depicting a single female figure standing or sitting in a languorous pose. Some are set against backdrops of Moorish architectural elements, holding peacock feathers, or in faux agricultural scenes. Others evoke the poses and physique of Classical sculpture.[23] Scroggy's catalogue and Comstock's blotter entries both illustrate that the Stanhope industry focused as much on the objects that concealed the tiny pictures as it did on the photos themselves. Scroggy's 1870 catalogue, for example, listed a wide range of small objects containing secret Stanhopes, including plated and ornamented rings, scarf

FIGURE 3.4 Transparent playing card, n.d. Paper. Courtesy, The Kinsey Institute. (397q a021.1-1)

pins, pocket knives, and watch charms in the shape of miniature opera glasses. "Hard rubber rings" were even available with "Fancy Views . . . for young gentlemen 'who like to have a finger in it.'"

French Transparent Playing Cards, another tricky entry in the *Grand Fancy Bijou Catalogue*, also show up in numerous Comstock raids. Scroggy described their effects with great enthusiasm: "These cards, when produced before the light, are perfectly transparent, and the exciting object, then clearly depicted, as it were by magic, create an extraordinary and startling sensation among the players, particularly the ladies." An example of this type of Transparent Playing Card (figure 3.4), photographed to make the hidden image apparent, confirms just how "startling" these "aids to seduction" could be.

Like Stanhopes and their holders, explicit transparent playing cards were by no means rare. Comstock seized approximately 6,000 transparent cards from George Ackerman early in his vigilante career. In 1876, these types of cards still were flooding into the country from France in large numbers. In the case of Guion Ferdinand and Lazare Dreyfus, the mechanism of importation completely avoided any potential difficulties from customs officers who might have figured out the trick. Comstock wrote that Ferdinand and Dreyfus were sailors "of the French Transatlantic Steam Ship Co. They have been engaged for months in smuggling Obscene Playing Cards, pictures &c. Ferdinand would bring them over, and Dreyfus would run them off the wharf, or bring customers to buy the same. . . . I have put the Customs Officers on track of several others, who are doing the same thing on board one or two other ships of the same line." Comstock also informed the postal inspector that he had brought the case in state court instead of federal, to "get them in jail the sooner."[24]

The customers who surreptitiously bought transparent French playing cards from the wharves undoubtedly were not buying them for personal use. Instead, they were sold to wholesale merchants who in turn supplied a wide variety of retail agents. "Devilish charms" such as these showed up especially often in raids on customarily male spheres: saloons, cigar stores, barbershops, and confectionary stores, as well as on city streets where boys and men peddled them, chiefly to other boys and men. The correlation between tobacco, homosocial environments, and the targets of Comstock's raids was especially close.[25]

The *Grand Bijou Catalogue* also offered a variety of tobacco-related items, including "French Fancy Magic Cigar Cases," which contained "in a secret compartment Ten very fine colored fancy engravings, and on the outside a beautifully executed French Painting." An example of a Trick Cigar Case (figures 3.5 and 3.6 / plates 4 and 5) from the Kinsey Institute demonstrates how the "secret compartment" worked, with a false door inside, opening in this case to a painted image showing a somewhat unsettling scene of a cat clawing bloody wounds onto the backside of a man interrupted in the act of fornication.

The popularity of objects that on the outside seemed innocuous but hid a sexual secret within also extended to some rare and eccentric homemade novelties. In the 1878 case of Louis Wingeroth, Comstock alleged that the defendant "kept a confectionary store in New York and one in Brooklyn, and sold the ordinary Round clam shell, with obscene figures of the private parts of a man on one side, and of a woman on the other, inside the shell."[26] In the Remarks column for this case, Comstock noted family

FIGURE 3.5 Trick cigar case (closed), n.d. Courtesy, The Kinsey Institute. See also color plate 4.

FIGURE 3.6 Trick cigar case (open), n.d. Courtesy, The Kinsey Institute. See also color plate 5.

trouble: "His bro. says W. and wife have not slept together since Oct. 77 and are not on good terms. She has all his money." As he often did, Comstock also pointedly took note of Wingeroth's connection with the city's notoriously corrupt municipal Democratic government as "President of a Tammany Ward Club in NY."[27]

Six years later, Comstock recorded the seizure of another amateurish and "ordinary" object that made copulation into a hidden gag. In 1882, he arrested an eighteen-year-old street peddler named Theodore Marulok and his partner Foster Jester on Broadway near the New York Herald building. The two men together had ninety examples of a "box containing figures of hen & rooster which by pulling out lid placed the two in an indecent posture."[28]

An example from the Kinsey Institute (figure 3.7) closely matches this description. Unlike the Stanhope holders, transparent playing cards, and trick cigar cases, the clams and chickens seem to have been made in small quantities by homegrown entrepreneurs.[29] Jerking open and closed these crude devices heightened the suggestive nature of the display. The popularity of these objects derives from their humor as much as their playful evocation of sex. As sexologist John Bancroft asserts, the prevalent connections between sex and humor can be explained by the fact that laughter serves as a "release of pent-up tension" and also aids the "many, if not most of us [who] are scared by or uncomfortable about sex and use humor as a way of reducing those anxious feelings."[30] These anxious feelings undoubtedly applied in proposals between same sex couples, as well as in proposals between men and women.

Another category of humorous and provocative visual culture Comstock seized suggests at least the possibility of having served particularly to ask a "pointed question" between men: humorous phallic objects, seized in raids on the male-only terrain of saloons. In August 1882, Comstock arrested Daniel McGuire and John Phillips in Buffalo, on the charge of "Exhibiting and loaning an Obscene figure in bar-room" described as "1 glass Penis filled with liquor."

An example from the Kinsey Institute (figure 3.8) demonstrates the strong association between phallic symbolism, humor, and fraternity at this time.

FIGURE 3.7 Trick box containing copulating hen and rooster, n.d. Courtesy, The Kinsey Institute. (ISR 759)

FIGURE 3.8 Penis-shaped glass liquor bottle, n.d. Courtesy, The Kinsey Institute. (ISR615)

McGuire and his bartender Phillips charged patrons to fill the bottle with liquor, which they then would share with other men. The penis-shaped liquor bottle was remunerative as well as simply funny.[31] The bulbous base of the Kinsey example suggests that it held a large quantity of liquor. One can imagine inebriated saloon patrons humorously considering where to grasp the evocative flask.

At McGuire's bar, Comstock also seized a "Telephone Box Containing a very obscene figure" which probably was a penis modeled in wax. The same object showed up in a saloon at 502 Bedford Avenue in Brooklyn the following year in the arrest of Edward Guild. "He had a most obscene figure, which he kept in his bar-room for exhibition. This figure was an immense penis encased in a telephone box. . . . He would exhibit the filthy article to draw trade or entertain customers."[32] The phallic shape of the receiver-transmitters attached to the very new invention of wall-mounted box telephones likely inspired this humorous visual pun.

Ten years later, phallic novelty items were still showing up in saloons, including what sounds like a very awkward drinking vessel: "1 obscene figure in shape of large chamber pot . . . with penis for handles, out of which patrons drank wine."[33] In all these cases, the owners of phallic drinking vessels and novelty items testified that they were popular with customers, and therefore great for business. Whether or not these objects were used to aid in homosexual seductions, they do suggest a playfulness and fluidity in sexual iconography in keeping with George Chauncey's observations on the "multiple cultural meanings" present in male relationships in the nineteenth century.[34]

Whether intended for opposite-sex or same-sex partners, all of these examples of "articles to aid seduction" in Comstock's arrest records prove that an underground private world of objects and images flourished in the service of nurturing intimacy in post–Civil War America. At a time when sex and other bodily functions could not easily be read about or verbalized, visual culture stepped into the void in the form of small objects that could pose a question such as "Can I Screw U" without words.

UNEQUAL JUSTICE

Despite his many losses in court, Comstock showed remarkable persistence in his first years on the job and soon began to see some positive results. In 1874, *The New-York Evangelist* offered its support, hoping that Comstock would "prove more and more a terror to those who make merchandise of indecency and lust."[35] In 1875, even the usually skeptical *Brooklyn Daily Eagle* admitted of the NYSSV: "The necessity for such a society may be deplored but cannot be denied."[36] And in 1876, the *New York Observer* covered the NYSSV's annual meeting in great detail, with lengthy quotations from the speeches offered.[37]

Both ministers and politicians in attendance praised Comstock for his perseverance, and for demonstrating the extent of an immoral business of which they had been unaware. The threat to the nation's youth was described in the gravest terms, with former Lieutenant Governor Stewart Woodford proclaiming that he would "rather that my boy and girl were brought home to me corpses than that these terrible suggestions of wrong should enter their bosoms."[38] In the same year, Christian newspapers demanded that the district attorney and courts "promptly dispose" of offenders.[39] The society's stories of Comstock's courage and persecution, and the increased discussion, albeit elliptical, of the immoral materials circulating in America, all began to change public sentiment, thereby winning hearts and minds for legal convictions as well.

The constant message of the NYSSV that the morals and future of children were at stake was especially compelling, and frequently emphasized in the growing body of newspaper stories and editorials sympathetic to the cause. One of the cases that may have especially accelerated this positive attention concerned an "immoral schoolmaster" named George H. Gaulier, whom Comstock arrested on November 25, 1876. Gaulier, a Frenchman born in Paris and educated in Florence, was charged with "exhibiting obscene pictures to boys & having same in his possession."[40]

Comstock noted in his remarks that Gaulier "made a practice of showing books, pictures, &c. to his pupils, also enticing lads about Cooper

Institute & Y.M.C.A. to his room for same foul purpose." Gaulier's positions as a French teacher included stints at some of the city's eminent
private schools, including Packer Collegiate Institute and Friends Seminary. The seizure of materials at his apartment on Broadway included
a wide variety of the types of merchandise advertised in catalogues like
Scroggy's to "aid in seduction," including two bound books, one cigar
holder, one package of French cards, thirty-three photos, fourteen ink
sketches, one "Tin figure of a man," one "Box containing obscene figures,"
and thirty-two stereoscopic views.[41]

Newspaper coverage of the case was extensive, with the *New York
Times* the next day titling its article "Important Arrest by Mr. Anthony
Comstock and Detective Britton—A Teacher Poisoning the Minds of his
Pupils." The article described in somewhat careful language the depositions of two men, seventeen and twenty-one years of age, who had been
lured to Gaulier's apartment and then shown "a number of lewd pictures,
books, and stereoscopic views." Newspapers used the terms "lewd," "vile,"
"filthy" and "disgusting" to describe the materials that were seized in his
possession. Gaulier countered that he had never shown them to any youth
"not old enough to take care of himself."[42]

Gaulier's sentence was unprecedented for Comstock's defendants up
to that point. He received six years at hard labor and then was ordered "to
stand committed at expiration of 6 yrs imprisonment till fine be paid." It is
doubtful that Gaulier was ever able to pay the extraordinary fine of $5,000.
Undoubtedly, this severe sentence was the result of his obvious homosexuality and the abuse of his trusted position as an educator. Throughout
Comstock's career, defendants who were homosexual like Gaulier faced
far worse treatment in the press and in the courts than others.[43]

Punishments for disdained sexual proclivities other than homosexuality were equally harsh, but generally involved commitment to an asylum
rather than prison time. This was ultimately the verdict in the case of
William A. Van Wagner. Comstock arrested him on February 17, 1876, and
carefully recorded the somewhat inventive exhibitionist scheme he had
concocted, presumably to "aid seduction." Van Wagner "would light his
gas at night & with a reflector would throw the light into ladies' windows

opposite & then turn it on himself, he being entirely nude in the window on a stand." Affidavits were produced testifying to Van Wagner's insanity, and the proceedings were suspended when he was committed. He was twenty-six at the time.[44] Comstock, as usual, was unsparing. The laws he had helped to pass were starting to be enforced more regularly, albeit unevenly and unfairly. Now, emboldened by some helpful turns of fortune, attention, and support, he tackled much more public and popular entertainments.

GUARDING THE (MORE) PUBLIC WEAL

Anthony Comstock began 1877 in an optimistic mood. Among his first entries for the year in the category of "persons not arrested but obliged to give up unlawful and questionable business," he recorded successfully threatening several managers of entertainments that both were public and popular. The first of these exchanges was held with Richard K. Fox, manager of the *National Police Gazette*, America's most successful and salacious tabloid. Comstock noted that he sent Fox a copy of anti-obscenity laws by registered mail, and then met with the *Gazette*'s editor, Gilbert Shearer.

During their meeting, Comstock "called his attention to articles in the *Gazette* on 'Seductions, Rapes, Brothels, Assignations, &c.' and told him so many cases set out with large heading & accompanied with lurid pictures & advertisements of vile matter made it exceedingly objectionable & could not be tolerated. He said it should be changed and it was changed the next issue very radically."[45] Fox did in fact subtly shift the focus of his *Police Gazette* in coming years, reducing the percentage of his stories involving "seductions," etc. But even though the amount of space devoted to sexy stories dropped in the *Gazette*, the outcome of Comstock's efforts to restrain newspapers still was not what he could have hoped. [46]

Joshua Brown points out subtle shifts in marketing made by publisher Frank Leslie in response to Comstock's threats, which did not result in lessening the "indecency" of his newspapers. Leslie changed the title of his most sensational publication from *Days' Doings* to the *New York Illustrated Times* and "veered away from the barroom to the parlor." His content, however, still focused on "pictorial coverage of news shunned by the respectable press." As a result, after 1876, everyone in the family was exposed to scandalous news stories, such as Comstock's arrest of the infamous abortion provider Ann Lohman, aka Madame Restell, and her subsequent dramatic suicide.[47] Following on the publicity bonanza of Victoria Woodhull, Leslie especially highlighted similar stories in *Days' Doings* about women who "took on the sexual frisson of notoriety" in part by "inhabiting male positions."[48]

With abundant copies on public view, Richard Fox's *National Police Gazette* likewise continued to offer stories of debaucheries, young women tricked into prostitution, and naughty wives, all with eye-catching illustrations. The *Gazette* also pandered to Comstock's robust ego by portraying him frequently as fearless, strong, and dapper, as in his arrest of a "vicious vendor and his pal" in 1879.[49] On a few rare occasions, Comstock did manage to stop the press, but mostly Leslie and Fox seem to have been too economically successful and politically powerful for him to suppress.

In the 1885 trial of a news dealer, Comstock was asked why he had chosen such a low target. The *New York Times* reported the dialogue in Court: "'Is there no way to get at the publisher of these papers?'" asked the magistrate, addressing Mr. Comstock. "No. I am afraid not," was the response. "Unfortunately the laws do not aim at the proprietors."[50] Comstock's answer was true only in practice rather than in law, in that he rarely could get a judge to interfere with publishers of men's "sporting newspapers," as they were known.

In the cases of both the *National Police Gazette* and *Days' Doings*, editorial self-censorship resulted in far less reduction of salacious stories than Comstock undoubtedly hoped. The clearest result of his campaign to clean up American newspapers was that they ceased publishing obvious advertisements through which "obscenities" could be ordered. Nevertheless, in his typical overestimation of his own success, Comstock counted both his settlements with the *National Police Gazette* and *Days' Doings* as great victories.

As his next target of coerced moral improvement in 1877, Comstock took on another popular venue for sexy stories about transgressive women: theatrical performances. Eleven days after pestering Richard K. Fox about the *National Police Gazette,* Comstock led a platoon of NYSSV leaders to see the "variety" show produced by Jake Berry (aka Jacob Schonberger) at the Columbia Opera House in the West Village at Twelfth Street and Greenwich Avenue, on February 27, 1877. Jake's wife Belle was the star of the show, along with a troupe of "Dizzy Blondes." Jake and Belle published a *Song and Dance Book* in 1873 that features wonderful chromolithographic portraits of the couple on the cover, accompanied by tendrils with lush strawberries (figure 3.9 / plate 6). While Jake looks out at us with direct command, we see Belle in a smaller medallion and from the side—a suggestion of her reduced significance as compared with her husband.

The style of theater they performed, however, typically offered the exact opposite of this gender power arrangement. As Robert Allen writes, after 1869 and the arrival of the British actress and producer Lydia Thompson in New York, "burlesque in America was inextricably tied to the issue of the spectacular female performer, and from then on burlesque implicitly raised troubling questions about how a woman should be 'allowed' to act on stage, about how femininity should and could be represented, and about the relationship of women onstage to women in the outside, 'real' world."[51] All of these questions came up in the court proceedings that followed the visit of the NYSSV to the Columbia Opera House.

The reason for Comstock's consternation is obvious. Shortly before the NYSSV's visit, Berry advertised that the show would be "Frenchy," "Racy," and "Piquant," with "LOVELY FEMALE BATHERS IN REAL WATER," and "naughty Parisian Dances." These were precisely the code words Comstock had been attempting to remove from newspaper advertisements for arousing materials that could be ordered through the mail.[52] Confronted with the "spicy" promise of "70 of the most attractive and best formed ladies on the stage," the NYSSV sent a large investigative squad to see the show, including many gentlemen from the society's executive committee. Samuel Colgate, John M. Cornell, Calvin C. Woolworth,

FIGURE 3.9 *The Berry's Song and Dance Book* (New York: R.M. De Witt, 1873), cover. Harris Collection of American Poetry and Plays, Brown University. See also color plate 6.

Charles H. Stevenson, and Comstock all attended, in addition to the society's new full-time detective, Joseph Britton.

After seeing the show, including its principal sketch "Mock Modesty," Comstock and the committee were unanimous that it should be suppressed. However, when Berry heard that the NYSSV was going before the grand jury to bring an indictment, he wrote to Comstock and promised to change anything "objectionable" and also to provide a private box any time Comstock or his friends "should choose to honor his Opera with a call."[53] Despite Berry's promises, when the NYSSV committee returned to see the show the following month with the Reverend Alfred Taylor now in tow, they still found it "vile & filthy in the extreme."[54] According to Comstock's notes, the court took no action at the time, but he happily recorded that Berry was successfully convicted the following year, following the complaint of a newly formed organization.

The prosecution of Jake Berry and the Columbia Opera House, in March 1878, was the earliest successful and well-publicized legal victory for the Society for the Prevention of Crime (SPC), an organization that went on to remain active for nearly eighty years.[55] The SPC was similar to the NYSSV in that wealthy Christian men devoted to eliminating vice formed both. The SPC's main difference was that it concentrated on illegal liquor sales, police corruption, and prostitution. By 1878, the NYSSV also had added gambling to its portfolio of vices to be suppressed, but still focused largely on obscenity prosecutions. The two societies sometimes worked together, as presumably in this case, but in later years largely operated separately.

When police stormed the Columbia Opera House on February 25, 1878, on the demand of the SPC, Jake and his wife Belle Berry could not be found, but twenty-eight performers were taken into custody, including twenty women and eight men. Berry was at home, and when he heard the news, he valiantly and promptly turned himself in and the performers were freed.[56] An advertisement for the show shortly before the new raid demonstrates that its "piquant" sketches had not been substantially changed since the NYSSV's complaints the previous year.[57] What had changed, however, was the strategy used by the anti-vice campaigners to shut the show down. This time, Berry was indicted on charges of maintaining a "disorderly house."[58]

When the Berry case came up for trial the following month, the audience in the courtroom included several theatrical managers who were watching closely, as well as New York reporters who covered the proceedings in great detail. Everyone knew this case would be important in determining where the line would be drawn between legal and illegal public displays of the body and sexuality, and who would get to draw the line.[59] The cast of characters, of course, was important to the way the trial unfolded. The judge in the Berry trial, Recorder John K. Hackett, was the same man who in 1877 had authorized Comstock to destroy seized materials even when charges against the defendant had been dismissed.[60] A surviving copy of the Berry trial transcript demonstrates the rapidly evolving legal and cultural terrain in which Hackett operated, and also describes in fine detail the public entertainments that straddled the line between moral and immoral in that moment.[61]

Assistant District Attorney Joseph Bell began his testimony for the prosecution with his most important witnesses, Moses Meeker and William Waite. Both had recently been hired by the SPC to visit saloons and liquor stores, ask for drinks, and then report the illegal sales that resulted.[62] In this case, they had been sent to see Berry's show. Both sets of attorneys grilled the men on the exact clothing worn by the women. Mr. Waite testified to seeing skits including an "Amazon Dance," a "Nuptial Chamber," and "Female Bathers," all performed by women wearing flesh-colored body-length tights. In some cases, skirts ended well above the knee, while in others only a wrapper was worn on top of the tights, open in the front. In the Female Bathers sketch, only tights were worn, but lace was used to simulate a shower between the girls and the audience.[63] During a cancan dance, the girls allegedly pretended to "peep at the privates" of other girls.

In the skit "Mock Modesty," which received much attention, Meeker testified that the plot involved two men at a house of assignation, and a wife who threatened to cheat as well in revenge. During the play, the male character scandalously said to his wife, "There will be no Peter between us tonight."[64] All of this testimony was meant to support Bell's insinuation that the suggestive skits were merely preludes to solicitations made by the actresses to male members of the audience. Meeker testified specifically that he was invited to treat actresses to liquor in a backstage "Wine Room," and that one asked him to take her home, stating, "If you will go with me, for the consideration of five dollars, I will give you one of the best diddles that you ever had in your life."[65]

During cross-examination, Berry's attorneys tried to establish that the show was no different from others being performed in the city. Meeker was grilled on his prior attendance at theater performances. Had he seen the Naiad Queen? The Black Crook? The White Crook? A ballet performance? Weren't the costumes similar in showing off the bodies of the performers? Even though no term existed then for what today we describe as "contemporary community standards," clearly this concept was already seen as relevant in the comparison of the costumes and performance with other theatrical exhibitions on offer in the city at the same time.

Testifying for the defense, Belle Berry also spoke in detail about the play Mock Modesty. She refuted Meeker's description of any double entendres. Instead, she said that her character in the skit was a burlesque actress who wanted to be a "melo-dramatic actress," so she went off to commission a play. In the piece, an Irish couple has a baby whom they misplace, leading to the dramatic line: "Nellie, Nellie, don't cry we have lost our Peter, we have got no Peter between us now!"[66] Belle firmly denied that the rag doll the "husband" held was positioned at an angle to suggest its relation to his penis.

In trying to determine the character of the entertainment, attorneys on both sides seemed to find it relevant whether a phallic joke had been made about "Peter," and also whether the female actresses performed in male costumes, which they did, for example, as brigands in the March of the Amazons.[67] As in other burlesque shows, Belle Berry's troupe "took wicked fun in reversing roles, shattering polite expectations, brazenly challenging notions of the approved ways women might display their bodies and speak in public."[68] Openly reversing gender norms in a theatrical performance was now part of the determination of criminal liability.

Speaking for the defense, the police captain who arrested Berry stated that he was only moved to shut down the show following "the action of a society in making charges against him before the Police Commissioners." Personally, he had seen the show several times and "never saw an immoral act." Several witnesses concurred, including one who thought "the young ladies on the stage were rather heavily clad." Another witness testified that he had taken his wife and daughters to see the shows and "did not think it was a bad place to take ladies." In her testimony, one of the actresses performed "one of the putatively naughty dramas," which a reporter described as "not at all glaringly indelicate, but seemed rather oppressively stupid."[69] All of this went to establish that the play was meant to amuse, not arouse.

These judgments, of course, were matters of taste rather than fact, thus presenting one of the earliest examples of the heated debates Comstock endured when he targeted public arts. In contrast to the leeway he was given in the 1870s to unilaterally determine obscenity with respect to privately circulated materials, his efforts to suppress public displays of art and culture inevitably led to complicated conversations with people holding vastly different opinions.

Even more pressing from the defense position was the question of who was qualified to judge. Only the agents for the SPC testified that actresses were soliciting men. Berry's attorneys asserted that testimony should not be valued from men who were "the hired agents of the Society instigating this prosecution, and paid for the procurement of the evidence which they testify to." With regard to both the very new SPC and its somewhat older cousin, the NYSSV, many Americans, and especially defense attorneys, were uncomfortable with the exercise of police powers by "a voluntary association" with "no lawful authority to appoint detectives, and empower them to induce the commission of offenses against the law, in order that the offenders might be punished." How could agents be credible when they were paid by a volunteer crime-fighting association to drink liquor, watch bawdy shows, and "inform" on fellow citizens?[70]

Ultimately, however, Hackett's charge to the jury refused to acknowledge any of these issues and asked the men solely to decide whether Berry knowingly and willfully maintained a disorderly house. Hackett defined that in broad terms. Premises could be deemed disorderly if they were "open promiscuously to the public, and resorted to for the purposes of prostitution or indecency, or of corrupting, debasing and depraving public morals." They could also be deemed disorderly if "the transactions within them are intrinsically innocent and legal, yet are so conducted as to be an annoyance to the neighbors." Even if the jury were to conclude that the premises were not disorderly and did not annoy the neighbors, Hackett continued, the jury could still convict if they felt that "acts and sights of indecency, depravity and lewdness were permitted by the defendant." Hackett acknowledged that this standard was new, "as I have observed the changing rules of society have imparted elasticity to the law protecting morals, social rights and property."[71]

After four hours of deliberation, the jury asked for "some points on the reliability of the testimony," or in other words, clarification on the credibility of witnesses' testimony. The judge responded grumpily that it was the jury's job to determine who was "entitled to be believed." The judge then further threatened to lock them up for the night if they did not reach a verdict within fifteen minutes. They quickly came back with a verdict of "Guilty, with a recommendation to mercy." The judge was not inclined to honor the plea for mercy. Despite the overall weakness of its case, the SPC was fortunate to be heard by a sympathetic judge. At the end of his trial, Jake Berry was convicted and sentenced to eight months in prison and a fine of $150. The sentence was upheld on appeal.[72] The standards and interpretations of the relevant law indeed had become "elastic," and much to Berry's harm.

In May 1878, a reporter from the *New York Sun* visited Jake Berry in prison on Blackwell's Island in New York's East River (since renamed Roosevelt Island). In his description of the trial that sent Berry to prison, the reporter pointed out the discrepancy in testimony and the source of the worst accusations. He then gave a sympathetic portrayal of Berry, writing that his "former friends would hardly know him as he appears now . . . no longer erect and proud in his confidence of political influence and means, but bowed and broken." Berry confessed that he had lost "more than $15,000," mostly by giving money to people who said they could help him. He was still waiting to hear from the governor about a pardon, which seems never to have come through.

The unnamed reporter next interviewed David Whitney of the SPC, who shared that enormous political pressure had been brought on Berry's behalf. He was happy to report that this effort had failed, and the Society had won a very important "test case." Now, Whitney proudly boasted, "more care is exercised in the granting of licenses to places of amusement than has been heretofore" and "in all cases where doubt exists" he was specifically consulted in his role as executive officer of the SPC. The reporter closed his piece by noting that the Columbia Opera House was no longer hosting any amusements. Where there had been "profane songs by brazen-faced females and the clatter of the resonant heels of clog dancers," now there were "hymns and exhortations" from preachers and lecturers renting the facility.[73] With Berry's conviction as example, Anthony Comstock added theatrical entertainments to his list of targets. His next venue proved, however, that he could not always rely on having the law applied in an "elastic" manner on his side.

THE BUSY FLEAS

One of the salient decisions the jury had to make in the Berry trial was whether to believe the prosecution that the audience was entirely male, or to accept defense witnesses' assertions that women also attended the shows. This mattered because entertainments offered only to men in the nineteenth century often were accompanied by solicitations from prostitutes. Comstock largely left regulation of "the social evil" to other preventive societies in future years, including the SPC, and the Society for the Prevention of Cruelty to Children.[74] Comstock did, however, continue to raid brothels when they offered visual entertainments on which he could bring an obscenity indictment. This division of efforts became especially clear following a notable prosecutorial debacle in 1878.

Less than a year after Berry's conviction, Comstock visited a brothel run by Emma De Forest and arrested her and four other women on the charge of violating "the law against giving an obscene exhibition." He noted in his arrest blotter: "This house, *224 Greene*" is just in the rear of 15th Precinct Station house. Girls solicit from the windows constantly to passers by on the streets." In his court testimony, Comstock provided even more explicit details of what he had seen. Customers sat in a comfortable parlor room setting while watching a troupe of female prostitutes called "The Busy Fleas" lick and stroke each other. The $5 price of admission included selection of a "Busy Flea" to take upstairs, and presumably repeat aspects of the performance that were most arousing. Despite his outrage, Comstock took time to interview all the women as they were taken into custody. One was "a bawdy foul creature, but rather good looking." Another "was seduced by her lover & for shame ran away from home. Promised to leave N.Y. & go home to her mother."[75]

When the De Forest trial opened in September 1878, Comstock bitterly recorded that only the brothel's madam was indicted, although he had arrested all the performers as well. A further irritation lay in the fact that both the prosecution and defense attorneys seemed utterly disinterested in the case. Comstock complained: "a jury was called without any care, but just as they came. [Assistant District Attorney] Herring opened the case for the People in a speech so decidedly for the defendant that persons asked which side he was speaking on?" Herring further directly attacked Comstock for "exceeding his duty," suggesting that he had gone to the brothel on his own authority and "induced the parties to commit a crime and give this performance."

Comstock had been warned beforehand that Herring planned to use the case to publicly smear his reputation and methods. Needless to say, he was furious when the Judge announced a verdict of not guilty, without even sending the case to a jury.[76] The difference in outcomes between the Berry and De Forest cases rested on more than just the attorneys and judges involved. Police and professionals in the judicial system were ambivalent, to say the least, about the vigilante efforts of New York's new private infrastructure for suppressing vice.

In the same year as the Berry and De Forest trials, an eloquent letter to the editor published in the *Brooklyn Daily Eagle* and titled "Informers" asserted: "But of one thing we may feel assured, that a government which finds it necessary to employ such spies and informers as this Anthony Comstock and his assistants cannot long retain the confidence and support of any rightly constituted citizen."[77] The *Tribune* also weighed in on the issue in 1878, publishing a lengthy condemnation of Comstock's investigative techniques: "The Comstock method involves a distinct and more questionable element; the tempting of persons into breaking the law in order to prosecute them for it."[78]

Adding to the new hostility against Comstock were two other highly publicized cases between the Berry arrest in March 1878 and the De Forest trial in September that year. In April, the famed abortionist Ann Lohman (known as Madame Restell), one of Comstock's targets, committed suicide rather than face imprisonment on charges of providing contraceptives and abortions from her Manhattan mansion. The story elicited a mixed response in the press, with some surprising sympathy for Restell. And in July, Comstock flagrantly ignored proper procedure by entering the grand jury room and providing evidence to obtain indictments in the trial of another contraceptive provider, Dr. Sara Blakeslee Chase, "without the knowledge or consent of anyone in the District Attorney's office."

Comstock was irate because his previous request for indictments had been denied, and Chase then initiated a lawsuit against him for false imprisonment and damage to her business. The district attorney and the judge in the case were furious.[79] The editors of the *Tribune* warned the members of the NYSSV that they "must either teach Mr. Comstock more discretion or lose a good deal of the cordial support they have hitherto received from the better portion of the public and the press of New-York."[80] Christian newspapers, in contrast, continued their hyperbolic praise, with the *Christian Advocate* in June 1878 insisting, "His work is most important and is attended with constant peril. He is brave and every way reliable. . . . Stand by him through thick and thin."[81]

In five short years as secretary of the NYSSV, Comstock had established himself as one of America's most polarizing figures, a lightning rod for both vilification and praise. In 1878 alone, Comstock was the subject of dozens of articles in newspapers across the country, including the *Cecil Whig* in Elkton, Maryland; the *News and Herald* in Winnsboro, South

Carolina; and the *Daily Globe* in Saint Paul, Minnesota.[82] In addition to reducing advertisements for "obscenities" in the nation's newspapers, Comstock had also become a standard character within them, in many cases feeding editors and readers with stories just as "piquant" as those he was trying to suppress, about erotic publishers, bawdy actresses, and abortionists. Comstock traveled the country with fierce energy in these prime years, chasing down potential defendants, giving speeches to like-minded congregations, and helping to organize fellow societies for vice suppression. By 1879, whether you were for or against Anthony Comstock was a test of your beliefs about civil liberties, private vigilantism, gender roles, sexual expression, literature, art, theater, and the roles of religion, government, and law in shaping American culture and social life. And he was just getting started.

By promoting himself as the face of American vice suppression, Comstock was gaining greater levels of publicity, much of it good but some of it terrible, especially because he now threatened the freedom, and finances, of the nation's very robust press. For the first time, he emerged as a standard butt of jokes, and his name became a widely recognized synonym for prudishness. In 1877, the editors of the wonderfully satirical magazine *Puck* added Comstock to their proposed Christmas gift list for the first time, wishing him "The Venus Anadyomene."[83] The following year, *Puck* proudly proclaimed: "Anthony Comstock colors to the roots of his hair, when he meets the naked truth, which is why he won't read *Puck*."[84] For the rest of his life, Comstock served as a target for witty writers and cartoonists whose efforts cumulatively eroded his credibility and, along with it, his cause.

THE HICKLIN TEST: AN ADVANCE FOR THE CAUSE

In retrospect, Comstock should not have been surprised at his very mixed coverage in newspapers. At the very outset of his public career in 1873, during the federal trial of Victoria Woodhull, the wealthy newspaper editor Frank Leslie complained about the Comstock laws in his popular publication *Frank Leslie's Illustrated Newspaper*. He found Woodhull's public accusations distasteful, but felt that Henry Ward Beecher had recourse against his accusers without the new law. If he was innocent and could prove it, then he could sue Woodhull for libel in state court. If he was guilty, then the press had every right to expose the truth. Woodhull was an odd bedfellow for an established man like Leslie, but nonetheless she was a compatriot; the precedent and possibility of government censorship boded ill for all members of the press.[85] Publishers' efforts to flout and repeal the Comstock laws continued for decades, keeping the antivice organization perpetually on the defensive.

Most vocal in the fight against the Comstock laws and the NYSSV were atheist "freethinkers" like attorney and orator Robert G. Ingersoll, who founded the nation's first organization devoted to free speech, the National Liberal League (NLL), in 1876. As Susan Jacoby writes, "Ingersoll praised the framers of the Constitution for deliberately omitting any mention of God from the nation's founding document and instead acknowledging "We the People" as the supreme governmental authority."[86] In keeping with his strongly held belief that America's founders had codified a strict separation of church and state, Ingersoll was quick to criticize the NYSSV as an organ of governmental power operating primarily to enforce Christian ideology as law.

During the tumultuous years following the establishment of the NYSSV, Ingersoll was joined in his free speech cause by a variety of other outspoken libertarians, including Doctor Edward Bliss Foote, an advocate for birth control; DeRobigne Mortimer (D. M.) Bennett, publisher of the most influential free-thought newspaper in the country, *The Truth Seeker*; Ezra and Angela Heywood, free love advocates and publishers of the magazine *The Word*; and the anarchist Moses Harman, publisher of a newspaper scandalously titled *Lucifer the Light Bearer*.[87] In 1878, Foote joined attorney Thaddeus Wakeman and several other free speech advocates to form the National Defense Association (NDA), an organization founded specifically and exclusively to provide legal and financial assistance to those arrested or threatened in cases involving "the Comstock Laws, State, and National."[88]

Although the libertarian radicals who formed the NLL and NDA disagreed on many particulars, they all believed in secular government, in their constitutional rights to publish and circulate their points of view, and in the importance of vehemently speaking out against Anthony Comstock and the NYSSV. David Rabban aptly summarizes the commonalities among this disparate group: "Just as individual autonomy justified freedom of conscience from religious and political authority, freedom to determine the use of one's sexual organs even within marriage, and freedom to retain the value of one's own labor, it justified freedom to express personal opinions on any subject."[89] Together, members of the NLL and NDA penned an enormous number of articles, pamphlets, and entire books outlining their many complaints about what they saw as an unconstitutional exercise of religious and governmental control. Petitions sent to Congress demanded repeal of the Comstock Law.

Despite the virulence of their opposition, however, most of these liberals and publishers were unwilling to be associated with explicitly erotic literature. As Donna Dennis notes, "It was Comstock's position that people who espoused free thought, sex education, contraception, and free love were all, as he called them, smut dealers. . . . But sex radicals and free thinkers, who were just as adamant about drawing a line between their allegedly legitimate speech and the allegedly unacceptable speech of erotica dealers, often went out of their way to convey their strong disdain for commerce in sexually arousing materials. In other words, they defended their own unorthodox speech in part by condemning and marginalizing the expression of those with even less social capital."[90] Disagreements abounded; Angela Heywood, for example, insisted in *The Word* that it would be critical to publish "such graceful terms as hearing, seeing, smelling, tasting, fucking, throbbing," etc.[91] That was further than most of her fellow libertarians were willing to go.

This split in the ranks of freethinkers and publishers of more risqué material undermined early efforts to win support for overturning the Comstock laws, both in Congress and in the U.S. Supreme Court. Instead, Congress ignored calls for repeal, and in *Ex Parte Jackson*, 96 U.S. 727 (1878), the Court upheld the conviction of an NYSSV defendant who mailed circulars for lotteries, asserting the government's right to suppress speech that was fraudulent or "injurious to the public morals." The only good news for advocates of free speech was the Court's insistence on the privacy of closed envelopes and packages, which could not be opened without issuance of a warrant.[92]

Before 1878, liberals had been dealt several stiff blows, but the worst was yet to come. Comstock had been pursuing freethinkers and their publications for several years, but with little positive result in skeptical courts. Several trials involving publishers, including Ezra Heywood and D. M. Bennett, had resulted in acquittals, pardons, paltry fines, and severe condemnations of Comstock's overreach. On December 10, 1878, however, Comstock's persistence paid off when he arrested Bennett for a third time.[93] A U.S. district court jury found Bennett guilty of sending obscene matter through the mail, in this case a copy of Ezra Heywood's anti-marriage diatribe *Cupid's Yokes*. This time, Comstock not only won his case but also set a legal precedent that would have an impact on American law for decades.[94] The following year, when Judge Samuel Blatchford upheld Bennett's conviction in federal circuit court, the opinion rested for the first time on language used in England to define obscenity. In the case *R. v. Hicklin* (1868), an anti-Catholic pamphlet titled "The Confessional Unmasked" was declared obscene and therefore subject to forfeiture. For the first time, a modern English court defined obscenity in this case as "the tendency to deprave and corrupt the minds and morals of those who are open to such immoral influences."[95]

In the course of rendering his verdict in New York, Judge Blatchford followed this English language and established a new test of obscenity in the United States: "whether the tendency of the matter charged as obscenity is to deprave and corrupt those whose minds are open to such immoral influences, and into whose hands a publication of this sort may fall." As a member of New York's elite "New-England Society," Blatchford's decision to adhere to this standard reflected both his Anglophilia and his affiliation with the types of evangelical and Republican Connecticut men who populated the board of the NYSSV.[96] Although Blatchford saw this language as clarifying, however, it did not have that effect on either side of the Atlantic.

In England, the *Hicklin* decision "in defining intentionality as imma-
terial to a judgment of obscenity, attempted to clarify legal and cultural
confusion about whether the term extended beyond clandestine smut . . .
but uncertainty continued, as for some years it remained unclear whether
or not a defence based upon intentionality—and, by extension, artistic value, was valid."[97] A series of challenges to the ruling followed in
English courts, and decisions continued to take into account the context
of distribution. A sexually explicit medical treatise that circulated only to
doctors, for instance, continued to avoid prosecution under the test, thus
maintaining long-standing practice in English law to consider the crime
of "obscene libel" only when matters disturbed the public peace and/or
threatened public morals.[98]

When *Hicklin* "migrated" to the United States in *U.S. v. Bennett*, however, this important caveat was left behind, and contextual questions of
motive, intent, distribution, audience, and even political purpose were
ignored. Stephen Gillers summarizes the result of the *Bennett* conviction
and precedent in stark terms: "If *Hicklin* was bad for writers and publishers, *Bennett* was far worse because of the far tamer content of *Cupid's Yokes*.
While *Hicklin* reported confessional dialogue that was fairly explicit, if
only in a roundabout way, *Cupid's Yokes* contained nothing of the kind. If
it offended, it was because of its ideas."[99]

When Blatchford decided to uphold the guilty verdict in the *Bennett*
case on the basis of the language from the *Hicklin* ruling, the lowering of
the prosecutorial bar significantly boosted the efficacy of the NYSSV's
efforts to vanquish the "ogre" of obscenity. Comstock touted the language
of *Hicklin* relentlessly for the rest of his career. Thanks to Blatchford's
more rigorous reading and application of *Hicklin*, Bennett's sentence was
affirmed and he served thirteen months of hard labor. Ezra Heywood
ultimately served two years in prison.

Because defense attorneys in Bennett's trial were denied their request
to read the entire text of *Cupid's Yokes* to the jury, or to offer exculpatory
evidence about its intended audience, it is tempting to see this particular
text as unimportant. Certainly, the *Hicklin* test could have been applied
to any of the provocative publications produced by publishers seeking to

protest the Comstock laws. However, if *Cupid's Yokes* is not unique, it is fitting that Anthony Comstock's great victory should involve this particular refutation of his beliefs. The subtitle of *Cupid's Yokes* is "An Essay to Consider Some Moral and Physiological Phases of Love and Marriage, Wherein Is Asserted the Natural Right and Necessity of Sexual Self-Government." Comstock resolutely believed in the power and necessity for the state to govern sexuality, a position in distinct and fundamental contradiction to free love philosophers, who felt such matters should be left to individuals.

In *Cupid's Yokes*, Heywood argued that the attempt to suppress sexual attraction and physical love through enforced marriage laws and monogamy led to a variety of evils, with particularly harsh consequences for women: "we have but to lift the roofs of 'respectable' houses to find the skeleton's [*sic*] of its feminine victims."[100] Enforced marriage laws, Heywood wrote, led women to lose the right to say no to sexual relations that were painful and/or unhealthy, and led men to satiate their sexual urges through abuse of their wives, and prostitution. The twin evils of sexism and capitalism made all of this worse, because women's low wages led them to prostitution as the highest-paying work available. The end result was that women were forced to choose between two forms of sexual slavery, marriage or prostitution, and clerics, Congress, and courts all were equally responsible.[101] Heywood believed that to fix this problem, adults first needed to embrace sexual feelings, and especially lust, which "properly means desire, prayer, exuberant strength."[102]

For Comstock, this line of argument simply was unacceptable apostasy. In his published writings, he referred alternately to "free-lovers" and "free-lusters" and labeled their religion as "infidels" and "blasphemers" in his arrest blotters. Because "lust was in itself dangerous; therefore Comstock and his allies attacked not only sexual literature sold for profit but also any dissenting medical or philosophical opinion that supported the belief that sexuality had any other than reproductive purposes."[103] After the *Hicklin* test was adopted, Comstock's belief became law: anything that could be perceived as arousing lust would "deprave and corrupt." And because the effect only had to be measured in (abstract) reference to "those whose minds are open to such immoral influences," no expert witness testimony, analysis of an author's motives, or discussion of comparative works was relevant.[104]

Emboldened by this progress, at the end of its *Annual Report* for 1878, the NYSSV addressed "A New Issue." Publishers and book dealers who were forced to stop selling works that had been declared obscene were now reprinting and selling "Classics" that previously had been available "only to meet what some consider the legitimate demand of the student, or gentleman's library." Previously, the board had "refrained, thus far, from touching these things," but now they were reconsidering. Since these might fall into the hands of youth and "awaken lewd and libidinous thoughts," they were now subject to prosecution. In Comstock's mind, the same rule applied equally to art, and especially to the "cheap copies or photographs hawked about the streets as a copy of a celebrated painting."[105] Thanks to *Hicklin*, the slippery slope had just become extremely steep. The war on classic literature and art had begun.

DISTINGUISHED OBSCENITIES

In 1882, Mark Twain penned a satirical essay supporting the efforts of the NYSSV and its Massachusetts counterpart, the New England Society for the Suppression of Vice (NESSV, later the Watch and Ward Society), to suppress the circulation of immoral literature. He took direct aim at the *Hicklin* test: "we surely do not make laws against the *intent* of obscene writings, but against their probable *effect*. If this is true, it seems to follow that we ought to condemn all indecent literature, regardless of its date. Because a book was harmless a hundred years ago, it does not follow that it is harmless to-day. A century or so ago, the foulest writings could not soil the English mind, because it was already defiled past defilement."

Twain went on to compose a list of works on his own bookshelves that were candidates for suppression, including works by Shakespeare, Byron, Rabelais, and many others. He specifically mentioned Balzac's *Droll Tales* and Boccaccio's *Heptameron* and *Decameron*, which Comstock had already been seizing and feeding into the incinerator at the American Tract Society building for several years. Comstock said of one of his defendants in these cases, "He is one of the respectable sneaks, who preserve their respectability & yet do the nastiest business through the mail."[106] As always, Comstock's choices for suppression of literature and art involved arousing sexual speech. Boccaccio's bawdy *Decameron*, a popular tale of seductions and other intrigues, for example, was produced in numerous illustrated versions in multiple languages throughout the nineteenth century.[107] These books usually differed from blatant pornography, such as *Memoirs of a Woman of Pleasure*, by avoiding discussion or illustration of explicit sexual acts. In most versions, we read about and see protagonists before or after, rather than during their sexual activity.

Twain went on in his essay to subject modern literature to the *Hicklin* test. He suggested that poems by Swinburne and Oscar Wilde, and Walt Whitman's *Leaves of Grass*, were contemporary versions of lusty literature comparable to Boccaccio's and should also be removed from his bookshelves.[108] Here, Twain's essay was specifically inspired by the attempt by the NESSV in 1882 to prevent publication of three of Walt Whitman's poems within the newest (sixth) edition of *Leaves of Grass*: "A Woman Waits for Me," "To a Common Prostitute," and "Dalliance of the Eagles." The first poem contained the lines "Without shame the man I know likes and avows the deliciousness of his sex, / Without shame the woman I like knows and avows hers"; the second began with the proclamation "Be composed—be at ease with me—I am Walt Whitman, liberal and lusty as Nature"; and the third eloquently described avian intercourse in flight. All of these, like the *Decameron* and other "classics" Comstock suppressed, offered precisely the type of narrative he hated, with male and female (and even avian) lust celebrated and satisfied, rather than penalized.

After Whitman refused to comply with the Boston district attorney's insistence that the poems be excluded, the publisher, James Ripley Osgood, canceled the contract. Osgood had printed Twain's work as well.[109] Twain protested only privately, failing to finish and publish his satirical response. In the same year, however, he did allow the first authorized edition to be published of his own stab at what he called "pornographic" literature, *1601: Conversation As It Was by the Social Fireside in the Time of the Tudors*, which became enormously popular in underground circulation.[110] Both Twain and Whitman chose to publish more sexually explicit literature in the face of censorship. Their artistic revenge against Comstock and the NESSV may have lacked overt courtroom confrontation, but it was powerful nonetheless.

In contrast, libertarian publishers were not at all subtle in their fight against Comstock's suppression of books. Ezra Heywood, for example, in 1882 published Whitman's three poems as a circular and mailed it to all his subscribers. Comstock was incensed when a sympathetic jury acquitted Heywood.[111] He was equally unhappy in 1882 when a New Jersey judge released on a technicality two defendants who had been selling the *Decameron* and the *Heptameron* at an auction in Asbury Park, New Jersey. The defense attorney in the case claimed that only one book had been sold to a "young lawyer" who was a "proper person," and thus the sale was justifiable.[112] Comstock countered in the NYSSV *Annual Report*: "one of them had to admit, on cross-examination, that to induce sales he had offered them to young men, with the suggestive expression of, 'You must not leave this on the parlor table, nor let the ladies see it.'" As in the Berry trial, materials that were seen only among men always were suspicious, and presumed obscene.[113]

Despite his uneven success in court, Comstock as usual was persistent, and after the *Hicklin* test was affirmed in the case of D. M. Bennett, he felt secure to go after both "high art" and literary works like the *Decameron* and *Leaves of Grass*. At the same time that he began his assault on classic literature, he also began to seize reproductions of European paintings of the nude that were sold in reputable bookshops and art galleries. These images, he believed, were equally capable of arousing passions and therefore deserved the same treatment under the law.

Comstock's incursion into this realm began in earnest in 1883, when he prosecuted a store clerk named August Muller at the E. A. Bonaventure gallery on the charge of selling 768 high-quality reproductions of popular paintings of mythological subjects by the French photographic studio

Goupil's. Many of the originals, including Alexandre Cabanel's *Birth of Venus*, had been exhibited in the Salon in Paris to great acclaim and were well known and admired in New York. Others were copies of old master paintings, such as Peter Paul Rubens' *Venus' Fest*. The stature of the original paintings was unquestionable. In the case of Cabanel's *Birth of Venus*, Napoleon III had purchased the first version of the painting in 1863. The American collector John Wolfe commissioned a smaller version of the work in 1875 that was on view for guests at his New York City home and then at the Metropolitan Museum of Art, to which he donated the work. The reproductions were printed in sizes and formats similar to many of the pornographic photographs Comstock typically seized, and both types included scenes of nude women; he made no distinctions based on mythological narratives or technical merits, and these were not considered in the course of the trial.

As a copy of the defendant's appellate brief in the Muller trial attests, the case was first heard on December 17, 1883, by Justice John Brady, with John D. Townsend serving as attorney for the defense and John O'Byrne as assistant district attorney for the prosecution.[114] The first witness Townsend cross-examined was Joseph Britton, the NYSSV agent who had made the original arrest at the behest of Comstock. Townsend first asked Britton if he did not "induce men to commit crime" by asking the clerk to obtain and sell him pictures of nude women.[115] Here he was trying to establish entrapment, but O'Byrne objected to the line of questioning, and the judge sustained his objection.

Townsend next tried to establish that the seized evidence was within the spectrum of common images in a variety of media, including stories in *The National Police Gazette* and souvenir cards featuring photographs of actresses in tights such as *Dolly Adams* (figure 3.10). In this advertisement for "Housewortth's Celebrities" ca. 1890, Adams's form-fitting bodysuit does little to conceal the contours of her body, narrowed at the waist by an extremely tight corset. Townsend clearly hoped that the actress's curvaceous figure and the example of a tawdry *Gazette* image would illustrate that the reproductions of the paintings fell within acceptable norms. Unfortunately, discussions of the aesthetic and symbolic differences

FIGURE 3.10 Houseworth's Celebrities, *Dolly Adams*, ca. 1890. Photographic print on cabinet card. Ohio State University, Jerome Lawrence and Robert E. Lee Theatre Research Institute.

between oil paintings and photographic reproductions, and mythological scenes versus contemporary staged plays, were never allowed to proceed. Instead, Judge Brady sided with Comstock, and the jury was not permitted to even look at the images Townsend attempted to introduce.

Finally, Townsend demanded that Britton admit that some of the original paintings were on display in New York and had not been seized, including Cabanel's *Birth of Venus*. Again O'Byrne objected, and the judge sustained his objection. In two full days of testimony, the jury was permitted to see only six of the seized images on account, the judge noted, of "the occult" character of the material.[116] In future years, attorneys would argue successfully that "peers" could not judge defendants when they were forbidden to see the evidence in obscenity cases. In 1883, however, this line of defense carried no sway.

In a last effort on behalf of his client, Townsend brought forward three expert witnesses—two artists and one amateur historian—whom he hoped would provide guidance for the jury "as to where the line between obscenity and decency [should] be drawn." Judge Brady permitted the experts, but when Townsend asked them to explain "the distinction between pure and obscene art," the judge found the question not germane to the discussion, ruling "it is self-evident to the mind of every juryman what is decent and what is indecent in art."[117] Brady refused to accept that copies of works on exhibition "in the finest public galleries" or works used for scientific or artistic study should be exempt from the law, and he ignored Townsend's complaint that the law itself violated the "liberties of the citizen." His final charge to the jury asked them to consider only the *Hicklin* standard: "If its effect be to excite improper emotions and inward thoughts, if it suggest an impure sense or is likely to produce a depraved state or condition of the mind, or it is treated in such a way as to arouse improper passions, then it would be indecent under our laws, as declared."[118]

In keeping with the judge's narrow charge, the jury rendered a swift guilty verdict. Bonaventure was forced to pay a fifty-dollar fine and suffered the much more significant loss of his stock. The verdict was upheld on appeal, and Comstock noted in his arrest record that he had scored a "Great Victory!" He happily reported in the NYSSV's next *Annual Report* that "we have advanced one step in 1883 over any previous year, and by a single verdict in the Oyer and Terminer Court in New York City, we have cleared many shop windows, and checked the tide of obscenity which had been coming from France and other European countries under the specious protection of art. We maintain that Genius has no more right to be nasty than the common mind."[119]

As this jubilant passage indicates, the implications of Muller for dealers and galleries were severe. By legally establishing that reproductions of fine art shared the same status as pornography, Comstock had created a situation of great uncertainty. While the actual fine for an obscenity conviction might be relatively minimal, the destruction of seized stock and legal fees could amount to a significant financial blow. Most damaging, the Muller verdict inflated Comstock's already robust self-estimation of his legal authority. Proverbially speaking, he "dined out" on the precedents set by the Muller decision in dozens of subsequent cases, seizing reproductions of French paintings across the mid-Atlantic states.

Comstock happily celebrated his "great victory" in 1883, but only because he could not see the future. By targeting reproductions of celebrated art, he had sparked a conversation that brought onto the stage many new players who soon would become aware of his efforts and mobilize to thwart them. These were not scrappy, struggling libertarian publishers but wealthy collectors, museum benefactors, cosmopolitan expatriates, artists, and art students.

Over the course of the coming decades, Comstock's attempts to suppress "high" art would reveal the fault lines between his own purist views and those of his employers, who belonged to a wealthy elite that in the 1870s began to adopt "notions of the unfettered rights of property and the social or even racial superiority of the holders of wealth."[120] Once the interests and tastes of the bourgeoisie were questioned, the game grew decidedly more complicated. As Comstock completed the last entries in Volume I of his Record of Persons Arrested in June 1884, he surely must have felt great satisfaction looking back on the laws he had helped to pass, the vice suppression societies he had helped to form, and the thousands of defendants he had valiantly tried to bring to justice in his first forty years of life. The effort, however, was not without its costs, and those were beginning to accrue.

FORTY

In 1913 and nearing the end of his life, Anthony Comstock took a large role in helping Charles Gallaudet Trumbull write his first biography, *Anthony Comstock, Fighter*. It must have been with his permission and encouragement, therefore, that Trumbull wrote an entire chapter on efforts to persecute Comstock, which he titled "Weapons That Did Not Prosper." The overview is comprehensive, including legal, journalistic, physical, and criminal attacks.

Members of the National Liberal League, of course, figured prominently. Comstock also clearly wanted less famous harassments to be stated for the record. "In city after city [civil] suits were commenced . . . on the ground of alleged illegal arrest and malicious persecution," sometimes landing Comstock in jail for a few days. In addition to nearly mortal wounds, he also received a constant stream of threatening letters, packages containing poison, and even "a collection of smallpox scabs, labelled as such, with a hearty message from the sender expressing the hope that they would do their full work. Mr. Comstock and his wife were at once vaccinated, and escaped." Trumbull also spent two pages describing in intimate detail a bomb that had been sent to the NYSSV office. The point of cataloguing all of these attacks was to demonstrate the truth of "God's word through Isaiah: *No weapon that is formed against thee shall prosper; and every tongue that shall rise against thee in judgment thou shall condemn. This is the heritage of the servants of Jehovah.*"[121] Despite his efforts to be comprehensive, however, Trumbull left out of his chapter one particularly painful weapon wielded against Comstock.

Unlike most of the men he worked with and prosecuted, Comstock had no obvious circle in which to fraternize. He certainly was not wealthy enough to socialize with his employers at the NYSSV in their fancy homes and clubs. Although executive committee members monitored the results of his raids frequently, and even participated in them on occasion, in general they left the dirtiest work to their secretary and agent. Anthony Comstock represented and worked for the city's elite, but in reality he was a clerk promoted to a supervisory position. In many instances, he revealed an active disdain for the rich in general, fitting with his middling class position. In 1883, for instance, he wrote: "Unpopular though this sentiment may be, yet these facts are forced upon my mind by the evidences of moral decay to be seen on every side. Elegant dress, lavish expenditure, proud position, and arrogant ways—none of them makes a pure mind, a noble character, nor prevents the evils of lust from exerting themselves upon the inner nature of mankind. Those who have money to gratify every wish and hide their crookedness are often the ones most susceptible to these influences."[122]

At the same time that he disdained great wealth, however, Comstock also had a difficult time enjoying the company of men of his own class status, given that they so often gathered in spaces that were saturated with objects, images, and speech he found distasteful and immoral, if not illegal. This situation was exacerbated after 1877, when the NYSSV began a fierce campaign against gambling and lotteries.[123]

An 1885 article in the *New York Times* helps illustrate the chasm separating Comstock from other men. With jocular derision, the *Times* reported on a flap between the censor and a Beekman Street barber around the corner from his office. Upon seeing a lithograph of a ballet dancer with "abbreviated skirts" tacked on the wall, Comstock ordered that it be removed and handed the barber "a set of laws, rules, and regulations." Although he ultimately relented and tore down the lithograph, the *Times* took delight in reporting the barber's final resolve: "'Here,' said Mr. Koechlein, 'is a razor. If Mr. Comstock calls here again I'll tell him I'll shave him, but he'll have to stand this razor.' The blade is at least two inches wide and weighs almost as many pounds."[124] The incident was trivial, but its notoriety illuminates the stark rift between Comstock and his fellow (male) New Yorkers, and the eagerness of (male) reporters to call him out as an unwelcome brother.

Confident in their legal standing, newspaper publishers were equally unafraid to openly criticize and caricature Comstock. They even took delight in reporting on his unsuccessful application to join fraternal organizations, even though this clearly was a painful personal embarrassment. In 1889 the *Brooklyn Daily Eagle* ran an article on this subject with the scornful title "Do Not Like Him—Anthony Comstock Blackballed by Veterans": "It has long been Comstock's ambition to become a Free and Accepted Mason, but the masons have not been free in accepting him. Two weeks ago Comstock prevailed on Harry W. Knight, of the Methodist Book Concern, to propose him for membership in U.S. Grant Post

G.A.R., this city . . . at their meeting . . . at which nearly two hundred members were in attendance last night, there was an avalanche of black balls such as no man in any society probably ever received."[125]

Despite the obvious delicacy of the matter and supposed secrecy of the vote, many of the men who blackballed Comstock were happy to articulate their reasons, citing in particular his clashes with members he accused of participating in gambling.[126] Whatever the truth of the vituperative back-and-forth claims, it is clear that few at the G.A.R. post thought Comstock would be fun to pal around with. At middle age, Anthony Comstock was one of the most unpopular men in America, unwelcome in male spheres that embraced exactly the type of humor and culture he spent his professional life trying to suppress and even eradicate.

Comstock never suffered the many weapons used against him without fighting back. Trumbull was careful to detail these moments as well. In one instance, a "big Irish ex-prize-fighter, standing six feet three" waylaid Comstock when he had just left a federal courthouse with his hands full of exhibits. "The young New Englander dodged, dropped the exhibits, and his fist somehow landed just between the eyes of the ex-prize fighter, whose head dropped helplessly back. Before he could recover, Comstock sprang at him, caught him by the throat, forced him backwards over one of the chains that kept people off the grass, throttled him with one hand while with the other he kept the crowd off, and waited for the arrival of a hastening policeman."[127] The account is probably overblown; nonetheless, the record is clear that Comstock used fists, warrants, laws, and persistence, and never left an enemy alone. He certainly was no shrinking violet.

In 1880, Comstock added another bludgeon to his arsenal; he began to publish bombastic tomes that laid out his positions and defended his methods. The first of these efforts, *Frauds Exposed*, took up nearly 600 pages. In the preface, Comstock declared that his objects were first to educate the public about fraudulent schemes, and then to defend his own good name. . . . Prejudices have grown up, because of libels and slanders that have been printed in newspapers."[128] He next broke down, in thirty-three tendentious chapters, from "Bogus Bankers and Brokers" to "The Louisiana State Lottery," the frauds perpetrated by criminals, the villains responsible for evil in America (including prominently gamblers and "liberals"), and the thoroughly reasonable methods he used to fight for good. Comstock generously specified that he used the term "liberal" to refer to members of the National Liberal League, rather than "decent infidels" like Unitarians.[129] Much of the heft of the volume came from Comstock's republication of the entire text of many of the diatribes published against him by the NLL, all answered in minute detail.

Although Comstock mentioned obscene literature and immoral art in *Frauds Exposed*, he did not attempt to clarify what those terms meant in 1880. In that moment, he relied on the *Hicklin* test to persuade judges, juries, and readers that sexual speech of any type could lead the vulnerable to ruin. Comstock's next tome, *Traps for the Young*, published in 1883, was more specific on the subject. The purpose of this book was to offer advice to parents and others who cared for children. First, he presented a series of warnings about particular "traps," including "half-dime novels," gambling, quacks, and infidels. He warned that these should be thought of like "a contagious disease. . . . It is the author's purpose to send a message in advance to parents, so that they may avert from their homes a worse evil than yellow fever or small-pox." Comstock placed responsibility for the avoidance of these traps squarely on the shoulders of parents: "It is in the home that we must look for first impressions. Here the foundation of the character of the future man or woman is laid."[130]

Comstock continued by offering a more extended discussion of his philosophy regarding what qualities made something an "evil." In the case of classic texts like the *Decameron*, he justified suppression in the following clear terms: "Do not forget that *lust breeds crime*. Crime begets public burdens to society, and to the victim misery and suffering. . . . Many of these stories are little better than histories of brothels and prostitutes, in these lust-cursed nations." Lust, beautiful mistresses, and sex outside marriage were all subjects to be avoided scrupulously. Only marriage afforded men "priviliges."[131]

In the case of art, Comstock complained that "Pompeii, the art galleries, and the museums of Europe are explored to find some new work of an obscene character which [men] can reproduce, which shall possess the quality to satisfy . . . low taste, and yet shall be labeled 'art' for their protection." All the elements of the *Hicklin* test are encoded in this language. Reproductions of lascivious scenes circulating among vulnerable persons of "low taste" inflamed the passions, and therefore were obscene and subject to seizure.

Comstock wasn't any happier about expensive European imports hanging in the homes of wealthy men and the city's new museums. He pleaded, "Few men or women who display beautiful paintings, or copies of the same, of the lewd in art, or of the nude, ever give a thought to what impressions are being made upon the budding lives about them."[132] But here his language regarding the status of obscenity was more circumspect: "with a work of art as compared to a copy; in the first there are things which call for a division of attention; the artist has expended much time to bring his picture to perfection. The lines of beauty, the mingling of colors, tintings, and shadings all seem to clothe the figures by diverting attention from that which, if taken alone, is objectionable, with a surrounding which protects its offensive character."[133] This distinction between copies and originals undoubtedly was not Comstock's choice, but rather emanated from his bosses who were sensitive to any suggestion that the expensive art hanging in the homes of their own bourgeoisie class might fall within his purview.

No person was more important in supporting Comstock as a "servant of Jehovah" and at the same time reining him in as the agent of a society run by wealthy men than Samuel Colgate, who served as president of the NYSSV from 1876 until shortly before his death in 1897. In a diary maintained over the course of these years, Colgate documented his relentless efforts to support Comstock and further the work of the society. On numerous occasions, Colgate personally traveled to various jails to bail Comstock out when he was indicted on charges of libel and assault. In at least one instance in 1883, Colgate and two other members of the NYSSV committee even paid off a defendant to avoid publicity. Colgate wrote, "The injured man was in the Sherriff's Office and in a private interview with him we settled the matter paying him $400. We felt Comstock was in the wrong and we were anxious to settle it without a suit."[134]

Colgate's diary also demonstrates the way he used connections within the evangelical community to organize campaigns in support of Comstock and the NYSSV, encouraging like-minded Christians to voice their praise through hundreds of editorials in religious newspapers, Sunday sermons, and published resolutions of support.[135] In just one example, in 1882, the Reverend James M. Buckley defended Comstock vigorously in a literary "symposium" written jointly with the censor on "The Suppression of Vice" and published in the influential *North American Review* at the same time that the sixth edition of Whitman's *Leaves of Grass* was suppressed.

In this publication, Comstock made his case for the necessity of the work and his methods in his usual hyperbolic prose. Reverend Buckley agreed with Comstock on every point, contending that even a single bad picture or book could ruin the purity of a child forever, insisting that the methods Comstock used were legal and necessary, and protesting that the general public "left to itself" would "take little interest" in this class of crimes.[136] Octavius Brooks Frothingham, the third author in the symposium, offered his contrasting point of view as someone who had spent most of his career as a Unitarian minister (hence a "decent infidel" in Comstock's parlance). Frothingham's critique was similar to that of many who had "no doubt there are evils to be removed, wrongs to be righted, stains to be obliterated. The question relates to the method of doing the work." While he allowed that Comstock's "supporters are men of character; his aims are high," he was skeptical: "Who is so virtuous as to be allowed to forbid the distribution of cakes and ale? Mr. Comstock makes frequent use of the words 'obscene,' 'indecent,' so forth. Are we prepared to accept his definition of such words or the definition of his society?"[137] As this passage indicates, in the course of their efforts, an unintended consequence quickly emerged for Comstock and the executive members of the NYSSV. By holding themselves out as arbiters of morality, they had opened themselves to charges of hypocrisy.

Samuel Colgate was in a particularly awkward situation regarding this charge. He had inherited and now ran his family's enormous (and enormously lucrative) soap and pharmaceuticals company. The Colgate Company "held exclusive U.S. distribution rights to Vaseline and in the mid-1870s launched an aggressive campaign advertising the substance's therapeutic value." The campaign's promotional pamphlet included a doctor's endorsement that Vaseline was effective at killing sperm, sporting the slogan that "prevention is better than cure." Critics fulminated against the blatant hypocrisy of Comstock's unwillingness to prosecute his employer for mailing materials advertising contraceptives, and Colgate was publicly embarrassed.[138] The claim of Vaseline's effectiveness as a spermicide, of course, had the added defect of being completely false.

Although most of the NYSSV's executive members avoided assaults quite as stinging as those aimed at Comstock, they nonetheless were forced in many instances to defend their agent and organization, and many of them simply quit. Samuel Colgate noted in his diary on January 28, 1878: "several of our old Board have resigned and I have had considerable trouble to get a new one."[139] Despite his frequent problems in running the NYSSV, and busy schedule in running several other philanthropies as well, Colgate always stood up for Comstock, fulfilling the role more of a father figure than a boss. This role flowed naturally from Colgate's significant experience and devotion to playing the role of father in his own family.

In 1866, Colgate commissioned a portrait (figure 3.11) depicting a moment of cheerful play at his bucolic estate in Orange, New Jersey, which he called "Seven Oaks."[140] In the scene, painted by Johannes Oertel, Samuel entertains his four sons with a puppet show while his wife Elizabeth observes the scene from the doorway of an adjacent sunny parlor. The family's wealth is amply displayed in Seven Oaks' imported carpets, sumptuous drapes, and polished moldings. Mr. Colgate's library is furnished with baronial Elizabethan furniture, signifying not only the masculinity of the room's principal occupant but also the long standing of the family in American society and business. To emphasize this point, a portrait of Samuel's father William hangs above the fireplace. Samuel's four sons demonstrate the dress of fashionable boys typical of the era, with the eldest child in the uniform of his military school, the next oldest at left in blousy knickers falling below the knee, and the two younger sons in the unisex dresses worn by both girls and boys not yet fully toilet-trained.[141]

FIGURE 3.11 Johannes Adam Simon Oertel, *The Colgate Family*, 1866. Oil on canvas, 85.1 ×
68.6 cm (33.5 × 27 in.). Museum of Fine Arts, Boston. Museum purchase by subscription in
honor of Theodore Stebbins, Jr., John Moors Cabot Curator of American Paintings, 1977–2000
and M. Theresa B. Hopkins Fund 2002.20.

Samuel and Elizabeth sit on a diagonal axis facing each other with the boys encircled between them, symbolically representing a protective familial nucleus. The boys are protected both by the parents who guard them and by an environment entirely devoid of any sculptures or images of nude or seminude figures. Comstock strove as much as possible to emulate the Colgates' warmth and propriety in his own family life, or at least to present that happy visage to the outside world. Unfortunately, that goal was far from realized.

Anthony Comstock could never have afforded such an impressive work of art as Johannes Oertel's testament to the virtuosity of the Colgate family. Even if he had the funds, his family could never have made such an appealing subject. Eleven months after Anthony and Maggie were married in 1871, Maggie gave birth to a little girl they named Lillie. She was initially a healthy nine-pound baby but lived for only six months. Anthony and Maggie were utterly grief-stricken, and the couple seems never again to have conceived a child. They were not, however, without family members. Maggie's bedridden sister Jennie continued to live with the couple for several decades, and at some point in the 1870s, Comstock's father and stepmother, Thomas and Bertha, came back to the United States.

In an unusually charitable moment, Margaret Leech writes that as a family man Comstock "performed many kindnesses. . . . Out of his small resources he had helped his father, whose second marriage had brought him four sons. Comstock rented a house in Brooklyn and installed the family there. After his father's death, he contributed to his step-mother's support. And, when one of his half-brothers left his wife, he gave financial assistance to her and her children."[142]

Following Thomas's death in 1881, Anthony and Maggie took the opportunity to buy land and build a spacious country house in the newly developed town of Summit, New Jersey. In 1883, they moved there with Jennie, leaving their tiny Brooklyn home. Nearing the age of forty, Comstock not only emulated Colgate by moving to New Jersey but also in many ways returned to the home environment of his youth in New Canaan. The two-acre property had few flowers, but abundant gardens and an orchard, as well as a horse and a milk cow.[143] Unlike his stark farmhouse in Connecticut, this new house was abundantly furnished, with clocks, profuse bric-a-brac, and several dozen oil paintings with subjects such as the signing of the Declaration of Independence and the signing of the Magna Carta.[144]

At this point in his life, Anthony Comstock had a wife and a proper country estate, and he had even carved out a role as a parenting authority. Around the time he published *Traps for the Young*, Comstock also increased the frequency with which he got involved in family dramas, helping parents who asked him for assistance and advice in dealing with "bad" children. On April 7, 1882, for example, he arrested Minnie Samuels, thirteen, for stealing from her mother. Mrs. Samuels and Comstock served as witnesses at the arraignment. He wrote in his notes: "She threatened to lead a life of shame. Even telling her mother when she refused to give her money to go to low theatres. If I was only a little bigger I could earn all the money I want. She systematically stole from her mother & father & from neighbors to go to Coney Island to low plays." The judge sent Minnie to live in a "House of Refuge."[145] Comstock saw himself as a protector of children, but he was not a father. Now settled in his estate, he set out to rectify that problem.

Although documentation is vague and contradictory, the story as Comstock told it recounts that in 1885 he came upon a pair of starving twins during a raid in Chinatown. The brother and sister were about one year old, orphaned by the death of their mother and the incarceration of their father. The boy died, and Comstock brought the girl, named Adele, home and claimed her as his "adopted" daughter, although this was an informal arrangement.[146] Whatever the actual situation, Adele's arrival seems to have provoked some rumors right from the beginning. On July 17, 1886, the treasurer of the NYSSV, Kiliaen Van Rennselaer, published a letter in support of his colleague in the *New England Messenger*: "All the rumors about Mr. Comstock's family have been thoroughly sifted by the society which employs him. And I pronounce them false."[147] Van Rennselaer's words were politely obscure, but they clearly referenced more definitively articulated speculations. Although it is impossible to identify the subjects of those rumors today, the timing of this comment suggests some suspicions about Adele, possibly that she was Comstock's own child, born to a prostitute. Comstock's many enemies were persistent in framing him as a hypocrite, voyeur, and worse.

As the years went on, Adele attended private school in Brooklyn, and then in Newark. During these school years, a number of problems reportedly surfaced. Adele had troubles that were ascribed to a low IQ. Margaret Leech described her as "a straggling, subnormal child, whom the employees in Comstock's office detested to take around with them, when he brought her in to see the sights of the city. She made herself conspicuous after the manner of stupid children, doing annoying and slightly malicious things."[148] The house must have been tense indeed, with Adele's and Jennie's problems, and Anthony often away.

Even when Anthony was home, the situation rarely seems to have been light-hearted. A neighbor summarized the effect of Comstock's arrival: "His residence here brought Summit to the attention of a greater number of newspaper readers than almost any other individual then here and while this attention was often in the nature of ridicule or censure of the man it certainly never did the town harm." Other neighbors were not as sanguine. One of Comstock's first acts after establishing himself in Summit was to form the "Law and Order Association" whose first target was unlicensed saloons. At the time, Summit was a town with a population of just 2,069; however, it contained twenty-two liquor stores and saloons, just two of them legal. Within a year of his residence, Comstock cunningly helped obtain indictments and fines for many of them, which made him unpopular with quite a few of his neighbors.[149]

Indeed, Comstock seems never to have been "off duty." On his way home from work on October 19, 1886, he recorded making arrests at a scene of "stealing chickens on Ferry Boat." The driver allowed two "pals" to steal eight chickens. Although one "pal" escaped, the two other defendants served several months in prison.[150] In summer months, it is possible to trace the dates and locations of Comstock family vacations, as the NYSSV records show the ever alert agent rounding up gamblers, carousing drunks, nasty mistresses, etc., in picturesque upstate New York vacation spots such as Saratoga and Tannersville. None of this seems to have made for much family fun.

Margaret Leech writes of Maggie: "Clear it is that she worried about her husband, that her life must have been a tense and protracted agony of anxiety. One neighbor in Summit, New Jersey, where she and Tony spent most of their married life, was to wonder how she went on living. He was always provoking quarrels, this mad, obstinate husband of hers, always running his opinionated head into something that was not his affair."[151] Comstock seems never to have considered the effect of his nonstop purification efforts on his own family. Instead, he had the great fortune of a worldview that allowed him to see every weapon thrown at him, and every hardship he faced, through the comforting lens of an unshakable faith in himself and God. Whether or not this certainty was justified, as with most adults at forty years of age, his hand had been dealt, and he would spend the rest of his life playing it out.

4

ARTISTS, LIBERTARIANS,
AND LAWYERS UNITE

....

The Rise of the Resistance (Volume II: 1884–1895)

INDECENT LOOPS AND SHADOWS

Although Anthony Comstock in general held far greater powers when he began writing in the imposingly empty new Volume II of his Records of Persons Arrested than when he began writing in Volume I, the switch occurred during the particularly frustrating spring and summer of 1884. His first entry, on June 30, recorded a case brought against a Michael Murray (aka Big Mike) who allegedly had been selling betting pools at the racetrack in Sheepshead Bay.[1] Although he could round up gamblers and get them into court, he could not often get judges and juries to convict them. That same spring, Comstock also spent a day in Albany testifying before skeptical members of Theodore Roosevelt's special committee of the New York Assembly charged with investigating waste and corruption in New York City government.[2] It would be another decade before these early stirrings of oversight and intervention would bear fruit. Comstock still would have to muck through Volume II with only grudging and inconsistent support from the city's police. In contrast, in the realm of obscenity prosecutions, in 1884 he had real cause for optimism.

In the fall of 1884, Comstock took a break from prosecuting gamblers and turned his attention back to two men he had arrested numerous times, Thomas Scroggy and Charles Conroy. On October 3rd, the censor was back in Philadelphia once again purchasing materials from Scroggy's store at 1232 Vine Street. The *New York Times* noted that Scroggy "had been convicted three times of similar offences, and served one term in the penitentiary." Nevertheless, the stationer was still well stocked with materials to support Comstock's case. He left the shop with "a box full of obscene photographs, and about 12 indecent books." Clearly, the profit Scroggy made on these items was worth tempting further prosecution, and to prove the point Comstock even noted in his arrest record that Scroggy sold books by Paul de Kock "at about two times regular price."[3]

At the end of his trial, Scroggy went back to prison again, this time for two years, thus adding to Comstock's recent success in gaining convictions in obscenity trials. Victory in the Muller trial, and implementation of the *Hicklin* test, were significantly helping to shift opinions and outcomes. Even better, from the NYSSV's point of view, the verdict in the Muller trial had inspired a burst of self-censorship. The society boasted in its *Annual Report* for 1884: "In our last annual report, we cited the arrest of a young man, for the offense of selling photographs of indecent works of art, the originals of which had been exhibited in the "Saloons of Paris. . . . These prosecutions have caused many, whose business was the manufacturing of semi-indecent pictures, to submit to us such pictures before offering them for sale, resulting in preventing many large orders from being executed."[4] Comstock's arrest blotters corroborate this optimistic statement, listing numerous instances in which dealers and printers brought images for Comstock to inspect prior to production. The *Report* did not let on, however, that some firms proved highly resistant to this arrangement.

The month after the Scroggy arrest, Comstock again took to familiar ground, prosecuting his old nemesis Charles Conroy, who had served two years in prison in 1874 for slicing a four-inch gash deep enough into Comstock's face to cut to the bone. Like Scroggy, Conroy served his time and promptly went back to work as a street peddler on the corner of

Broadway and Fourth Street. For this last arrest, Comstock's notes were strangely brief: Conroy was "oft arrested" and picked up for just "one ob. picture." The case was noted as dismissed.[5] What Comstock didn't bother to record in his own Record of Arrests was that his prosecution of Conroy this time had resulted in a major setback, if not in law then certainly in public relations.

By 1884, Comstock was a ubiquitous subject in newspapers, from the lowbrow *Police Gazette* to the tony New York *Sun* and *Tribune*, with frequent laudatory editorials in the Christian press and with telegraph wires spreading all of this across the country. The ample coverage of this last Conroy case may seem unwarranted from the perspective that Comstock's seizure of just one picture was so small. But the story held many other claims to public interest. Newspapers delighted in retelling the story of the great hatred between the two men, who had been sparring for twenty years. They also spilled gallons of ink describing their arresting physical attributes—Conroy had been born missing one arm, and still took a swipe at Comstock in court when he felt unfairly attacked. An eloquent *Herald* reporter added: "The famous scar on the broad and capacious cheek of Anthony Comstock is like Hawthorne's scarlet letter. Sometimes it is pale and almost invisible, but if anger or fright causes the blood to leave his face it stands out distinct and clear, as if it was traced in crimson fire."[6]

Equally remarked upon in the courtroom drama was the particular picture Comstock presented to the judge as evidence. The subject in the image was Annie Sutherland, a popular actress who was frequently photographed among the city's many "footlight favorites." The photographer was the highly regarded and romantic Jose Maria Mora, a wealthy Cuban exile whose family had been forced to flee their estate at the time of a populist uprising against Spanish rule in 1868.

Originally trained as a painter, as David S. Shields recounts, Mora began work in New York a few years after fleeing Cuba, at the extravagant Sarony & Co. Photography Studio. In a bold and innovative move in 1871, Napoleon Sarony and his son Otto opened an enormous salon in Union Square, filled with contemporary paintings, sculpture, decorative arts, and lounging areas. There, Sarony pioneered the use of elaborate painted

backdrops for scenes of actors and actresses in specific roles, made by artists who visited the plays to research the correct atmosphere to heighten
the drama. Mora absorbed all of Sarony's innovations, and then struck out
on his own, opening a studio nearby. Just the year before the Conroy trial,
he reached the social apex of his career when he photographed the outrageously lavish fancy dress ball hosted by Mrs. Alva Belmont Vanderbilt in
1883 as a housewarming party for her new Fifth Avenue mansion.[7]

As the trial began, and probably much to Comstock's surprise, the
courtroom was packed with reporters and observers, including women.
At first, under cross-examination, Comstock answered questions from
Conroy's lawyer "by commenting upon them, protesting against them
and quoting decisions of the Court of Appeals."[8] Comstock then asked
the judge to get rid of the case by declaring the picture obscene but letting Conroy off with a suspended sentence. Conroy's lawyers refused.
Although Comstock heartily attempted to suppress any discussion of the
evidence under the precedent established in the favorable appeals court
decision in the Muller case, this time he had no luck.

In 1884, a legal team far outstripping his own small pocketbook represented Charles Conroy. This time, the gifted attorneys Colonel Charles
S. Spencer and Edward Chamberlain were engaged by a group of publishers and photographers to defend Conroy as a "test case." The year
was propitious for the success of a lawsuit on behalf of photography.
In that same year, Napoleon Sarony won an important victory in the U.S.
Supreme Court in the case of *Burrow-Giles Lithographic Co. v. Sarony*.
Sarony had sued the lithographic firm for printing 85,000 unauthorized
copies of his gorgeous portrait of *Oscar Wilde, No. 18*, and prevailed at
trial. Burrow-Giles appealed the judgment against him, and the case
went all the way up to the Supreme Court. On March 17, 1884, the Court
affirmed that just like an author, the photographer was an "originator" of
intellectual property.

Sarony, the Court said, had created a work "entirely from his own original mental conception, to which he gave visible form by posing the said
Oscar Wilde in front of the camera, selecting and arranging the costume,
draperies, and other various accessories in said photograph, arranging

and disposing the light and shade, suggesting and evoking the desired expression, and from such disposition, arrangement, or representation, made entirely by plaintiff, he produced the picture in suit." As Jane Gaines notes, the decision was limited in scope and ultimately overhauled by future justices. However, the legal ambitions and victories of the Saronys and their fellow photographers in these years should not be overlooked.[9]

On the day of Conroy's trial, Otto Sarony was in attendance in the packed courtroom, along with Mora and other well-known New York photographers "ready to testify," including K. W. Beniczky, Benjamin J. Falk, and Edward Anthony.[10] Outside the courtroom, these men were in fierce competition not only to create the greatest aesthetic and technical innovations in their field but also to secure the highest-profile clients. Now, however, they sat in common cause. If photographs of women in tights were held to be obscene, they could not be sold; all of these noted photographers faced the possible loss of the value in their intellectual property that they had gained through copyright protection.

Edward Chamberlain was the star of Conroy's defense team. As treasurer of the National Defense Association (NDA), he had already spent much time and effort defending the cause of free speech. Colonel Spencer, an equally eminent criminal defense attorney and former state legislator, started off the defense's presentation by handing Judge Edward Patterson a pamphlet published by the NDA, titled "Something to Read," which contained "extracts from the sayings and writings of great men, including Henry Ward Beecher, Thomas Jefferson and many others, concerning what might and might not be considered immoral and what ought to be permitted and what suppressed."[11] Comstock was outraged, but Judge Patterson insisted that the trial move on. Spencer next tried to establish that Comstock had a long-standing hatred for Conroy and that the case was brought simply for revenge on account of his scar. Comstock countered that he had warned Conroy many times against selling cards such as this one and had given the defendant ample opportunity to cease the practice.

Next, once again over Comstock's vehement protests, Judge Patterson allowed Spencer to force him to comment on the evidence in the case.

A reporter summarized the result: "After a good deal of trouble Mr. Comstock, in reply to Colonel Spencer's question: 'What do you find indecent in the picture?' defined the fault as being: 'The figure of a woman divested of her proper womanly apparel and sitting in a posture that is lewd and indecent.' The Colonel tried hard to get a more specific answer, but did not succeed."[12] Perhaps on the expectation of an appeal, the case was put off for a week so that a stenographer could be obtained. When the trial resumed, Chamberlain conducted the cross-examination, forcing Comstock to be more specific about the alleged indecency of the picture. Finally, and presumably with some embarrassment, Comstock identified that loops on the fringe of Sutherland's short jacket, or a shadow beneath them, looked like women's "private parts."

In a handwritten description of the case, Chamberlain went on at length about the poor quality of notes taken during testimony, even when the stenographer was present on following days. He therefore gave his own lengthy account of the cross-examination of Anthony Comstock. According to his own notes, Chamberlain began his cross-examination by describing the picture in question: "Miss Sutherland was represented sitting on a rock with the ocean behind her. Her position was a natural and not ungraceful one, and her leaning slightly forward heightened the look of earnestness which appeared in her exceptionally pretty face. The figure was entirely clothed except the arms which were bare, the bust even was not exposed." No further description, or an actual copy of the picture, seems to have survived. Chamberlain continued:

I then asked Comstock to take the point of a pen and with it point out to the judge just what it was in this picture that he meant when he testified that it "represented the private parts of the woman or indicated them." This he refused to do and his refusal was sustained by the judge. My object in asking this was very properly to fix just what the witness meant. The picture as I have said was of an actress in the usual costume of the ballet with the short skirt surrounded by a border of fringe. In this case the fringe was made of a chenille or some heavy substance and was put on in loops so that all around the thighs and across the figure was a row or series of these loops. . . . I maintain notwithstanding the ruling of the judge that I had an absolute right to know just which one of these loops Comstock testified to as "representing the private parts of the woman" or if none of these loops then the shadow below or if neither of these then what other part of the picture was the subject of the criticism.[13]

Chamberlain here was going well beyond typical defense tactics in Comstock's obscenity cases, which usually consisted of claims of entrapment, followed by a discussion of comparative works and contemporary standards, the unassailable status of the recipient, and sometimes the work's "classical or artistic" merit.

Chamberlain's demand here specifically was formal and aesthetic. Could Comstock articulate an element in the picture that made it obscene? He continued his cross-examination with extraordinary pluck and daring:

In order to test the knowledge of the witness concerning the matters of which he was so free to testify I asked him how many "private parts of women" he had ever seen that looked like anything he could point out in the picture and to simplify the question I asked how many "private parts of women" he had ever seen. Now this was a perfectly appropriate pertinent question and proper to be put and the only valid legal objection that could have been made to it was that to answer it would tend to degrade the witness. This objection was not made. Objection was made however that the question was scandalous . . . it was ruled out after a long argument.[14]

Chamberlain went on to confess his strategy: if Comstock had admitted to having seen women's "private parts," his character would be put in question. If he answered in the negative, then the attorney would submit that Comstock was unqualified to judge whether the "loops" in the fringe, or the shadow beneath them, looked like the "parts." Comstock's unwillingness to comment even briefly on the case in his arrest blotter may perhaps be attributed to his deep humiliation during

Chamberlain's questioning—especially in front of women who were present in the audience.

In another blow to Comstock, Judge Patterson allowed a series of photographers to testify, as long as "their opinions about the picture" did not go into the record. A *Telegram* reporter summarized only: "The parts objected to as indecent in the picture were explained by Mr. Mora, the photographer, and others to be the shadow of a finger on the jacket."[15] Otto Sarony's deposition, which is preserved with Chamberlain's account, went much farther, angrily insisting that it was "not different in essential details from a great number of similar photographs that are being constantly manufactured sold and exhibited all over the United States."[16]

Notwithstanding Sarony's strong denial of any wrongdoing, at the end of the trial Mora promised the judge that he already had destroyed the plate and the image would not circulate further. Judge Patterson followed by ruling "that the shadow should not be there if it gave the picture an indecent appearance," but also that the case was postponed "indefinitely." The matter ended without establishing any precedent regarding the use of expert witness testimony, or the legality of actress card images in general.[17] But there really can be no question as to who "won" the case. Comstock had been humiliated in front of a packed courtroom, and photographers felt emboldened to test even further the limits of the law.

WOMEN IN MEN'S CLOTHING

Despite Jose Maria Mora's acquiescence in destroying his plate of *Annie Sutherland* during the trial of Charles Conroy in 1884, the actress did not stop posing for photographs in similar garb. Although court documents suggest that part of the testimony in the Conroy case involved a debate over whether Comstock called Sutherland a "strumpet," the publicity seems only to have helped her career. A photograph of Sutherland taken in 1888 shows her once again seated, wearing a man's wide-brimmed hat and vest, with tights, leather shorts, and the addition of large "loops" strung at

FIGURE 4.1 Issued by Allen & Ginter (American, Richmond, Virginia), *Annie Sutherland*, from the Actors and Actresses series (N45, Type 1) for Virginia Brights Cigarettes, ca. 1888. Albumen photograph, 2/3/4 × 1 3/8 in. (7 × 3.5 cm). The Jefferson R. Burdick Collection, Gift of Jefferson R. Burdick. Metropolitan Museum of Art. (63.350.203.45.546)

the level of her crotch (figure 4.1). Indeed, photographer Benjamin Falk exhibited enormous skill at emphasizing loops in every part of the picture—in the fringe on her hat, edging on her tights, round boot buttons, and even in the perfectly fake smoke rings Annie blows into the perfectly fake sky. Two other images of Annie Sutherland wearing crotch-length fringe four years after the Conroy trial also survive in the Jefferson R. Burdick Collection at the Metropolitan Museum of Art. The "loops" and "shadows" that had been termed suggestive of her "private parts" were now a part of her brand. Perhaps most damaging to Comstock's hope of suppressing these "indecent" features is the fact that by 1888, they also were part of the brand of "Virginia Brights Cigarettes."

While Comstock was focused on his attempt to remove Conroy from the busy corner of Broadway and Fourth Street, vast industrial and technological forces were gathering that ultimately would prove far more damaging to his efforts than his old foe. The invention of mechanized rolling machines in the early 1880s enabled an exponential boost in the production of cigarettes. By the end of the decade, the Duke Company alone was manufacturing four million cigarettes every day. These were then shipped to consumers nationwide using the extensive train networks that had been completed in the years following the Civil War.[18]

Such vast production and national distribution, in turn, merited a similarly large investment in advertising, thus prompting the growth of trade cards with attractive visuals to stimulate the interest of male consumers.[19] Trade cards were distributed both as giveaways in packages of tobacco products and by vendors and street peddlers. In 1888, when Comstock made a raid on a supplier in New York, his seizure of "cigarette cards" included more than 10,000 ready to be delivered to peddlers like Conroy.[20] A large number of these images, like *Annie Sutherland*, depicted women wearing men's dress and engaging in male-gendered activities such as smoking. The torrent of provocative pictures of women with tights, loops, and shadows now barreling across the country at unprecedented speed also brought copious images of gender-bending women to the attention of male consumers.

While it might seem surprising to find images of women in men's dress used to sell products to men, in fact these followed on ample precedents in theatrical entertainments such as Lydia Thompson's and Belle Berry's "Dizzy Blonde" sketches. Pictures of men actively subordinated by women were popular as well, with examples ranging from the illustration of Fanny Hill flagellating Mr. Barquist in *Memoirs of a Woman of Pleasure* at mid-century to a hand-colored stereograph (figure 4.2 / plate 8) made in Rochester, New York, decades later by the large firm Webster & Albee. Prominently, on the right side of the card, thin but bold letters spell out "Sold Only by Canvassers," thus alerting wholesale dealers that

FIGURE 4.2 Webster & Albee, Stereograph of a woman standing on a man's back, ca. 1885. Hand-colored stereograph card. Courtesy, The Kinsey Institute. (2009.86.2). See also color plate 7.

circulation of the image should be private and man to man in expectation of legal difficulties.

Presumably, in the privacy of his own home, the purchaser could enjoy the amusing sight of a grown woman, dressed as a girl, riding her male companion like a horse and guiding him with gauzy reins held in his mouth like a bit. Hand-coloring provides decorative accents to the pair, as well as to a Japanese folding screen at left. All of this was made more dramatic through the technology of the stereoscope, which of course could be passed along to share the intimate and piquant view with a partner, as a proposal to play along. The popularity of images of gender-bending and dominant women made by Jose Maria Mora, Benjamin Falk, Webster & Albee, and many other photographers at this time is a good reminder that then, as now, men's sexual inclinations were enormously varied.

Scholarly interpretations of gender-transgressive women in popular culture have ranged widely in past decades. For some, these images have been viewed chiefly as biting parody, a demonstration that men's confidence in their superior status was so entrenched and justified that they could view women "wearing the pants" as obviously ridiculous.[21] Others have suggested that these images helped men to process the anxiety they felt at a time when "New Women" were gaining greater educational and professional opportunities. Images such as these may also have satisfied repressed homosexual fantasies.[22] The high volume of these images and performances in the late nineteenth and early twentieth centuries suggests that all of these explanations are probably true, and additionally that many men may simply have been sexually aroused by the fantasy of being submissive to a dominant woman.

Around the same time that cigarette cards featuring cross-dressing women began spreading across the country, the early sexologist Richard van Krafft-Ebing was shifting the course of early research "from a physiological to a more psychological understanding." The terms "fetishism," "sadism," and "masochism" were all introduced around 1890.[23] On the basis of numerous case studies in his psychiatric practice, Krafft-Ebing determined that, in addition to individuals who enjoyed flagellation, many "masochists did not desire to experience actual physical pain, but they derived pleasure from the inner feeling of being dominated and abused." Most of these patients were men.[24] Although many aspects of Krafft-Ebing's theories have since been disproven, nonetheless his contemporaneous assessment based on case studies is still a useful reminder that then, as now, men indulged in a wide variety of sexual fantasies. It certainly would have come as no surprise to Krafft-Ebing, based on his research, that images of cross-dressing and dominant women were marketed to men.

Recent scholarship suggests that we take a nuanced view of the numerous and varying versions of male gender expression and sexuality at the turn of the twentieth century.[25] Whether men were tickled, terrified, unmoved, entertained, or some combination of these when they viewed *Annie Sutherland*, one thing seems relatively certain: many experienced sexual desire when they looked at images of women in masculine garb and dominant positions. For Anthony Comstock, who believed that patriarchy was unquestionably the correct and proper order of the universe, this phenomenon must have been endlessly perplexing—or perhaps he viewed this all much more simply as a further example of the work of Satan. In either case, the images he worked so hard to erase from his day, and from the historical record, prove that diverse American fantasies during his reign were profitable. By 1890, Comstock had created an extremely complex legal situation for a wide variety of art and advertising professionals seeking to satisfy the fall gamut of American lust.

PICTURES IN FRAMES

In 1885, the most famous misbehaving women in New York City were not on a burlesque stage or smoking in a cigarette advertisement, but rather depicted in a large oil painting on the wall of the Grand Saloon in the Hoffman House Hotel. The painting was William-Adolphe Bouguereau's *Nymphs and Satyr* (figure 4.3 / plate 8). For much of each day, only the wealthy male patrons of the saloon could see the work. However, Bouguereau's masterpiece was also known to the public through its many photographic reproductions, which had been ruled obscene in the trial of August Muller in 1883 but nonetheless circulated widely. Like the Webster & Albee view of a woman imperiously riding on the back of a man, *Nymphs and Satyr* similarly featured a male figure in a humorously submissive position.[26]

The lighthearted subject of the work undoubtedly contributed to its popularity. For thousands of years, nymphs and satyrs had symbolized hedonistic pleasures, including sexual desire. In Bouguereau's playful evocation of the theme, the satyr has been caught spying on a group of nymphs who now are taking their vengeance by dragging him into a nearby pond. Satyrs can't swim, and so his lust has been swiftly transformed into mortal terror. The eroticism of the scene is highlighted not only by the copious exposed flesh we see, but also especially by the flesh that is pressed together in the scene, including most prominently the satyr's left arm against the breasts of the nymph behind him. The artistry of Bouguereau's technique in these passages is exquisite. As Fronia Wissman writes, "the brushstrokes are almost invisible. The contemporaneous term was *leché*, 'licked.'"[27]

FIGURE 4.3 William-Adolphe Bouguereau, *Nymphs and Satyr*, 1873. Oil on canvas, 102 ½ × 72 in. (260.4. × 182.9 cm). Sterling and Francine Clark Art Institute, Williamstown, Massachusetts. (1955.658) Image @ Sterling and Francine Clark Art Institute, Williamstown, Massachusetts, USA (photo by Michael Agee). See also color plate 8.

Whether or not Anthony Comstock was aroused we never will know, but we do know that he was not amused. In the NYSSV's *Annual Report* for 1885, he noted: "There has been quite a disposition among a certain class of liquor men to advertise their places, by exposing more or less publicly, lewd pictures to attract customers. These saloons are called "first-class" with "Artistic Attractions. At one stroke they defile the mind of our young men, and encourage intemperance." Although Comstock was determined to address this problem as part of his new attack on "classics" and immoral art, this certainly was not the first year he had tackled what he referred to as the "glittering embellishments of the barroom." As William Gerdts writes, this was "the day of the barroom nude."[28]

Throughout the nineteenth century, lower Manhattan was dominated by boarding houses catering to single young men who had immigrated to New York for its available factory work. Crammed into small rooms with little shared space, these men sought roomier gathering places in which to enjoy their own company. Many saloons in the nineteenth century served as workingmen's clubs that provided "close-knit camaraderie" for regular clientele. As smaller, less elevated, and cheaper versions of rich men's clubs, these bars similarly provided highly decorative spaces for fraternal socializing. Beer companies helped with the "glitter." Starting in the 1870s, they began providing their affiliates with funds to upgrade amenities and decorate lavishly—with oak and mahogany bars and brass foot-rails and spittoons.[29] As Anthony Comstock's arrest blotters attest, many saloon owners also enhanced their "opulence," and their profitability, by hanging framed erotic prints and oil paintings.

In 1875, the first unlucky target of Comstock's campaign against saloons was Alexander Clarke. It was no accident that Clarke earned this dubious distinction. His bar, located at 114 Nassau Street near the corner of Ann, stood in the city's Second Ward, just below the infamous Five Points neighborhood and near the markets, ferry docks, and slips adjacent to the East River.[30] Like many of the saloons Comstock later targeted, this one was on his walking route, just two blocks from his NYSSV office at 150 Nassau Street. From his office door, Comstock would have turned left to walk to Fulton Street, where he made another left turn to reach the ferry for Brooklyn. Clarke's saloon undoubtedly was a noisy distraction on his daily commute.

On March 12, 1875, Comstock visited Clarke's saloon with an officer from the Second Precinct and hauled him off to the police court. Three days later, Comstock reported that Clarke had been indicted "for exhibiting obscene pictures. He kept a bar-room and advertised his picture gallery through various papers through the mails and otherwise. I seized some 13 framed pictures." Clarke waited six months until his case was heard. In the meantime, Comstock continued his investigation and discovered that Clarke and his brother-in-law Reagan "did a thriving business fitting up Rum-holes, advertising them by their oil pictures & then selling the same." Comstock proceeded to arrest two of their clients, seizing nine framed pictures at 312 Park Row, on the edge of the Sixth Ward, and 52 West Thirty-First Street in the Tenderloin.[31]

Although Comstock neglected to title the first pictures he seized in these saloons, we may reasonably assume that most were copies of erotic European works.[32] Occasionally, Comstock's arrest records are more descriptive. For example, in August 1875, five months after his raid at Clarke's, Comstock reported to his supervisor at the Post Office Department that he had arrested Mr. James Trainor, a "Rumseller at 95 Bowery," on the charge of "exhibiting obscene pictures on the walls of his Barroom. One picture, entitled 'Belshazzar's Feast,' was the most infamous thing I think I ever saw. He was held in $1000—bail." The picture further was described as a "wood engraving in frame."[33]

The image Comstock seized was probably a copy of a late-nineteenth-century orgiastic print (figure 4.4). The image is based on a story in the Old Testament Book of Daniel (5:1–6) in which Belshazzar, king of Babylon, holds a banquet at which he and his nobles, sons, and concubines drink wine from sacred vessels looted from the temple in Jerusalem. God writes a message on the banquet room wall in burning letters that only the virtuous Daniel can decipher, foretelling the demise of Belshazzar and his kingdom.

Artists typically depicted the story as a cautionary tale, as in a version by Rembrandt focusing on the terrified face of Belshazzar as he

FIGURE 4.4 *Belshazzar's Feast*, late-nineteenth century. Print. Granger.

fearfully confronts God's inscrutable warning. In contrast, the "infamous" late-nineteenth-century version relegates the moral of the story to small details, including the tiny and dazed Belshazzar with goblet and candelabra seen at left. Daniel appears here at center right not as a virtuous biblical hero, but rather as a hungover partygoer who has been caught on the scene the morning after. God's warning is not visible at all in the picture.

The most prominent features in the foreground of the image are the exposed, naked thighs and buttocks of drunken concubines lying atop and alongside Belshazzar's nobles and sons. This "vile" version of the scene emphasizes the drinking and the sex rather than the retribution, thereby converting the story from uplifting parable to bodice-ripper. In the sphere of the saloon, images such as *Belshazzar's Feast* actively subverted the messages of restraint and respectability proselytized by moral reformers such as Comstock and instead affirmed their opposites—lust and the prominent display of its sensual satisfaction. Despite its obvious lack of moral message, the bawdy biblical scene seems not to have bothered New York judges especially. Clarke, Reagan, and Trainor all received minor punishment consisting of a few days in prison and seizure of their pictures.[34]

When Comstock returned his attention to saloons a decade later in 1885, his selection for a first target was ambitious, no doubt owing to the confidence he had gained from the Muller trial. No barroom in late-nineteenth-century New York was more "glittering" than the Grand Saloon of the Hoffman House Hotel. The luxurious experience of drinking there began even before a man entered the doors. Situated at the convergence of Fifth Avenue and Broadway between Twenty-Fourth and Twenty-Fifth Streets, the Hoffman stood at the epicenter of fashionable bourgeois culture in Gilded Age America. The hotel's elegant white marble Italian Renaissance façade faced both the serene and leafy Madison Square Park and the posh steakhouse Delmonico's. Within a few minutes' walk, patrons could shop in the city's newest department stores and see the latest productions on Broadway.

Just as the hotel stood at the convergence of two preeminent avenues, the Hoffman House Saloon metaphorically occupied a uniquely important position at the nexus of conventions regarding both respectability and "low" life. The saloon's visual culture and climate were much more titillating and exciting than the city's evangelical parlors and elite private clubs, but the Hoffman was also far too expensive to be considered low class. The clientele at the Grand Saloon, including powerful Democratic politicians, sporting men, and wealthy gamblers, enhanced its chic allure.[35]

The Hoffman's coproprietor, Edward S. Stokes, had a fitting resume to fashion one of the most notorious drinking establishments in New York City. Wealthy and intemperate, Stokes served four years in Sing Sing prison for the crime of murdering his sexual rival, the financier James Fisk. After he was released from prison in 1881, Stokes inherited partial ownership of the Hoffman House and in short order fitted its bar as an elegant space for hedonistic enjoyment, chiefly by filling it with brilliant examples of French academic nudes. These were not necessarily any less erotic than regular barroom nudes, but they did have the added cachet of being expensive. In 1882, Stokes bought *Nymphs and Satyr* as the show-piece of his saloon. The painting had been celebrated since its first exhibition at the annual Paris Salon in 1873. By 1885, the nymphs had become so famous that a guide to New York's "Art Attractions" printed that year advised, "Ladies can see this superb work any morning before ten o'clock," which must have made Comstock especially irate.[36]

On January 2, 1885, he recorded in his arrest blotter that a committee from the NYSSV visited Stokes at the Hoffman: "Composed of W. C. Beecher & A. Comstock, and he promised to remove certain objectionable pictures in his bar-room. Afterwards it was done."[37] Despite the terse confidence expressed in Comstock's report on his conversation with Stokes, in retrospect he was either overly optimistic or deceptively self-aggrandizing (or, quite possibly, both). Judging by newspaper descriptions, prints, and photographs, Stokes seems to have made no effort whatsoever to clear his hotel of the sensual display that made it so popular. Later in the same year as Comstock's visit, Stokes even issued a large and lavish publication celebrating the hotel's "attractions," including illustrations of the many paintings and sculptures of nudes on display. The Grand Banqueting Hall, for example, is shown to include full-size nudes in sculptural niches, as well as cavorting nude allegorical figures in the band of murals forming an alcove above the coffered Romanesque arcade. Intricate interlaced decorative patterns in gold and silver heightened the opulence of the room.[38]

Two years later, *Nymphs and Satyr* was still rising in popularity and fame. A critic writing in *The Connoisseur* in 1887 went so far as to credit the infamous bar and its celebrated painting "with the distinction of inaugurating the alliance between art and cocktails."[39] As Comstock's arrest records demonstrate, the alliance between alcohol and nudes was long-standing, but now it had leapt from the workingman's barroom to a hotel salon with gentlemen, and sometimes even proper ladies. The nude was becoming normal.

King's Handbook of New York, published in 1892, confirms that Stokes did not tone down the sensuality of the works on display one whit following the visit of Comstock and Beecher, noting the continuing presence of many nudes: "The bar-room is a veritable art-gallery. . . . Its great attraction for visitors lies in its collection of works of art, which includes Bouguereau's famous painting, 'Nymphs and Satyrs'; . . . Etienne's 'Boudoir of an Eastern Princess'; and also . . . Schlessinger's 'Pan and Bacchante,' in bronze; and 'The Egg Dancer,' a fine piece of old bronze."[40] Many of these works can be seen in an *Interior View* of the saloon made by Thomas & Wylie in 1890 (figure 4.5 / plate 9), showing the *Nymphs and Satyr* in its premier position at the center of the room.

Thomas & Wylie's dazzling chromolithograph documents not only a thorough absence of female patrons in the Grand Saloon in 1890 during regular business hours, but also takes delight in conveying the fashions, manners, intimacy, and environment shared by the men who gathered there. The attire and hairstyles in the scene catalogue the full range of personal and sartorial choices for New York's wealthy men in 1890, including cutaway morning coats on the men at left, more formal Prince Albert style double-breasted coats on the men at right, and even the relatively new and more casual sack suit on the man at center, worn with a patterned silk waistcoat to make it suitably stylish for an office setting.

Interior View provides insight into two other components of the comfortable and exclusively masculine culture of the time: taxidermy and tobacco. The 1880s was a vibrant period of time for New York taxidermists, with ample work from residential, commercial, and institutional patrons such as the American Museum of Natural History and the New York Zoological Society. The objective for those types of displays was to render and stage the animals with a specificity that captured their behavior in the wild. On a lighter note, "Novelties in Taxidermy" were also popular, including humorous dioramas such as a scene of frogs sitting for a portrait, and an orchestra of squirrels.[41]

In the Hoffman House, Stokes included both types of taxidermy work, with one deer and two wolves' heads hung prominently at the entrance to the saloon, as seen in Thomas and Wylie's *Interior View*. At both corners of the bar, the print also shows "novelties" in the form of preserved bear cubs holding miniature versions of ornate gilded lampposts. Presumably, these growling cubs were meant to evoke the ferociousness of wild beasts,

FIGURE 4.5 H. A. Thomas & Wylie, *Interior View of the Hoffman House Bar,* 1890. Chromolithograph, 61 × 46 cm., on sheet 71.1 × 55 cm. Library of Congress Prints and Photographs Division. See also color plate 9.

and the courage (and unabashed cruelty) of the men who killed them.[42] This evocation of man as predator, paired with the vision of the chiseled Satyr meeting his doom at the hands of naked women on the opposite wall, ensured that male fantasies of both dominance and subjugation were equally represented.

Finally, no institution catering to gentlemen could be complete without tobacco. In the back of Thomas and Wylie's print on the right side we see a large case and attendant devoted to the sale of cigars. The gentlemen in the foreground have already made their purchase and are prominently depicted smoking cigars while also drinking champagne. *Interior View* also illustrates that Stokes was brilliant at using his art collection for branding and marketing. The box of cigars facing us on the table at lower right shows that the label is Hoffman's own, with Bouguereau's *Nymphs and Satyrs* prominently decorating the inside of the lid.

The men depicted at the Hoffman House saloon share not only an interest in fashion, taxidermy, and tobacco, but also in each other. Almost all the men in the scene gaze intently at another man, as they sit or stand in close proximity to each other across small tables or the narrow bar counter. The intensity of these gazes reflects the perfect ease with which men shared close friendships in this age of both sex segregation and "mixed" sexual orientation in saloon culture.[43] Whatever proclivities a patron at the Hoffman House saloon held, there was ample visual fuel to titillate his senses.

Despite the openly lusty and hedonistic atmosphere Stokes presided over in the Hoffman House, Comstock clearly was restrained from more vigorously prosecuting this eminent target. In contrast to his prosecutions of less well-heeled barkeepers, Comstock and Beecher issued their warning and left; there is no evidence that the NYSSV ever bothered Stokes again, despite the hotel's continued display of immodest nudity. Comstock's decision not to follow through with his threat to prosecute probably was not his choice. The astute leaders of the NYSSV undoubtedly would have been concerned that prosecuting the favored haunt of powerful Democratic politicians would result only in an unsuccessful slog and even more public criticism of their work.

Comstock also restrained himself from seizing art displayed in private homes, although concern that he might is evident in a *Brooklyn Daily Eagle* editorial from 1886 warning him, in stark terms, not to try: "It has been told to me that Anthony Comstock considers himself empowered by the same law that allows him to open letters passing through the United States mails, . . . that he had a perfect right to enter the house of any citizen and to take down from the walls such pictures as did not meet with his approval. Happily for himself he has never undertaken to exercise this autocratic privilege—a privilege that would never be granted in Russia—for more than one law abiding citizen when made aware of this claim of Mr. Comstock has said, with a flush in his cheek and a menace in the voice, 'I'd like him to come into my house on that errand. I'd blow his brains out.'"[44]

Technically, there was no reason Comstock couldn't get a bench warrant to seize work from inside a private home if he could demonstrate that it contained what he felt to be obscenity. Practically, however, he and his employers probably surmised that this was, in fact, an "autocratic privilege" Americans would not abide. Pictures in frames, both in the public and private haunts of the wealthy, would remain outside the limits of Comstock's power. In these domains, he could only hope for self-restraint.

In this regard, he might have been heartened to know that his youthful hero in the dry goods trade, A. T. Stewart, had voluntarily kept painted nudes out of his enormous art collection. When the American Art Galleries auctioned his valuable works in 1887, a critic noted: "The three examples of the painter [Bouguereau] in this collection . . . are entirely free from objection on the score of deficiency in raiment, and Anthony Comstock . . . could survey them without a blush."[45] Like Stewart, Morris Jesup and his wife Maria also prevented any "objectionable" figures from infecting the paintings in their Madison Avenue mansion.[46]

Although statistics are not readily available to ascertain the percentage of nudes purchased by wealthy American collectors before 1883, it is fair to say that this was a relatively small market. Generally speaking, early collectors of French academic nudes like John Wolfe were celebrated outliers. The tides turned quickly, however. After the formation of the American Art Association in 1883, buying imported French art at auction came to represent the pinnacle of excess, and therefore success, for wealthy Americans. For a variety of reasons, the works sold in this manner were so expensive that they were available only to an elite new class of entrepreneurs interested in "a novel means of art consumption that articulated, valorized, publicized, and habituated more hierarchical concepts of social class than before the Civil War."[47] As this fetish for European works took hold among American captains of industry, more nudes like Bouguereau's *Nymphs and Satyr* crossed the Atlantic, providing ever more visual proof of the nation's rising wealth and power in relation to its European forbears.

Reviewing Comstock's prosecutions of pictures in frames in light of this sea change makes clear the constraints he experienced in seeking to impose moral restraint in this sphere. As might be expected, Comstock's limitations were defined less by qualities of form or even subject matter, but rather by the realities of wealth, power, and taste. In 1883, Comstock achieved the apex of his authority to cleanse America of obscenity. Just two years later, shuffling away from the Hoffman House with the NYSSV's attorney in the winter of 1885, he was effectively forced to acknowledge the limits of that power: he could not target rich people, and he had to stay away from respectable private homes.

Comstock's clearer discernment of the scope of his beat was a positive sign of the greater wisdom that came with experience and middle age, but his actions had obscured the legal terrain for many others. While Stokes and those who drank and smoked in the Hoffman House probably never worried that Comstock might arrive on the scene and haul them off to the police court, other individuals and institutions interested in displaying nudes in America could not be so unafraid of Comstock's moralistic rhetoric and prosecutorial powers. This was especially true for a rising group of American artists who had studied abroad and were ready to seize new authority to study and represent the nude in art in a manner similar to their European counterparts. For these men, and the lawyers who advised them, Comstock presented a very clear and present danger.

PHOTOGRAPHS OF THE LIVING MODEL

On May 19, 1885, the celebrated artist John La Farge was arrested on charges of grand larceny. Anthony Comstock did not bring this specific complaint; however, the dangerous legal situation he had created for artists using photographs of "living models" in America definitely was germane to the case. At the time, La Farge's many innovations in stained glass had already made him a favorite of the nation's wealthiest patrons. By 1883, he had completed spectacular windows in Boston's Trinity Church, as well as for George Washington Vanderbilt's Biltmore Estate in Asheville, North Carolina. As James Yarnall notes, however, despite his many successes, by 1883 La Farge also had major problems: "While widely acknowledged as an artistic genius, in terms of balancing his books he came to be regarded as hopelessly inept." As he was on the verge of bankruptcy, a group of businessmen came together to form a managerial partnership. La Farge would continue to oversee all artistic matters, and persons with more financial experience would handle the rest. The arrangement began to deteriorate almost immediately, with conflicts over such matters as artistic control and physical ownership of preparatory works. By the time of the arrest, the relationship between the trustees of the La Farge Decorative Art Company and the artistic genius for whom the business was named had soured into the bitterest of divorces.[48]

The transcript of *George Chamberlain v. John La Farge* at first appears rather straightforward. Charles E. Brooke, attorney for George Chamberlain, a trustee of the company, claimed that La Farge refused to remand to the trustees photographs and watercolors assessed at the value of $3,750. Brooke produced evidence clearly showing that the company had title to the work. La Farge's attorney, Ira B. Wheeler, did not dispute the evidence showing the company's rights, but rather asserted that this property was different because it included "solar photographs" and enlarged reproductions of small tintype photographs of nude models.

The photographs in question were of female models who had posed for the figures of "Help," "Need," and "Sorrow" in a stained glass window commissioned by Frederick Lothrop Ames for the Unity Church in North Easton, Massachusetts. The *Angel of Help* window (figure 4.6),

FIGURE 4.6 John La Farge, *The Angel of Help*. Helen Angier Ames Memorial Window, 1883–1887. Unity Church, North Easton, Massachusetts.

considered among the greatest achievements in American stained glass, includes these three allegorical figures in the bottom half of the design. Despite the financial and legal mess surrounding its production, the *Angel of Help* remains one of La Farge's crowning achievements.[49]

La Farge and his assistants used an extraordinary array of materials in his finest stained glass works, and even painted directly on the glass for great verisimilitude in rendering the human body. Presumably, this is why he commissioned photographs of models to assist in the design and production of the work. Even though the figures were ultimately depicted as clothed, gauging their postures and proportions was much easier with knowledge of the underlying anatomy. Small photographs were enlarged so that proportions could more easily be scaled up to the enormous finished piece.

Although Brooke clearly established the trustees' property right to all the preparatory works for the window, Wheeler countered with a creative and effective line of defense, establishing that photographs and drawings of nude models effectively had a different status "in custom" than other preparatory works. During cross-examination, Wheeler established that the subjects were "living models that posed in more or less of a nude form." He then deposed two assistants in the La Farge Company—William A. Williams and John Johnston—and also the sculptor Augustus Saint-Gaudens. All three testified that the custom for photographs of the nude was to keep them "private" and "sacred," so that only those who needed to work from them directly would see them. Because the models could be identified "as in a portrait," it would be a "violation of every obligation of honor and of custom for an artist to part with the photographs of any model." The three witnesses spoke at length and in concert, testifying to the customary use of this type of image and the care taken to protect the identity and privacy of the models.

At the end of the trial, in utter frustration, Brooke moved to strike all of the evidence "relating to the custom of the profession," but the motion was denied. Clearly, the judge had been convinced by Wheeler's arguments. In July, the La Farge Decorative Arts Company not only voted to withdraw its complaint, but also further stipulated that "the property in question is the property of said John La Farge and not of this company, and the said company have and claim no ownership, interest, or control in or over the same." By distancing itself from Chamberlain and voting with such strong language to disavow the photographs, the company was also effectively inoculating itself from any possible liability on charges of obscenity. While Comstock was not involved directly in the case, his aggressive campaign against photographs of "artistic" nudes beginning in 1885 certainly had an effect, rendering La Farge's preparatory studies legally toxic. In this case, the toxicity worked in the artist's favor, but far more commonly, the reverse was true.[50]

In 1885, the murky legal status of photographs of the nude used by artists was indeed causing a great deal of trouble, especially in Philadelphia. Throughout his career, Anthony Comstock had relatively little luck sending defendants to jail on obscenity charges in municipal and state courts in the City of Brotherly Love. That does not mean, however, that his prosecutions did not cast a long shadow. Philadelphia even had its own Quaker version of Comstock, Josiah Leeds, who sponsored a comprehensive anti-obscenity bill in the city in 1884.[51]

During the same years Comstock and Leeds were on a rampage to get rid of photographs of nudes, Philadelphia's most famous artist, Thomas Eakins, was engaged in producing exactly the type of preparatory studies the La Farge Decorative Arts Company decided it could live without. Eakins had first been introduced to the use of these photographs as sources for artistic work during his training in Paris, 1866–1870. After he purchased a camera in 1879, Eakins began making his own versions, using a small circle of students, colleagues, and family members (including himself) as models. He was so convinced of the efficacy of using photographs of nudes that he produced them in classes at the Pennsylvania Academy of the Fine Arts, where he taught and then served as director of the schools from 1876 to 1886.

In these same years, Eakins was also involved with experiments by Eadweard Muybridge in the development of motion photography at the University of Pennsylvania. Muybridge photographed dozens of nude models in sequence as they completed a variety of activities including running, leaping, wrestling, etc. The stated purpose of the project was to study comparative anatomy and motion; in addition to human models, Muybridge also photographed many animals. However, the burlesque-type skits he also recorded undermined the credibility of Muybridge's effort. Despite the many differences between their projects, for both Eakins and Muybridge, the specter of prosecution loomed large. In 1887, the *Brooklyn Daily Eagle* reported a scare at the nearby Photo Gravure Company that produced the plates for Muybridge's *Animal Locomotion*, a publication based on his experiments. A spokesperson for the company reported that a "queer person" visited who was suspected of being "an agent of Anthony Comstock. The human and animal locomotion pictures are intended only for artists and scientists, but it is feared that if Comstock saw them he would gather them in."[52]

In light of this anxiety, great care was taken in the way the work was presented. *Animal Locomotion* was issued only in an extremely expensive volume with limited circulation. For one hundred dollars, subscribers received one hundred plates, which could be selected from categories including men—draped, pelvis cloth, or nude; women—draped, trans-parent drapery and seminude, or nude; and children—draped or nude.[53] Because subscribers had to affirmatively choose the level of bodily expo-sure with which they were comfortable—and pay steep prices for the photographs—there was less likelihood of complaint. The tactic seems to have worked, because Comstock and other censors stood down regarding circulation of *Animal Locomotion*. The identity of the "queer person" seems never to have been discovered.

Thomas Eakins, unfortunately, received far worse treatment than his colleague for making photographs from living models. In 1885 and 1886, he became embroiled in scandal regarding the young female art students who posed nude, and soon thereafter he was fired from his position at the Pennsylvania Academy. His "Naked Series" of photographs (figure 4.7) studying the alignment of the spine in various postures ended up locked away in a safe deposit box, where its potential damage to the "honor" of the models was neutralized. Eakins protested his censure vehemently, insisting that the photographs were an essential aid to good figure

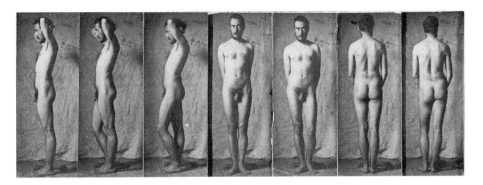

FIGURE 4.7 Circle of Thomas Eakins, *Naked Series: Thomas Eakins*, c. 1883. Albumen silver prints (seven), mounted on card, image and sheet (overall): 3 1/16 × 8 3/8 inches (7.8 × 21.3 cm) Mount: 3 1/16 × 10 inches (7.8 × 25.4 cm). Philadelphia Museum of Art, Purchased with the SmithKline Corporation Funds, 1984. (1984-89-3)

painting: "My figures at least are not a bunch of clothes with a head & hands sticking out but more nearly resemble strong living body's [*sic*] than most pictures show, & my subjects have always been decent . . . you at least can imagine that painting is with me a very *serious* study, that I have but little patience with the false modesty which is the greatest enemy to all figure painting." At the Academy, his words fell on worried and therefore deaf ears. But he was not alone in his opinions.[54]

In 1885, Charles Montgomery Skinner, editor of the *Brooklyn Daily Eagle*, published a long editorial titled "The Vexed Question of the Nude in Art." In it, he offered a strong defense of artist's models: "A deal of talk has been made of late about living models. . . . The *can can* dance in long dresses is demoralizing; study from the nude in art classes is purifying." Skinner went on to insist: "There may be dissipated people among models, but I am persuaded that they do not form a majority. As soon as a model shows the effect of immorality, fast living, gluttony, or drink he or she becomes useless as a model. . . ."[55] Skinner's remarks refuted a common association between display of the body and dissipated or "low status." In Thomas Eakins's case, concern about the reputations of the women who modeled had been at the heart of his problems. In sum, Eakins "broke many of the basic rules of voyeurism operative in the age. . . . Photographing naked middle-class Philadelphians, and then making those images available for consumption by other middle-class Philadelphians, including women, transgressed rules about class and gender distinction."[56] During the past two decades, both Muybridge's experiments and publications and Eakins' involvement with producing photographs of the nude have received substantial scholarly attention and analysis.[57] Less well studied are the courtroom trials, in both Philadelphia and New York, that served to create the chilled and dangerous atmosphere in which artists like La Farge, Muybridge, and Eakins all made decisions in the mid-1880s. These were, in fact, precisely the years that Comstock specifically targeted photographs of living models used by artists for obscenity prosecutions.

In the first of these major cases, Comstock arrested the "Fine Art Photographer" Frank Hegger in New York City on October 27, 1886, and promptly wrote to the chief Post Office inspector William West in Washington to announce his accomplishment. Hegger, who maintained three separate stores on Broadway, was accused of selling "unmounted photographs" that were imported through the mails from Paris. Comstock described these as "of the most obscene and filthy character," and went on to specify that "one package contained 134 pictures, most of them from life, and I am satisfied from my investigation that there is a large amount of nude and obscene pictures imported by various dealers in the City of New York, on the plea that they are designed for artists, and then, when they reach here, are distributed promiscuously."[58]

Comstock was not wrong about the "promiscuous" circulation of French *académies*, which were studies of nudes "in poses ultimately inspired by life-drawing classes."[59] Typically, these photographs were ordered as enlargements from numbered catalogue sheets featuring one or more professional models holding poses often seen in classical sculpture and mythological painting. Because they were designed for serious professional study and based on life drawing class practices for male students, there was nothing coy about the poses in *académies*.

As an example from the Kinsey Institute (figure 4.8) demonstrates, models took no care to hide sexual anatomy, but neither did they engage

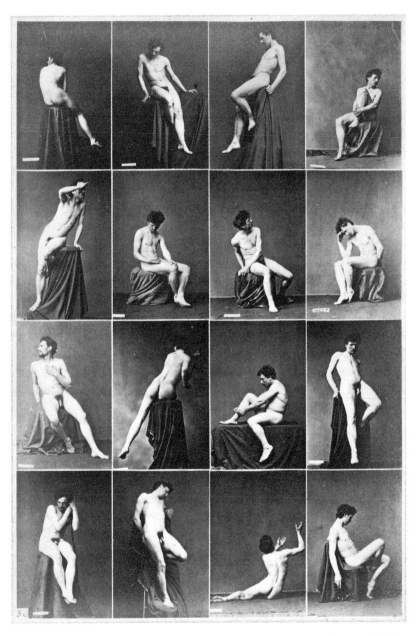

FIGURE 4.8 Catalogue card: male models, n.d.. Photographic catalogue card. Courtesy, The Kinsey Institute. (kidc2723)

in sexual acts. Male models always appear in a flaccid state. Notwithstanding their elevated intentions, in short order even "the most functional of anatomical studies became fodder for leering wankers as well."[60] Many of the same European studios that produced *académies* also produced sexually explicit pornography in the same formats, making it unsurprising that Comstock conflated the two categories as "most obscene and filthy."[61] Nonetheless, in the Hegger case, it was clear that the defendant was operating as a serious artist, with a comprehensive assortment of photographs on sale.

The other works Comstock seized in the Hegger raid were still in the package in which they had arrived, addressed from the firm of Adolphe Braun & Co. in Paris. In 1883, the Braun firm had been designated as the first official photographer of the Musée du Louvre, with the sole license to photograph and circulate copies of the museum's many treasures.[62] The photos received from Braun undoubtedly included many paintings and sculptures of the nude as their subjects. In addition to selling photographs from life and after art, Hegger also had a thriving practice as a photographer of New York City scenes. Numerous examples of his work are preserved, including a wonderful view of men bathing at *Coney Island* in 1885 (figure 4.9) in the Museum of the City of New York.

In his defense at the time of the raid, Hegger showed Comstock that he had imported all the photographs legally, and had even paid customs duties on them. Comstock reported this to the Post Office inspector with consternation and asked him to direct the attention of the "proper authorities to the matter." In his report, Comstock insisted that "pictures which have been condemned by the courts of this State, and which come within the definitions of obscenity as laid down by the courts universally, may not be permitted to pass through the Customs House, or Post Office."[63] He conveniently elided the fact that the nation's courts had not yet "universally" declared a standard for obscenity; the Supreme Court did not affirm the low bar of the *Hicklin* test until 1896 in *Rosen v. United States.*

FIGURE 4.9 Frank Hegger, *Coney Island*, 1885. Albumen print. Frank Hegger / Museum of the City of New York (X2010.11.7645)

Nevertheless, West promptly wrote to Henry G. Pearson, the postmaster in New York who had cleared the photographs, and on November 1st received the following lengthy reply:

One of the packages mentioned by Inspector Comstock was shown to me by him, and contained photographs which would undoubtedly have been withdrawn from the mails had their character been observed at this office, and also some which, although displaying human figures wholly or partially nude, would not be considered by me as obscene or indecent.— being essentially of the same character as many pictures openly exhibited in places of public resort in this city. . . . And while I do not question the good faith of his statement that "obscene" pictures are displayed in the Paris *Salon* (the annual exhibition in that city of carefully selected works of the best and most renowned artists of all countries) it seems to me open to reasonable doubt whether pictures actually deserving of the epithet "obscene" would be accepted by the eminent persons charged with the duty of choosing from among the large number of pictures offered those which, on the scores of merit and propriety, are worthy to form part of the display.

Pearson went on to use the language from the *Hicklin* test, asserting that he did not feel that every picture representing the "nude or partially draped body" had the " 'positive' tendency to deprave and corrupt the morals."[64]

Pearson's response to his supervisor in Washington is telling, both of a more cosmopolitan and nuanced approach to the determination of obscenity that was brewing, and also of a new professionalism that soon would make private organizations like the NYSSV seem anachronistic. Pearson trusted the "eminent persons" who selected works for the Salon and, in doing so, acted forthrightly in the charge of their "duty." He drew on his own experience in this regard: Pearson was celebrated in the United States for his fastidiousness as vanguard of a rising class of civil servants in the Progressive Era who were devoted to public service over party politics. A cartoon published in *Puck* in 1885 (figure 4.10) depicted President Grover Cleveland handing Pearson papers specifying his "Re-appointment for Honesty and Efficiency" while the editors of the *New-York Tribune* and *New York Sun*, Whitelaw Reid and Charles A. Dana, stand in the background holding daggers, incensed that their own favored candidates were not selected for the job of leading the nation's largest post office. Pearson is shown prominently at the center, carrying a locked case labeled "The People's Trust."

Although Pearson's letter and the Hegger case in general do not seem to have received public attention, several other prosecutions of these types of reproductions in late 1886 were discussed in the press, revealing attitudes similar to Pearson's. On December 9th, for example, Comstock and two agents went "on the warpath" in the vicinity of Wall Street. At the saloon of John Bittner, they seized "a haul of steel engravings and fancy tobacco signs," including a *St. Anthony's Temptation* and Bouguereau's enormously popular *Nymphs and Satyr*. At the café of Pierre Bernard,

FIGURE 4.10 Frederick Burr Opper, *Consistent Civil Service Reform*. Chromolithograph. Cover illustration for: *Puck* XVII, no. 422 (April 8, 1885). Library of Congress Prints and Photographs Division, Washington, D.C.

Comstock seized colored photogravure copies of a Hans Makart painting. He also ordered a reproduction of Édouard Dubufe's *Sacred and Profane Music* out of a print dealer's front window.[65] The press was relentlessly snarky in covering these small cases, making reference to "the hanging committee of the 'Comstock Academy of Fine Arts'" and reporting, "It was said last night by several New York artists that if the old masters were alive they would be 'doing time.'"[66] In the more substantial Hegger case, in the end the judge made no distinction between photographs of living models and photographs of European paintings. Despite Pearson's judicious statements and growing sentiment in favor of artistic nudes, Hegger was convicted, fined $100, and lost both sets of photographs. New York in 1886 still was relatively friendly terrain for Comstock.[67] As usual, he would not be as welcome in Philadelphia courtrooms.

Just one month after the raid on Hegger, on November 29, 1886, Anthony Comstock initiated a string of raids in Philadelphia on "venders in improper photographs": John C. Ripka, John Francis, F. C. Pfeiffer, Frederick Junior, Lewis Kohn, and Albert Snyder were all arrested that day and released on bail. All of these men worked for and/or owned reputable shops in the center of the city, which made the case especially newsworthy. Comstock told a reporter for the *Philadelphia Press* that "the present evil was of recent origin and was carried on under the guise of French high art." He was especially concerned about the ease with which his agents had purchased the photographs, which suggested that the dealers had become "very bold in their operations."[68] Despite Comstock's anxiety, prosecutors do not seem to have been terribly concerned. They freed the defendants on a total of $600 bail and then delayed the trials for a year. When they did bring them to court, the matter was quickly settled.[69]

The first defendant tried by Assistant District Attorney William W. Ker was Frederick Junior, a clerk at Janentzky & Weber. This artist's supply store at the time was the most substantial in the city, with a catalogue offering more than 260 pages of paints, easels, brushes, canvas, paper, ceramic materials, books, etc.[70] What the catalogue did not divulge was that the retail outlet also sold photographs of living models. Comstock had obtained the photographs through the simple expedient of asking Junior if they were available. The young clerk promptly responded by bringing a box from the rear of the store. Comstock rifled through the box, chose a dozen, paid his bill, and then had Junior arrested.

On cross-examination, the defendant's attorney, Henry D. Wireman, peppered Comstock with questions designed to humiliate him. First, he established that Comstock was not an artist, had never traveled in Europe, and had never visited the Pennsylvania Academy of the Fine Arts. As the *Philadelphia Press* reported, Comstock was asked whether he understood that "those are nude pictures necessary for the study of art." The judge, however, refused to allow the question, on the grounds that "Mr. Comstock's opinion, which Mr. Wireman insisted upon, would not be worth anything." The crowded courtroom exploded in laughter. In a move that must especially have galled Comstock, all the seized photographs were then presented to the jury.[71]

Speaking for the defense, Wireman asserted that the photographs were imported, they had passed through the customs office, and duty had been paid on them as works of art. He further provided justification for their use, stating, "It was too expensive for artists to obtain living models for their work and photographs were substituted." Wireman's next witness was the proprietor of the store, Frederick Weber, who "testified that he imported the pictures in 1881, in response to a call for them from artists." Finally, Thomas Eakins took the stand, presented as "artist, painter, sculptor, and formerly of the Philadelphia [*sic*] Academy of the Fine Arts."[72]

Although it would have been fascinating to hear Thomas Eakins's testimony just two years after his own forced resignation from the Pennsylvania Academy for producing similar photographs in February 1886, unfortunately at that point Judge James Craig Biddle's patience was exhausted. With Eakins on the stand, he looked "up from a paper before him, and said it was not necessary to carry the case any further, as Mr. Junior was but an employee of a firm and was not responsible before the Court. The jury then returned a verdict of not guilty."[73]

Two further defendants' cases were heard in a purely perfunctory manner, and the jury was about to hear a third when Assistant District Attorney Ker dramatically rose and interrupted the proceedings to make an
eloquent speech:

> I have not had time to consult with the District Attorney on this case, but
> I think I will be justified in not presenting it. I am here to perform a duty,
> and I am a moral coward if I do not do it. But it can not now be the wish
> of the State to destroy art. I believe in the Bible and in God and I know
> he made nothing imperfect. He made man in His own image, and by the
> fall of man alone came indecency. However, I can not reconcile my mind
> that the pictures before me are obscene, lewd, and indecent. They are of
> the highest state of art, and any man who says they are obscene ought to
> go to a less civilized community than Philadelphia.

Judge Biddle concurred: "It is not very easy to define actually what the
terms nude and obscene mean. In every Catholic house in the country
there is a nude representation of Christ, and all the pictures of Adam and
Eve are familiar to all. Nude pictures are not necessarily lewd or indecent."
He then dismissed the remaining cases, even ruling that the county was
responsible for paying all costs of the proceedings.[74]

Comstock insisted on a final statement, during which he indignantly
protested that "these pictures are the same which the New York Court
of Errors and Appeals decided to be obscene." The *Philadelphia Press*
reported that a voice was heard from the crowd in response: "Yes, but
they did not see them." Unmoved and "caustic," Biddle sent Comstock
on his way with a stern rebuke: "It won't do, and it seems absurd for New
York detectives to come over here and try to demonstrate that recognized
works of art are obscene. . . . There may be a higher standard of virtue
then in New York which we here do not have."[75] With pride in his less
"virtuous city," Biddle sent Comstock packing. There is much that we, in
turn, may learn from the legal drama involved in both the Hegger and
Philadelphia cases.

The first observation is that Henry Pearson's reaction in New York
reveals an emerging belief that the judgment of professionals mattered

as to the determination of obscenity. In his judgment, the evaluation of "depravity" should not reside solely with Comstock, especially when there were many "eminent persons" responsible for choosing works for the Salon. In Biddle's Philadelphia courtroom as well, defense attorneys took pains to establish that Comstock was uninformed about art, having never studied the subject or even visited many museums. This line of attack directly refuted the logic of the *Hicklin* test, which required only a determination of whether the effect of the work might be "depraving" to those whose minds were susceptible to harm. Refuting this definition, many professionals charged with cultural regulation in the mid-1880s were newly expressing the sensible idea that trained professionals should be relied upon to judge the determination of art versus obscenity.

A second significant observation that arises from the Philadelphia testimony is how quickly religious beliefs were brought to bear on questions of bodily display. In refusing to bring forward the last defendants, Assistant District Attorney Ker testified to his own understanding of the perfection of the body as made by God in refuting Comstock's more Calvinist views. Although he acknowledged the "fall of man" as responsible for indecency, still he could not bring himself to disavow the beauty of the body arranged in the postures seen in Salon paintings and classical sculptures. Judge Biddle concurred, adding the perspective of Catholic customs regarding the nude even in religious works. As freethinkers had warned, it was impossible to define obscenity without in essence choosing between sectarian religious doctrines and establishing one as law.

Biddle's nonchalant remittance of the evidence to the jury in the Philadelphia cases marks a third potent attack against Comstock's power as an arbiter of obscenity. As compared with the judge in the Muller trial in New York, Judge Biddle worried not at all about the "occult" character of the photographs. American jurisprudence relied on an individual's being tried by a jury of peers, and in Biddle's mind that meant that the jury had to examine the evidence of the alleged crime. Comstock was outraged at treatment of the evidence in these Philadelphia cases from the outset. In his arrest blotter, he wrote, "Could not seize his stock as there is no law in Penn. to permit it" and "This is an outrage on Justice!"[76] In future years, Comstock increasingly was refused his requests that juries be denied access to the evidence in trials and that he be allowed to destroy evidence before the completion of courtroom proceedings.

In addition to greater access for jurists to evidence in these obscenity cases, many more expert witnesses were now coming forward on the stand, including America's most renowned artists. In evaluating the significant difference between the conviction of Frank Hegger in New York in October 1886 and the acquittal of the seven defendants on similar charges in Philadelphia in January 1888, regional differences and attitudes are of course relevant, as are the individual temperaments of the players and relevant state laws.[77] But a great new conversation had also intervened in the public discourse about nudity and censorship.

In November 1887, Comstock broke the cardinal rule he should have learned earlier, that he should not go after rich people. In abrogating this rule, he made a blunder of epic proportions that damaged his cause more than any single adversary. The precedent of the *Hicklin* rule was not reversed in law, but public opinion changed so dramatically in 1887 that judges and juries after that time rarely agreed to adhere to its strict standards. Comstock wasn't given to regret his failed efforts, but if he was, the prosecution of Edmund Knoedler would have been the perfect occasion.

MORALS VERSUS ART: THE TRIAL
OF EDMUND KNOEDLER

Before 1887, the legal status of reproductions of paintings depicting nude and seminude figures was debated mostly within courtrooms, and among post office and customs officers. Photographers, artists, and other arts professionals were occasionally involved in court cases after the Muller trial of 1883, but newspaper coverage of their efforts was still modest. All this changed in November 1887, when Comstock arrested Edmund L. Knoedler and a clerk, George Pfeiffer, at Knoedler & Co.[78]

Knoedler's was an enormous step up from the Bonaventure Gallery where August Muller worked as a clerk, in terms of both geography and the price of its wares. Located opposite the Waldorf Hotel at Fifth Avenue and Thirty-Fourth Street in the 1880s, the Knoedler gallery catered to a steady stream of clientele drawn from the nation's wealthiest collectors. Regular patrons in the post–Civil War years included Cornelius Vanderbilt, John Jacob Astor, Henry Osborne Havemeyer, William Rockefeller, Jay Gould, and Henry Clay Frick.[79] The firm took pride in advertising itself as the New York successor to Goupil & Cie., a prominent Paris firm. Knoedler's was one of only a few galleries in the city that procured the most sophisticated and desirable works currently popular in Paris for American buyers. Because of its high stature, and in distinct contrast to the Muller trial, the Knoedler prosecution was covered voraciously by the press and debated throughout every stratum of the art world. The time was ripe for a fierce national debate about the nude in art, censorship in general, and Anthony Comstock in particular.

Comstock seems to have been aware of Knoedler's high-profile status at the outset of this case, as he was particularly cautious. He recorded in his arrest blotter that Roland Knoedler Edmund's father, and the head of the firm, had been present at the Muller trial and had helped to pay the costs of the appeal, and that a copy of the law had been delivered to his gallery in 1884. Despite Knoedler's clear knowledge of Muller's conviction and the defeat of the appeal, the gallery continued to sell reproductions of the same artworks as Bonaventure. As his cases against Philadelphia art dealers were still waiting to come up for trial, Comstock sent the NYSSV agent Joseph Britton to purchase "photographs of nudes" at Knoedler's, clearly hoping that he would be offered photographs of living models, which most jurists considered to be obscene. Britton returned only with 117 "photographs of original paintings" by artists "of the modern French school," including William-Adolphe Bouguereau, Alexandre Cabanel, and Jean-Léon Gérôme.[80]

Convinced that these were also illegal, Comstock took the evidence to a district attorney and a judge before making his arrest, and both affirmed that they were clearly within the scope of the law. In light of his success in the Muller and Hegger cases and his careful preparation in this instance, Comstock had every reason to believe that Knoedler's wares would be held to be obscene in a relatively speedy proceeding. Contrary to his expectations, however, he added to his blotter notation: "A most outrageous assault by Press followed arrest, upon A. C. & Soc."[81] This "assault" began immediately.

In its first article on the Knoedler arrest, the *New York Times* gave a brief description of Britton's visit to the gallery and then included lengthy comments by Roland Knoedler, the head of the firm, who insisted: "His customers were among the most refined and intelligent people in the country, and he was sure they would repel with indignation the imputation that they were purchasers of improper pictures." Daniel Huntington, president of the National Academy of Design, also weighed in, asserting that "he did not think it was within the capacity of any man to draw the line sharply between pictures which were intentionally obscene and those which were classically artistic and pure."[82] Two days later, the *New York Herald* reached out to artists for interviews. William Merritt Chase supported a proposal to raise money to send Comstock to Europe for "a careful tour of the great galleries" that would improve his "taste and judgment." Augustus Saint-Gaudens also chimed in, insisting that "the decision as to the morality of a work of art should not be left to a man like Comstock."[83] On the following day, the *Times* dropped any pretense of neutrality and concurred with Saint-Gaudens, assessing in an even more hostile manner that Comstock exemplified "persons of a low grade of intelligence and a prurient turn of mind" who threatened to permanently discredit the work of the NYSSV.[84]

On the same day that the *New York Times* declared Comstock unintelligent, the *Evening Telegram* in New York offered an even more jarring stab. The *Telegram* titled its article "Our Art Censor: Anthony Comstock and the Harmless Objects of His Misguided Criticism" and published line drawings of all thirty-seven subjects of the seized photographs (figure 4.11). Comstock immediately tried to persuade the district attorney in New York to indict the *Telegram* and bring the case before a grand jury, but the district attorney turned him down, and even gave his correspondence with Comstock to the press. All of this was spread via telegraph wires across the nation, with the *New Orleans Times-Picayune* declaring on November 22nd: "It is characteristic of Comstock to expect

FIGURE 4.11 www.fultonhistory.org "Our Art Censor," *The Evening Telegram*, New York (November 16, 1887), 1. Accessed at:

the whole machinery of the law to run or stop as he may direct. Unless he subsides pretty soon the community will get mad and rise at him."[85] Across the nation, many communities were indeed "rising at him."

A case in point is the reaction of the Society of American Artists. Some members, including Augustus Saint-Gaudens and John La Farge, had already been feeling the ill effects of Comstock's designation of photographs of living models as obscene. And reproductions of European art were extremely valuable for American artists who did not have the means to travel abroad. In his memoir, the painter Will Low recalled "how a single photograph from a Salon picture would be passed from hand to hand among the younger artists, and provoke more discussion than would the entire illustrated catalogue of the same exhibition to-day [in 1910]."[86] In 1878, Low had joined together with other progressive artists to form a society that would be more open and vibrant than the stodgy National Academy of Design. From its inception, the Society of American Artists exhibited more nudes than the Academy, including in its very first exhibition two works that represented nude artist's models, Howard Roberts's *La Premiere Pose*, and Thomas Eakins' *William Rush Carving His Allegorical Figure of the Schuylkill River.*[87] In 1887, the Society responded to the Knoedler arrest both with haste and with unequivocal condemnation.

Just two days after the raid, members of the Society of American Artists met at the Tenth Street Studio Building in New York City and penned a formal rebuke, which was published in several newspapers:

> *Whereas,* We believe that the study of the nude is necessary to the existence of any serious art whatever, and that the proper representation of the nude in art is not only innocent, but is refining and ennobling in its influence; and,
>
> *Whereas,* We believe the popularization of such works of art by photography to be of the greatest educational benefit to the community;
>
> *Resolved,* That we protest against this action of the Society for the Suppression of Vice as the work of incompetent persons, calculated to bring into bad repute one of the highest forms of art, and denounce such action as subversive to the best interests both of art and morality;

> *Resolved*, That it is the sentiment of this meeting that the cause of art education in the United States and of higher education in general demands that measures be taken to restrain the agents of the said society from exceeding the limits of the field in which its work properly belongs.[88]

The denunciation was clear: serious art required study of the nude, photographs of works of art held educational value for the public, nude figure painting was among the "highest forms of art," and professional artists were best fitted to police "art and morality" themselves. The cause of higher education in the United States demanded that the NYSSV stay away from art.

The Society of American Artists' solidarity in response to the Knoedler arrest signaled both a small uprising and a much broader change across the spectrum of the American art world in the late nineteenth century. The year 1883 was significant not only for Comstock's victory in Muller but also because it was the year in which Congress raised the tariff on imported art to 30 percent of the value of the work, hoping to stem feverish collecting of European art by American buyers. This dramatic and unpopular increase not only spurred the wealthiest American collectors to display their fortunes even more ostentatiously by participating in sales at New York auctions but also, as Kimberly Orcutt notes, "initiated a broad public dialogue that helped to establish the idea of art not as property but as a sacred instrument of public education with the power to impart culture."[89] Many of the same artists who battled Comstock also lobbied against tariffs in Washington in following decades.[90] These larger conversations about the value of art strengthened the claim of American artists to professional authority, and also raised concerns that censorship, like the new tariff, would impede the advancement of American culture.

The post–Civil War years also constituted a ripe "period of intense organizational effort in the cultural sphere" that further elevated the importance of the national conversation about art. Expositions, exhibitions, and public and private commissions all increased dramatically during this era.[91] Philanthropists in these same years joined forces to create and expand major public art museums, including the Metropolitan Museum of Art (1870), Boston Museum of Fine Arts (1870), Philadelphia Museum of Art (1876), and Chicago Art Institute (1879). To promote and publicize all this expansion, American artists gained a wider public than ever before through "the vigorous growth of the book and magazine publishing industry."[92] Comstock was an inadvertent part of this promotion; his notoriety and flare for the dramatic provided ample opportunity for visual culture to be discussed and debated. Comstock, as much as or perhaps even more than any other figure in American history, put art on page one, beginning in the 1880s.

Comstock was understandably furious at all of the vitriol directed at him and the NYSSV, but even his fury was covered in the press to his detriment. One particularly jarring story in the *New York World* alleged that, seeing some newsboys carrying copies of the *Telegram*, he had assaulted one of them: "It may have been the sight of the latter which excited his fury. Whatever the cause . . . he caught Flynn by the collar and, to the horror of the spectators, knocked the lad down and began kicking him violently. Those who saw the assault say he acted like a madman."[93] Whether or not the story was true as reported, it is undeniable that November 1887 was one of the worst months of Comstock's life. On November 16th, the *Springfield Daily Republican* printed an assertion that he was "the most preposterous ass that walks on two legs," and three days later the *Chicago Tribune* surmised that the "utterly hopeless task of regulating the morals of New York" had rendered him "insane."[94]

Thankfully for Comstock's sake, Samuel Colgate, still president of the NYSSV, was at his side during all this tumult, and led a strong defense by the society. In his diary, Colgate wrote that the NYSSV held meetings on November 15th and 16th to discuss the "seizure of photographs at Knoedler's on 5th Avenue." Colgate personally composed an open letter to the *New York Post* proclaiming that the entire board "heartily approve of all that [Comstock] has done, and as a society are willing to take the entire responsibility of the whole matter." On November 19th and 21st, he met with the editors of religious newspapers and ministers. And three days later, at the Twenty-Third Street YMCA, Colgate rallied 100 ministers

at an "enthusiastic" meeting at which they drafted resolutions to be published in the press.[95] Comstock's own defense, with which Colgate likely
assisted, was published in the form of a thirty-nine-page pamphlet titled
Morals Versus Art.

Supportive talking points elicited by the NYSSV are fully evident in
published editorials, including an anonymous reviewer for the conservative *New Englander and Yale Review*, who wrote: "Yet we hope that
Parisian toleration of lewdness under the guise of Art will never set the
standard of decency in this country."[96] This favorable view of censorship in New England publications is not surprising given that American
Anglo-Saxonism was so deeply rooted in these states, a region representative of the nation's mythologized "Puritan" past. NYSSV members
were almost all raised in New England and clearly agreed with the line
of reasoning that found the influence of Catholic France to be detri-
mental to American culture. This attitude was reinforced by anxieties
especially potent in the mid-1880s. Those years witnessed a strong bout
of "WASP panic," with a spate of polemical essays expressing anti-immigrant anxiety, including Josiah Strong's *Our Possible Future and Its Present
Crisis* in 1885, and *Harper's New Monthly Magazine*'s "Does the Puritan
Still Survive?" in 1886. These essays, and the leaders of the NYSSV, all
presumed the existence of a "racio-cultural hierarchy," with "Teutonic/
Anglo-Saxons at the top."[97] Given their belief that Anglo-Americans
already possessed the greatest culture on earth, it seemed natural to view
French influences generally as a form of pollution.

Comstock voiced this opinion in the very first section of *Morals Versus
Art*, asserting that American youth were endangered by "lewd French
art—a foreign foe."[98] This "foreign" threat was visceral for Comstock,
given that consistently more than 50 percent of defendants in his cases
were born in another country, a percentage not far removed from overall population statistics in New York in the late nineteenth century.[99]
In response to the rapid growth of urban areas and the rapid influx of
immigrants, "American Protestantism intensified its long-standing effort
to develop institutional modes that would enable it to exert moral influence, if not ecclesiastical authority, over the increasingly non-Protestant

urban masses."[100] The NYSSV stood as a perfect example of this type of institutional mode of social control. The Metropolitan Museum of Art similarly enacted changes in these years to keep the working classes out of its galleries, for example by limiting its weekend hours.[101]

In the next section of *Morals Versus Art*, Comstock confronted the most difficult strand of criticism directed against him—that he personally was unfit to evaluate art. In this second section, he tried to articulate in a convincing manner the aesthetic standards that guided his work as the person who "drew the sharp line." Here Comstock asserted, "the closer art keeps to pure morality the higher is its grade." To back up this idea, he cited the poet and essayist Sidney Clopton Lanier, who opined on the subject of morality and art: "Let any sculptor hew us out the most ravishing combination of tender curves and spheric softness that ever stood for woman; yet if the lip have a certain fullness that hints of the flesh, if the brow be insincere, if in the minutest particular the physical beauty suggests a moral ugliness, that sculptor . . . may as well give over his marble for paving stones." Rephrasing this position, Comstock summarized that nudity in art was fine, as long as it was "free from any unchaste posture or expression."[102] This distinction was not new to discussions of art in America.

The artist George Inness generally agreed with Lanier, and wrote in a more precise vein in 1879 that nudes painted with an "excess of realism" resulted in images that were "disgusting." Therefore, the nude figure should be painted only if viewed from a distance of thirty or forty feet for a "subdued effect." If an image of the nude was too "literal and sensuous" then the tendency was "inevitably to the lustful."[103] In the mid-1880s, several American artists began depicting the nude with precisely the "literal" and "sensuous" formal elements observable in photographs of living models, and of course much pornography.

Kenyon Cox, in particular, advocated for and exhibited paintings of nudes that crossed the line toward the "literal" in the 1880s. In 1886, his work won over the influential critic Mariana Griswold Van Rensselaer, who praised his depiction of a robust woman, in a (now lost) work *Evening*, as "no bloodless abstraction, no classicizing nonentity, but a very handsome, very healthy, very superb specimen of femininity—one who would be characterized by the simple term woman better than by any other."[104] Comstock's arguments were having precisely the opposite effect on the art world than he might have hoped. By 1887, even the relatively conservative artist William Merritt Chase was no fan of Comstock's censorship, providing negative criticism to the press and eagerly signing on to the Society of American Artists' rebuke.

In answer to the claims of the Society of American Artists and others that only trained professionals could judge works of art, Comstock questioned the premise of the complaint: "Do ladies and gentlemen of ordinary intelligence require an artist to inform them whether a book or picture contains lewd and indecent suggestions or not?" he asked.[105] In another passage of *Morals Versus Art*, he further explained his philosophy with a series of "slippery slope" fallacies: If an artist could make money selling images of beautiful nudes, why then couldn't a father be permitted to exhibit his own beautiful nude daughter for money—"something more chaste, perfect and beautiful in form than that figure on the artist's canvas. . . . Would this be allowed? Would the father be permitted to even photograph his nude child and sell those photographs upon the public street?" The resounding answer of "no" for Comstock lay not in the damage to the child, but rather to the "hundreds of thousands of young men who would, inevitably, be unable to stop themselves from "secret vices."[106] Comstock's obsession with lust and masturbation had not shifted an iota in twenty-five years. One can only conclude that at least a part of the "effect" Comstock referred to here was his own "uncomfortable" arousal, and he didn't need anyone to tell him when he was feeling it. His connoisseurship was rooted not in the head or the heart, but rather in the groin. And as censor-in-chief for the United States, it was his groin, in effect, that determined legality.

What had changed, with the help of the gentlemen members of the NYSSV, was that Comstock now applied a filter to his assessment of the danger of arousing images that had not been relevant in his impoverished youth. His new employers, grappling with the political realities of their situation, tacitly accepted the idea that wealth was an inoculant to the "disease" of the nude in art. Expensive original paintings with nudes were not a danger, but when this "high art" was reduced to the same medium as cheap photography, it lost the protection that came from circulating among the "right sort of people," who presumably were capable of viewing it with aesthetic detachment rather than erotic pleasure.

The anonymous critic for the *New Englander* who agreed that the Paris Salon was not a fitting standard of decency for Americans, defended Comstock's point of view on this subject as well, stating: "The very cheapness of these photographs, with which the country is now being flooded, is a proof that they are intended to be sold among people who have not the slightest thought or appreciation of Art."[107] Even some art gallery owners agreed that reproductions of works might "cheapen" the value of the originals, and thus merit suppression.[108]

This condescending point of view was not lost on Americans reading the newspapers. By 1887, those paying attention to the arts knew well that examples of French academic nudes were hanging in the parlors of wealthy merchants, as well as in the Hoffman House saloon and Metropolitan Museum of Art. Critics and defense attorneys alike were relentless in calling Comstock out as a hypocrite for seizing reproductions but leaving the originals in place. As an editor in the Richmond, Virginia, *Daily Times* quipped: "Comstock has been capturing pictures in New York in which there are nude figures, but when asked why he did not capture Bouguereau's 'Nymphs and Satyr' in the Hoffman House bar, he said because it was an original work of art. But then, according to that a copied picture of Adam and Eve might be let off if it represented 'original' sin."[109]

Despite Comstock's concerted efforts to answer each and every one of the arguments of his sneering adversaries, he was not able to control the narrative at any moment of the Knoedler fiasco. Nevertheless, in 1887 he probably wasn't terribly worried about his future ability to police art. In *Morals Versus Art*, fully half of the text consisted of legislation and case law on his side, much of it a product of his own efforts and including of course the Muller decision and the *Hicklin* test. What he could not foresee was the possibility that the public dialogue surrounding the Knoedler case could trigger a change in attitudes that would effectively overrule the letter of all this law.[110]

As Nicola Beisel recounts, on the day after the arrest at Knoedler's, one of the many individuals interviewed in newspapers was the presiding judge in the Muller trial, John R. Brady, who was quoted as saying that because the pictures in Muller were never entered as evidence, they had not actually been declared obscene. In an even more startling passage, he asserted that he "would never have voted for this law. . . . I think that too large and too dangerous a discretion is lodged in the hands of the officer who is charged to see that the law is obeyed." Not every judge interviewed agreed with Brady's strong rebuke, but still this was an ominous statement from a member of the New York bench.[111]

When the Knoedler case was finally heard on March 23 and 26, 1888, the court proceedings disappointed anyone waiting for fireworks. The trial was held in the city's lowest criminal "police" court, without a jury. Judge James T. Kilbreth looked through the pictures submitted and declared that two of the thirty-seven subjects were obscene using the standard operative in Paris—both were photographic reproductions of paintings specifically illustrating scenes of prostitution. One of these was Henri Gervex's *Rolla*.[112] If Comstock had taken the time to learn more about *Rolla*, he might have found its theme exculpatory—the painting illustrates Alfred de Musset's cautionary poem about a young man about to commit suicide after luring a poor young woman into prostitution and spending all his family's money on gambling.

Despite the moral message of the poem, however, Kilbreth was not impressed with its virtue. Knoedler and Pfeiffer pled guilty, and they were sentenced each to pay the minimum fine of fifty dollars.[113] Knoedler's decision to plead guilty and not bring an appeal was probably not due to a lack of interest in overturning the precedent in Muller, but he was a busy man and was soon reported to be on his way back to Paris to buy more French paintings for his American clients. Comstock technically had scored another win, but the bright line separating naughty and nice had shifted significantly from the 1883 case. Reproductions of Bouguereau's *Nymphs and Satyr* were now, at least legally, on the nice and not the naughty side.

Samuel Colgate, at the same time, had to spend much more effort cleaning up the mess that had resulted from the Knoedler public relations disaster. Conversations at the NYSSV cannot have been comfortable. Among his many well-heeled clients, Roland Knoedler "assisted in forming the collections" of Morris K. Jesup, and probably sold art to other society leaders as well.[114] Although on the surface, and in the news, Colgate presented a united front on behalf of the NYSSV, his diary records a very rocky stretch. In 1888, Colgate increasingly noted that he traveled all the way into Manhattan for a meeting of the society from his home in New Jersey, only to discover that there was no quorum. And in October 1888, Colgate noted: "This has been a very unpleasant day, principally with the SSV internal trouble in our Board, but I hope all will come out straight." Within a few months, the society made major changes, including firing Joseph Britton, the agent who initiated the Knoedler raid. William C. Beecher, the society's long-serving attorney (and the son of Henry Ward Beecher), resigned.[115]

Although the Knoedler trial did not result in court proceedings that overturned Muller and the *Hicklin* test, the public outcry against censorship and Comstock and in favor of artists and art did lead to major changes in the types of arrests attempted by the NYSSV in future years. Perhaps an even more important outcome was that the controversy effectively put censorship on the map of major political issues that were debated widely, and nationally. Comstock's arguments increasingly were serving as a foil for evolving tastes and standards, rather than as ideas to be taken seriously.

The Knoedler fiasco is an excellent example of just how effective Comstock was as a measure of cultural and intellectual change. His hyperbolic language regarding the dangers of obscenity had not changed at all from his earliest literary tirades, and in fact had grown even more overblown. In *Morals Versus Art*, he wrote that obscenity was "like a parasite, fattening upon carrion. Its very presence poisons the moral atmosphere. Its breath is fetid, and its touch moral prostration and death. . . . When art thus lends its enchantments to vice the law quarantines it, and justice applies a disinfectant."[116] A thoroughly unconvinced book reviewer for the *New York Sun* responded with a scathing assessment of the pamphlet: "Mr. Anthony Comstock comes to the rescue of the Society for the Suppression of Vice in a pamphlet entitled 'Morals vs. Art' . . . in which he shows how incompetent he is to discuss the question and how ill fitted by nature or education to fill the office he occupies. . . . His remarks about New York artists are bitter, but harmless, and his attacks upon the press ridiculous."[117]

A decade earlier, such scathing criticism was limited to radical free-thinkers and free lovers. However, from the mid-1880s on, such flaming insults would become standard within newspapers across the country. The *Sun*'s book reviewer assessed that Comstock's "one-sided" approach might "gratify his self-complacency," but would not "satisfy common sense people."[118] This appraisal was both concise and correct. Comstock had already reached the apex of his power. He would spend the next eighteen years of his career unwittingly disarming the weaponry he had amassed in his first fifteen years as a Soldier of the Cross.

LOSING THE WAR WHILE WINNING SOME BATTLES

Anthony Comstock's arrests of art dealers and professional photographers decreased dramatically after 1887. In the wake of Knoedler, Samuel Colgate and other leaders of the NYSSV probably thought it best to stay away from the contested sphere of "art," both to maintain internal solidarity and to avoid further loss of public support. However, this does not mean that Comstock and the fear of censorship diminished. Instead, his name began to crop up across the country as a shorthand way of expressing anxiety about anything that might be considered morally suspect. This might be seen as progress for the cause of purifying America, because fear undoubtedly fueled an unknown level of self-censorship. We must wonder what paintings, novels, sculptures, and other works do not exist because of the specter of Comstock's disapproval. In reality, however, Americans reacted to this new situation, in which the threat of censorship was frequently and broadly publicized, in an extraordinarily diverse number of ways. This phenomenon was underway even before 1887, and accelerated rapidly thereafter.

A case in point is the story of the "Society Belles" of Boston. On June 7, 1887, newspapers reported that Boston's highly respected portrait photographer Elmer Chickering had been arrested. His alleged crime was photographing fashionable young women from the Back Bay who sat for their portraits "in various poses, after famous pictures in the French Salon, and in reproduction of Greek ideals." The poses included single figures such as "Venus Rising from the Sea," and also large multi-figure compositions such as "Nymphs at the Bath." Although the photographs were supposed to remain private within the group and did not carry Chickering's customary signature, some of the negatives managed to escape the small circle of young women, and reproductions were now being offered for sale around the city. The character of the photos was described as certainly coming "within the provision of Anthony Comstock's interpretation of the law." Even though Comstock was nowhere on the scene, his judgment nonetheless was invoked as the national yardstick for determining obscenity.[119]

Despite the national uproar, the case ended without much trouble for anyone involved. The women's names were never revealed, Anthony Comstock never showed up in Boston, and all the evidence mysteriously disappeared before the trial, so in the end the prosecution was forced to drop the case. Chickering went on to continue his successful career as a photographer of high society and celebrities for many years. Nevertheless, the arrest scare is instructive. Chickering and the well-educated young women who chose to bare their bodies as "devotees" of art certainly knew of Comstock and the parallel activities of the New England Society for the Suppression of Vice. The questionable character of paintings from the Paris Salon was frequently in the news. Rather than cowering in fear, however, they were emboldened to demonstrate their refutation of the politics of prudishness. In their defense, the young ladies claimed that "as devotees of true art there can be nothing improper in the exposure of natural beauty."[120]

This, in short, amounted to Comstock's worst nightmare—youth from respectable families "depraved" by seeing French paintings. He was less conscious of a related scenario that should have kept him up more often.

Thanks to his widely publicized and overreaching censorship, Comstock had actually made nudity and French painting more fashionable. In addition, the profits for risk-taking became so great that the enterprise was worthwhile even for mainstream producers such as Chickering, who most certainly was paid a hefty fee for his prints, negatives, and discretion. By the mid-1880s, the threat of an obscenity prosecution by Comstock was indivisibly wed in the American mind to the promise of both cultural cachet and profits. Anthony Comstock's name had become shorthand for "sex sells." Even Comstock was well aware of the boost in sales his censure could provoke. In 1891, he authored an essay published in the *North American Review* titled "Vampire Literature" in which he began his tirade with the story of a young actress who came to him and confessed that she had written a "spicy book" to try and "bring her name prominently before the public."

The young woman "with perfect *sang froid*" described the story and "being informed that such a book would surely be seized if published," offered a bribe in exchange for lenience. When Comstock summarily turned her down, the young woman "asked whether, if she should change the book so as to make it conform to the law, we would not 'attack it just a little,' and seize a few copies if she paid us for doing so, so as to attract attention to her book and get the newspapers to notice it." Comstock expressed outrage that there seemed to be such "criminal indifference and recklessness" on the part of so many writers and publishers.[121] He obviously did not know many writers and publishers.

As usual, Comstock was oblivious to the fact that original cultural production was always a measured gamble. The best scenario, as the young lady hoped, was to push to the edge of obscenity as closely as possible without crossing over the line. The intimation that censorship *might* occur was golden. Theatrical productions in particular benefited from being branded as a potential target for Comstockian rage. When the actress Sibyl Johnstone appeared on stage in New York in 1890 as an artist's model in *The Clemenceau Case*, the *Wheeling Register* in West Virginia reported that the production threw "Anthony Comstock into a fit and packed the theater."[122] As a result of its notoriety, the play appeared in New York for many months, and then toured the country for many more, staged in theaters large and small. Everywhere the play traveled, newspaper stories of its outrageous nudity generated ticket sales. As in the case of Chickering's Boston Belles and their interest in French Salon nudes, the producers of *The Clemenceau Case* were also inspired by stories relevant to Comstock's censorship campaigns.

The novel *L'Affaire Clémenceau* by Alexandre Dumas was loosely based on the dramatic life and criminal trial of a sculptor named Pierre Clemenceau. William Fléron translated the novel into English in 1890, and that same year produced a Broadway play. This fictional version of the life of Clemenceau begins with Pierre at the age of fourteen, when he leaves school for an apprenticeship with a sculptor named Mousier Ritz. Clemenceau exhibits some talent at copying antique sculptures, so Ritz decides to "examine" him with the rite of passage of a true artist—sculpting from a nude model. Ritz refers to this as an "experiment": "Which would have the mastery, the artist or the man? . . . It would seem quite probable, I admit, that . . . these men, stretched by the tension of their faculties, should feel the need, during the interval of work, of unusual excitements, only to be satisfied by extraordinary indulgences." Clemenceau passes the test by immersing himself in his work without suffering from any "unusual excitements," thus proving that he is a real artist, for whom "true genius is chaste."[123]

The student's triumph over his baser impulses is merely temporary. Clemenceau is soon besotted with a beautiful fifteen-year-old girl named Iza, and the two fall in love and marry. Eventually, Clemenceau learns that Iza has been carrying on an affair with a wealthy Russian count at the urging of her evil mother. After discovery of the treachery, and much torment, Clemenceau duels with the count and kills him. Eventually, he kills Iza as well, and the novel ends as he turns himself over to authorities.

Prosecutorial action upon the play was extremely uneven. Comstock's name appeared frequently in reviews worrying about, and therefore advertising, its potential to be shut down. In New York, however, the play was relatively undisturbed except for some terrible reviews. The *Evening World* was particularly scathing, especially regarding the actress playing

Iza: "ladies with such curves are, as a rule, only too glad to hide them."[124] The production replaced its leading lady soon thereafter with the highly praised Sibyl Johnstone.

Johnstone appears in an actress card by Napoleon Sarony in an early scene in the play in which Clemenceau meets Iza at a fancy dress ball at which she is dressed as a page. At the tender age of fifteen, she falls asleep during the party, and he sketches her (figure 4.12). Sarony chose to show Johnstone asleep in her page costume, so that we may gaze on her undisturbed and fall in love as Clemenceau did. The costume also enabled Sarony to show Johnstone cross-dressing as a boy, which provided some added *frisson*, but not as much as if she were shown in the play's most infamous scene, in which Iza poses on a pedestal in the 1890s stage version of one of Comstock's favorite targets—a photograph of a living model. The Baltimore *Journal* described the scene in detail: "Probably nine-tenths of the audience came principally to see 'the model.' . . . For less than half a moment they saw a shapely head, neck and shoulders

FIGURE 4.12 Napoleon Sarony, *Miss Sybil Johnstone in The Clemenceau Case, by Alexandre Dumas*, ca. 1890. Billy Rose Theatre Division. The New York Public Library Digital Collections.

and a well moulded arm given a pure white color by the black back ground of the white silk tights in which the model was clothed."[125]

Because of the modeling scene, the play was shut down in Boston by the action of aldermen who went to see it and who then threatened to revoke the theater's license if it went on. Angered audiences called them "hogs" in protest of the censorship action.[126] After Boston, however, the play's notoriety seems only to have helped ticket sales. In Montana, the *Helena Independent* made sure to let audiences know that "the company which will appear here is the same that gave the play in Boston and New York which caused so much sensational talk."[127]

The "sensational talk" ended up being lucrative for Sibyl Johnstone, as well as the play's promoters. In May 1891, the *Salt Lake Herald* reported that "the leading lady in 'The Clemenceau Case' has been offered $2,000 to use her influence during the season of '91-'92 in forwarding the interests of a well known firm of dealers in light ribbed underwear."[128] As the young writer in Anthony Comstock's office well knew, sensational coverage could bring lucrative advertising offers, in addition to ticket and book sales. And judging from the popularity of the artist's model theme, Sibyl Johnstone probably sold a lot of ribbed underwear. Comstock had helped to make figure painters and sculptors, and their nude models, extremely sexy.

Just as the image of Johnstone on a pedestal in silk tights offered the right amount of sexual tension to bring in crowds and sell products, so too did other images of artists and models. One of these was Édouard-Joseph Dantan's *Un Moulage sur Nature* (A Casting from Life) (figure 4.13). To heighten the sex appeal of his painting, Dantan included a cast of Michelangelo's anatomically complete *Dying Slave* in the background at left. He also added a note of humor in the three busts in the background gazing in amusement at the artistic action. The model's pale, clean shaven skin is intended to represent the aesthetics of classical and Renaissance sculptures like Michelangelo's, but Dantan has made her face and lower arms quite visibly pink from exposure to sun—a touch of the "real" that reviewers often complained about in contemporary French academic paintings. When the *Evening Telegram* published line

FIGURE 4.13 Édouard-Joseph Dantan, *Un Moulage sur Nature* (A Casting from Life), 1887. Private Collection. Photo @ Christie's Images / Bridgeman Images.

drawings of the pictures seized in the Knoedler arrest, Dantan's painting was featured on page one at the bottom (figure 4.11).

Although (and probably because) it had only ever been seen in America in a reduced and censored black-and-white state, an enterprising artist at the George Schlegel Lithography firm in lower Manhattan recognized the allure of the quasi-justifiable nude and used the painting as inspiration for a cigar box label titled *The Altogether* (figure 4.14 / plate 10) in 1896.[129] As a frame for the picture, Schlegel's artist added a border of gold medallions and easels signifying the approval of the French Salon. The title of the label was well known in the mid-1890s as a key bit of dialogue in George du Maurier's novel *Trilby*, which appeared in serial form in *Harper's New Monthly Magazine* and then as "the first novel to be named after an artist's model" in 1894.[130] The phrase was also used as shorthand for the moment in an infamous sketch titled "Ten Minutes in the Latin Quarter" in 1896, in which the actress Hope Booth portrayed

FIGURE 4.14 George Schlegel Lithographic Co., *The Altogether*, 1896. Cigar Label. Courtesy, The Winterthur Library: The John and Carolyn Grossman Collection. See also color plate 10.

a poor young woman who, like Iza, takes up modeling for an artist in "the altogether."[131]

The Schlegel lithography firm produced several other cigar box labels with artists and models in the 1890s. These striking decorative labels, as always, were reserved for the interior of the cigar box, therefore presumably to be viewed only in homosocial environments. While the nudes stayed on the inside of the box, the exterior label often sported a bowdlerized version of the picture showing only the artist and not the model. In this manner, the men wealthy enough to buy an entire box of cigars could feel specially privileged—nudity once again served as a homosocial inside joke.

Given Comstock's pique at theatrical presentations with tights, and especially those like *The Clemenceau Case* that generated great public excitement, it may seem surprising that he was not more actively involved in trying to suppress the play and novel in New York. This lacuna was probably due not to his opinions on the production but rather to some irritating and messy complications of vice-fighting in the 1890s. In yet another way in which Comstock personally was losing his war against indecency, many more individuals and organizations took up the "business" of suppression in the 1890s. Comstock had managed the neat trick of popularizing both vice *and* vice suppression.

Copies of Fléron's novel *The Clemenceau Case* were in fact suppressed, but not by Comstock on behalf of the NYSSV. Instead, Joseph Britton, the agent who had been fired following the difficult times around the Knoedler trial, had formed his own rival vice-fighting society in June 1890: the New York Society for the Enforcement of Criminal Law (NYSECL). Fléron's publisher, the American News Company, was one of the new society's first targets. From the beginning, the NYSECL seems to have been devised mostly as a front for various nefarious schemes. The logo and the language of advertisements for its work published in newspapers seems hastily concocted, and the "society" never solicited contributions. Britton and his "director" Robert Gunn instead were cunning opportunists who made their money in other ways. The NYSSV recently had moved out of its offices at 150 Nassau Street to brighter quarters nearby, and Britton and Gunn rented the exact same rooms in which the NYSSV previously was housed. Whoever came to the door, and whatever mail came there mistakenly, was seized and the "business" of vice suppression effectively usurped from the NYSSV. The *New York Sun* quipped: "The history of BRITTON and the officers of his Society would make, it is said, interesting Summer reading."[132]

Comstock was absolutely enraged by the existence of this new society, described in the *New York World* as "Rivals in Vice Crushing." He told the paper that Britton had been fired "on account of the alleged discovery that Mr. Britton was a gambler, a handler of police hush money, and up to all sorts of sharp practices." In his continuing critique of his rival's "sharp practices," Comstock related the recent story of a man who mistakenly came to the 150 Nassau Street offices with an embarrassing personal story involving hostile mail, which Britton promptly sold to newspapers.[133] As much as Comstock rightly protested, he personally had helped to invent a remunerative industry ripe for opportunists like Britton. After years of working for the NYSSV, Britton had figured out that you didn't need to go to court often to make the work pay. You only needed to make yourself *seem* powerful. From there, collecting "hush money" made the business lucrative.[134]

Stories about Britton continued to surface in New York newspapers. In 1891, for instance, he was sued for "welching" on gambling debts. His accuser asserted that he had "$30,000 worth of rare paintings, picked up during his connection with Anthony Comstock." Britton admitted to being a connoisseur with substantial real estate and art investments, and also acknowledged that he was a "plunger," or gambling addict. But he strenuously protested: "It is insinuated that I am a blackmailer . . . I wouldn't be loose in the streets of New York if that were so. The police hate me." Their ire made sense, since several reports claimed that Britton was being paid by Republicans in the state Senate to bring them evidence about Tammany-appointed police on the take. Britton's hatred of Comstock is evident in his unconvincing defense: "I don't go along with my hand in the hand of the Lord. I am not a hypocrite." Britton claimed to undertake the work as "a good citizen" rather than for "religious motives."[135] He continued to be a thorn in Comstock's side for most of the 1890s.

On the other end of the spectrum of new vice fighters was a group of committed and virtuous would-be censors that, nevertheless, Comstock equally had difficulty with—women. As Alison Parker documents, "a significantly broad base of Americans" supported censorship efforts, including groups dominated by women such as the WCTU and the American Library Association (ALA). Under Frances Willard's leadership after 1879, the WCTU diversified its mission, and in 1883 it formed its own Department for the Suppression of Impure Literature. While the WCTU passed judgment on bad and good cultural expression via a grassroots movement, the ALA stressed that professionals should make these decisions, as in the case of the Society for American Artists. Both types of organizations focused on prevention of harm to children, and both competed with and gradually diminished Comstock's authority as an arbiter of morality.[136]

On the horizon as well was the Progressive Era. The mid-1890s was an extraordinary period of forward motion for reform efforts to clean up New York City's corrupt police force, which protected much of the trade in vice. In 1894, the Lexow Committee launched investigations into police corruption in New York's state legislature, generating a 6,000-page chronicle of the city's vice. During the committee's hearings, a "greengoods swindler named Streep" accused Comstock of corruption, in a "monstrous libel" published across the country, once again causing NYSSV leaders to have to defend their agent.[137] The following year, Theodore Roosevelt was appointed to the New York City Police Commission and famously walked his own beat at night, collaring roundsmen on the take. Eventually, these efforts would succeed enough to erode the perceived need for private vice-fighting societies.[138]

The mid-1890s were not completely unhappy for Comstock and the NYSSV. It was in 1895 that obscenity law made its way into United States Supreme Court doctrine for the first time, with three cases that Whitney Strub describes as "nearly unqualified victories for the vice crusader." In *Grimm v. United States*, the court upheld the tactic of using decoy letters in a case that originated with Robert McAfee in Chicago. In one of Comstock's cases, the Court also upheld the conviction of Lew Rosen, who published a newspaper with tidbits from New York's racy Tenderloin scene. The innovative Rosen added nudes covered with "lamp black," which could be rubbed off with a piece of bread. Supreme Court justices, including Samuel Blatchford, the judge who upheld the Muller decision when he was on the New York State Court of Appeals, "cited the *Bennett* case and quoted its obscenity criteria in full, promoting the *Hicklin* standard to the law of the land." In a third clarification of obscenity law and procedure in 1895, the Supreme Court also ruled in the case of a radical editor named Dan Swearingen that the term "obscene" could only be applied to "that form of immorality which has relation to sexual impurity."[139]

While these advances in law were significant, opposing legal forces were also moving ahead. In the journal *Arena* in 1894, Edward Chamberlain, the NDA attorney who had represented Charles Conroy, defended the publications of his client Mrs. Lois Waisbrooker. Waisbrooker continued the tradition of feminist sex radicals like Angela Heywood by publishing explicit sexual health information that affirmed women's sexual desire and right to control their reproductive lives. In his essay, Chamberlain pleaded: "To the patriot who sees an inquisitorial censorship enforcing its law to silence arguments not otherwise answerable and restricting freedom of opinion and expression on American soil . . . this appeal will not be made in vain."[140] Over the course of the next several decades, gifted attorneys like Chamberlain would increasingly uphold the principle that even the most radical sexual speech should be allowed to circulate in a nation that supposedly promised "freedom of opinion and expression." Although the NDA ceased its operations for lack of funds in the same year Chamberlain published his essay, as Janice Wood chronicles, in 1902 a new group of activists founded the Free Speech League, whose prominent members included attorney Clarence Darrow and journalists Lincoln Steffens and Hutchins Hapgood.[141]

In one sense, the spread of the conversation about culture and censorship can be viewed as a victory for the NYSSV. Censorship efforts and the discussions about them, no matter their source, created fear of suppression, which in many places begat self-censorship that served the same repressive purpose. In New York, Boston, and other cities, many publishers, producers, and others agreed to have their materials approved by grassroots, preventive, and/or professional societies to avoid protest and possibly prosecution. Police officers increasingly conducted their own investigative efforts to enforce anti-vice laws.

But in other important ways, the spread of the conversation about decency actually doomed the overall effort. Once the dialogue about culture at its sexy edges shifted from the inner sanctums of preventive societies, district attorney's offices, courtrooms, and the Post Office Department to the public arena, it was impossible to constrain. The negotiated boundaries between decency and indecency that provoked chilling anxiety in some people provoked enthusiasm in others who were happy to demonstrate their courage in breaking down a barrier, as well as capitalistic opportunism in still another, sometimes overlapping camp. Vice, vice suppression, and defense of vice grew symbiotically together in their appeal across the nation.

BRIDGE JUMPERS, LOVERS, AND BACHELORS

Following his unsuccessful attempt to suppress racy art in the Hoffman House Saloon and his more famously unsuccessful attempt to suppress reproductions of French Salon nudes in the mid-1880s, Comstock's focus shifted, but not his resolve. He continued to make raids on (cheaper) barrooms, and to frighten picture dealers into voluntarily destroying their stock. He also continued whenever possible to make a splash in the news by targeting a popular new attraction. In this attempt in 1891, he visited two bars owned by Steven Brodie, New York's most celebrated daredevil, in a case all but guaranteed to generate press coverage.

Steven Brodie had grown up as a newsboy and bootblack in lower Manhattan's dangerous Fourth Ward, a neighborhood near the docks filled with boarding and disorderly houses. The source of his later fame, the Brooklyn Bridge, loomed large during Brodie's childhood, as much of the neighborhood was torn down during his youth to make way for its gigantic piers. In the 1890s, Americans came to know him as "Steve Brodie, B.J." (bridge jumper) because in July 1886, he supposedly became the first man to jump off that spectacular span and survive.

Many contemporary observers and recent historians have suggested that Brodie's leap from the Brooklyn Bridge into the chilly and turbulent waters of the East River was a hoax, and that Brodie had a friend throw a dummy from the bridge while he swam to a rescue boat from the shore.[142] Hoax or no, the numerous newspapers across the country who covered the story were happy to have a tale to tell, and Brodie capitalized on his fame in future years by performing swimming and jumping feats outdoors across the country, as well as in staged theatrical productions.

Less well remembered is Brodie's fame as an art collector. In the years following his "jump," Brodie's fortunes increased, and he purchased two saloons, at 114 and 335 Bowery, to capitalize on his fame. He filled both venues with pictures of nudes.[143] When Comstock raided Brodie's saloons on October 14, 1891, he seized "24 pictures framed on wall. 10 obscene Cards . . . 1 album containing 41 Pictures."[144] Brodie was enraged, especially because he claimed to have traveled to Paris personally with his wife to select and bring back the pictures for his saloons. He protested to a newspaper reporter: "There ain't one of them photos that can touch that big picture of the feller with the horns being hauled all over the lot by a crowd of naked women, that hangs in Ned Stokes's place up in Madison Square. But, yer see, that's the difference. I'm only on the Bowery, and I'm Steve Brodie.[145] Brodie, of course, was referencing Bouguereau's *Nymphs and Satyr*, famously hanging in the saloon of the Hoffman House Hotel.

Despite his legitimate argument about disparate treatment, Brodie was unsuccessful in convincing the jury of the refinement of his collection. Although he was fined only fifty dollars, his pictures were seized, and he was warned that if he displayed any again, "another complaint would be made." Later that afternoon, Brodie told another reporter: "I want me pictures, and I'm going to have them. I don't want the ones from my place at 114 Broadway. I'll own up they're a little off and will give them to Comstock, but the ones from No. 355 was all dead swell high-art bluffs an' I want 'em back."[146] The results of Brodie's demands in 1891 are unclear, but he must either have prevailed in the return of his "swell" pictures or bought more, because four years later Comstock again raided Brodie's saloon, arresting his bartender Charles Reiley and seizing "70 pictures on walls." Reiley was sentenced to sixty days in prison on two separate counts.[147] Both Brodie's awareness of his persecution in comparison with "Ned Stokes" and his persistence in replenishing his pictures and thus courting renewed prosecution are noteworthy.

A colored lithograph by Strobridge & Co (figure 4.15 / plate 11) shows Brodie in 1896 as the star of his own Broadway show, *On the Bowery*. He is the hyper-masculine daredevil "Champion Bridge-Jumper of the World," but also a nattily dressed "swell" sporting hefty jewelry—a diamond tie pin, gold watch fob, and impressive cufflinks stand out above white-collar business attire. Through the swinging louvered doors behind Brodie we see a profusion of framed pictures, packed onto the walls. Brodie's connoisseurship and collection of European paintings of nudes had become as much a part of his "Bowery" act as his alleged courage and athletic prowess.

FIGURE 4.15 Strobridge & Co., *On the Bowery*, 1896. Color lithograph poster, 75 × 50 cm. Library of Congress Prints and Photographs Division, Washington, D.C. See also color plate 11.

This rich mixture of class and gender symbolism is deeply evocative of complex social shifts in the late nineteenth century. During these years, an enormous influx of immigrants changed the character of cities and rural areas alike. Industrialization and the growth of cities brought pockets of greater segregation according to wealth. Women increasingly took advantage of new educational and professional opportunities and campaigned for political power, and men were encouraged to beef up their bodies to counter the feminizing effects of urban life.

Many scholars writing about this period observe a hardening of identity classifications—urban and rural residence, ethnicity, religion, sex, and gender—and a loss of the fluidity and multiple meanings that existed in earlier periods.[148] Steven Brodie's example is a good reminder of the individual particularities that always make such generalizations suggestive rather than conclusive. Brodie is both a boxer "on the Bowery" and a connoisseur who travels to Europe to buy paintings, a perfect melding of "low" and "high." Equally fluid is Brodie's evocation of masculinity. He stands with his fists raised as an exemplar of superior strength, but he is also fastidiously dressed and groomed, wearing expensive accessories. All this may seem even more paradoxical given Brodie's presumed audience.

Besides his many remunerative theatrical performances, Brodie increased his fame and wealth by engaging in a very particular type of tourism in the 1890s. His saloons were iconic attractions on the many "slumming" tours popular with middle-class and wealthy New Yorkers and adventurous visitors to the city in the 1880s and 1890s.[149] Much of the plot of the show *On the Bowery* in fact revolves around a visit to Brodie's saloon as the most important stop on a slumming excursion; when he appears in Act Two, "he takes control of the story and leads the uptown characters from his Bowery saloon, across Brooklyn Bridge (where he reenacts the jump), and to the East River."[150] This scene in Act Two is clearly what we see in Strobridge's lithograph; Brodie is standing in front of the doors to his saloon, as if he is performing for us as visitors on a slumming adventure.

Chad Heap has profitably mined the loaded phenomenon of slumming, concluding that it ultimately promoted the demise of the more fluid social arrangement evident in "mixed" saloon culture. As imperious visitors passed judgment on "slum" saloons, they shaped "an increasingly polarized white/black racial axis and a hetero/homo sexual binary that were defined in reciprocal relationship to one another."[151] While overall this tourist activity may have served a larger process of polarization, *On the Bowery* shows us something more complex and surprising.

Brodie's persistence in hanging French paintings of the nude in the 1890s testifies to his conviction that they were essential to his performance of the Bowery for middle- and upper-class tourists. Rather than symbolizing "high" art in this locale, they signified that his saloon was an avantgarde outpost of chic sexual culture, akin to Hoffman's. Women and men both took part in slumming tours, eroding the strict gender segregation that had marked saloon spaces in the nineteenth century. In that sense, Brodie's bar really did have something in common with Stokes's more upscale establishment, which had begun to admit women, if only before business hours.[152]

As the cases of both Stokes and Brodie attest, by the end of the century Americans were choosing from a much richer array of symbols to express their particular combinations of characteristics, circumstances, and choices. Brodie's polished presentation of the Bowery may even be seen as a subtle form of resistance to the stereotyped expectations of the tourists who chose this somewhat obnoxious form of recreation. Whatever Brodie's intentions, we may observe from twenty years of Comstock's saloon raids that he had not achieved his intention of eliminating the display of sexual images and objects in "glittering" barrooms. Instead, changes in American attitudes toward gender, class, and sexuality had prompted larger viewing audiences who sought out the very "obscenities" Comstock tried so hard to eradicate. Americans continued to exhibit myriad ways of blatantly rejecting the aesthetics of respectability, celebrating desire, and inventing new cultural paradigms in the years nearing the twentieth century.

A similar rich array of individual expression is evident in the haul of underground pornography Comstock continued to seize and destroy. While he might have hoped that his tight grip on New York City would reduce the trade in America as a whole, producers and distributors instead simply moved their operations farther away from his threatening surveillance. By the 1890s, the business had shifted significantly beyond city limits, as "the difficulties of pursuing a business in bawdy books and pictures within New York City nonetheless opened up opportunities for resourceful erotica entrepreneurs elsewhere in the country."[153] Using both public and private express mails, businesses operating in rural areas collaborated together to produce low-quality, high-volume pornography.[154] Some examples of these materials survive in the Case Files of the U.S. Post Office Department in the National Archives and Records Administration.

The most remote large-scale producer Comstock helped to prosecute was Oscar Saemann of the Mexican Picture Company, aka Sunbeam Gallery.[155] Breda, Iowa, is an unlikely setting for a large publishing operation. Located ninety miles from Sioux City and more than a hundred miles from Des Moines, Breda in 1890 boasted a population of just 256 people.[156] Breda's distance from major urban centers (and from Comstock) was helpful in staving off prosecution for at least some years. In this case, as in many others, however, Comstock was able to extend the reach of his prosecutorial zeal by working with a network of postal inspectors and agents for vice societies across the country that he had helped to create.

The case was initiated in 1894, when Comstock discovered pictures stamped with the name "O. Saemann, Photo., Breda, Ia." in the course of raids on large distributors in Lancaster, Pennsylvania and Brooklyn, New York. He asked his colleague Robert McAfee to look into the case. McAfee held a position modeled on Comstock's, both working as an inspector for the U.S. Post Office Department in St. Louis, and also as an agent for the Western Society for the Suppression of Vice with branches in Cincinnati, Chicago, and St. Louis.[157]

Thanks to his ample archival records, we know that McAfee first collected advertisements in newspapers, including a small entry in the

Chicago World promising "PHOTOGRAPHS of Mexican Girls." In Breda, he and another agent discovered that Saemann was "a German, 47 years old and unmarried," who produced his goods both at his home and by employing a boy working in the office of "a weekly Democratic paper of small circulation, the *Breda Watchman*." Saemann was arrested "in the act of making the pictures" and the agents seized 100 negatives, 2,000 prints, and several hundred books. McAfee sent the chief postal inspector numerous examples of the printed circulars and photographs, as well as a copy of a soft-cover book titled *The Bride's Confession*, drafted in the form of a first-person narrative detailing an extremely satisfying evening for a virginal bride and her new husband. Samuel Colgate might not have been pleased to learn that Vaseline was mentioned.

The evidence McAfee included in his report tells us a great deal about the flow of sexually themed materials across the United States at the height of state-sponsored censorship. In a letter to Eugene Le Beuf in Brooklyn, dated August 1894, Saemann not only advised Le Beuf (operating under the pseudonym Joseph Harkin) to buy mounted rather than unmounted pictures, but also wrote, "You have told me long ago that you would send in some photos to copy. If they are good I will certainly make negatives out of them *but they must be of Cabinet Size* or larger." Presumably, New York was an easier place to locate new source material than Breda, and the flow of images between rural and urban areas could therefore go both ways. Comstock's seizure of 2,000 pictures and 500 circulars from Le Beuf was one of his several leads back to Saemann.

Another letter included in McAfee's case file on Saemann came from a railroad employee named Herman Harkness seeking "fancy pictures salable on trains. . . . Ordinary business on road is very dull and if there is anything to be had that I can handle on the quiet & make some money I want to get on." The evidence McAfee included in his report suggests that Saemann was more than willing to supply images that would spice up a dull train ride. He divided his photographs into two categories: "mailables" and "second grade."

"Mailables" would be shipped for free anywhere in the United States or Canada using standard postal services. These included photographs with titles such as *The Morning Toilet, Shoe-Lacing,* and *Alone in the Timber.* Saemann would only ship his "second grade" photographs, however, by private express carrier. This line included "our Mexican girls strictly taken from life in all kinds of positions and showing everything. Not old grandmothers taken in tights, but charming girls, suitable for plain work." These photographs cost one dollar for three, as compared with twelve cents each for the "mailables." Both the profit margin and the risk were higher for this group, and private carriers benefited from the extra business.

Among the several photographs included in the Saemann case docket is a scene that certainly belonged among the more expensive group (figure 4.16). The three individuals shown include a person wearing a train engineer suit, with mustache and muttonchop whiskers. It is unclear whether this figure is a man, or a woman dressed as a man. This person sits back against the crook of a couch while stiffly kissing a naked woman pushed close by the pressure of another woman who is kneeling behind the second and reaching through her legs to grab the man's penis, or perhaps a dildo, from the opened front buttons of workpants. The engineer's uniform reflects the dominant importance of the railroad in sparsely populated regions of the country such as Breda, as well as the fact that lonely railroad men were also typical customers for both brothels and pornography, as several of Comstock's cases attest. If the scene does show three women involved in simulating heterosexual play, this would not be unusual given the frequent appearance of cross-dressing in American theatrical and brothel performances around this time.

McAfee's report to the postal inspector included not only Saemann's own products (such as examples of his "second grade" photographs) but also circulars advertising the wares of other distributors, including several signed "Frank B. Teel Hurleyville, N.Y." The Teels, (father Ambrose) and son, specialized in reprinting and distributing photographs, pamphlets, and books. Comstock noted, when he arrested the pair in 1894, that they printed twenty-four different images and at the time of arrest had 11,402 copies of those, all made "from Electro's." The popular industrial process of electrotyping was an efficient way to produce large quantities cheaply.[158]

FIGURE 4.16 Photograph of three figures engaged in sex play, ca. 1894. Photograph. Evidence included in case file: *U.S. vs. Oscar Saemann, alias Sunbeam Gallery &c.* (September 13, 1894); Entry 231, Box 111, Case Files of Investigations, Post Office Department, National Archives and Records Administration, Washington, D.C.

One of the advertisements bearing the Teel name included in evidence seized in Iowa promised:

PHOTOS of Pretty GIRLS!
LOVELY FEMALES UNDRAPED.

Photos! En Deshabbile![sic] The Loveliest Damsels you ever saw in careless and bewitching attitudes. There are short women, tall women, fleshy women, graceful women, women with black hair, brown hair, blond hair, red hair, and not a single coarse face or poor form in the lot. They were taken in warm rooms and will be found to be all that could be desired. No actresses. No ballet girls. No tights. Fresh and Rosy, Plump and Pretty.

No. 1. Scenes in an "Electric Message [sic]" bath room; how a young man received shocks from pretty female assistants. . . . Five different scenes! These are "NEW PHOTOS" of the loveliest females. No padded tights here! . . .

No. 4. "A High Old Time." A husband hides, and catches his pretty wife with a male caller in peculiar antics; and "on the sly." . . .

No. 5. "The Modern Venus." A beautiful girl is comparing her own charms to the famous statue. (sent securely sealed.) for only 50 cents . . .

F. B. TEEL, HURLEYVILLE, N.Y.

Several of the adamant assertions in these ads speak to the common frustrations of mail-order pornography customers during Comstock's era. Distributors who promised "spicy," "racy," and "rich" scenes often mailed photos far less "en deshabbille" than desired. Tights clearly were a particular annoyance. The emphasis on *new* photos in the Teels' ad also speaks to the rampant circulation of prints produced with terrible quality, many generations removed from the original negative.

Irritation with the poor quality of ordered pictures was so great that a customer named G. W. Wilson wrote to his postmaster to complain about the terrible products and service provided by a distributor named George Watts (alias Ralph): "Dear Sir! I beg the ability to state to you,

FIGURE 4.17 *Scenes in an Electric Massage Parlor*, ca. 1894. Photographic reprint. Evidence included in case file: *U.S. v. George Watts and Ralph Watts* (September 10, 1894); Entry 231, Box 111, Case Files of Investigations, Post Office Department, National Archives and Records Administration, Washington, D.C.

in this letter, that one, Ralph Watts of South Fallsburgh, N.Y. is engaged in the business of sending obscene photographs through the U.S. mails. And also swindling through the mails. . . . his little photographs are vulgar things, that he sends out. But he sometimes forgets to send any at all." The Post Office Department case file Comstock prepared for Watts, who was located just seven miles south of the Teels, includes several pictures matching the Teels' advertisements, including *No. 1. Scenes in an Electric Massage Bath Room* (figure 4.17) and also *The Modern Venus* (figure 4.18), who gazes at a tabletop *Venus de Milo* in a fancy parlor. The disparate subject matter in these images, pairing a masochistic delivery of electric

FIGURE 4.18 *The Modern Venus*, ca. 1894. Photographic reprint. Evidence included in case file: *U.S. v. George Watts and Ralph Watts* (September 10, 1894); Entry 231, Box 111, Case Files of Investigations, Post Office Department, National Archives and Records Administration, Washington, D.C.

shocks by women in bathing costumes with a seminude figure who compares herself to "classic" art, suggests that some customers may have been more curious than prurient. Certainly, many were less than satisfied as Wilson's letter attests.

The seized evidence further included copious pictures of women wearing tights, proving Wilson's claim of false advertising. The terrible quality of these samples attests to the difficulties of producing illicit images at this time, and also bears out the frustration of customers like Wilson. Despite Watts's promises, the pictures mailed to Wilson only showed females fully dressed as actresses and in tights, with the exception of *No. 5. The Modern Venus*, which perhaps did not present the model quite as "En Dishabbille! [*sic*]" as the customer wanted.[159]

Many of Watts's other products were also likely to have been disappointing, but for very different reasons; the full product line claimed to offer solutions to a comprehensive array of heterosexual male desires, including courtship and marriage. For example, Watts's "Lover's Package" presumably contained everything a man would need for courting his beaux, including "Whip and Fan Flirtations; also Window and Dining Table Signaling, The Language of Flowers." The quirky collection presumed that a young man and woman would develop their own coded system of communication that would be unintelligible to watchful parents. Watts also sold sample love letters and sexual health information of dubious quality, including a "Book of Nature! The Greatest Book Ever Published by Which to Know Thyself, Containing a full and explicit explanation of all that can or ought to be known of the structure and uses of The Organs of Life and Generation in Man and Woman." "Spicy Prose and Poetry! For Gents Only!" included the titles "How to Do It, or the Acts of Fascinating Pretty Girls"; "The Bashful Man's Experience on His Wedding Night"; and "Adventures of a Newly Married Couple." As Watts's disgruntled customer Wilson testified, these items were not especially spicy.

At the opposite end of the spectrum of illicit men's images, many of the "spiciest" or very "worst" pictures Comstock seized were foreign imports, which continued to flow into the country in large numbers despite his best efforts to prevent their circulation. In 1891, for example, Comstock arrested Carl Casper in Milwaukee, who imported catalogue cards from Rome. Comstock's letter to his Post Office Department supervisor described Casper's methods in detail: "Before the arrest I had an interview with him, in which he informed me that he had to charge very high prices, as it was very dangerous business. . . . He had specimens to order from, some containing 15 and 25 different scenes grouped together on a card, which he charged $2.50 each for. These, he informed me, came from Rome, Italy, and that in order to have large pictures, it would be necessary to send over to Rome to get them."[160]

Frank Partridge of the "Elite Art Co." in Carlstadt, New Jersey, also imported catalogue cards "of the most pronounced and outrageously obscene character," but in this case from Paris. Partridge was not as picky about the quality of what he sold, and simply made negatives from each of the individual scenes in his catalogue cards, which he then used to manufacture large numbers of photographs. Convinced that Comstock was a customer, Partridge showed him a recent envelope from France "containing over 900 variety of obscene pictures," and was promptly apprehended.[161]

Although evidence was not preserved in either of these cases, imported catalogue cards survive in the Kinsey Institute collection in large numbers that undoubtedly are similar to those procured and sold by Caspar and Partridge. Catalogue cards typically included between twelve and twenty-five individual scenes that were numbered, providing a range for the dealer or individual customer to choose from and order in a larger size. Their inclusion of a variety of images placed them at the heart of the pornography industry, as men could choose what most assisted them in achieving arousal and satisfaction.

The variety among the Kinsey Institute's catalogue cards is immense. In some, scenes are arranged to form a narrative in which individuals meet, disrobe, and engage in a series of increasingly explicit acts in settings similar to the book titles Comstock listed in his arrest blotters. Men appear as sailors in same-sex play, women are shepherdesses in trysts with shepherds, and newlyweds experience the "first time." Saint Anthony always succumbs to temptation without much hesitation—a standard trope. Images that depict exploitative or injurious scenes are not common, but they do appear; there are examples of children appearing nude together (although not engaged in sexual acts), and others that appear to depict bondage (although it looks extremely fake). In some cases, it is a bit of a challenge to figure out how many figures are in the frame, as the images are small and the entanglements quite complex.

What quickly becomes evident is that the Kinsey Institute's catalogue cards really do constitute a catalogue. They illustrate the very diverse tastes and desires of men at the end of the nineteenth century, desires that include the urge for straightforward sex acts, romantic seduction, and the earnest hope of finding fulfillment with one partner—in other words, to be the happy "gent" seen in George Watts's advertisement for "The Lover's Package" (figure 4.19)

Societal approval for this more romantic view of male desire over frank sexual expression is evident in the punishments meted out in the courts in these cases. Oscar Saemann, for example, was quickly convicted and given the extraordinarily harsh punishment of a $6,000 fine, plus costs of prosecution, and "imprisonment at hard labor in the Penitentiary at

FIGURE 4.19 *The Lover's Package*, ca. 1894. Newsprint. Evidence included in case file: *U.S. v. George Watts and Ralph Watts* (September 10, 1894); Entry 231, Box 111, Case Files of Investigations, Post Office Department, National Archives and Records Administration, Washington, D.C.

Fort Madison, Iowa for a term of Eight years." Eugene Le Beuf spent two years at hard labor in the Kings County Penitentiary, and Frank Partridge served two years and six months at Sing Sing prison. In contrast, Comstock advocated for a lighter sentence for George Watts on the basis that his materials were not as bad, and he only paid a fine of $500.[162] In sum, we may note that the wide range of "obscene" images, objects, and texts American men purchased through the mail provides further evidence that sexuality and masculinity were not experienced or expressed *en masse*, but rather as deeply personal, individual, and varied aspects of life that changed over time.

No work of art makes this point more beautifully than John Haberle's *A Bachelor's Drawer* (figure 4.20 / plate 12), which pictorially conveys the transition in a man's life from bachelor to husband. In 1894, the same year that George Watts paid a $500 fine in part for selling products designed to ease the troubles of America's many unmarried men, the gifted still life painter John Haberle completed an utterly anti-Comstockian, cheeky take on bachelor life. Haberle might easily have been one of Ambrose

FIGURE 4.20 John Haberle, *A Bachelor's Drawer*, 1890–1894. Oil on canvas, 20 × 36 in. (50.8 × 91.4 cm). Metropolitan Museum of Art. Purchase, Henry R. Luce Gift. (1970.193). See also color plate 12.

Teel's or George Watts's customers. Strewn among theater tickets and playing cards are a series of photographs of the "En Deshabbille!" type that put some men in prison and resulted in fines for others. Actress cards and a plainly nude photograph from a living model are included here in thoroughly nonchalant fashion along with other symbols of homosocial spheres—playing cards, a corncob pipe, and cigar and cigarette stubs. Metaphorically, we go "slumming" through his drawer, now turned inside out and exhibited mysteriously as an exterior vertical plane: a "low" photographic cigarette card with a nude is presented to us through an exquisitely crafted and technically sophisticated example of a premier "high" art form—trompe l'eoil painting. Haberle incorporated the symbols both of his bachelorhood and also of his own recent transition from bachelorhood to marriage and impending fatherhood, indicated by the inclusion of a book titled *How to Name a Baby*.[163]

Haberle's witty aggregation of symbols of both bachelorhood and marriage demonstrates his fluid acceptance of both aspects and phases of his life, each with its own visual expression. The artist included his own self-portrait as a faux tintype at the bottom, thus acknowledging ownership of his changing desires, habits, and situation. Despite all of Comstock's efforts, Haberle's only obvious concern for legality rests in a small clipping at the center of the painting, alluding to charges that his depictions of currency were so precise that they amounted to counterfeiting. Whatever social sensibility the NYSSV might have hoped to impose after twenty years of effort clearly had not taken hold in Haberle's studio in New Haven, Connecticut, not far from Comstock's ancestral Eden, New Canaan.[164] Despite trying so hard and for so long to legislate, police, and inflict fear of "dread punishment," by 1895 Comstock had not achieved his goal of making images of the nude feared and rare.

An early sexology study made of 1,000 male college students born in the early to mid-1890s found that, on average, boys received their first "striking and permanent" impression of sex at the age of ten, from another boy. More than three-fifths of the students reported masturbating, which was judged to be a "very conservative number." Comstock might have been happy that the study also noted, as John D'Emilio and Estelle B.

Freedman point out, "Most of the young men viewed their sexual behavior as a problem, as a sign of moral weakness and a failure of manly self-control."[165] These men born after twenty years of concerted censorship efforts still lived in a world filled with arousing sexual materials, and they still masturbated—the major difference perhaps was that more of them felt bad about their natural inclinations.

As he penned the last entry in Volume II of his arrest blotter on May 10, 1895, Comstock closed the book on 275 pages of efforts to reign in American sexual culture over the span of a decade. In that time, in contrast to his earnest hopes and relentless efforts, he had witnessed the muddling of boundaries between high and low and watched public culture become steadily more risqué. In private realms, pornography was still widespread, although its quality in many cases was diminished. As the end of the century neared, Comstock could take heart that he had survived attacks of many types and still managed to keep on with his sacred work. He had not changed in his beliefs, mission, or methods. The world around him, however, was transforming with astonishing speed.

5

NEW WOMEN, NEW TECHNOLOGY, AND THE
DEMISE OF COMSTOCKERY

....

(Volume III: 1895–1915)

COMSTOCK AND THE LADIES

Anthony Comstock began to pen entries in Volume III of his arrest records for the NYSSV in June 1895. This third volume would be his last. Signs were ominous that this enormous chronicle of effort would not recount many happy moments for the aging censor, nor for the aging society that employed him. The NYSSV's *Annual Report* for 1895 included an update from the treasurer mourning the deaths of twenty previously loyal donors in the past two years who had not been replaced by new benefactors. Further adding to the dark tone of the report was a lengthy discussion of the "Depressing Beginning" to the year.

Comstock had been sick for a month, and then accused of blackmailing potential defendants during the widely publicized hearings in the New York State Assembly's Lexow Committee investigating police corruption. Supportive letters had been received from some involved with the committee, but the effort was not soon enough, and "this base assault seemed almost entirely to stop contributions." The *Annual Report* also included a lengthy tirade on a sore subject regarding an even more intractable problem, "Legislation for New Evils."

This unhappy entry began by describing a marked rise in entertain-ments that had become popular since the World's Columbian Exposi-tion held in Chicago in 1893: "Pictures and photographs of nude women, exhibitions and photographs of living pictures of young women in flesh-colored tights, lascivious dances in imitation of those performed by heathen women upon the Midway Plaisance at the World's Exhibition, and the exposing of the sacred form of woman for advertising purposes, have rendered stricter laws in the interest of public morals a necessity." Comstock went on at length to tell the tale of aborted efforts to craft legislation barring the display of the body nude, seminude, or wearing only tights in public. According to his version of the story, the failure of his legislative efforts was all to blame on the ladies of the Woman's Christian Temperance Union.[1] Comstock had long had difficulty in fraternizing with men. Now, troublesome collaboration with "ladies" was added to his miseries. Comstock's new woman problems began with the Exposition, and plagued him throughout the waning years of the nineteenth century.

The World's Columbian Exposition was the product of three years of planning to celebrate the 400th anniversary of Christopher Columbus's pivotal voyage. By the time the gates closed, an astonishing 30 million people trekked via new railroads to see its wonders. Alan Trachtenberg writes that the fair was "an oasis of fantasy and fable at a time of crisis and impending violence," opening at the same time in the spring of 1893 as the worst financial panic in the nation's history unfolded. A debate about indecency must have felt like a welcome conversation instead.[2]

The spectacular campus of the Exposition was dominated by the strict neoclassical designs of architect Daniel H. Burnham, who sought to demonstrate orderly possibilities for urban life. The Exposition's nick-name "White City" derived from its uniform white stucco surfaces and abundant streetlights, which made it possible to visit exhibitions even at night. Almost every element of the vast site was carefully managed to convey sophisticated acceptance of neoclassical European style, includ-ing the creation of a medal by the nation's premier sculptor, Augustus Saint-Gaudens.

FIGURE 5.1 Louis Saint-Gaudens, *Study for World's Columbian Exposition Commemorative Presentation Medal, reverse,* 1892–1893. Cast, Plaster, 20.3 cm (8 in.). Harvard Art Museums/ Fogg Museum, Gift of Agnes Mongan. (1974.63) Photo: Imaging Department (c) President and Fellows of Harvard College.

Initially, Saint-Gaudens designed his medal with Christopher Columbus on one side and a nude male youth on the reverse (figure 5.1). This slender version of a Greek *kouros* figure evoked America as a young country, surrounded by ancient symbols of war, peace, and freedom. While the Columbus design was accepted, the United States Senate Quadro-Centennial Committee rejected the reverse with the nude male. To the sculptor's outrage, the committee rejected his final design based on a sketch, refusing even to acknowledge the value of seeing a cast. Saint-Gaudens told a reporter for the *New York World*: "As for the idiot who drew his monstrosity from memory after seeing my chaste figure, he is an ass, a consummate ass—the worst kind of an ass."[3]

The Senate committee's prudishness was protested by the National Sculpture Society and covered extensively in newspapers. In a true example of irony, while the commissioners were arguing about the small medal, Saint-Gaudens's other major work for the Exposition was being hoisted

FIGURE 5.2 Augustus Saint-Gaudens, *Diana* 1892–1893. Gilded copper sheets, height of figure: 13 feet 1 inches (398.8 cm); figure including ball: 14 feet 6 inches (442 cm). Philadelphia Museum of Art, Gift of the New York Life Insurance Company, 1932. (1932-30-1)

to the top of the Agriculture Building.[4] This was *Diana*, an eighteen-foot-tall sculptural portrait of the artist's mistress Davida Johnson Clark, entirely nude. Representing the goddess of the hunt, the 1,800-pound gilded sculpture had proved too large for its initial spot atop Madison Square Garden, and so was repurposed to crown the Exposition. A later version made to better fit its New York City home today graces the Philadelphia Museum of Art (figure 5.2). As Jennifer Greenhill observes, the "dignified ideality" of this nude cheekily contradicted the fact that it was "a monument to the sensual pleasure the sculptor and his circle sought in their extramarital lives, no matter how austerely that pleasure registers in the virginal goddess's lithe form and dispassionate expression."[5]

In addition to this artful form of protest, Saint-Gaudens led the Society of American Artists in proclaiming to newspapers that its annual exhibition for 1894 would be filled with nudes so that he would be "triumphantly vindicated."[6] Like Mark Twain and Thomas Eakins, Saint-Gaudens responded to censorship by creating more work that pushed at perceived boundaries of appropriateness. Now he had a small army of artists ready to join the fray with him.[7] As Michele Bogart notes, "professional and civic elites" began in 1893 to form organizations and "contended that expertise, whether gleaned through the experience of superior practitioners or that of cultivated and learned connoisseurs, should determine the delegation of authority for decisions affecting the aesthetics of the public realm."[8] Comstock's opinions on art never would go unchallenged again.

Other American sculptors also used the occasion of the Exposition to show off their European training and extensive work with living models, producing monumental nudes that could not be avoided. At the central Court of Honor, Frederick MacMonnies's *Barge of State* rested in an enormous fountain. The massive work represented the nation as a ship rowed by allegorical figures signifying Arts and Industries, capped by the figure of Columbia enthroned. As seen in a detailed view (figure 5.3), the level

FIGURE 5.3 *World's Columbian Exposition, Columbian Fountain.* Illustrated in: *Inland Architect,* vol. 19, no. 3 (April, 1892). Ryerson & Burnham Libraries, The Art Institute of Chicago. (IA 1903_0934b)

of anatomical detail in this central figure was unprecedented in such public American sculpture. Columbia's erect nipples are reminiscent of the
promises made by the Teels of upstate New York in their circular advertising pornography, also from the 1890s:

FIGURES FULLY REVEALED

Are you tired of Actresses in stuffed tights; Grandma's of the Ballet
Corps, and 20 Minuet [*sic*] photos on a single card? If so, here are some
genuine good ones, POSITIVELY NO TIGHTS.[9]

MacMonnies undoubtedly understood the connection between his
own freedom as an artist and Columbia's in baring all, with "positively
no tights." Thomas Eakins similarly took the opportunity to display his
massive *Agnew Clinic*, with a nipple at the apex of the composition, which
had previously been rejected even by the Society of American Artists.
And this was just the respectable part of the Exposition.[10]

As an antithesis to the refined display of neoclassical planning and
design orchestrated by Burnham, the managers also agreed to incorporate
an outlet for less high-minded cultural expression in order to avoid competition outside the gates. The "Midway Plaisance," a mile-long carnival
inside the grounds of the Exposition, offered an unruly display of faux
architecture and culture from around the world. If Burnham's design
for the main sections of the Exposition offered a fairy tale of American
ambition and idealism sugarcoated in aesthetically pleasing white stucco,
the Midway was an ugly hodgepodge of the nation's worst prejudices.
As Frederick Douglass pointed out, the labor of African Americans was
fully on view in the buildings constructed for the Exposition, but their
intellectual and artistic accomplishments were purposefully excluded.
He was appalled by the presentation of Dahomeans on the Midway as
half-naked "savages."[11] In more than fifty elaborate Midway displays,
inauthentic performances set in fake habitats confirmed the assumptions of white audiences about the perceived superiority of "white,"
"Western" culture. Unsurprisingly, these were not the issues that concerned Anthony Comstock.

When Comstock arrived at the Midway Plaisance in August 1893, a *New York Recorder* reporter described his reaction as "shocked," "horrified," and "irate." He stated that he did not want to promote vice with too much description, so he vaguely stated that he had seen all fifty performances on the Midway, and three were "groveling filth." The reporter was not so circumspect, noting that Comstock was most upset by what he called the "Hip Dance" at the Streets of Cairo Theater (which the reporter discussed in detail). This was Comstock's translation of the better-known term *"danse du ventre,"* known today as belly dancing.[12] To suppress the Streets of Cairo dances, Comstock called upon the Lady Managers of the Exposition. At his request, five of them went to see the show with him, and their petitions to have it shut down were temporarily successful. The *Recorder* article, reprinted in newspapers across the country, included sketches of a *danse du ventre* performer, as well as a rude caricature of Comstock pushing a lady manager behind him at the Midway, with his hand firmly on her buttock.[13]

On the same day as the *Recorder* skewering, Joseph Pulitzer's more high-minded *New York World* took the opportunity to publish diverse opinions on the subject of the *danse du ventre*. A priest named Father Edward McGlynn defended Comstock as "a great public benefactor" and insisted, "I have no patience with those who pretend by enthusiasm for science or art [that] they cease to be men tempted to yield to their passions. The brute is their [*sic*] still, and our holy religion and the restraints of civilization and law are needed to keep it in subjection." McGlynn analogized that allowing the dance would be similar to allowing Native Americans to practice scalping for the purposes of an educational exhibition.

On the affirmative side of the debate, the famed "Serpentine dancer" Loie Fuller declared that she would not perform the dance herself because she "could not do it justice." But her approach was much more nuanced: "I am well aware that dancing may be immoral and graceful and artistic at the same time, but the dancer I saw impressed me only with her art. She really expressed thoughts and ideas in her graceful pantomime." Fuller was already perhaps the most acclaimed dancer in the world, a pioneer in costume, lighting, and performance who influenced a rising generation of avant-garde artists in France and America. In the 1890s, her twirling "serpentine" movements with billowing layers of silk were among the first images captured on film. In her approach to the *danse du ventre*, Fuller spoke from her own perspective as an artist, considering the entire context of the performance, its surroundings, music, authenticity, and the expressive quality of the dancer as essential to deciding whether "immorality" overshadowed grace and artistry.

The final testimonial offered in the *World* was provided by Ida Craddock, an eccentric lecturer and author on ancient "Phallic" religions (among many other topics), who offered a somewhat cryptic defense of the "real significance of this dance as a religious memorial of purity and self-control."[14] When Craddock published and circulated advocacy for her unusual views on sexuality and spiritualism in Chicago in 1894, Clarence Darrow defended her, in the same year that he also represented Eugene V. Debs before the United States Supreme Court. In two blows for free speech, Darrow struck a plea deal on Craddock's behalf and lost the Debs case, but in that year he firmly established a career path that would eventually score significant victories for civil liberties.[15]

After moving to Philadelphia in 1895, Ida Craddock published a much longer explanation of the "*danse du ventre*" in a lengthy pamphlet. She began her tome with a preface that confirmed Comstock's statement that the dance had proliferated following the Exposition: "Under the names of the Koochy-Koochy, the Huta-Kuta Dance, Muscle Dance, etc., it has spread into most of the large cities and summer resorts of the United States, and is being witnessed daily and nightly by crowds of men and by young people of both sexes." Craddock went on to explain the symbolic features of the movements and concepts involved in the dance. Six tassels worn on the skirt represented the ancient practice of abstaining from sex until the sixth day after "tapu time" (menstruation), thereby creating the conditions for a joyous marital union on the sixth "most passionate day of all the twenty-eight." Craddock believed that men especially needed to practice restraint so that their wives would not be forced into having uncomfortable or unpleasurable sex.[16] Her concerns were similar to those of many other female sexual health authors Comstock prosecuted, although her solution was more exotic.

Craddock's legal troubles unfortunately continued. Comstock hounded her with numerous prosecutions until she finally committed suicide in 1902, thereby emulating Madame Restell's sad alternative to imprisonment. Notwithstanding her tragic and untimely demise and her lack of a serious following, Craddock did make a significant impact on American culture as a loud and full-throated advocate for her rights to freedom of speech and religion. At the time of her suicide, she became a cause célèbre for her attorney Clarence Darrow, as well as for other members of the Free Speech League. Within this fledgling organization, a new consensus began to emerge: "those who believe in the general principle of free speech must make their point by supporting it for 'some extreme cause.' Advocating free speech only for a popular or uncontroversial position would not convey the breadth of the principle."[17] Once again, successful censorship brought with it the seeds of its own demise.

The fact that Fuller and Craddock were called upon to provide their opinions on the *danse du ventre* in the *New York World* in 1893 is revealing of several shifts in social attitudes that especially bode ill for Comstock. Many more women were now in the public eye as pundits as well as performers. The increasing prominence of women was equally true in the realm of vice suppression. Women in both spheres had a major influence on Comstock's professional life in ways that he found profoundly challenging in the last twenty years of his life. Once set onto the national stage, America's powerful "ladies" would not be sidelined again without loud protest.[18] Yet another public relations disaster began rather innocuously, as a quite welcome and promising collaboration between like-minded censors.

In 1890, Emilie Martin was appointed head of the Department of Purity in Literature and Art of the WCTU. Over the next several years, she became an unusually close ally of Comstock, even establishing an office for the WCTU's department near the rooms of the NYSSV in the Times Building on Park Row. The department became extremely active soon after Martin's appointment, and the National Minutes for the WCTU for 1892 even alerted members that they had the " 'power to seize anything improper in character' and turn it over to the District Attorney, who 'may have the offensive matter destroyed.'"[19]

When Martin heard about the *danse du ventre* in the Streets of Cairo exhibition, she helped rally women to write letters in opposition to the performances. She and other WCTU members also were adamant that the dance be stopped in New York. In December 1893, four dancers from the Midway show traveled to New York; at Martin's urging, Comstock visited the show with police on December 4, 1893, and arrested three of them. The women and their attorney protested that this was a "dance of the Nation," and a press agent for the show claimed "the dance represented a woman in ecstasy paying her devotions to her deity." Both arguments used language set forth in the *World* article of the previous summer. This was a novel legal defense on the grounds of educational value and religious freedom, but the judge was unimpressed. In short order, the dancers were each fined fifty dollars.[20] Although Comstock thought it best to leave the matter alone and avoid more publicity for the show, Martin and other members of the WCTU would not let the matter lie. They directed their efforts at another new enemy in New York in the mid-1890s: living pictures.

In 1896, Comstock's description of "New Evils" was not limited to "lascivious dances in imitation of those performed by heathen women upon the Midway Plaisance" but also referenced an explosion of innovative displays of the body in theatrical settings. Both sensual dancing and living pictures had been popular in theatrical productions for decades, but now they were part of a crowded variety of entertainments that were much more sexually charged and popular amongst mixed audiences. Robert Allen documents this shift as part of the rise of vaudeville, which "absorbed a number of forms of popular entertainment that previously had been relatively independent of any particular presentational venue: shadowgraphy, magic lantern shows, puppetry, and magical illusion among them." And, in the mid-1890s, living pictures.[21]

Living pictures, also known by their French name *tableaux vivants*, had been popular both as a parlor entertainment and public spectacle for decades. In their most elevated form they were entirely chaste.[22] Regardless of their subject matter, *tableaux vivants* generally were not judged on the quality of their narratives, but rather on how elaborate the preparations were for the short display. When the curtain rose, audiences saw actors standing still in an elaborate set that either created or recreated a particular scene. Typically, full performances included several scenes in sequence, and the audience was meant to be impressed by the skill of the producers and cast in managing all the changes. Living pictures were often accompanied by music and a narration from others offstage and thus were experienced as a series of shadow box scenes, separated by a curtain rising and falling.[23]

Living pictures certainly didn't have to display the body, but beginning soon after the Exposition in 1893, promoters added much more flesh to their *tableaux*, in an action akin to the Society of American Artists' exhibition of many more nude paintings. The two were not unrelated. When *The Famous Rahl and Bradley Living Bronze Statues: Orpheus and Euridice* was staged at the Casino Theater in New York in 1895, five men and women connected with the production were arrested. Prosecutors may have been especially eager to shut the show down given that Euridice's left breast is fully exposed in the souvenir photograph taken of the show that year (figure 5.4). William Merritt Chase appeared for the defense, as president

FIGURE 5.4   Knowlton, Photographer, *The Famous Rahl and Bradley Living Bronze Statues: Orpheus and Euridice*, ca. 1895. Albumen print on card mount, mount 17 × 11 cm. (cabinet card format). Library of Congress Prints and Photographs Division, Washington, D.C.

of the Society of American Artists, testifying "there is nothing immoral in the human frame."[24] Chase was among the most vocal proponents, and organizers, of artistic living pictures in New York in the 1890s.[25]

While the "bronze sculptures" in the Casino Theater case caused a public sensation in 1895, white powder was more typically used to simulate the effect of marble statuary, as in the case of *Adam Forepaugh and Sells Brothers, 8 Lovely Ladies: Living Statues Illustrating Famous Art* (figure 5.5). Here, the "ladies" acted out scenes including "The Sabines," "The Three Graces," and the "Youth of Bacchus" that required seeming nudity to achieve the promised "perfect facsimiles of master marble groups and pictures." This display of "faultless female forms" was billed as "elevating, educating, and entrancing," and many actress cards of this era portray models wearing tights in Living Pictures poses. In 1894, Napoleon Sarony took advantage of the craze to publish an innovative series of staged

FIGURE 5.5 Strobridge Lithographic Co., *Adam Forepaugh and Sells Brothers, 8 Lovely Ladies. Living Statues Illustrating Famous Art*, ca. 1896. Chromolithograph poster, 105 × 292 cm. Library of Congress Prints and Photographs Division, Washington, D.C.

photographs of models acting out paintings in a journal titled *Sarony's Living Pictures: Photographed from Life*.[26]

Emilie Martin was among the many WCTU women who were not impressed with any of this. In 1894, she turned her attention from police action against performances to legislative advocacy.[27] Working with Mrs. Mary Burt, a seasoned legislative draftswoman for the WCTU and chair of its New York branch, the organization presented a comprehensive bill in the New York State Assembly to prevent "the degrading of women and girls," and to "preserve the respect due to women." Within days, Comstock presented his own competing version, setting off an angry and very public argument that dragged on for several years as the two competing bills made their way through various stages of consideration and revision.

Both of the competing bills were broad-ranging and deeply upset theater managers, who vehemently protested against them. The public had grown to expect this sort of back-and-forth vitriol between purity forces and their targets. What was less usual was the angry dissension between censors who wanted very similar results. Since the mid-1880s, Comstock had appeared at WCTU conventions to rally support for his censorship efforts and to advise women on the various dangers faced by youth. Publicity was positive on these occasions, but behind the scenes, "Comstock could be both condescending and self-aggrandizing" as he "was often unwilling to acknowledge that his organization needed women to work actively against the 'impure.'"[28]

Although Emilie Martin was an unwavering acolyte willing to play a supporting role with Comstock, other WCTU leaders wanted to make their own progress on these issues without his help—and to be credited for the power of their own organization. WCTU women publicly accused Comstock of trying to take credit for their bill. They also preferred their own version, which had a narrower scope. Comstock had tacked on criminal penalties related to contraceptive use, which the women were unwilling to support, and they also objected to some more explicit language in his bill, which they felt made the legislation itself indecent.[29] In a series of open letters published in newspapers, WCTU and NYSSV censors turned on each other, playing a game of one-upmanship as to whose efforts could be more "pure."

Ultimately, the rift between the two camps went well beyond the specific elements of their competing bills and rested more deeply on issues of gender and power. The WCTU sought political empowerment for women, and the language it used in its own version of the bill emphasized the importance of preventing women from degradation. In contrast, as Alison Parker notes, Comstock after twenty years was still obsessed by "the problem of the masturbating boy," rather than any "program of maternal activism."[30] In other words, the members of the WCTU wanted to exercise their power as women to help other women, which never was the focus of Comstock's efforts. In his single-minded quest for power to identify and suppress vice, Comstock lost a golden opportunity to build lasting alliances and support for his cause.

The NYSSV's *Annual Report* for 1896 detailed more negative developments for the organization over the course of that year. Nine more contributing members had died, and Samuel Colgate was forced to resign due to his poor health. In a worrisome turn, expenses had exceeded income for the first time. Comstock also sadly noted in this *Annual Report* that his bill to expand the penal code regarding displays of the nude had failed. He thought it unwise to support the "loosely drawn," "adverse bill" proposed by the WCTU, and as a result no new law had been passed. As a direct result, he concluded, New York had been "flooded with most atrocious displays in theatres and low play houses, and with open and flagrant indecencies in private halls of entertainment."[31] He failed to mention in his gloomy report that New Yorkers were also now flocking to an entirely new form of low entertainment.

Comstock might never have been able to keep up with the changes that carried what he considered to be obscenity into an ever-changing landscape of technology and culture. He undoubtedly was not alone in marveling at the pace at which his world was transforming. In 1910, the *New York Times* published an obituary for one of the most outrageous theatrical institutions in New York in the 1880s and 1890s, Huber's Museum. Comstock prosecuted Alfred and Alice Thompson there in

November 1895, noting in his arrest blotter that Alfred was "manager of 6 fat women at Huber's Museum, who dress in tights & ride Bicycles. A nauseating display. Alice, Wife of Alfred S. T. Sells pictures of herself in tights in a bawdy attire & posture."[32] Their show presumably faded from the limelight long before Huber's closed. Nevertheless, the *Times* author waxed nostalgic as it bid adieu:

> The visitors at Huber's formed the most heterogeneous gathering to be found anywhere in New York. People from out of town, east side folks, women and children, young men of the Bowery stamp, sailors on shore leave—all of them mingled in the crowds that went to Huber's. These last few years the crowds have not been so large—there are five-cent motion pictures next door—but they have been just as heterogeneous.

The author of this tender testimonial concluded with a sanguine reflection: "So, in a very short time all that is left of the museum will be a memory and a regret on the part of those New Yorkers who always intended going there some time and kept putting it off because they could go anytime."[33]

While Comstock was mired in his fruitless arguments with the WCTU, artists, engineers, and entrepreneurs did not wait for the outcome of their deliberations. An extraordinary new entertainment provided an unprecedented opportunity to multiply the performances of the mid-1890s and distribute them in a way that would prove even more impossible to constrain than the *danse du ventre* or living pictures on stage. "Five-cent motion pictures" proved to be the demise not only of Huber's Museum, but also of the censorship tactics of the past.

GOD MOVES IN A MYSTERIOUS WAY

Although the last decade of the nineteenth century had proved difficult for Anthony Comstock and the NYSSV, the news was not all bad as the twentieth century neared. New investigations, commissions, and organizations bolstered reform efforts generally as the Progressive Era took hold. Although the Lexow Commission was no friend of the NYSSV, it had in fact generated some new efforts to clean up corruption in the city's notorious police department. The WCTU proved a difficult and sometimes prickly ally, but still they were helping with the cause of cultural "purification," albeit in parallel rather than in concert. And the NYSSV and other like-minded purity crusaders across the country had already been remarkably effective on the legislative front. "By 1900, forty-two states had either enacted [anti-obscenity] laws or amended existing laws to further crack down on vice and obscene matter."[34]

Despite these successes, social reformers devoted specifically to reducing sexually explicit culture were thwarted by unforeseen new threats. As Comstock's arrest records attest, technologies emerged beginning in 1895 that spread vice to the masses in wondrous displays of pride-inducing American innovation. Ultimately, Thomas Edison proved to have far more sway over public attitudes and morals than Anthony Comstock, or any other Progressive Era activist. As a devout Christian, Comstock must have thought that God was moving in extremely mysterious ways, as the popular hymn promised.

In his first confrontation with miraculous vice in the era of Edison, on April 16, 1895, Comstock recorded seizing a phonograph and eleven "cells" at a cigar store on Broadway. This machine represented a relatively new development in entertainment and technology. Originally envisioned by Edison and other engineers as a labor-saving recording device for stenographers, in 1890 an entertaining coin-in-the-slot version was introduced that proliferated rapidly.[35] When the drop of a nickel was registered, cylindrical wax cells rotated, and the patron could listen on a receiver to a brief recording. As Comstock discovered, bawdy songs and dirty jokes rather quickly dominated these recordings.

Needless to say, Comstock's initial assault on the phonograph did not stem the flow of its importation into saloons and other entertainment venues, or clean up the content on cells. Just the next year, Comstock arrested Charles Fitter and John Lee in Jersey City on February 14, 1896.

Comstock discovered that the two men had created a traveling business, "going from place to place, exhibiting most obscene & blasphemous stuff at 5cts per head. They were in saloons."[36] Continuing his investigations, Comstock traced the producer of their cells back to one of the first recorded comedians in American history, Russell Hunting.

The *Brooklyn Daily Eagle* reported Comstock's delight at finally finding the man whose voice had "flooded" cities and towns in New York and other states. Hunting admitted that he had just shipped fifty cylinders to various saloons and resorts at Coney Island, which was in the process of being transformed into an enormous and raunchy version of the Midway at Chicago's Columbian Exposition, with rides and a wide sandy beach for people-watching and swimming.[37] Perhaps because of the novelty of the technology, Hunting was dealt a relatively harsh sentence.[38] Nevertheless, after five months in jail, he was back to his usual stage act, which was probably no less rude, performing "the original Michael Casey" stories "in Irish dialect." Hunting performed alongside other vaudeville actors who similarly produced humor unfortunately laden with poisonous sexual, ethnic, and racial stereotypes.[39]

Religious organizations tried to promote group phonograph concerts that were uplifting, rather than singular coin-in-the slot entertainments that replicated vaudeville humor. Very soon, though, "cultural prejudices were forgotten in the face of commercial opportunity, and when Edison sought to extend his phonograph into the visual realm, the inventor developed a method of exhibition modeled after the arcade machine— the peephole kinetoscope."[40] Slot machines bearing still photographs and motion pictures turned out to be even more popular and profitable than the scratchy phonograph recordings.

The NYSSV's *Annual Report* for 1899 for the first time worried about the increase of "Obscene Pictures in Slot Machines," claiming that "drastic measures are required to suppress this mighty evil."[41] Arrest blotter entries bear out this concern; the quantities of kinetoscopes, and pictures within them, was staggering. In December 1900, Comstock seized 13,000 photographs destined for slot machines, and in September 1901, another raid yielded 625 pictures and forty-three slot machines.[42]

By 1903, it was clear that this technology was spreading rapidly, rather than receding. The NYSSV reported that year: "These slot machines are very seductive to young men, and are, particularly, a curse to boys. In the machines where pictures are exhibited, one picture usually a very bad and seductive one, is exhibited *Free*. The boy presses the button, an electric light is turned on, and the free picture appears to view, behind a magnifying glass. Then by dropping one cent in a slot, and pressing the button again, the light is again turned on, the machinery is started, and fifteen other bawdy pictures appear."[43] Some estimates suggest that 30 to 60 percent of kinetoscopes offered "sexually-oriented pictures."[44]

While nickel-in-the-slot amusements were spreading vaudeville-style New York theatrical scenes across the country, another Edison invention also burst onto the American cultural landscape, one that ultimately would be immeasurably more influential. On April 23, 1896, Edison premiered his "Vitascope" at the Koster & Bial's Music Hall, located at Sixth Avenue and Twenty-Fourth Street. The Vitascope projected motion pictures onto a white screen within a gilded frame. Within one year, "several hundred projectors were in use across the country" and even small villages "had been visited by showmen not once but two or three times."[45] During that first presentation night at Koster & Bial's, Edison showed six scenes replicating vaudeville's typical mix of short skits, including one serpentine dancer. The motion picture industry thus was born.

The mid-1890s were especially ripe years for film to take up the subject of fleshly display, as "the agitations for and against the nude in American culture came to a head just when Motion Pictures first established themselves as vehicles of entertainment." Instantly, the popular risqué themes of the New York stage of the mid-1890s migrated to film. As David S. Shields documents, in 120 early productions of Thomas Edison's American Mutoscope and Biograph company, twenty-six took as their subject artists' models, another twenty described living pictures, and one of the earliest dances to be recorded in 1897 was Fahred Mazar Spyropoulos (Fatima, or Little Egypt), of Chicago Midway fame, performing the *danse du ventre*.[46]

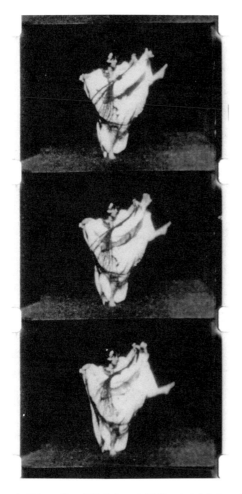

FIGURE 5.6 Thomas A. Edison, Inc., *Ella Lola, a la Trilby*, 1898. Motion picture. Paper Print Collection, Library of Congress, Washington, D.C.

An excellent example of this genre is a brief film made in Thomas Edison's New Jersey studio in 1898, which captures fifteen-year-old Ella Lola performing a dance "a la Trilby," the artist's model in George du Maurier's sexually provocative novel (figure 5.6). In Edison's brief evocation of the "fallen" model, Lola's flowing robes allow a full glimpse of her naked leg as she kicks and twirls. In another early film preserved in the Library of Congress, Lola's quick shimmies and forceful thrusts are captured in a "Turkish Dance" that closely follows Ida Craddock's censored descriptions of the *danse du ventre*.[47] Edison does not seem to have been concerned by previous successful prosecutions of performances of seductive dances. Nancy Mowll Mathews further demonstrates the intertwined fascination of painters and filmmakers in this early era for censored subjects, documenting early examples in film such as *The Draped Model*, in which a female in living-pictures-style body tights poses for a photographer, while both pose for a filmmaker.[48] Comstock worked to pass legislation against new technologies, including slot machines, in the New York State Assembly, but he was always a step behind.[49] After 1903, Comstock prosecuted just a few cases involving film, leaving regulation of that burgeoning industry largely to other players.[50]

Although Comstock mostly left film to others to police, his prosecutions in other media were deeply influenced by a rapidly changing standard for vice as Americans absorbed a new cultural Zeitgeist. When Comstock attempted to prosecute Richard Fox's *Police Gazette* in 1898, the judge told him that it was "no worse than Koster and Bials," which was still the prominent showplace in America for Vitascope pictures.[51] The dazzling technology of film left few Americans behind as it ratcheted down American expectations for propriety in entertainment.

Artists also were transformed by this new technology and its social implications, especially in New York City. In 1905, the artist John Sloan captured a scene of young women crowding around kinetoscope slot machines, watching "Girls in Their Nightgowns" and "Naughty Girls!" As Katherine Manthorne notes, Sloan began his art career at the same time as film emerged, thereby developing a "moving-picture eye" along with many other members of his generation. In early prints such as *Fun, One Cent* (figure 5.7), Sloan displayed both a vibrant new pictorial style and intellectual engagement with the new social relationships and perceptual experiences of Americans in a visually and technologically changing nation.[52] The girls Sloan depicts exhibit amazement, joy, and camaraderie as they huddle around the machines, presumably making the most of their money by sharing the experience. Undoubtedly, Sloan was as fascinated with the new technology as he was with the new phenomenon that

FIGURE 5.7 John Sloan, *Fun, One Cent*, 1905. Etching, plate: 4 15/16 × 6 7/8 in. (12.5 × 17.5 cm),
sheet: 9 7/8 × 12 15/16 in. (25.1 × 32.9 cm). Gift of Mrs. Harry Payne Whitney, 1926. Metropolitan
Museum of Art. (26.30.20) @2017 Artists Rights Society (ARS), New York.

women were accessing sexually themed pictures in public equally with
men. By leaving two of the kinetoscopes free for us at left, Sloan invites us
to make our own choice as to whether we would prefer to see our fortune
or "spicy" scenes.

While Americans were falling in love with kinetoscopes, vitascopes,
and a slew of further inventions that followed, they were developing
another new passion as well: postcards. On this beat Comstock was on
much more familiar ground, since the postcard industry relied upon photographers, printers, and, of course, the U.S. mail. He invested an enormous amount of time and effort in his attempt to clean up this popular
medium. Postcards first became popular in the United States as souvenirs
at the 1893 World's Exposition in Chicago. After 1898, when Congress
lowered the mailing rate for postcards to a penny, consumption and production soared. Between 1905 and 1915, "literally millions of postcards

were printed, imported, sold and mailed." In 1908 alone, the Post Office Department reported that 700 million postcards had been mailed.[53]

In the NYSSV's *Annual Report* for 1905, Comstock complained: "The business of uttering indecent post cards has been sprung upon us, to a marked degree, the past year. . . . In the early part of the year it seemed as if the streets were flooded and shop windows filled with foul pictures, displayed upon post cards." Once again, the quantities were simply enormous. In 1905 alone, NYSSV agents seized more than 300,000 post cards in Manhattan. In Brooklyn, in just one day they captured nearly 110,000.[54]

Although Comstock never listed the title of a kinetoscope in his arrest blotters, he took pains to record the titles of postcards, including "Honeymoon," "A Pipe Dream," "Hold on I'm in for That Too," "A Good Thing Coming," "What Happy Saw," "Through the Keyhole in the Door," "A Bulls Eye," "A Fellow Feeling," "Labor & Capital," "Naval Engagement btwn Alice Roosevelt & Longworth," "A Curious Mistake," "Sitting on a Peg," "Wrestling Girl Cards," "Tim's Pipe Dream," "Suffragette Speech," "Little Willies—Pissers," "How to Make a Motor Run Better," "The Maiden Dream," "Under the Garden Wall," and "Early Bird Catches the Worm."

Another Comstock habit is also evident in his work to suppress postcards: he was simultaneously angered and flattered by his own contribution to the spicy postcard fad. In the same *Annual Report* in which he complained about the enormity of the problem, he also reported "An Amusing Incident": "In one case on Broadway, up near Herald Square Building, we found a man, his wife and daughter, selling some of these vile cards. They had them displayed in the store windows, so that little boys and girls could see them from the public street. When one of our assistants visited the place on the 20th of October, the wife of the proprietor was present, and informed him that prices had gone up, doubled on these cards, because 'Comstock was making trouble.'" The shopkeeper's mention of his name clearly "amused" Comstock, but he was not softened.

A week later, Comstock arrested all three family members. He explained: "Ordinarily we would not have arrested the women; but when women so far forget themselves as to sell degrading pictures . . . this Society will make no distinction because of sex."[55] Comstock's arrests in his last decade indeed record a growing number of women who had "forgotten themselves" and were forced to face the consequences of indictment and incarceration. As more women came into the public worlds of entertainment and business, both as consumers and as workers, they also came onto Comstock's radar, and even his patronizing sympathies evaporated.

The complicated situation for workingwomen at the turn of the twentieth century not surprisingly found its way onto postcards. Many of these, including *Early Bird Catches the Worm* (figure 5.8), included a coded double entendre inscribing workingwomen as sexually available. Stenographers here were "wanted," but more for the sexual pleasure of the male boss than for their expertise and professional qualifications. This type of scene visualizing non-procreative sex between unmarried partners certainly met Comstock's qualifications as degrading and therefore obscene. Consumers seem not to have been bothered at all, and these types of cards were purchased and mailed in huge numbers.

FIGURE 5.8 *The Early Bird Catches the Worm*, 1909. Postcard. Collection, Frederick S. Lane

In addition to visualizing new tropes such as the available working-woman, artists and photographers also responded to the tremendous new opportunity presented by postcards by plagiarizing a wide variety of subject matter from other media. Both elevated art and the popular and profitable spheres of vaudeville, kinetoscopes, and film were ripe for plundering. Another popular series of risqué postcards, "What I Saw Through the Keyhole" (figure 5.9), directly paralleled a kinetoscope of the same title that was popular in penny arcades.[56]

The appearance of this theme in both media reflects not just the steep rise of sexual imagery in the public sphere, but also the normalization of the peephole view that Americans widely experienced when they looked into slot machines. Both modes of seeing were voyeuristic, privileged, and titillating, and promised an engagement with the realities of sexuality unhindered by censors determined to slam the door shut between private encounters and the public domain. For the price of a penny or a nickel, almost anyone in America now could look at images of other people involved in sexual play.

FIGURE 5.9 *What I Saw Through the Keyhole*, n.d. Postcard. Collection, Frederick S. Lane

Ironically, nobody in America looked through more proverbial keyholes than Anthony Comstock. His self-made career introduced him to more sexual expressions, predilections, and acts than any man in America in the nineteenth century. This was perhaps even truer in the early twentieth century, when he took on a relatively new target that probably was an education even for him. In two charged instances, Comstock encountered the world of private sex clubs in New York, in which he was confronted by sexual expression entirely liberated from the "normative" standards he had been trying to impose for thirty years.

On October 5, 1900, Comstock led a team of more than a dozen "ununiformed policemen and private detectives" into a small warren of rooms at 183 Bleecker Street in Manhattan's bohemian Greenwich Village. The "resort" was known as the Black Rabbit. Comstock told a reporter that he had received numerous complaints about the club, and that he had "never before raided a place so wicked."[57] Compared with the performances by young women at Emma De Forest's Busy Fleas brothel, which Comstock had visited in 1878, the Black Rabbit offered a far wider range of entertainments.[58]

Perhaps stung by the controversy following his lengthy visit to the Busy Fleas, or because he was so easily recognizable, Comstock initially did not investigate the Black Rabbit himself, but rather sent three detectives. Louis F. Dittman had been employed by the NYSSV for seven months; James Hanse testified that he was a professional who ran his own agency for more than ten years; and John Derring described himself as a wagon salesman who sometimes moonlighted as a detective. In more than 150 pages of depositions, testimony, and cross-examination, the men described their evening. After they arrived at the club between 10 and 11 p.m., the men first paid an entry fee of ten cents each and were admitted to a back room, which housed a bar serving whiskey and beer. Male and female guests sat at tables, drinking and enjoying piano music and dancing.

Once seated and served, Dittman claimed that a character known as "Jarbeau Fairy" joined the table of NYSSV detectives and inquired whether they would like to see an exhibition by a hermaphrodite named Pauline Sheldon. She charged one dollar per head, plus a dollar for a room in which the exhibition would be made. Jarbeau told the men that proper terms should be used, "prick, prick, and balls, balls, and cunt, cunt, and don't be beating around the bush." After collecting the money from the men in a small upstairs room, Dittman reported that Sheldon seated herself, "lifted up her dress and skirts and exposed testicles and what she described as a penis . . . then made further display by lifting up the testicles and penis and said 'underneath was the vagina, the same as a woman's.'" The men were not invited to do anything but look; they claimed that they left "after sufficient time to secure the proper evidence of a gross and indecent exhibition" and then went back to the barroom.[59]

Here, they drank more beer, and were offered the opportunity to see "a circus," to receive oral sex from a man or woman, or "anything you want us to do." A piano played, and Jarbeau Fairy danced with a woman named Myrtle Queen. The dance was described as extremely seductive. Dittman reported the music as "what is known as the 'Ragtime Dance.' Said Jarbeau drew the said Myrtle close up to him and put her arms around his waist, Jarbeau's legs were between the legs of Myrtle; then as the piano played, they moved their bodies in time with the music, rubbing their private parts together and acted as if in the sexual embrace." Another dancer performed in a short skirt with a magic lantern.

After the dances, the detectives were urged to go upstairs once again and see "the circus" for fifteen dollars, which they paid. Once again in a private upstairs room, one female and two male performers—Myrtle Queen, Opera Fairy, and Gertie Fairy—performed oral sex on each other sitting, lying down, and in the "Sixty nine." Afterwards, they demonstrated complicated athletic poses in which they engaged in more oral sex, including "the bridge" and "the triangle." Opera Fairy offered to drink beer and urinate at the same time, evoking a "fountain." The detectives declined to pay for the beer necessary to see that, but as a final act Opera put a lit cigarette in his rectum and replicated smoking.

During cross-examination, the defense attorney, James Oliver, tried to prove that the detectives were drunk. Before visiting the Black Rabbit they had already been to another "similar institution" on Thirteenth Street called the Horse Exchange, where they smoked cigars and were approached by a man called Ivy, described as a Fairy, who in turn introduced a woman known as "The Circus Queen." In total, each of the men admitted to imbibing two or three drinks at the Horse Exchange, and six more at the Black Rabbit. Derring denied under cross-examination that he got paid more than his daily wage "in case of a conviction."

Although Oliver tried very hard to implicate Comstock as somehow a bad actor in the affair, none of his arguments were effective in court. Two of the defendants, Sheldon and a door manager named Michael Davis, were found guilty only of misdemeanor crimes because they were not present during the "circus." Davis served eight months in jail for keeping a disorderly house, and Sheldon served eight months for indecent exposure. The other defendants were convicted of much more serious crimes and received correspondingly harsh sentences. Edith Myrtle Lynch was convicted of sodomy and sentenced to seven years in prison, and Jules Dumont received fourteen years at hard labor for the same crime. Comstock noted in his arrest blotter that Dumont was French, and a fashionable dressmaker. The unequal length of his sentence was entirely typical of the fate of homosexual defendants in Comstock's cases.[60]

In some ways, the existence and subsequent trial of the Black Rabbit is not especially surprising. By 1890, a subculture of male sex workers had emerged in New York and in cities across the country, "dominated by self-consciously feminized men who called themselves 'fairies.' Many cross-dressed and posed as 'female impersonators.'"[61] George Chauncey documents the rise of similar nightclubs offering "fairies" and "circuses" in New York as early as the late 1870s. Dives like the Black Rabbit, the Slide, and Paresis Hall were all popular on slumming tours "among middle-class men (and even among some women), in part as a way to witness working-class 'depravity' and to confirm their sense of superiority."[62] Comstock's description of the Black Rabbit affirms this assessment: "Between midnight and 3 or 4 o'clock A.M., it was no uncommon sight to see the street in the immediate vicinity of this den lined with handsome carriages or automobiles, in waiting for the aristocratic patrons of this den of Moral Perverts."[63]

As much as these clubs may have perpetuated and furthered disempowering stereotypes, they were also important to the men who called themselves fairies. In 1892, "the Slide was a place where they felt free to socialize with their friends and to entertain not only the tourists but also the saloon's regulars and one another with their campy banter and antics." Men wore female clothing and makeup if they felt like it, and danced. "'Normal men' and 'fairies' intermingled casually at many saloons some of which were known as 'fairy places' in their neighborhoods." Newspapers gave increasingly detailed descriptions of "orgies" in these clubs beginning in the 1890s, with the effect both of raising alarms and publicizing their existence and offerings.[64]

Although the Black Rabbit was by no means unique, it does represent an extraordinary shift, at least as compared with the brothel cases Comstock prosecuted at the start of his career. In contrast to those earlier cases, Comstock farmed out this investigation to others, but he still listed himself as a witness even though all he had done was inspect the premises on the day of the arrest. He may have done this so that he was entitled to a portion of any assessed penalties, or just so that he could take the stand, pass judgment, and receive credit for the convictions. At this advanced point in his career, he may also have recognized that his reputation could not withstand another pummeling as had occurred following his much-mocked in-depth reporting on the Busy Fleas entertainments at Emma De Forest's brothel.

Much water, indeed, had passed under the bridge in the twenty-two years since that first brothel case in Comstock's arrest blotters. In the sham De Forest trial, Comstock had suggested to the assistant district attorney that he depose six police officers and a *Tribune* reporter who had seen the performance, but he refused. The defense followed by not bothering to offer any evidence or witnesses, but simply moved to release the defendant "on certain points of law." In a fitting conclusion, the district attorney stood to announce that the one witness he had planned to call could not be found. The case was quickly thrown out.[65]

In the case of Emma De Forest, the police clearly were on the take, and the proceedings amounted to a brief farce. In the Black Rabbit case, however, Judge Rufus B. Cowing took pains to make sure that every detail of the detectives' visit was recorded without censorship in court documents. He read to the jury the entire language of the sodomy law: "A person who carnally knows in any manner any animal or bird, or carnally knows any male or female person by the anus or by or with the mouth, or voluntarily submits to such carnal knowledge, or attempts intercourse with a dead body." Cowing further insisted in the course of the proceedings that Davis and Sheldon be exonerated on their original charges, reindicted under lesser misdemeanor charges, and granted new and separate trials with the opportunity to change their initial guilty pleas, "that justice may be done."[66]

A final observation on transformations from 1878 to 1900 involves Comstock himself. He no longer was the wide-eyed, Jesus-quoting zealot he had been in his thirties. During the Black Rabbit trial, Dittman testified that when the arrest was made, "Mr. Comstock was standing down there, and I told Mr. Comstock that this was Jarbeau and Mr. Comstock says, 'Oh, this is Jarbeau, the cock-sucker, the head one down there?' and I told him that it was." Comstock had become inured to sexual speech, as had the judge, the jury, and the lawyers. The overall rise in the professionalism of the court is extraordinary, as is the coarsening of the conversation during trial. This was an American legal system denuded of its nineteenth-century euphemisms.

All of the peering Comstock had done through America's peepholes clearly had changed him into a much more street-tough and jaded man. In some ways he had become more like the agents he hired, as much a private investigator seeking opportunities to win convictions and garner fees, as a "roundsman for the Lord." This revised role was also evident in 1905, when he had the opportunity to peer into another private club in which sexuality was untethered from any illusions of respectability.

In 1905, a wealthy young man named Harry Thaw asked Comstock to investigate the architect Stanford White. White at that point in his career was wealthy and successful, known throughout New York for his design of the city's most-loved building, the second Madison Square Garden. The building was adored for its "modern cosmopolitan" entertainments as well as its attractive architectural details, including a tower "modeled on the Giralda bell tower in Seville." After 1893, the tower was capped by Augustus Saint-Gaudens's second version of *Diana* (figure 5.2), a gilded nude thirteen feet high and illuminated with electric lightbulbs so that she glistened as one of the highest points in the city, day and night.[67]

White was famous not only for his grand entertainment palace and many other popular architectural designs, but also as a scandalous celebrity. He and Augustus Saint-Gaudens operated as the quintessential men about town, visiting each other's all-male clubs, dining at expensive restaurants, and attending theatrical events. Elizabeth Lee notes that "letters filled with telling obscenities, vulgarities, and explicit sexual drawings have led scholars to suggest that one or both men probably had bisexual inclinations." In 1888, White organized the "Sewer Club" with five other friends, including Saint-Gaudens, in rented rooms in a Washington Square Park building.[68] Here, the men caroused with models and other mistresses, and helped each other hide affairs from wives. White also had a studio in the tower of Madison Square Garden. In both locations, he famously held parties where young models and actresses were invited to pose nude surrounded by elaborate decorations, including a multitude of painted and sculpted nudes and an infamous red velvet swing.[69]

Harry Thaw entered the scene as the wealthy scion of a high-society Pittsburgh family. Thaw developed an infatuation with a young actress named Evelyn Nesbit after seeing her on the stage. After courting her for some time, Thaw took Nesbit to Europe and then married her in 1905. Later that year, after the couple moved back to New York, Thaw became obsessed with the idea that Stanford White had robbed Nesbit of her virginity and jealous of what he perceived to be their continuing relationship. In a mental state later ruled "dementia," Thaw sought help in proving that the architect was still debauching his wife and other young women. At some point in the development of his paranoia, he asked Comstock to investigate. For the seasoned vice hunter, this was a grand opportunity to strike at a high-profile target. Unfortunately for Comstock, White was dead before the NYSSV could take credit for bringing him down.[70]

On June 25, 1906, Thaw shot White dead on the rooftop restaurant at Madison Square Garden, in front of a large number of horrified patrons. The story consumed American newspapers for months.

In the wake of the murder, Comstock was only too happy to join in the public circus of the scandal, telling reporters that he had "testimony damaging to the character of the late Stanford White and three of his associates, and that if he is subpoenaed he will give that testimony." With utter disregard for the secrecy of the grand jury, Comstock at the same time volunteered to reporters that his testimony would describe "revolting orgies" and "atrocities perpetrated upon girls."[71] Although he had only a bit part in the unfolding drama of the White murder trial, still he was happy to have his story told, and members of the press were always happy to print his spicy quotes regarding juicy scandals. As a *Philadelphia Inquirer* editorial summarized in 1906, "Anthony Comstock is undoubtedly the best-posted man in this country on things nobody ought to know."[72]

Comstock was, indeed, often the first to know about whatever scandalous entertainment one ought not to know about. In 1905, he confiscated posters for a newly popular form of entertainment at Madison Square Garden—physical culture exhibitions. In October that year, Comstock's seizure of 12,000 fliers advertising Bernarr Macfadden's "Beauty Show" so ably publicized the event that a crush of 20,000 people showed up to Madison Square Garden for a parade of athletic bodies in clinging outfits; 5,000 had to be turned away.[73] A publication by Macfadden promoting physical culture demonstrates the style of his form-fitting suits (figure 5.10). In addition to raging against Macfadden's new exposure of muscular women and men, Comstock was also back on familiar turf that year, pulling oil paintings out of a brothel managed by Rosina Arnedo at 167 Hester Street.

To excite her male patrons and make more money, Arnedo asked men to pay an entrance fee to look at four large oil paintings in a front room, where patrons waited before going upstairs with a prostitute. At the time of Arnedo's arrest, Comstock wrote that there were "10 women in house. 38 men—5 upstairs with women & 33 waiting turn. Bah!" Arnedo was sentenced to pay a fine of fifty dollars for exhibiting the pictures and another

FIGURE 5.10 *Bernarr Macfadden's Women's Physical Culture Competition*, 1903. Photograph. H. J. Lutcher Stark Center for Physical Culture & Sport. The University of Texas, Austin.

fifty dollars for operating a disorderly house, and the paintings were destroyed.[74] Despite Comstock's evident disgust, the practice of blending art and prostitution had a long history. In the ancient world, "the Greeks had frescoes in their bordellos showing various sexual positions that made it easier for the customer to explain what was desired."[75]

A final infuriation in 1905 came from overseas. On October 30, 1905, Arnold Daly staged George Bernard Shaw's play *Mrs. Warren's Profession* at the Garrick Theater in New York, with his wife Mary Daly in the lead role. The play had been banned from the stage in England because its subject matter focused on the "profession" of prostitution. Although Shaw conveyed a moralizing take, nevertheless any creative work that took prostitution as its subject was the literal definition of pornography. Newspapers in New York extensively covered preparations for the opening, citing concern about Comstock's potential interference. They also made clear that they knew Daly's expressions of anxiety were a now well-trodden ploy to sell out the house. On the day before the opening, the *New-York Tribune* mocked the producer for warning that children would be refused admission and "young people are respectfully requested to keep away. Fine, Mr. Daly! You know how to get them there!"[76] Indeed, some tickets ultimately sold for an astounding thirty dollars each.

As opening night approached, the critical tenor of the newspaper coverage convinced Daly to cut "every line that is capable of a double construction," and Mary Daly declared that "the play is more likely to shock men than women. Women may not be supposed to know about these things, but they do know about them, and they take a deep interest in these social problems."[77] On the day after opening night, newspapers offered lengthy and vigorous debates over the play's value, but almost all of them expected Comstock's imminent prosecution.

They were correct, but not entirely. The play was stopped after the first performance, but this time it wasn't Comstock who led the censorship effort, but rather New York City's police commissioner. Rumors also spread that Shaw's works had been moved to a locked cage in the New York Public Library.[78] Newspapers in both London and America printed an angry response from Shaw, including his assertion that "Comstockery is the world's standing joke at the expense of the United States." Notwithstanding the fact that Comstock had not been involved in closing down Shaw's play, the term stuck and became synonymous with unreasonable prudishness for the better part of a century. Shaw added in his remarks a further caustic takedown of Comstock in the form of a quotation from his play *Man and Superman*: " 'Hell is paved with good intentions, not bad ones.' "[79]

In his *Annual Report* for 1905, Comstock provided his own definition of the term "Comstockery" in rebuttal: "The applying of the noblest principles of law, as defined by the Higher Courts of Great Britain and the United States of America, in the interest of Public Morals, especially those of the young."[80] There certainly were plenty of Americans who agreed with him, even in New York City. In the last decade of his life, Comstock was a featured speaker around the country, receiving invitations from YMCA branches, WCTU conventions, and Social Purity conferences, at which he was welcomed as a famed champion of Christianity, temperance, morality, and decency. He also of course continued to attend church services and to speak to church congregations regularly. It is through these lenses that Comstock undoubtedly made sense of the many extraordinary changes and cultural expressions he witnessed in early-twentieth-century America, including belly dancers, bawdy phonograph songs, risqué films, orgies, debauched artists, and even a hermaphrodite.

One of the most popular hymns sung by Protestant denominations in Comstock's era was William Cowper's "God Moves in a Mysterious Way":

God moves in a mysterious way
his wonders to perform;
He plants His footsteps in the sea
and rides upon the storm.

Deep in unfathomable mines
of never-failing skill
He treasures up His bright designs
and works His sovereign will . . .

His purposes will ripen fast,
unfolding every hour.
The bud may have a bitter taste,
But sweet will be the flower . . .[81]

If God was performing "wonders" guided by "bright designs," Comstock must sometimes have had difficulty discerning them. Indeed, many of the wonders of the new century were quickly turned to prurient use.

In 1905, Anthony Comstock, now age sixty-one, was no longer a young and idealistic man, and he was not well. Two years earlier, newspapers reported him close to death with "la grippe," which kept him in bed for two months. Shortly after his recovery, he was thrown down stairs by an alleged perpetrator during an arrest, landing him back in bed. In that year, too, more of his stalwart supporters at the NYSSV died, including William E. Dodge, Jr. During the last decade of his life, the NYSSV's arrest blotters show a blizzard of cases either suspended or settled quickly for the minimum fine of fifty dollars. Income was down, as was respect for the work of the society. The bud indeed had a bitter taste at the start of the twentieth century, and the last decade of his life would not provide much proverbial relief from the storm.

1906

The year 1906 started badly and ended worse for Anthony Comstock and the New York Society for the Suppression of Vice. In its *Annual Report* for that year, the society listed half the number of donors and donations than it had twenty years earlier. And its balance sheet would have looked far worse without the handsome contributions of John D. Rockefeller, who gave $250, and Mr. and Mrs. Andrew Carnegie, who each gave $500; their combined gifts of $1,250 amounted to nearly a quarter of the total collected.[82] Perhaps in response to its much-reduced fundraising, the society dropped gambling prosecutions from its beat, claiming that "there were others to look after" this vice.

In the society's main stock and trade, obscenity prosecutions, there were more targets than ever to try and tame. In the report's list of "New Foes," for example, there was a seizure "in Maiden Lane, of 468 watches, each provided with a revolving disk in the back which, when the watch was wound up, kept the disk revolving, showing six obscene pictures."[83] The categories of "obscene pictures and photographs," and rubber articles "for immoral use" continued to supply tons of material for incinerators in New Jersey.

Although the society persisted into its thirty-fourth year in a reduced state, it still counted a variety of successes that justified its existence to anyone interested in reading its lengthy and detailed descriptions of the "perverts" and "reprobates" that agents had encountered in 1906. The society's biggest problem was not, in that moment, its diminishing funds or any lack of targets, but rather the reputation of its secretary and agent, Anthony Comstock. In fact, most of the Society's *Thirty-Third Annual Report* was devoted to defending his honor and countering his critics. It was a valiant but ultimately unsuccessful effort at reputation rehabilitation: 1906 marked a tipping point, after which Comstock was fair game for a wider and more hostile circle of detractors than he had ever encountered before.

That circle had always included law enforcement officers, with whom Comstock had particularly bad relations. Of the sixty-one defendants who were convicted or pled guilty to crimes prosecuted by the NYSSV in 1906, forty-seven "absconded," and only one was rearrested—indicating the disinterest, if not outright apathy, of the police toward the work of the society, similar to its situation when it started its work in 1874.[84] After thirty years of dealing with Comstock, court officers had grown so hostile toward him that in March 1906 the *New York Times* reported that he had been punched by a defense attorney, Hugh Gordon Miller, three times in a federal court hearing. Comstock had arrested Miller's client, Ernest Richards, along with a codefendant, J. J. Koch, as proprietors of the "Parisian Preventive Co." at 1609 Broadway, which sold "articles to prevent conception." Their product was listed in Comstock's blotter as "womans safeguards."[85]

Miller claimed that Comstock had set up his client and allowed the man responsible for the crime, Koch, to escape. When Comstock interrupted Miller by exclaiming "That's a lie!," the young attorney "sprang at Mr. Comstock with the agility of a toreador" and delivered "three resounding whacks. One caught Mr. Comstock in the eye. The second was stopped by his chin. The third smashed his hat and sent it flying across the room." Despite Comstock's numerous attempts to obtain a warrant for the lawyer's arrest, nobody involved in the judicial system was willing to help him, and the scrappy defense attorney ended up as the hero in news coverage of the trial.[86]

Comstock's next bout with his detractors was far more damaging to his reputation. As usual, his troubles began as a response to a complaint. A mother had sent him an illustrated publication of the Art Students League of New York, which had been mailed to her daughter.

FIGURE 5.11 Photograph of Anthony Comstock in his New York office, ca. 1900. Wisconsin Historical Society (WHS-4995)

She considered the pictures "highly indecent" and asked Comstock to investigate.[87] Similar letters regarding objectionable material arrived at the office of the NYSSV on a daily basis, and Comstock used a mail sorting table and a rolltop desk, seen in a photo taken around this time (figure 5.11), to organize his work.

In keeping with his usual methods, Comstock personally examined the publication and declared it to be "obscene, indecent, filthy, and disgusting," and therefore fair game to be seized and destroyed.[88] He was especially concerned by the reproductions of life drawings of nude models on pages 161 and 168 (figures 5.12 and 5.13). Believing that he had grounds to take action against the League, Comstock traveled to the school with his deputy, Charles Bamberger, just a few days after receiving the letter.

FIGURE 5.12 Drawings by John Carlson and George Macrum reproduced in: *The American Student of Art* 1, no. 6 (June 1906), 161. Art and Architecture Collection, Miriam and Ira D. Wallach Division of Art, Prints, and Photographs, Astor, Lenox, and Tilden Foundations, New York Public Library.

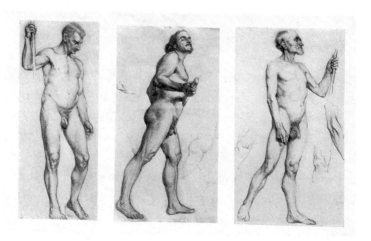

FIGURE 5.13 Drawings by E. E. Clark, C. J. Martin, and W. D. Koerner reproduced in: *The American Student of Art* 1, no. 6 (June 1906), 168. Art and Architecture Collection, Miriam and Ira D. Wallach Division of Art, Prints, and Photographs, Astor, Lenox, and Tilden Foundations, New York Public Library.

The facility they entered was far happier and grander than their more typical haunts in the slums of lower Manhattan. League students shared a joyful camaraderie derived at least in part from an ethos established at the time of the school's formation thirty years earlier in 1875. The Art Students League was "the radical school: It had separated from the tyranny of the [National] Academy; it had grown out of a desire on the part of a group of students to better their education; it was student controlled and managed."[89]

In 1905, a group of students began to organize a new journal that would show just how far art education had evolved at the League and in the United States. The first issue of the *American Student of Art* included an introductory essay, presumably penned by its student editor André Champollion, which set forth the journal's aims: "It must be understood that the paper will be devoted entirely to the discussion and reproduction of the work of American rather than to that of foreign artists . . . who have not yet won the desired recognition because lacking a fair opportunity to call the public's attention to their efforts."[90]

From January through May 1906, publication of the *American Student of Art* proceeded according to plan. The journal included essays by and about League faculty, and both teachers and students offered practical advice on topics including proper depiction of drapery, drawing from casts, and the use of color in landscape painting. Although the first five issues of the *American Student of Art* were published, sold, and circulated within and outside the League with no discernible controversy, the June edition offered a twist that led to the drama of Comstock's raid. From January through May, the magazine was distributed only to those who purchased it. In June, however, "the number" was "made a sort of catalogue for the League," including detailed information about courses for the upcoming quarter, with lists of faculty, fees, times, and class locations. This enlarged, illustrated publication not only proved the point that outstanding art education was on offer at the League's spacious facility on West Fifty-Seventh Street, but also supplied the information necessary to enroll immediately. Rather than mailing the journal only to paying subscribers, the June issue was mailed, free of charge, to everyone on the League's mailing list, including the offended mother who complained to Comstock.[91] Ever vigilant and responsive, he wasted little time in launching his raid.

Unfortunately, at the time of his visit, the sultry August weather had chased most of the League's artists and administrators out of the city to breezier summer homes, and the only person Comstock could find in the office was a young clerk named Anna Reibley, who physically handed him the June edition when he requested a copy.[92] Obsessed, as always, with saving the youth of America from the dangers of lust, he arrested Reibley on the spot, and seized all of the remaining issues of the *American Student of Art*. His momentary victory, however, was classically Pyrrhic given the personal and professional injuries he suffered in the ensuing political firestorm.

Even if the *American Student of Art* had been an obvious source of smut, his sympathetic and blameless young defendant was a disastrous choice for success in the courts of either law or public opinion. A very short time after her arrest, Reibley was released into the custody of her attorney, but the shy young woman's brief incarceration helped ensure that over the ensuing months, debate about the case would rage in the pages of magazines and newspapers across the city and nation. Comstock's arrest record entry for the Art Students League case was similar to the one he wrote for the trial of Edmund Knoedler in 1887: "This arrest led to violent abuse before the public."[93]

The "violent abuse" started almost immediately. On August 4th, two days after the raid, the *New York Times* detailed the responses of various members of the city's art aristocracy, as well as its hoi polloi. According to the *Times*, League officials raced back to New York, promising not only to fight the case, but also to "bring an action against Comstock, to punish him, if possible." The shocked reaction of League administrators to Reibley's arrest demonstrates that they had not imagined any potential criminal liability when they made their decision to merge the magazine and circular. Reibley herself protested in court, declaring "You do not look at this thing in the right light. . . . This is pure art."[94]

The same article noted that "incidentally, New York artists, whether they have been students at the league building or not, are taking up the fight." Artist Everett Shinn was prominent among those ready to wage war. Shinn was quoted as saying "Why if he were in Paris he would have been tossed into the Seine last night. Hully gee! That human moral mothball!"[95] Other newspapers printed mostly exclamation marks to reflect the unprintable character of many of Shinn's remarks.[96]

The most powerful weapon wielded by artists against their nemesis, appropriately enough, was caricature. At the League, "students drew cartoons of Comstock wherever they could find a space on a wall for a sketch. A small group of them hung out of a window a plump figure supposed to represent the Summit [New Jersey] moralist." Everett Shinn reportedly called on the League students to keep drawing: "Boys, you know what to do with him. Cartoon him until the cows come home. . . . Get at him! Get at him!"[97] In similarly defiant mode, the *New York World* illustrated the "PICTURES WHICH COMSTOCK CALLS LEWD AND FOR WHICH HE RAIDED ART STUDENTS" on the day following the raid and provided reproductions of the "Caricatures of Antony Comstock and His Latest Raid, as Drawn To-Day by Members of the Art Students' League, Whose Home Was Raided" in its evening edition.[98]

During 1906 and 1907, while the League case was debated and adjudicated, cartoons and jokes featuring Comstock abounded in newspapers and magazines. Across the country, editorial staff including those of the *Duluth News* made great sport of his prudishness: "When dining at a friend's home, Mr. Anthony Comstock is said to have blushed a rosey red when his host removed the dressing from the fowl."[99] *Life* published a snarky fictional dialogue between a cupid representing the editorial staff of the magazine and a wary Comstock:

"Don't you think I am doing a great work?"

"You are indeed, Anthony."

"Do you really mean that?"

"Certainly. There wouldn't be any standard of comparison . . . How big an ass some one else is, all we have to do . . . is to place him alongside of you."[100]

FIGURE 5.14 Louis M. Glackens, *St. Anthony Comstock: The Village Nuisance*, 1906. Lithograph. J. Ottmann Lithograph Co., New York, publisher Keppler and Schwarzmann. Reproduced in: *Puck* 60, no. 1538 (August 22, 1906), centerfold. See also color plate 13.

All totaled, *Life* published five caricatures of Comstock related to his prosecution of the Art Students League.

Louis M. Glackens took his turn lambasting *St. Anthony Comstock: The Village Nuisance* in the most elaborate visual barb of this period, published in *Puck* (figure 5.14 / plate 13). At center, we see a scene labeled: "The Temptation of Saint Anthony (Revised)." The "temptation" here is a chorus of mannequin "formes" sporting hosiery and corsets. While he holds up his hands in protest, Comstock at the same time fixes his gaze firmly at his enticement. The scene is a clear reference to his ineffective campaign to rid shop windows of such suggestive displays. At the upper left, Comstock leads clothed horses down a park path, and below that he attempts to serve a warrant on "a shameless French poodle." On the right side of the pastiche we see Comstock bathing fully clothed and, finally, in the last scene, what happens when he "gets what is coming to him," tormented by winged devils in the fiery abyss of hell—in which he wears only a peek-a-boo carnival mask across his ample posterior.

PLATE 1 Kelloggs & Thayer, *The Good Tree or Hieroglyphics of a Christian*, 1846–1847.
Hand-colored lithograph, 32.4 × 23.8 cm. The Connecticut Historical Society.

PLATE 2 D. W. Kellogg & Company, *An Evil Tree, or the Natural Heart*, ca. 1830–1840. Hand-colored lithograph, 32.9 × 25.4 cm. The Connecticut Historical Society.

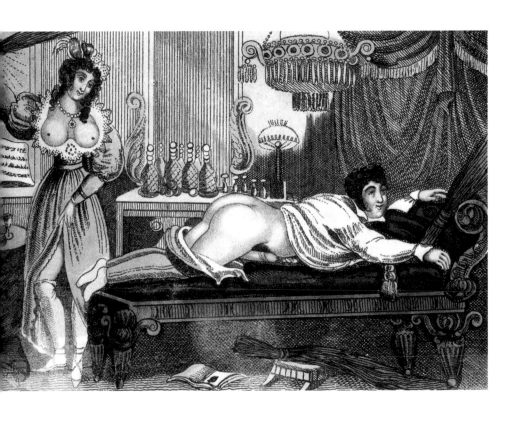

PLATE 3 *Fanny Whipping Mr. Barville*, scene from *"Memoirs of a Woman of Pleasure,"* ca. 1850. Engraving with hand-painted color. Included in: *Deposition of Officer Augustus Furnald against John Sweeney, with five pornographic images.* Courtesy, American Antiquarian Society.

PLATE 4 Trick cigar case (closed), n.d. Courtesy, The Kinsey Institute.

PLATE 5 Trick cigar case (open), n.d. Courtesy, The Kinsey Institute.

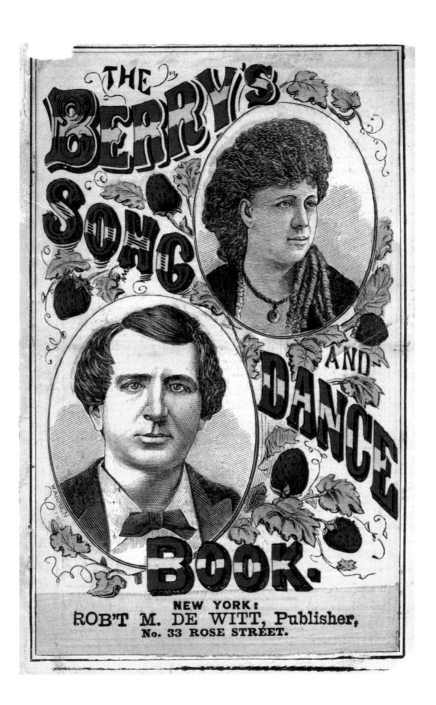

PLATE 6 *The Berry's Song and Dance Book* (New York: R.M. De Witt, 1873), cover. Harris Collection of American Poetry and Plays, Brown University.

PLATE 7 Webster & Albee, *Woman Standing on a Man's Back*, ca. 1885.
Hand-colored stereograph card. Courtesy, The Kinsey Institute. (2009.86.2).

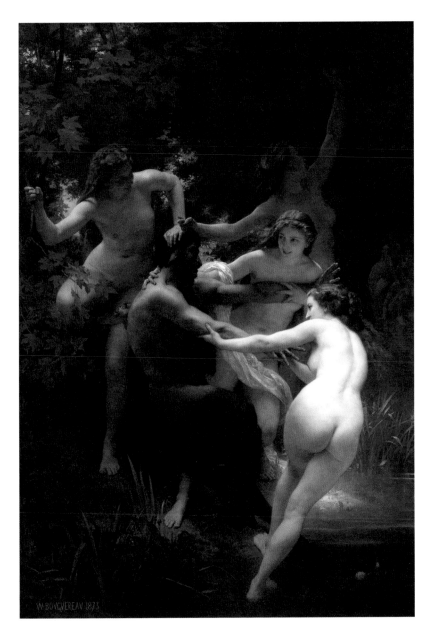

PLATE 8 William-Adolphe Bouguereau, *Nymphs and Satyr*, 1873. Oil on canvas, 102 ½ × 72 in. (260.4. × 182.9 cm). Sterling and Francine Clark Art Institute, Williamstown, Massachusetts. (1955.658) Image @ Sterling and Francine Clark Art Institute, Williamstown, Massachusetts, USA (photo by Michael Agee).

PLATE 9 H. A. Thomas & Wylie, *Interior View of the Hoffman House Bar*, 1890.
Chromolithograph, 61 × 46 cm., on sheet 71.1 × 55 cm. Library of Congress
Prints and Photographs Division.

PLATE 10 George Schlegel Lithographic Co., *The Altogether*, 1896. Cigar Label.
Courtesy, The Winterthur Library: The John and Carolyn Grossman Collection.

PLATE 11 Strobridge & Co., *On the Bowery*, 1896. Color lithograph poster, 75 × 50 cm. Library of Congress Prints and Photographs Division, Washington, D.C.

PLATE 12 John Haberle, *A Bachelor's Drawer*, 1890–1894. Oil on canvas, 20 × 36 in. (50.8 × 91.4 cm). Metropolitan Museum of Art. Purchase, Henry R. Luce Gift. (1970.193).

PLATE 13 Louis M. Glackens, *St. Anthony Comstock: The Village Nuisance*, 1906.
Lithograph. J. Ottmann Lithograph Co., New York, publisher Keppler and Schwarzmann.
Reproduced in: *Puck* 60, no. 1538 (August 22, 1906), centerfold.

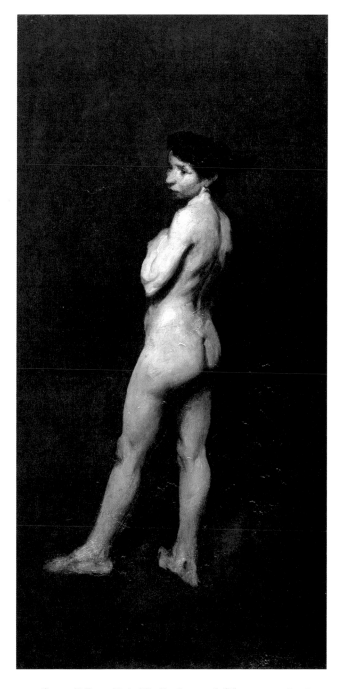

PLATE 14   George Bellows, *Nude: Miss Bentham*, 1906. Oil on canvas, 181 × 89.5 cm.
The Barber Institute of Fine Arts, University of Birmingham / Bridgeman Images.

PLATE 15 Robert Henri, *Salome*, 1909. Oil on canvas, 77 ½ × 37 inches.
Collection of The John and Mable Ringling Museum of Art the State Art
Museum of Florida, Florida State University. (SN937).

PLATE 16 Robert Henri, *Plate in Motion*, 1913. Oil on canvas, 77 ¼ × 37 ¼ in.
Daniel J. Terra Collection, Terra Foundation for American Art. (1999.69)
Photo: Terra Foundation for American Art, Chicago / Art Resource, NY.

PLATE 17 Thomas Eakins, *William Rush and His Model*, 1907–1908. Oil on canvas, 35 ¼ × 47 ¼ in. (89.5 × 120 cm). Honolulu Museum of Art, Gift of the Friends of the Academy, 1947. (548.1).

By 1906, Comstock had become so universally known as a comic figure that he was an easy trope to apply to almost any newsworthy story. In September, *Current Literature* surveyed August's slew of articles and editorials and summarized that "Mr. Comstock's recent action in raiding the Art Students' League, in New York has given to the word [Comstockery], especially in art circles, a new and additional potency not dissimilar from that which a red flag exerts upon a herd of long-horned bovines."[101] Although the most vocal factions of the American art world in 1906 agreed entirely with the students at the League, Comstock still enjoyed some support for his actions, especially along nativist lines that reflected growing isolationism. Weighing in on his side, the *New York Evening Journal* published an editorial proclaiming that Comstock had "acted properly to prevent the publication of a magazine which might well have served as the introductory feature of a mass of indecent periodical literature such as is circulated in Germany and in France under the name of 'Art.' This country . . . prefers common sense and self-respect to any sort of indecency, no matter how large the word 'art' may be written upon it."[102] A critic writing in *Brush and Pencil* likewise felt that study of the nude was "wholly worthless" in many lines of artistic production, as well as simply un-American. Whatever "Germany" did, "was it any reason why America should throw down the bars?"[103]

Comstock of course concurred with these authors. However, he went much further in describing exactly where the bars between decency and indecency stood. Just weeks after the League raid in 1906, he clarified his aesthetic and moral standards once again in an essay, this time published in *Leslie's Weekly* and titled "The Crime of the Nude." Here, he repeated the arguments he had made in the past, unchanged: "The Nude, as uncovered by so-called art, is a web which has enmeshed many a youth to his or her ruin. At its best it has a tendency to suggest to the minds of the young and inexperienced thoughts of an impure and libidinous character. . . . In the heart of every child there is a chamber of imagery which the spirit of evil seeks to decorate with defilement."[104] In directly justifying his seizure of the *American Student of Art*, Comstock repeated the *Hicklin* standard upheld in the Muller trial and expanded upon this argument by condemning the League reproductions as even worse: "Not one of these pictures was as brazen and gross as the pictures under discussion."[105]

The unarticulated difference in the case of the *American Student of Art* is easy to see: this publication included full frontal male nudity. Presumably, nothing could encourage libidinousness more than a picture of the organ of libidinousness itself. Indeed, it was quite unusual to see images of a penis in the Progressive Era outside of outright pornography. Many American artists got around the problem through a visual version of bowdlerism, for example by sculpting a stump in the place of male genitals. Other popular solutions included placing a leaf or loincloth over the penis or posing male figures to face away from the picture plane, as in the clever cartoon "Let Anthony's Punishment Fit the Crime" (figure 5.15).[106] Even many medical publications shied away from illustrating male reproductive anatomy during Comstock's reign, and medical and artistic schools alike ensured that women were never asked to view the penis in coeducational situations, and in most cases never at all.[107]

In most art schools, as in the Art Students League in 1906, students were separated by sex in life class, and female artists were limited to female

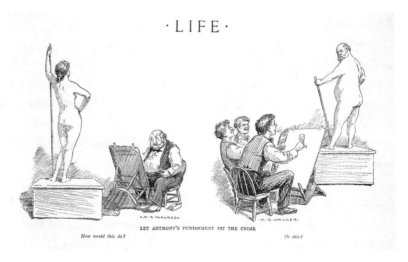

FIGURE 5.15 A.B. Walker, *Let Anthony Comstock's Punishment Fit the Crime*, 1906. Cartoon reproduced in: *Life* 48, no. 1246 (September 13, 1906), 287.

FIGURE 5.16 *A Popular Eviction*, 1906. Cartoon reproduced in: *Life* 48, no. 1244 (August 30, 1906), 221.

models or male models wearing loincloths, while male students worked from fully nude models of both sexes.[108] The *American Student of Art* metaphorically removed these normal bars of decency by allowing women to see images of penises. Cartoonists responded to the subtleties of the situation by depicting a female allegorical figure of "Public Opinion" and a coeducational pair of students linked arm-in-arm as the figures giving Comstock "the boot" from the Art Students League in *A Popular Eviction* (figure 5.16).

Comstock's pique regarding this aspect of the case became particularly evident during the course of the trial when he protested to a *New York Sun* reporter: "I have forty envelopes in my possession which I took from seized magazines, each of them addressed to an unmarried woman" and complained during the trial that he was appalled to see "two women looking at pictures of the nude unclothed" within the League. He accused "these young men of the Art League who are influencing 60,000 young girls annually to turn to lives of shame!," insinuating that the arousal of the girls themselves most concerned him because it might lead them to prostitution.[109]

While protectionist and paternalistic arguments could easily have helped his cause in the Art Students League case, Comstock was effectively barred from pursuing this line of argument by the simple fact that it was the young, "helpless" Anna Reibley who visibly wilted on the witness stand when the case was finally heard in police court on October 15, 1906. League attorneys staunchly refused to produce an alternate (male) defendant in the case.[110] Comstock arrived in New York's police court to find the seats packed with female and male art students, with pencils ready to lampoon their archenemy once again. The arguments in this first round chiefly laid out the facts of the case. The prosecution established that Miss Reibley had been the person who distributed the journals to Comstock and his deputy and who later handed over the remaining stock when presented with a search warrant. Comstock also presented his best argument against the idea of professional necessity. He voiced his shock and dismay at seeing young people look at pictures of "unclothed beings" on the wall at the League. "Were they studying those pictures from motives of art? No, Sir; they were not. They were actually enjoying them."[111]

On the second and final day of testimony, the League's attorney, C. C. Crowley, was brutal, blunt, and personal: "Comstock during most of his life has followed the single profession of looking for the worst. . . . He is a degenerate so far as the consideration of certain subjects is concerned. He is blind to the beauties of life."[112] With the testimony concluded, Magistrate Mayo took the matter into his chambers, and finally, on December 31, 1906, he issued his verdict: the case was dismissed. Thus, 1907 rang in as the first year in which a publication with depictions of pubic hair and a penis had prevailed in a highly publicized American obscenity case.

As it turned out, Comstock's opponents were wrong to think that the outcome was entirely favorable to the cause of artistic license. At the time he arrested Reibley, Comstock also confiscated all the copies of the *American Student of Art* that he could obtain. This amounted to "3650 books. 44 envelopes. 1000 lbs." Unbeknownst to the students and teachers, the League's attorney cut a backroom quid pro quo deal with the magistrate that resolved the case. The charges were dropped, but in exchange Comstock got what he most wanted: he recorded in his blotter that all the copies in his possession were destroyed, as per orders of the district attorney. Today the publication is recorded as having endured in fewer than six complete sets.[113]

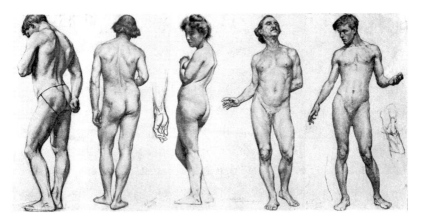

FIGURE 5.17 Art Students League of New York, *Course Catalogue, 1907–1908*, 12. Photo, Courtesy of Art Students League of New York.

Much more damaging than simply the loss of this issue of the publication, the fearful board of control of the League acted swiftly to discontinue the *American Student of Art* entirely—before the case even came up for trial.[114] The 1906–1907 course catalogue did include reproductions of male nudity in life drawings (figure 5.17) and photographs of female students drawing from a male model, but in both instances the images were less provocative than in the *American Student of Art*. The male model in the women's life class is clearly wearing a loincloth, and the penises of the men facing the viewer in the life drawings are obfuscated in a manner suggesting bowdlerized aesthetics. In this case, self-censorship was enacted through literal erasure.

This conservative response to potential legal liability is typical of the ways institutions often respond to censorship threats with self-censorship that stifles provocative voices. Comstock's victory in this regard, however, was as usual fleeting. Once again, the images he managed to remove from the public sphere were more than matched by the outpouring of work featuring fully realized and anatomically complete nudes in following years made by artists who stood in opposition to his efforts. Comstock's actions at the Art Students League had made nudity even more of a cause célèbre and great inspiration. Thanks to Anthony Comstock, obscenity was the newest American modernity.

THE MARRIAGE OF OBSCENITY AND MODERNITY

After the court's dismissal of the Art Students League case in late 1906, artists and art students were jubilant; they had vanquished their foe and defended their professional license. In March 1907, an overstuffed Comstock impersonator presided at the League's annual auction of artistic spoofs created by student members of the satirical "Society of American Fakirs."[115] Newspapers reported that at the event a "grotesquely costumed" Comstock auctioned off "most unblushing" nude pictures, and a student presented Anna Reibley with a statue showing Comstock holding a mallet above the *Venus de Milo* "on which his foot—a covered one—is resting. The art magazine is clasped tightly in his arm."[116] Comstock had galvanized a rising generation of artists and their teachers around the idea that their future was free of Comstockery. Making art that challenged American prudishness and censorship certainly was not a new concept in 1906, but the significant attention paid to the issue at this moment brought a fresh vigor and energy to the task of producing visual "reactions to limits."[117] In homes and studios, artists affirmed their allegiance to the faithful, full, and frank representational aesthetics of the life studies published in the *American Student of Art*.

In 1906, John Sloan, who had already been intrigued by censored subjects like kinetoscopes, recorded in his diary that he and several friends painted murals in a basement and "Comstock would not be pleased." As John Fagg points out the following year, Sloan also recorded in his diary that his wife Dolly read sexually explicit passages from a censored novel while the artist Robert Henri took notes. "This was at once a bohemian entertainment in which a woman read aloud a man's frank recollection of his sexual experiences in the company of her husband and best friend, and a further challenge to Comstockery, the serious intent of which was marked by Henri's dedicated act of transcription."[118]

The anti-censorious daring of Henri and Sloan reflects not only their desire for artistic freedom, but also their experiences as natives of Philadelphia, a city that was much less inclined towards censorship than New York. Whereas Henri came from a fine art background, however,

Sloan was one of a group of young men, including Everett Shinn, George Luks, and William Glackens, who all got their start as artist-reporters. As employees of newspapers including the *Philadelphia Inquirer*, the *Public Ledger*, and the *Philadelphia Press*, these men were undoubtedly aware of the many controversies in which Comstock was involved, and the generally hostile attitude of Philadelphia journalists in covering them. The example of newspaper reporting was foundational to the idea of "truthful" art for these men in several ways. As Sylvia Yount notes, when Shinn transitioned to working as an artist in a variety of media in New York, his "response to the urban spectacle encompassed the street subjects favored by the sensational metropolitan press—fires, accidents, and poverty—as well as the vaudeville theater."[119] At the same time as he was quoted in newspapers cursing Comstock during the Art Students League trial in 1906, Shinn also painted an orgy of nudes as murals in the Belasco Theater, adding his own contribution to the "urban spectacle."[120]

John Sloan was not in the news as much as Shinn, but his response was similarly vehement. After 1906, his etchings and drawings brought even greater attention to the "filthy" things Comstock thought should be private—or nonexistent. Although in his diary Sloan criticized the drawings in the *American Student of Art* as "indecently bad studies made under bad influences, no thought and no effort to say anything but copy, baldly, the model," he also called Comstock "ridiculous" and continued depicting censored subjects in following years.[121] In 1907, Sloan painted *Movies, Five Cents*, in which a rowdy Nickelodeon crowd watches a couple kiss on screen. And in future years, he devoted himself to political groups pitted against Comstock, making cartoons for the socialist newspaper *The Call* and later serving as art editor of *The Masses*, which represented a variety of radical causes but always took delight in skewering Comstock.[122] In the pages of *The Masses*, Anthony Comstock was "a symbol for all the forces of repression and ignorance they opposed."[123]

Another New York artist inspired by the events of 1906 was George Bellows. In that year, Bellows was moved to paint his first nude, *Nude: Miss Bentham* (figure 5.18 / plate 14). Bellows's life was intimately connected with the Art Students League. He married a League student,

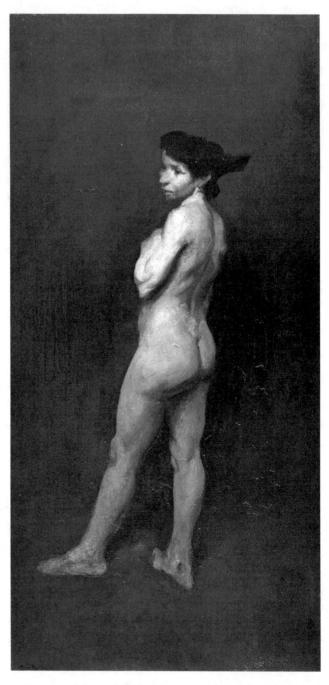

FIGURE 5.18 George Bellows, *Nude: Miss Bentham*, 1906. Oil on canvas, 181 × 89.5 cm. The Barber Institute of Fine Arts, University of Birmingham / Bridgeman Images. See also color plate 14.

Emma Louise Story, and later taught there. Here, in his extremely ambitious first painting of a nude, we engage the aesthetic of the artist's studio,
and the nude artist's model within it, free of idealization and stripped
bare of any mythological or allegorical justification. Her warm pink
skin and strong shadows suggest a woman who has not primped for the
occasion of her portrait, and the freely painted figure does not carry
the legitimizing technique of a classical or academic French approach.
The female figure even bears resemblance to the model depicted in the
American Student of Art, suggesting that Bellows might have hired the
same woman to pose for him.

For the next several years, Bellows continued to paint unembellished
nudes, sometimes on enormous canvasses, including *Forty-Two Kids*,
which attracted a fair amount of attention related to the frank nakedness
of its youthful male subjects. Critics discussed these paintings using
terms including "actuality," "alive," "representative," "vitality," and " 'actual
life.' "[124] However we might debate or define the artifice of realism or the
idea of representation today, it is undeniably true that many Americans
in the early twentieth century felt that seeing what previously had been
censored felt "real" and "modern" to them in that moment.[125]

Robert Henri in particular preached to his many students and followers "a compelling form of contemporary realism that depended less
on the imitation of an external 'reality' than on the ideal of an art that
was real in itself. This realism became a moral virtue, equated with truth,
honesty, and direct experience."[126] Unfortunately, patrons did not always
want to pay for art that looked so "real." In response to their own problems with censorship within the art world, Henri, Sloan, Bellows, Shinn,
and four other men exhibited their work together in a show called *Eight
American Painters* in February 1908 in New York, and then in cities across
the country. Their group became known as "The Eight," and later as the
"Ashcan School." With great savvy acquired from observing the effects
of censorship, the artists strategically capitalized on coverage of their
more controversial works to bring in viewers, in the best tradition of
Comstock's opponents.[127]

One of the foremost of those opponents was the anarchist Emma Gold-
man, who was a great influence on The Eight, and in particular on Robert
Henri.[128] In her essay "The Hypocrisy of Puritanism," Goldman asserted:
"The visionless and leaden elements of the old Young Men's and Women's
Temperance Unions, Purity Leagues, American Sabbath Unions, and the
Prohibition Party, with Anthony Comstock as their patron saint, are the
grave diggers of American art and culture."[129]

As the most influential and outspoken New York art teacher of his
generation for male, and especially for female, students, Henri infused his
philosophy of art with the radical politics of Goldman.[130] Both believed
that artists needed to be unshackled from censorship and all restraints
based on sex in order to tackle the realities of life in America in the twentieth century. In keeping with this philosophy, Henri sent both his male
and female students to downtown slums to view prostitution, destitution,
and "low" culture, day and night. He also painted censored subjects, as did
other artists of his circle in the years after 1906.

In 1909, Robert Henri painted two versions of *Salome*, inspired by "the
soprano Mary Gordon, [who was] . . . notable for her overtly sensual
interpretation and passionate acting" (figure 5.19 / plate 15). Censors had
forced the opera to close in a variety of theaters in New York beginning
in 1907, thus piquing Henri's interest in the outlaw subject.[131] His *Salome*
provocatively stares directly at us, as if to provoke our censorious response
to her bared flesh. For Henri, the pedigree of this scandalous subject
was impeccable: the opera was a controversial interpretation by Richard
Strauss of Oscar Wilde's already disreputable play, and the subject was
also a favorite of striptease halls and pornography. By 1909, "Salomania"
had taken hold, with actresses relentlessly compared as to their success at
the famed "dance of the seven veils."[132]

Given Henri's political ideals, it makes sense that in 1913 he wanted
to make a grand statement on behalf of freedom and truth for the most
important artistic event of his lifetime. The opportunity was the International Exhibition of Modern Art, known today simply as the Armory
Show. This massive display of painting, printmaking, and sculpture was
conceived by a small group of New York artists who sought to bring

FIGURE 5.19   Robert Henri, *Salome*, 1909. Oil on canvas, 77 ½ × 37 inches. Collection of The John and Mable Ringling Museum of Art the State Art Museum of Florida, Florida State University. (SN937). See also color plate 15.

together in one vast space all the strains of modernism that had been developing across Europe and the United States. For this purpose, they rented the cavernous space of the Sixty-Ninth Regiment Armory on Lexington Avenue, between Twenty-Fifth and Twenty-Sixth Streets, a fitting shift from more traditional art exhibition spaces in the city. Eventually, the number of works swelled to 1,400, and the number of visitors to 90,000.[133]

Henri helped with the initial planning stages for the exhibition, and in Paris saw the radical abstract nudes by Henri Matisse and Marcel Duchamp that were on their way to New York. In response, he hurriedly produced *Figure in Motion* (figure 5.20 / plate 16), a work that, for him, represented the best of American modernism.[134] In contrast to the angular, distant, and otherworldly nudes painted by European radicals, Henri's was a decidedly specific, unclothed, and unabashed young woman boldly striding toward the viewer on a massive scale.

In *Figure in Motion*, the model's bright red lips, bobbed hair, and confident stride all signify that she is not afraid of any accusation of moral deprivation or censorious judgment. Even more provocatively, Henri painted the work on such a large scale that on most walls the average viewer is confronted directly at eye height with a small tuft of pubic hair, this former signifier of pornography now simply represented as a modern assumption of freedom. Once again, in the wake of the League raid, the aesthetic of the life drawing and the projection of an unapologetic nude grounded in experience had been freed from captivity within the interior spaces of the professional art school.[135]

Even the last holdout of censored anatomy—the adult penis—came out of its loincloth and into the public sphere for the Armory Show in 1913. Arthur Lee, a student at the Art Students League in the years leading up to Comstock's raid (and later a teacher there), contributed a striking bronze male nude titled *The Ethiopian* (figure 5.21). The sculpture was widely understood to be a portrait of Jack Johnson, the first African American to win the world heavyweight boxing championship. Despite its anatomical specificity, the work failed to incite criticism or censorship and went on to win a gold medal at the Panama-Pacific International

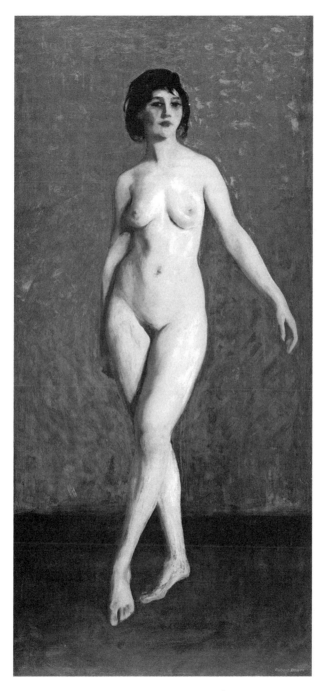

FIGURE 5.20 Robert Henri, *Figure in Motion*, 1913. Oil on canvas, 77 ¼ × 37 ¼ in. Daniel J. Terra Collection, Terra Foundation for American Art. (1999.69) Photo: Terra Foundation for American Art, Chicago / Art Resource, NY. See also color plate 16.

FIGURE 5.21 Arthur Lee, *The Ethiopian*, 1912. Bronze, 27 7/8" (overall). Museum purchase made possible by William T. Evans, William Franklin Paris, and Helen L. Spear, Smithsonian American Art Museum. (1990.30)

Exposition in 1915.[136] Even more than the Columbian Exposition, the Panama-Pacific was notorious for its excessive displays of nude art. Perhaps it is fitting that Comstock's life ended in the same year.

Young men were not the only artists to respond to the events of 1906. Thomas Eakins, for example, had spent a long career battling censorship, beginning in 1875 when the jury of the Centennial International Exhibition in Philadelphia relegated his now venerated *Gross Clinic* to the confines of a medical display. Eleven years later, he lost his position as director of the School of the Pennsylvania Academy of the Fine Arts for his unflinching coeducational program of study and photography of the nude.[137] In 1888, he directly challenged Comstock by testifying in a Philadelphia courtroom on behalf of seven men accused of selling indecent photographs. And in 1889, his masterpiece, the *Agnew Clinic*, offered a provocative bare breast at its fulcrum. As Jonathan Weinberg summarizes, "Eakins was above all an exhibitionist: as a realist par excellence he wants us to look at things rather than hide them."[138] Probably, then, it is no coincidence that Eakins began his most explicit painted image of a nude in 1907, shortly after the League trial.

For this feat, he revisited the theme of *William Rush and His Model*, which illustrated the scene of a young society woman posing for a venerable early-nineteenth-century Philadelphia sculptor (figure 5.22 / plate 17). Although Eakins had pointedly interpreted this scene on several occasions in the past, it was not until 1907 that he depicted the model with full frontal nudity, pubic hair, and an erasure of almost all the narrative elements in the work. The ship's scroll still stands in the foreground to remind us that the artist is Rush. Nevertheless, the model is decidedly no longer an allegorical figure.

With paint, the greatest tool in his arsenal, Eakins declared his kinship with the aesthetics and politics of the student drawings reproduced on pages 161 and 168 of the June issue of the *American Student of Art*.[139] The portly artist who bows to his muse while extending his hand maintains a respectable distance, albeit with an evocative mallet at his side. Indeed, the female figure for Eakins's last *Rush* (like Bellows's *Miss Bentham*) looks surprisingly like the model on page 161, with short dark hair and full hips.

FIGURE 5.22 Thomas Eakins, *William Rush and His Model*, 1907–1908. Oil on canvas, 35 ¼ × 47 ¼ in. (89.5 × 120 cm). Honolulu Museum of Art, Gift of the Friends of the Academy, 1947. (548.1). See also color plate 17.

Although the painting was never finished, the artist's intentions in 1907 are clear. For Eakins and The Eight, as for Mark Twain, Augustus Saint-Gaudens, Kenyon Cox, and many other artists and writers, censorship clearly produced mostly the reverse of its intentions. In the process, the coalition of those opposed to Comstock, and in favor of free expression, had grown in breadth and depth.

THE BITTER END

At the same time that the Art Students League debacle and its aftermath were unfolding, Comstock was also dealing with several other crises that made 1906 a nightmare for him. After the initial federal hearing in March

1906 at which Hugh Gordon Miller punched Comstock, J. J. Koch was convicted and sentenced to eighteen months in Sing Sing prison. Miller's client Ernest Richards, on the other hand, had his case dismissed by a federal commissioner, and then was acquitted of state charges after a jury trial. With typical tenacity, Comstock was unwilling to relent and, according to Miller, coerced Koch into making statements against his client. On July 24th, with new "testimony" in hand, and angry about his inability to bring Miller to justice for striking him, Comstock rearrested Richards. Miller again went on the attack, but this time threw more devastating blows than he had landed in March.

In court on October 17th, Miller cross-examined Comstock in his new case against Richards, with almost no reference to the charges currently under consideration. Instead, he intended to destroy Comstock's credibility and reputation by using information he had gleaned from a small network of defense attorneys united in their hatred and disdain for their nemesis. Miller set out to prove that Comstock was embezzling money from the NYSSV on a small scale through sales of office gifts, and to a much greater extent by defrauding the U.S. government through improper claims of travel expenses. Comstock did not have good answers to these charges, and Miller thus had served his friends in the press exactly what they wanted—yet another scandalous story involving the self-designated arbiter of American morality.[140] The accusations were covered extensively in newspapers across the country.

As usual, Comstock did not accept this negative coverage without a response. In a letter to the editor of the *New York Times* two days later, he denied everything, including being present in the courtroom for much of Miller's examination.[141] But Miller's final retort on November 25th was four times Comstock's in length. He started by offering a blistering assessment of Comstock's abuse of government travel fees: "there seems to be one standard of morals and of conscientious scruples with reference to art and such matters, and another standard of morals and conscience as to a little matter of money."

Miller then went on to address directly the growing sensibility that private vice-fighting was incompatible with Progressive Era ideals of good governance: "The Government employs a competent staff of conscientious Post Office Inspectors at New York as well as elsewhere, who are amply able to attend to this part of the Post Office business. After my experience and observations in connection with this particular trial I am convinced, however, that with Mr. Anthony Comstock with these matters it is merely a moneymaking business and a case of the "devil rebuking sin."[142] Comstock never was formally prosecuted on any of Miller's charges, but much damage was done to his reputation, and that of the NYSSV. Just as artists were no longer willing to accept the judgment of "unqualified" censors, Miller's battle was indicative of a similar movement on the part of defense attorneys. With the help of a great enemy against which to muster opposition, the Free Speech League was rapidly gathering steam.

As secretary of the Free Speech League in 1907, Theodore Schroeder published a "Statement of Contentions" in the *Albany Law Journal*, asserting that "the framers of the Constitution changed liberty of the press by permission, to Liberty as a right, because thus only can all citizens be protected in their proper opportunity to hear and read all that others have on offer, and without which freedom unrestricted there is no intellectual liberty at all as a matter of right." The purpose of this First Amendment language, as Schroeder defined it, was that citizens should enjoy access to the fullest presentation of "all that others have on offer" so that they could use their own informed reason in contributing as citizens to participatory democracy.[143] Schroeder's text in many places reads as a parallel legal evocation of the ideas of artists like Robert Henri, who felt a moral obligation to present the "real" as they understood it, unedited and, more importantly, without self-censorship.

Four years later, Schroeder authored the first trial manual for attorneys fighting obscenity prosecutions. In more than four hundred pages of legal analysis, *"Obscene" Literature and Constitutional Law: A Forensic Defense of Freedom of the Press* dissected the Comstock Acts, on the grounds of both "freedom of speech and of the press" and "due process of law."[144] Many of Schroeder's ideas were not new, but they were articulated more clearly and comprehensively than in the past, and many more lawyers were now reading and listening.

As Comstock's difficult year wound down to its bitter end, a variety of newspapers reported on December 29, 1906, that Comstock had been fired from his Post Office inspectorship, and that members of the Art Students League operating as the "Society for the Prevention of Anthony Comstock" were responsible for petitioning Washington officials for his removal.[145] Both stories turned out not to be true; instead, Postmaster General George B. Courtelyou stood by his agent and denied any suggestion that Comstock would be fired. Nevertheless, the enthusiasm with which the story was reported was telling. The general tenor seemed to be that Comstock's retirement was overdue.[146] The editors of the *Philadelphia Inquirer* summarized his beleaguered state with unusually sympathetic language: "The story that Anthony Comstock had been dismissed from his position as post office inspector turns out to be a cruel falsehood. No man is too virtuous for the shafts of calumny."[147] "Shafts of calumny" is an apt description for the assessments of Comstock that followed in the last decade of his life.

Comstock was by no means powerless after the debacle of 1906; nonetheless, if he ever allowed himself an honest moment of reflection on the year's events, it could not have been either pleasant or affirming. The following year, John D. Rockefeller declined to donate to the NYSSV, and for several years that followed, the society's patron list and total donations shrank to a small trickle. Critics and reporters increasingly associated Comstock's name with the promotion of vice, rather than its suppression. In June 1907, for example, an article on J. P. Morgan's outstanding art collection offhandedly noted: "Mr. Morgan probably knows as well as another that the presence of water doesn't necessarily make a horse thirsty. There are still plenty of Americans who couldn't be dragged into an art gallery unless Mr. Anthony Comstock had just been seen coming indignantly out of it."[148]

True to his character, Comstock did not go out without a fight. In his last years, he especially targeted homosexuals and women whom he considered to be "sex radicals." His blotter notations and annual reports also became more inflected with the anti-immigrant and isolationist sentiments generally taking hold among those who feared the loss of

Anglo-American cultural dominance. In the *Annual Report* for 1908, for instance, Comstock included a chart to show the "Nationality and Religious Creed of Persons Arrested." It was intended to sound an alarm about how many more foreigners were included in Volume III of his arrest blotters compared to the first two. He then expressed his hope that these numbers would "go far" in "sustaining our noble Commissioner of Immigration in his heroic efforts to keep undesirable classes from our shores."[149] The statistics regarding religion are by far the most startling, with arrests of "Hebrews" more than doubling from Volume II to Volume III, reflecting increased immigration as well as rising anti-Semitism.

Although Comstock's power and credibility were waning, his ability to destroy lives was still fearsome. One of the four defendants from Japan listed in Volume III was a young man named Kosen Takahashi. Comstock first arrested him in December 1909, when he was "caught in the act" of making forty-eight "pictures & sketches" of the "vilest" sort. Judging by other records of Takahashi's life, we may conjecture that the pictures Comstock referred to as "vilest" were homoerotic.[150] In the 1890s, Takahashi lived on the West Coast, where he "worked as an illustrator for the Japanese-language publication *Shin Sekai* and co-creator of the literary journal *Twilight*." Correspondence between Takahashi and Yone Noguchi, father of famed American sculptor Isamu Noguchi, suggests that the two were lovers in those years, and that Takahashi was deeply in love with Yone and heartbroken when the affair ended. The breakup, combined with the fierce prejudice faced by Japanese Americans on the West Coast, may have spurred Takahashi to move to New York sometime around 1903.[151] Although he was sentenced to thirty days in municipal jail in 1909, Takahashi managed to escape from custody, and lived as a "fugitive from justice" until Comstock arrested him again in July 1912. This time he served thirteen months in a penitentiary in Atlanta, and he died the following year in Saint Louis.[152] We will never know what contributions Takahashi might have made as an artist if Comstock had not prosecuted him for the crime of sketching and drawing erotic scenes.

Comstock was similarly unsympathetic and persistent in his pursuit of outspoken activists who campaigned for access to birth control in the early years of the twentieth century. One of his longest-running nemeses in these arguments was Emma Goldman. In 1906, Goldman was gingerly stepping back onto the national stage after two punishing decades of activism and retreat as a radical anarchist. During those years, she had been involved in a failed attempt to murder Henry Clay Frick, spent a year in Blackwell's State Penitentiary on the charge of "inciting to riot," studied nursing and midwifery in Europe, and been publicly vilified following accusations of complicity in the murder of President William McKinley by a fellow anarchist.

Ready to advocate for a less violent path to her agenda, Goldman joined forces with Theodore Schroeder, Leonard Abbott, Clarence Darrow, and others to help organize the Free Speech League in 1902, and also published *Mother Earth*, a journal devoted to disseminating the ideas of American and European provocateurs, including George Bernard Shaw, Marcel Proust, and Alexander Berkman. Comstock was a favorite topic in *Mother Earth*. In the very first issue, John R. Corvell compared his career with the "days of the Inquisition" and termed him "the arch enemy of society."[153] Comstock seized and burned several issues of *Mother Earth* during the course of its publication. His irritation and willingness to engage Goldman were undoubtedly fueled by her notoriety and influence, which of course in turn were vastly aided by his loud, attention-grabbing complaints.

Comstock had many reasons to be irritated in the last five years of his life, far beyond the biting criticism of activists such as Emma Goldman. At the NYSSV, his stalwart supporters were almost all dead. Morris Jesup had died in 1908, and Welcome Hitchcock in 1909. The society's arrest blotters after these years are filled with Comstock's rationalizations as to why cases were suspended or thrown out, or defendants ruled innocent. By the start of 1911, the NYSSV reported that it was $2,000 in debt and "the outlook was very dark and depressing."

Then, there was a bright spot. A "noble friend" appeared on the scene who anonymously paid the debt, and a new president took over the society after a year in which none was appointed, supposedly "in honor of" Hitchcock. The benefactor, Fred E. Tasker, whipped the NYSSV into shape by soliciting more donations, hiring more agents, and fundamentally shifting the working methods of the society. His main strategy to achieve all this turned out to be effective; Tasker first quietly signaled and then made it blatantly clear: Comstock's reign was over.[154]

In November 1913, an unusual blot appeared in the NYSSV's arrest records. Comstock crossed out an entry, which he had rarely done at any time during his entire career, and then wrote that the error was made because "of great pressure of business & constant interruption."[155] The intended reader of the post was undoubtedly John Saxton Sumner, who had recently been hired essentially to serve as the NYSSV's new Comstock. The transition was awkward, to say the least. Sumner's handwriting does not appear in Volume III until December 1914, more than a year after he was hired, and then Comstock took over briefly again. In January 1915, the society's *Annual Report* included a lengthy essay by Sumner, reporting on his first two years at the society. He never mentioned Comstock, but was obviously referring to him in smugly reporting that he had been able to shut down an offensive vaudeville show with "none of the objectionable publicity which sometimes accompanies the activities of this Society in regard to matters likely to attract public attention, and which sometimes militates against the effectiveness of our action by the advertising which it gives to the offensive matter."[156]

On June 13, 1915, the *New-York Tribune* ran a lengthy story on page 1, titled "Comstock's Rule in Vice Society Near Overthrow." The author, John J. Leary, Jr., described the NYSSV as an organization undergoing profound changes: "Whatever individual members of the society may think of the nude in art and undraped statuary, the society and its agents will not try to regulate questions of personal taste. That will be left for the individual to settle for himself. If he wishes a copy of a masterpiece in the Louvre or Tate galleries in his office or drawing room, that will be considered his own affair."

Leary described that the new direction of the organization had begun to bear fruit, with former members returning now that it was no longer a society of the "one-man class." The knives clearly were out. Either Tasker or Sumner, or both, provided inside dirt: "Comstock has protested against many changes. He has been as bitter in his charges of bulldozing at times to Fred E. Tasker, the president of the society, as he ever was to United States district attorneys who refused to do his bidding." Leary also reported that Comstock had been asked to resign but refused, accusing the district attorney's office of conspiring against him. When interviewed, lawyers in the D.A.'s office laughed at the accusation, but made "no effort, however, to conceal their amusement at the charge of satisfaction over Comstock's passing."[157]

Despite the ridicule and humiliation he faced on many fronts, Comstock was not done yet. In 1915, he took on Margaret Sanger, the century's most high-profile female advocate for birth control. Sanger had been indicted for her publication, *The Woman Rebel*, and fled to England to escape arrest. In doing so, she left behind her husband William Sanger, a painter and draftsmen for architectural firms, and their two children. Without Comstock's prosecutorial intervention, Margaret Sanger might not have made much of a mark.[158]

William and Margaret married in 1902 and "embarked on a life of decorous middle-class socialism" in Greenwich Village. As a public health nurse, she was an advocate of what she called "family limitation" and began writing about contraception in the socialist magazine *The Call*. When Comstock banned her column, "contraception turned into a free-speech issue and all of Greenwich Village jumped on board to protest Sanger's right to publish her views." Of course, Comstock had been suppressing birth control advocates and their literature for more than forty years, but now Sanger could rely on several overlapping networks of concerted anti-censorship activists, including attorneys, to help her cause.

Sanger came fully onto the national stage only in 1915, when Comstock decided to arrest William in an attempt to force her return.[159] He sent an agent early on the morning of January 19th to Sanger's apartment, who asked whether he had any copies of "Family Limitation." When Sanger produced the publication, he was taken into custody.[160] William Sanger's trial was high drama. The case was in the papers day after day, with birth control, censorship, suffrage, anarchism, and class politics seemingly on trial all at once. On September 10, 1915, the courtroom was packed. Emma Goldman's anarchist colleague and lover Alexander Berkman was there, as well as Leonard Abbott, head of the Free Speech League.

Sanger had brought a long statement "defending the doctrine of birth control and denouncing the law and 'Comstockery.'" When convicted and given the opportunity to just pay a small fine, Sanger jubilantly chose prison: "'The law is on trial here, not I,' cried the prisoner. 'I would rather be in jail with my convictions than free at the sacrifice of my manhood and self-respect, and under Comstock rule.'" The crowd burst into applause and cheers, and then held an indignation meeting in the corridor. Leonard Abbott vehemently decried "the right of the state to exercise dominion over the souls and bodies of our women by compelling them to go into unwilling motherhood," and declared that the Free Speech League already had the funds to publish a million copies of Sanger's pamphlet. Suffragists denounced the court for the burden the ban on information about birth control placed on the working classes.[161] Sexual speech had become indistinguishable from political speech. William Sanger was sentenced to thirty days or $150, and dramatically chose to take the thirty days. Margaret came home while he was still imprisoned in the Tombs.[162]

Two weeks later, Anthony Comstock abruptly died. His last entry in the NYSSV's Record of Arrests is dated September 10, 1915, the same day William Sanger was sentenced. The defendant was Allan van Slyke, charged with "indecent exposure . . . of private to 3 young girls in Morningside Park." Sumner penned in the result: "Acquitted—gave him benefit of doubt."[163] Newspapers credited the tension of the Sanger trial with exacerbating a previous illness, as well as the fact that Comstock had caught a cold while attending a purity conference in San Francisco, which developed into pneumonia. He died at home on September 21, 1915. The timing was auspicious. He had walked onto the public stage while prosecuting Victoria Woodhull, and now was leaving it while prosecuting Margaret Sanger.

Over the course of the following year, the trials initiated by Comstock ran their courses without him. Margaret Sanger was indicted by a United

States grand jury and then discharged by prosecutors overwhelmed by newspaper coverage of her cause.[164] Emma Goldman scorned Margaret Sanger for avoiding jail, although eventually she served time on other charges; Goldman herself chose to spend fifteen days in a prison workhouse for the crime of lecturing on birth control.[165] In 1916 as well, Margaret Sanger challenged New York State's laws by opening the nation's first family planning clinic in Brooklyn. It lasted only ten days, but Sanger managed to build on the publicity Comstock had first helped to provide to raise money, accrue allies, and eventually help to found Planned Parenthood with her compatriots.[166]

If the course of free speech in America demonstrates anything with clarity, it is that there certainly are times when a fierce and dogged opponent may in the end be a great gift. As Christine Stansell notes, the battle to protect free speech "linked artists, writers, and professionals of a progressive bent to working-class militants."[167] These factions disagreed on many subjects, but they all wanted the opportunity to be heard, and to be read. In following decades, that right has waxed and waned both in law and custom, but it never again has been as diminished as during the reign of Anthony Comstock.

At the time of his death, Comstock served in the public imagination not only as the embodiment of government censorship, but also as the greatest representative of a "Puritan." In 1910, the art critic Sadakichi Hartmann echoed Emma Goldman in complaining about the terrible effects of that legacy: "The artist as well as the public bear the troubled conscience of sinners . . . . Puritanism still deals out banishment, confiscation, punishment to unfettered poetic souls."[168] The truth of this damning critique is born out in Comstock's own words, and the evidence of his professional and personal life.

In the NYSSV's *Annual Report* for 1900, Comstock related the story of a sixteen-year-old girl who committed suicide. She left a note for her father quoted in the report: "Dear Papa: Do not be cross that I do this. A girl who has gone down as far as I have does not belong with good people. I have been at McGurk's three times and I can never go home again. Farewell and forgive me. Your sorrowing Emma." Two other girls the same week committed suicide under similar circumstances. Luc Sante writes that McGurk's, a saloon located in the Bowery, was called "Suicide Hall" because so many women who had reached desperate straits committed suicide there, including six girls in 1899 alone. Drinking carbolic acid was the most popular method. In the NYSSV's *Annual Report*, Comstock ascribed the deaths of all these girls to "reading light novels."[169]

Comstock also viewed child sex trafficking as largely the fault of the victims. In the *Annual Report* for 1912 Comstock placed the blame for "White Slavers" squarely on girls who had already been "dragged down to perdition by the perverted imagination. We recognize the fact that often the White Slaver forcibly entraps and imprisons young women in these dens, but the larger number are first debauched in mind before the physical downfall." "Some book or picture" secretly placed was the cause of the problem; "the trap is thus baited and set by the devil."[170] Comstock's self-aggrandizement as the savant on vice and its origins was matched only by his certainty that unmarried girls and women who engaged in sex, no matter the circumstance, deserved only judgmental scorn and condemnation. A final bitter irony is the impact of this burden even within his own home.

Although Comstock had achieved his bucolic ideal of a large home and gardens in New Jersey, many unpleasant problems yet remained within their small family. In the mid-twentieth century, the brilliant and brash journalist Ralph Ginzburg researched the Comstock family in preparation for a biography he never completed. Using formidable research skills, Ginzburg traced the childhood path of Adele, the daughter Comstock had informally adopted as a toddler. He discovered that shortly after Anthony's death, Maggie committed Adele to the Vineland Training Institute for Backward and Feeble-Minded Children. Ginzburg traveled there in 1959 and claimed to be a family member. As such, he was permitted to take notes on Adele's case files from the time she was admitted in 1917. Maggie and a family physician had completed the admissions paperwork. She reported that Adele in her teen years "began associating with persons of immoral character and maintaining illicit relationships with several young men." In 1912, she gave birth to an illegitimate child who lived one week and then died.

Five years later, a social worker transcribed Adele's confession that "she has been immoral since she was 19. Was promiscuous and does not know who was father of child. She mentions illegal relations with a nephew of her adopted mother, and other men . . . . She weeps as she tells her story. Is given to self pity." Adele's psychiatrist diagnosed that a somewhat low IQ combined with "heavy pressure at home" had caused her difficulties. He concluded that an unhappy home life had contributed to Adele's emotional problems; he noted: "She was apparently constantly picked on, battened down. Always told she was no good."[171]

The psychological evaluation of actors long dead is a futile endeavor. Nevertheless, it is fair to say that this was a "mysterious way" for God to move, indeed. Anthony Comstock had taken in a poor and starving child, and provided a home assuredly devoid of any of the "traps" he knew all too well. He had built a career as America's greatest moralist, including profuse instructions for righteous living. And yet, within his own home the debaucheries he had spent a lifetime combatting had taken place. In the world Anthony Comstock had helped to create, men and women continued to experience lust, masturbate, have illicit sex, use contraceptives, obtain abortions, and deliver illegitimate children. The chief consequence of Comstock's lifelong crusade was that all of this, even within his own home, was carried on with greater secrecy, shame, and psychic harm. Few authors of obituaries wished God had waited longer before calling him home.

CONCLUSION

....

Postmortem

A t the time of William Sanger's trial and Anthony Comstock's death, both in September 1915, nearly every observer
of American society and public health agreed that social
reform was necessary. Birth rates and infant mortality were perilously high
among immigrant populations swelled by war in Europe. Urban poverty
and disease were rampant, and in many cases poor young women had
few remunerative opportunities other than prostitution. While reformers
agreed on the need for change, the politics of how to accomplish it were
enormously divisive. Margaret Sanger, along with many other targets of
Comstock's prosecutions, believed that the answer lay in women's economic, political, sexual, and reproductive empowerment, which would
only be possible with free speech rights.[1] Her position was not new.

For decades, astute observers of the American scene including Walt
Whitman had noted the particular toll censorship had taken on women's
health and opportunities. In 1882, the year Whitman refused to bowdlerize
Leaves of Grass to facilitate its publication, he penned a brief essay on
censorship, "A Memorandum at a Venture." The essay begins with Whitman
comparing two "points of view" on the discussion of sexuality: one associated with Puritanism, and the other with pornography. This second point

of view was better than the first in Whitman's estimation because at least it was a "disease which comes to the surface, and therefore less dangerous than a concealed one."

In place of these two flawed discourses, Whitman believed America was ready for a new discussion of sexuality that would be redeemed "from its hitherto relegation to the tongues and pens of blackguards . . . as something not in itself gross or impure, but entirely consistent with the highest manhood and womanhood, and indispensable to both." A critical reason to do this was to end the repression of women. Whitman proclaimed in strong language: "To the movement for the eligibility and entrance of women amid new spheres of business, politics, and the suffrage, the current, prurient, conventional treatment of sex is the main formidable obstacle."[2] Many women (and some men) among Comstock's defendants, from Victoria Woodhull to Margaret Sanger, all agreed with Whitman that censorship of discourse about sexuality in America had devastating consequences for women in particular.

Comstock, in contrast, rejected both frank discussion about sexuality and any efforts towards female empowerment; he believed that the only solution to pressing social problems was the eradication of lust through suppression of erotic materials and birth control. The respective outcome of these two competing crusades should give pause to those who believe that Comstock's route was and still is the right way to go.

After 1916, Margaret Sanger regrouped, built her base of support through compromise and wise use of publicity, and eventually founded the American Birth Control League with allies in 1921. The league's successor organization, Planned Parenthood, today operates approximately seven hundred reproductive health services clinics throughout the United States. Despite a constant stream of threats to its survival by followers of Comstock's ideology, the organization enjoys broad support and seems likely to survive far beyond its first hundred years.

The NYSSV, on the other hand, continued to shrink from its already diminished state after 1915 to a condition of near irrelevance by 1920.[3] The organization finally shut its doors in obsolescence soon after the retirement of John Saxton Sumner, Comstock's successor, in 1950. Sumner's retirement may not have been by choice. In his last *Annual Report*, published in 1948, he recorded only $1,459 in donations and an operating loss of approximately $6,500 for the year.[4] Beyond the narrow question of institutional legacies, we may also wonder about the success of the cultural causes to which Sanger and Comstock were devoted.

On the birth control front, Andrea Tone points out that even at the height of Comstock's career, as he shoveled hundreds of thousands of rubber goods into incinerators, "an abundance of evidence" demonstrates that although "not openly endorsed, contraceptives were nonetheless accepted as Americans of all backgrounds created a zone of tolerance in which birth control was routinely made, sold, bought, and used."[5] Efforts to suppress birth control providers ultimately enhanced public support for family planning. A contemporary editorial noted of Margaret Sanger's incarceration in 1916: "Instead of squelching the doctrine preached by her, public sentiment is being strongly aroused in her favor."[6]

Similarly, American visual culture indisputably was filled with far more sexual images at Comstock's death than at the beginning of his career, notwithstanding his forty-three years of concerted efforts to eradicate them. Comstock himself traced the course of this path in 1902: "There are many living to-day who can remember the first production upon the stage of the 'Black Crook,' who will recall the storm of indignation which its gross features aroused. That was an entering wedge. Little by little since then, the managers of play-houses have been catering to depraved tastes, until, now, things indescribably vile are placed upon the public stage to meet the demands of a debauched public taste and desire. Dives of blackest hue are run openly, patronized by well-dressed persons, persons often moving in decent society and in the churches, who sneak into these abominable pest holes for personal entertainment."[7]

The situation had degenerated further between 1902 and 1915, with new technologies catering to the "debauched" tastes of far wider swaths of American society. Comstock lived just long enough to see the effect these fast shifts in popular entertainments had on the law. As Geoffrey Stone notes, in *United States v. Kennerley* (1913), Judge Learned Hand began the process of dismantling the language of the *Hicklin* rule, "noting that however 'consonant' that standard might 'be with mid-Victorian morals,' it 'does not seem to me to answer to the understanding and morality of the present time.'"[8] Comstock was at least partially responsible for these developments, so anathema to his cause.

In its lengthy obituary in 1915, the *New York Times* assessed the mixed results of Anthony Comstock's campaigns: "Few have attempted to criticize Mr. Comstock for his efforts to suppress books and pictures manifestly intended to be sold chiefly for their licentious character." He did cause great controversy, however, "because of the differences of opinion over what constituted the dividing line between indecency and art. Where public opinion and the courts held that Mr. Comstock had been wrong in finding evil in what purported to be art, the controversy was the finest of advertising."[9] The Art Students League case and the 1915 failed effort to suppress reproductions of Paul Chabas's saccharine painting of a nude young woman bathing in a stream, *September Morn*, were the two cases most often cited in assessing the pyrrhic successes of Comstock's life's work.

Certainly, we should not dismiss Comstock's effectiveness. Self-censorship was rampant during his era. As Geoffrey Stone summarizes, "Prudish editors routinely excised even relatively tame sexual references."[10] Galleries, museums, and art collectors in many cases made similar bowdlerizing choices. For many of Comstock's defendants, prosecution was little different in effect than the Inquisition or the witch trials of Salem. At Comstock's insistence, old men like Ezra Heywood were put to work at hard labor for publishing their political views; more than a dozen defendants chose suicide over imprisonment; and gay men served horrific sentences far longer than other defendants on the basis of similar "crimes." The persecution was no less real when it was internalized, as for example in the cases of the teenage girls Comstock cited who committed suicide because they believed that their sins were irredeemable. Heywood Broun summarized the thoughts of many who reflected on the consequences of Comstock's work: "It is not lustful thoughts which mar human personality, but only the sense of shame. Comstock spread shame about very widely and it was a force much more debilitating than any exotic notions which might have come from the books he seized."[11]

In "Puritanism as a Literary Force," H. L. Mencken decried that there had been broad support for the cause of censorship: "jury after jury has acquiesced in this; it was old Anthony's boast, in his last days, that his percentage of convictions, in 40 years, had run to 98.5 percent."[12] Mencken's assertion reflects his acceptance of Charles Gallaudet Trumbull's aggrandizing and frankly incorrect statements about Comstock's effectiveness. Even the fiercely incisive Mencken could not draw perfect conclusions from flawed data. In fact, Comstock's conviction percentage at its height, between 1887 and 1891, was 76 percent, with only 11 percent of defendants sentenced to jail. Between 1912 and 1915, his conviction rate fell to 40 percent, with only forty-five defendants in a four-year period serving jail time.[13]

Anthony Comstock is still a hero to some evangelicals, particularly for his long campaign against sexual health information, birth control, and abortion. For these purposes, Trumbull's hyperbolic text has been revived and treated as a record of fact by those who wish to valorize him.[14] We should all be awed by the depth of Comstock's faith, but facts matter, and I hope that even those who believe a return to Comstockery is a good idea will consider the vast evidence in *Lust on Trial* that disproves much of the success Trumbull claimed.

Trumbull, and indeed almost everyone else who has written about Comstock, has relied on Comstock's own self-aggrandizing numbers of defendants punished, published in the NYSSV's annual reports. But his arrest blotters are far more truthful. American judges and juries, far more often than Comstock liked to admit publicly, threw out his cases or assessed paltry fines.[15] Perhaps Comstock felt the need in those weighty tomes to be honest in penning what he must have seen as essentially a record of the damned. In Comstock's mind, those many, many "foxy" and "vile" defendants who escaped punishment surely were headed for hell. With all the details he provided of their lives, addresses, and crimes, God would know exactly where to find them. Nevertheless, there were fewer of them than Comstock would have liked to admit.

Mencken was more clear-sighted in recognizing the effects Comstock's legislative campaigns had in fostering the evangelical political opportunism that remains with us today. "The moral gladiators, in brief, know the game," Mencken wrote. "They come before a legislature with a bill ostensibly designed to cure some great and admitted evil, they procure its enactment by scarcely veiled insinuations that all who stand against it must be apologists for the evil itself, and then they proceed to extend its aims by bold interferences, and to employ it as a means of persecution, terrorism and blackmail."[16] These obfuscating and disingenuous politics are with us still.

Despite all of the suffering caused by Comstock and the NYSSV, "vice" as they defined it persisted, and in fact thrived. Whether we believe that censorship as a practice is right or wrong, or that sexually explicit images are helpful or harmful, the story of Comstock's efforts undeniably calls into question the efficacy of trying to control morality and sexuality by statute and prosecution. Comstock's ultimate failure lay chiefly in the single-mindedness of his desire to serve as a "weeder in the garden of the Lord." He was entirely unable to assess the power of the oppositional forces that amassed in resistance to his efforts to make America a more Christian nation. Rather than build his power by cultivating allies and broader support through compromise, he smugly insisted on the perfection of his own point of view and unique authority to certify right from wrong. "We the people," then as now, held far greater power than Comstock ever could, bolstered a by a growing class of civil servants like Henry G. Pearson who were committed to the rational and professional rule of law.

The story of the evolution of free speech and due process rights in America has largely been told as a twentieth century tale. Comstock's story, however, shows that the modern conceptualization of these civil liberties has deep roots in American history.[17] As Lyman Beecher well knew from the era of the early republic, many Americans carried forward a founding libertarian and "sceptical [sic]" narrative of freedom from government interference. In light of this history, we should make sure to remember that Comstock's era was an aberration from the American norm, not a baseline from which civil libertarianism evolved.

Comstock and the NYSSV, however, are unquestionably pivotal figures in this story. The National Defense Association in 1878 and Free Speech League in 1902 were organized specifically to raise awareness of constitutional rights and to fund lawyers who defended clients prosecuted under the Comstock laws. These organizations served as precursors to the National Civil Liberties Bureau in 1917 and then, in 1920, the American Civil Liberties Union.

Well beyond these formal organizations, surviving court records and newspaper accounts of Comstock's many trials prove that the nation's civil libertarianism and First Amendment ethos went far beyond the names we know of committed attorneys like Edward Chamberlain, Theodore Schroeder, and Clarence Darrow. Even in Comstock's earliest cases, we see long forgotten lawyers like William F. Howe and Henry D. Wireman demanding many of the statutory and procedural practices officially recognized in celebrated court cases of the twentieth century. During Comstock's time, both individual criminal defense attorneys and those who were members of professional organizations promoting civil liberties worked diligently to expand the rights of defendants, even when their "crimes" were roundly condemned in the court of public opinion.

These attorneys, brilliant at times, demanded that jury members be permitted to examine all the evidence and that testimony from expert witnesses be heard and entered into the record. Artistic and scientific merits were proffered as exculpatory justification, and contemporary community standards were invoked. The principles of separation of church and state, protection from unwarranted search and seizure, the right to privacy, and freedom from entrapment were all cited by attorneys defending Comstock's clients, even when these concepts were not articulated with the same language used in courts today nor recognized as concepts applicable to their clients' defense. The sheer, massive volume of cases initiated by Comstock, as well as his often suspect investigatory tactics, dramatically accelerated the evolution in American law of all these legal concepts. Ironically and significantly, Comstock can be credited almost single-handedly with instigating the foundations of a First Amendment Bar.

Ultimately, the language of the Comstock laws was so expansive, subjective, and difficult to articulate and enforce that prosecutors and judges turned their attention to more easily won cases. In 1964, ninety years after Comstock's successful lobbying trip to Washington, Justice Potter Stewart admitted defeat in his attempt to define a judicial standard for obscenity. He famously wrote: "I shall not today attempt further to define the kinds of material I understand to be embraced within that shorthand description [of "hardcore pornography"]; and perhaps I could never succeed in intelligibly doing so. . . . But I know it when I see it."[18] Stewart's oft-quoted line is an implicit acknowledgment that the determination of "obscenity" is inherently subjective, that it inevitably resides in the eye (and groin) of the beholder.

Stewart's honest but ultimately unhelpful "definition" of obscenity never had the force of law and in any case was soon superseded by the three-part test adopted by the Supreme Court in *Miller v. California* in 1973.[19] Nonetheless, in thinking about the role of arts and letters in this story, we should take seriously an important logical extension of Stewart's famous statement: if we know it when we see it, it also is true that we *can't* know it *until* we see it. Producers of visual and literary culture played a critical role in defining the bright line between acceptable and unacceptable culture throughout Comstock's career. The works of some of our greatest artists, photographers, and writers, including Augustus Saint-Gaudens, Thomas Eakins, John Sloan, George Bellows, Robert Henri, Napoleon and Otto Sarony, Benjamin Falk, Mark Twain, and Walt Whitman, recorded, reflected, expressed, interpreted, and shaped attitudes toward gender, sexuality, class, ethnicity, and race, as well as the vibrancy of constitutional ideals in our democracy. Patrons and consumers added their voices as well, helping to shape American culture through the choices they made of what to view, buy, and disseminate. For those who found and represented the edge of acceptability, whether for profit, politics, or artistic passion, each act of pushing against restraint changed the possibilities that lay ahead.

It is fair to ask, with the benefit of the hindsight provided by Comstock's story, how much good and lasting work could have been accomplished if all his fierce energy and passion and the abundant resources of his backers had been used to promote virtue, rather than criminalize and punish "vice." In 1873, when the YMCA chose to cast out its Committee for the Suppression of Vice, the organization's leaders made a deliberate decision about where to expend their time and efforts. The choice to advocate for and fund a punitive society whose aim was to incarcerate and incinerate was, for the YMCA, the road not taken. Those leaders who disassociated themselves from Comstock and the work of vice suppression chose instead to focus on providing safe housing, moral instruction, and healthy alternative entertainments for young men.

This rift did not take place in a vacuum, but rather reflected a broader shift in Protestantism at the time. While Comstock and his supporters continued to see themselves as avengers of Christ in the battle against evil, YMCA leaders instead took a less punitive turn toward the newer ideal of "Social Christianity," which sought to "reorient Protestant ethics to the needs of a newly industrialized society," thus spurring the creation of an enormous number of benevolent charities aimed at addressing specific societal needs. Responding to the ministry of progressives like Henry Ward Beecher, "the sympathizing Jesus gradually replaced the Christ of Calvary."[20]

By adopting the ideals of Social Christianity, consistently recognizing changes in society, and adapting to meet the needs of new and broader populations over the course of decades, the YMCA gained allies and evolved into an effective and far-reaching charitable organization that has made an extraordinary difference in the lives of millions. The lesson that Comstock offers us today is that those who devote their time and talents to educational and social welfare organizations ultimately have far more potential to influence national culture and individual lives than judgmental crusaders.[21]

Finally, we may observe that vague laws relying on subjective opinion always result in unequal application based on prevailing power structures and prejudices. Anthony Comstock's laws, which were disproportionately applied through a century of American history to the most vulnerable citizens of the day, offer a profound cautionary tale about legal efforts to "purify" the nation and their unintended but inevitable consequences. His fierce efforts and their outcomes prove that while it is certainly possible to put lust on trial, the effort is ultimately fruitless. A better democracy, capable of addressing our many challenges, cannot be achieved through censorship. In its place, we should invest our time and resources wisely in building our nation's intellectual, social, critical, creative, physical, spiritual, and self-reflective capacities. Our endurance as a democratic nation will be determined far more by our openness, our honesty, and our empathy than by our purity.

ACKNOWLEDGMENTS

....

Wwith great optimism in 2007, my husband Frederick Lane
and I decided to write a book together. Our first and
only thought was that we would write a biography of
Anthony Comstock. We had both mentioned him briefly in the books
we had just finished, and, given his significance, he seemed relatively
understudied in recent years. The project seemed promising given Fred's
expertise in the history of law and technology and my own prior experience writing about American visual culture through an interdisciplinary
lens. The goal of writing together unfortunately fell apart for a variety of
reasons, but our mutual fascination with the subject survived. This book is
largely the result of an in-house seminar in which I have been fortunate
to engage with a consummate expert in the fields of law, technology, and
efforts to police American morals. At the same time, I have benefited
from a husband who is an infinitely supportive, compassionate, patient,
and helpful partner and companion. Needless to say, this book would not
exist without Fred.

When I first branched out on my own in 2008 to undertake a book
about Comstock rooted in my specialization as an art historian, mentors
including David Lubin and Marc Simpson gave me initial advice as I began

to flesh out my research questions. I am also grateful for early and generous support from my colleagues at Saint Michael's College, my academic home from 1994 to 2013, including Jeffrey Trumbower, Susan Ouellette, George Dameron, Douglas Slaybaugh, James Millard, and Peter Harrigan. At the Fashion Institute of Technology (FIT), to which I moved in 2013, Anna Blume, the late Adam Gray, Deborah Stein, Ellen Brennan-Hearn, Giacomo Oliva, Patrick Knisley, David Drogin, Sam Albert, and Nanja Andriananjason were cheerful and helpful in supporting my scholarship efforts. Andrew Weinstein, Daniel Levinson-Wilk, Lourdes Font, and Justine De Young at FIT all contributed their expertise in answering specific questions regarding writing, history, and especially fashion. David Drogin and Patrick Knisley were instrumental in funding the costs of rights and reproductions. Parts of chapter 5 were honed for publication in "The Crime of the Nude: Anthony Comstock's Raid on the Art Students League of New York and the Origins of Modern American Obscenity" in *Winterthur Portfolio* under the expert guidance of Amy Earls.

Extra special thanks are owed to colleagues at the Kinsey Institute for Research in Sex, Gender, and Reproduction, at which I spent several weeks during two separate trips. Expert guidance from Catherine Johnson-Roehr, Garry Milius, and Shawn C. Wilson contributed immeasurably to *Lust on Trial*. Likewise, I spent a wonderfully productive summer as a Senior Fellow at the Smithsonian American Art Museum in 2010, and while there benefited from the guidance of Eleanor Jones Harvey, William Truettner, Amelia Goerlitz, the late and truly great Cynthia Mills, and Douglas Litts. Liza Kirwin served as an ideal liaison to the Archives of American Art. Alan Wallach also generously took the time to discuss my project with me at length in Washington that summer.

A year teaching and traveling in China as a Fulbright Scholar in 2011–2012 gave me enormous insight into the ways pervasive government-sponsored censorship can permeate a society, and especially educational institutions. Seasoned Fulbright officers, including Nathan Keltner and Victoria Augustine, and delightful colleagues and students at Guangdong University of Foreign Studies all contributed to making this a productive, safe, and joyful year for our entire family. In 2013, I was again fortunate to take part in an illuminating scholarly opportunity as a participant in a National Endowment for the Humanities Summer Institute at Bard Graduate Center for Decorative Arts, Design History, and Material Culture. The topic, "American Material Culture: Nineteenth-Century New York," brought together brilliant faculty, fellow scholars, and artists. During our weeks of study, I gained inspiration and advice on this project from generous colleagues, including the late and much missed David Jaffee, Catherine Whalen, Joshua Brown, Katherine Grier, Jessica Lautin, Julia Cathleen Ott, Diana Greenwold, and Dael Norwood, among many others.

Tracking down the records of Comstock's life and the surviving examples of his censorship campaigns required extensive travel to archives across the country, during which time numerous individuals offered kind assistance, including Stephanie Cassidy at the Art Students League of New York; Elizabeth Call and Chela Scott Weber at the Brooklyn Historical Society; Eric Robinson and Marybeth Kavanagh at the New-York Historical Society; Judith Ellen Johnson, Nancy Finlay, Barbara Austen, Susan Shoelwer, and Sierra Dixon at the Connecticut Historical Society; Carolyn M. Picciano and Mel E. Smith at the Connecticut State Library; Janet Lindstrom and Sharon Turo at the New Canaan Historical Society; Harry Miller at the Wisconsin Historical Society; Ryan Bean, Louise Merriam, Dagmar Getz, and David Klaasen at the Kautz Family YMCA Archives and Social Welfare History Archives at the University of Minnesota; Kim Reynolds and Sean Casey at the Boston Public Library; David Warrington and Lesley Schoenfeld at the Harvard Law School Library; Thomas A. Horrocks, Emily Walhout, and Wallace Dailey at Houghton Library, Harvard University; Marilyn Dunn and Lynda Leahy at the Schlesinger Library, Radcliffe College; Samantha Nelson and Brian LeMay at the Bostonian Society; Jane Becker at the Massachusetts Historical Society; Nancy Horan and Paul Mercer at the New York State Library; David J. Kelly at the Library of Congress; Bill Creech at the National Archives and Records Administration; Tripp Brinkley and Jennifer Lynch at the United States Postal Service; Diana Thompson and Bruce Weber at the National Academy of Design; Katherine Ott at the National Museum of American History; Leonora Gidlund, Kenneth Cobb, and Barbara Hibbert at the Municipal

Archives of the City of New York; Elizabeth Watts Pope and Paul J. Erickson at the American Antiquarian Society; Trina Yeckley and Kevin Reilly at the National Archives at New York City; Laetitia Barbier at the Museum of Morbid Anatomy; Gina Piastuck, Head of the Long Island Collection at the East Hampton Library; and Jeanne Solensky at the Winterthur Library. Roderick Bradford, Michael Ravnitzky, Nicola Beisel, and Henry Voigt all served as helpful correspondents offering their knowledge on related areas of my research.

Travel to these collections was facilitated by generous faculty development grants from Saint Michael's College and FIT, as well as travel grants from the New England Regional Fellowship Consortium, Gilder Lehrman Institute of American History, University of Minnesota Libraries, and New York State Library. I am grateful for the gracious hospitality, during my stay in Massachusetts, of Kate and Matt Van Sleet in Somerville. Keith and Penny Pillsbury were exemplary hosts and supportive friends through difficult times when they served as my hosts in beautiful Burlington, Vermont. Thanks also are due to Glenda and Harvey Werbel, who allowed me to hide out in their beautiful home for two months while I completed the first draft of the text in 2016. Their home could not have been a better place to flee all distractions and bring this project nearly to completion.

In the final writing phase of this project, once again I was fortunate to benefit from many wise and generous colleagues. Sylvia Yount and I cofounded a New York City American art history reading group in 2014 together with scholars and curators including Katherine Manthorne, Sally Webster, Jennifer Wingate, Randall Griffey, Bruce Weber, Connie Choi, Kimberly Orcutt, Michele Bogart, Jillian Russo, Isabel Taube, Matthew Postal, Michael Lobel, Margaret Laster, Harriet Senie, Lisa Peters, Peter Hayes Mauro, Anne Monahan, and Elizabeth Hutchinson. Conversations about new books and exhibitions in our field with this seasoned group have added considerable perspective to my own writing project. I have also profited from general advice provided by an extremely collegial and expert group of fellow writers working in the Allen Room at the New York Public Library (NYPL), including most notably Susan Jacoby.

NYPL collections, librarians, and staff, including Kyle R. Triplett and Melanie Locay, contribute to making the NYPL the best place in the world to write a book requiring constant access to primary and secondary sources.

During these many years, I relied as well on research assistants to help with some of the more tedious aspects of my archival excavations. Ryan La Rochelle spent a year as my work-study student at Saint Michael's College, during which time he downloaded hundreds of newspaper articles from the *New York Times Archive* and the *Chronicling America Historical Newspapers* database and organized them with meticulous care, while also working on his excellent senior thesis on censorship efforts following the assassination of William McKinley. My son Emmett Werbel tackled a similar task, retrieving and organizing relevant articles in the *Brooklyn Daily Eagle*. Shelby Superneau added copious research to my files regarding Emilie Martin and Comstock's relationship with the Woman's Christian Temperance Union in the course of writing her own excellent senior thesis. Kevin D. Steele organized hundreds of photographs I took at the Library of Congress into manageable PDF files. Molly Schoen at FIT provided expert help in finding promising collections of relevant materials, as well as securing rights and reproductions. Her patient and diligent efforts are much appreciated. Editors and peer reviewers at *Common-Place Journal, Winterthur Portfolio*, and Panorama including Susan Schoelwer, Amy Earls, Ellen Wiley Todd, Sally Webster, and Kevin Murphy provided wise guidance and assistance in publishing some previous essays on this material. Whitney Johnson, Miriam Grossman, and Marielle Poss provided gracious and timely support at Columbia University Press, in addition to Ben Kolstad at Cenveo Publisher Services, who oversaw production of *Lust on Trial* with professionalism and efficiency.

Throughout this project, individuals both dead and alive provided motivation for me to continue with this effort through the inspiration of their examples and stories, including many of the defendants and defense attorneys I was privileged to write about. Ralph Ginzburg's brilliant, fierce, and regrettably unfinished efforts to promote free speech by writing about Comstock in the mid-twentieth century nevertheless resulted in a treasure trove of materials I was fortunate to consult in the Wisconsin Historical Society. I was privileged also to interview his wife and creative partner Shoshana Ginzburg as part of this project, and her example and staunch friendship continued to provide great affirmation in the years since. I was grateful to be able to share a draft of this ms. with her before her unfortunate passing.

Finally, I would like to acknowledge the superlative combination of support and wise guidance I received from several devoted readers of this manuscript as it evolved, including Jonathan Weinberg, Joshua Brown, Daniel Levinson Wilk, and Michael Ravnitzky, and most especially Ellen Handler Spitz, who embodies the finest traditions of scholarship in every possible way. All of these kind and dedicated readers provided valuable advice as I grappled with the structure and substance of my argument. Geoffrey Stone demonstrated enormous generosity when he took the time to review a late draft of the manuscript. My editor at Columbia University Press, Philip Leventhal, has remained an enthusiastic supporter of this project from the outset. I am enormously honored and grateful to him for accepting the challenge of publishing *Lust on Trial* and for working with me for several years to improve the manuscript. To all of these individuals and organizations, I offer my profound gratitude.

ABBREVIATIONS

....

AC   Anthony Comstock

CFI   Case Files of Investigations, Postal Service Inspectors, General
          Records of the Post Office Department, Record Group 28;
          National Archives Building, Washington, DC, National
          Archives and Records Administration

Kautz   Kautz Family Young Men's Christian Association Archives,
          University of Minnesota Libraries

NYSSV   New York Society for the Suppression of Vice

RGP   Ralph Ginzburg Papers (1848–1988), Wisconsin Historical Society
          Library and Archives MSS 862 (Boxes 1–7 contain the files of
          Theodore Schroeder; Boxes 7–12 hold Ginzburg's own research
          files)

ROA   Report of Persons Arrested Under the Auspices of the New York
          Society for the Suppression of Vice, Library of Congress
          Manuscript Division, MSS34587; MMC-3288

YMCA   Young Men's Christian Association

NOTES

·············

INTRODUCTION

1. "Brooklyn's Elite Aghast," *New York World* (Evening Edition), September 21, 1888, 1.
2. Ibid; and "Photos Seized," *Brooklyn Daily Eagle*, September 22, 1888, 6.
3. "Died in Exile," *Brooklyn Daily Eagle*, October 24, 1889, 6.
4. This phenomenon fits within a broader American tradition. Stephen M. Feldman notes that "countervailing" traditions of dissent and suppression "have persisted throughout the course of American history and have contributed to the experience and understanding of free expression." Stephen M. Feldman, *Free Expression and Democracy in America: A History* (Chicago: University of Chicago Press, 2008), 3–4.
5. Charles Gallaudet Trumbull, *Anthony Comstock, Fighter: Some Impressions of a Lifetime of Adventure in Conflict with the Powers of Evil* (New York: Fleming H. Revell, 1913); Heywood Broun and Margaret Leech, *Anthony Comstock: Roundsman of the Lord* (New York: A. & C. Boni, 1927); Anna Louise Bates, *Weeder in the Garden of the Lord: Anthony Comstock's Life and Career* (Lanham, MD: University Press of America, 1995).
6. These include the Ralph Ginzburg Papers, Wisconsin Historical Society [hereafter RGP] (Ginzburg prepared research files to write a biography of Anthony Comstock, but never completed the project); and Case Files of Investigations, Postal Service Inspectors, General Records of the Post Office Department, Record Group 28, National Archives Building, Washington, DC [hereafter CFI]. Many newspaper articles quoted are clippings within RGP or have been accessed at the following digital sites: National Endowment for the Humanities and Library of Congress, *Chronicling America: Historic American Newspapers*, http://chroniclingamerica.loc.gov/; *New York Times Article Archive, 1851–1980*, http://query.nytimes.com/search/sitesearch/#//; Brooklyn Public Library, *Brooklyn Daily Eagle, 1841–1955*, http://bklyn.newspapers.com/title_1890/the_brooklyn_daily_eagle/; and *New-York Tribune*, archived at www.fultonhistory.com.

7. Helen Lefkowitz Horowitz, *Rereading Sex: Battles Over Sexual Knowledge and Suppression in Nineteenth-Century America* (New York: Vintage, 2003); Donna Dennis, *Licentious Gotham: Erotic Publishing and Its Prosecution in Nineteenth-Century New York* (Cambridge: Harvard University Press, 2009); Geoffrey R. Stone, *Sex and the Constitution: Sex, Religion, and Law from America's Origins to the Twenty-First Century* (New York: Liveright, 2017).

8. Helen Freshwater notes: "In some parts of the world censorship can be equated, all too literally, with death. Incarceration, death, and disappearance possess an inarguable finality." Helen Freshwater, "Towards a Redefinition of Censorship," in *Censorship and Cultural Regulation in the Modern Age*, ed. Beate Müller (New York: Rodopi, 2003), 240.

9. For a concise overview of theories about censorship, see Robert C. Post, "Censorship and Silencing," in *Censorship and Silencing: Practices of Cultural Regulation*, ed. Robert C. Post (Los Angeles: Getty Research Institute, 1995), 1–12. Another excellent compilation of essays on censorship theory is Beate Müller, ed., *Censorship and Cultural Regulation in the Modern Age* (New York: Rodopi, 2003).

10. I am grateful for Helen Freshwater's expansive "redefinition" of censorship, which "acknowledges that censorship is a process, realised through the relationships between censorious agents, rather than as a series of actions carried out by a discrete or isolated authority." Freshwater, "Towards a Redefinition," 225.

11. Richard Meyer, *Outlaw Representation: Censorship and Homosexuality in Twentieth-Century American Art* (New York: Oxford University Press, 2002), 13.

12. Catherine Cocks, "Rethinking Sexuality in the Progressive Era," *The Journal of the Gilded Age and Progressive Era* 5, no. 2 (April 2006): 96.

13. Whitman lived at 99 Ryerson Street, and Comstock at 354 Grand Avenue, both in Brooklyn.

14. David S. Reynolds, *Walt Whitman's America: A Cultural Biography* (New York: Vintage Books, 1996), 35.

15. Ibid, 203.

16. Ibid, 482.

17. Stone, *Sex and the Constitution*, 91.

1. ANTHONY COMSTOCK: FROM CANAAN TO GOTHAM

1. Quoted in Heywood Broun and Margaret Leech, *Anthony Comstock: Roundsman of the Lord* (New York: A. & C. Boni, 1927), 39.

2. Geoffrey R. Stone, *Sex and the Constitution: Sex, Religion, and Law from America's Origins to the Twenty-First Century* (New York: Liveright, 2017), 13–14.

3. "Address by Mr. Anthony Comstock," *Historical Account of the Celebration of the One Hundred and Fiftieth Anniversary of the Organization of the Congregational Church of New Canaan, Conn. June 20, 1883* (Stamford, CT: Gillespie Brothers, 1883), 96.

4. "Opening Remarks by the Chairman, Mr. A. B. Davenport," *Historical Account of the Celebration of the One Hundred and Fifteeth Anniversary of the Organization of the Congregational Church of New Canaan, Conn. June 20, 1883* (Stamford, CT: Gillespie Brothers, 1883), 7–8.

5. Leslie Young, "Notes on the Second School District," *The New Canaan Historical Society Annual* 2, no. 2 (June 1948): 49, 54; and "The Map of the Homesteading Period of Canaan Parish Circa 1772," *The New Canaan Historical Society Annual* 1, no. 2 (June 1944): 26. For genealogies of the Lockwoods and Comstocks, see Frederick A. Holden and E. Dunbar

Lockwood, *Descendants of Robert Lockwood. Colonial and Revolutionary History of the Lockwood Family in America from A.D. 1630* (Philadelphia: privately printed, 1889); and Johns Adams Comstock, *A History and Genealogy of the Comstock Family in America* (Los Angeles: privately printed, 1949), 1, 99.

6. Mary Louise King, *Portrait of New Canaan: The History of a Connecticut Town* (New Canaan: New Canaan Historical Society, 1981), 120.

7. New Canaan's enfranchised men voted 96 to 35 against Connecticut's more nondenominational revised state constitution in 1818—one of only two towns in Fairfield County to do so. King, *Portrait of New Canaan*, 135.

8. Isabel C. Cutler, "A History of the Fourth, or Old Church, School District of Canaan Parish and New Canaan," *New Canaan Historical Society Annual* 2, no. 2 (June 1948): 27.

9. Charlotte Chase Fairley, "A History of New Canaan 1801–1901," in *Readings in New Canaan History* (New Canaan, CT: The New Canaan Historical Society, 1949), 262.

10. John G. Pennypacker, "The Comstock-Burnham House," *Landmarks of New Canaan* (New Canaan, CT: The New Canaan Historical Society, 1951), 69.

11. Thomas and Roger were born in 1847 and 1849, then Caroline in 1852 and Harriet in 1854. Polly died soon after the birth of her seventh surviving child. Comstock, *A History and Genealogy of the Comstock Family*, 99. For more genealogical details, see Anna Louise Bates, *Weeder in the Garden of the Lord: Anthony Comstock's Life and Career* (Lanham, MD: University Press of America, 1995), 29.

12. Charles Gallaudet Trumbull, *Anthony Comstock, Fighter: Some Impressions of a Lifetime of Adventure in Conflict with the Powers of Evil* (New York: Fleming H. Revell, 1913), 24–26.

13. Most of the family's possessions were directly related to subsistence farming and lumber production at the family's sawmills. The family's personal property was valued at $583, while their real estate was valued at $8,800. Records of the Court of Probate for the District of Norwalk, 1847–1851, Index Vol. 8, 361, Documents Microfilm Reel #3538, Connecticut State Library.

14. Indeed, Connecticut was at the heart of a "new and decentralized world of workshop manufacture and 'fancy' goods" in the antebellum era that the Comstocks seem quite consciously to have avoided. David Jaffee, *A New Nation of Goods: The Material Culture of Early America* (Philadelphia: University of Pennsylvania Press, 2010), x.

15. Mrs. C. H. Demeritt, "Reminiscences," *Historical Account of the Celebration of the One Hundred and Fiftieth Anniversary of the Organization of the Congregational Church of New Canaan, Conn. June 20, 1883* (Stamford, CT: Gillespie Brothers, 1883), 33.

16. Fairley, "A History of New Canaan," 199–200.

17. James S. Hoyt, "Historical Discourse," *Historical Account of the Celebration of the One Hundred and Fiftieth Anniversary of the Organization of the Congregational Church of New Canaan* (Stamford, CT: Gillespie Brothers, 1883), 46–48.

18. Horace Mann complained, "Only one of the New England states proves recreant to duty in this glorious cause . . . the State of Connecticut." "The Hundred Years of School District Number One of New Canaan, Conn.," *The New Canaan Historical Society Annual* 1, no. 3 (June 1945): 22.

19. "New Canaan," *The Connecticut Common School Journal* 3 (1840–1841): 199.

20. A former student in Smith's weekend Bible class recalled, "We commenced with the first chapter of Genesis. . . . We made our own genealogical and historical chart and calculations, bringing in contemporaneous facts in profane history, and deducing practical truths." Hoyt, "Historical Discourse," 61.

21. Fairley, "A History of New Canaan," 210.

22. Quoted in Broun and Leech, *Anthony Comstock*, 39.

23. All biblical references derive from the King James version, which was uniformly used by Congregationalists through the nineteenth century.

24. General Land Index Grantees, New Canaan Land Records and Deeds, Microfilm Reel #2440, Connecticut State Library.

25. Edward J. Balleisen, "Vulture Capitalism in Antebellum America: The 1841 Federal Bankruptcy Act and the Exploitation of Financial Distress," *The Business History Review* 70, no. 4 (winter 1996): 476.

26. "Census—1850, New Canaan, Connecticut, Compiled by Lois B. Bayles, Librarian, 1968," New Canaan Historical Society.

27. Comstock, *A History and Genealogy of the Comstock Family*, 99.

28. Ibid.; see also "Schedule 1—Free Inhabitants in New Canaan in the County of Fairfield State of Connecticut," *Census for 1860, State of Connecticut*, 205, Connecticut State Library.

29. Thomas Anthony Comstock Passport Application, 1871 England Census, and England and Wales Marriage Index, all accessed August, 2014, at http://search.ancestry.com /cgi-bin/sse.dll?gl=allgs&gss=sfs63_home&new=1&rank=1&msT=1&gsfn=thomas %20anthony&gsfn_x=0&gsln=comstock&gsln_x=0&MSAV=0&cp=0&catbucket=rstp.

30. Gretchen Townsend Buggeln, *Temples of Grace: The Material Transformation of Connecticut's Churches, 1790–1840* (Hanover, NH: University Press of New England, 2003), 127–128.

31. Ibid.

32. Fairley, "A History of New Canaan," 198.

33. Quoted in Nancy Finlay, ed., *Picturing Victorian America: Prints by the Kellogg Brothers of Hartford, Connecticut, 1830–1880* (Hartford: Connecticut Historical Society, 2009), 1.

34. Stephen A. Marini, "Evangelical Hymns and Popular Belief," in *New England Music: The Public Sphere, 1600–1900*, ed. Peter Benes, The Dublin Seminar for New England Folklife Annual Proceedings (Boston: Boston University, 1996), 121.

35. Onesimus reputedly "refused to be freed" and therefore was considered the last remaining slave in the state in 1857. King, *Portrait of New Canaan*, 197.

36. This broad definition of the noun "lust" was prevalent in "Biblical and Theological" use through the nineteenth century according to the *Oxford English Dictionary*, accessed October 20, 2016, at http://www.oed.com/view/Entry/111374?rskey=YwX4d4&result =1&isAdvanced=false#eid

37. I am indebted to the generosity and insight of Ellen Handler Spitz, who reminded me of the specific language of Genesis 3 and its relationship to these lithographs.

38. Elaine Pagels, *Adam, Eve, and the Serpent* (New York: Random House, 1988), 12. Geoffrey Stone notes that "it was Augustine who crystallized the early Christian understanding of sex, and who, in so doing, ultimately helped shape traditional American views of sexuality more than a millennium later." Stone, *Sex and the Constitution*, 17–20.

39. I am indebted to my colleague Lourdes Font for her thoughtful and informed analysis of this image.

40. "Indecency in Works of Art," *Bulletin of the American Art-Union* 3 (June 1, 1851): 49. I am indebted to Kimberly Orcutt for sharing this source with me.

41. Edward J. Blum, "The Kingdom of Satan in America: Weaving the Wicked Web of Antebellum Religion and Politics," *Common-Place Journal* 15, no. 3 (spring 2015), http:// www.common-place-archives.org/vol-15/no-03/blum/#.WAJAbpMrJyw; see also Kathryn

Gin Lum, *Damned Nation: Hell in America from the Revolution to* Reconstruction (New York: Oxford University Press, 2014).

42. Trumbull, *Anthony Comstock*, 30.

43. Amy Werbel, *Thomas Eakins: Art, Medicine, and Sexuality in Nineteenth-Century Philadelphia* (New Haven: Yale University Press, 2007), 23–24. For a thorough review of anti-masturbation literature, see Helen Lefkowitz Horowitz, *Rereading Sex: Battles Over Sexual Knowledge and Suppression in Nineteenth-Century America* (New York: Vintage, 2003), 86–122; see also Stone, 147–148.

44. David S. Reynolds, *Walt Whitman's America: A Cultural Biography* (New York: Vintage Books, 1996), 201.

45. Catharine E. Beecher, *A Treatise on Domestic Economy for the Use of Young Ladies at Home, and at School* (New York: Harper & Brothers, 1845), 233, accessed October 13, 2016, at http://www.gutenberg.org/files/21829/21829-h/21829-h.htm#Page_220.

46. *Private Circular, for Gentlemen Only: No. 2*, 186?. Collection, American Antiquarian Society.

47. Horowitz, *Rereading Sex*, 33. See also Stone, *Sex and the Constitution*, 63–64.

48. Ibid.

49. As Lourdes Font notes, the lace that frames Fanny's breasts was referred to at the time as "van Dykeian," referencing portraits by the popular seventeenth-century artist (personal communication, March 2016).

50. Cleland is careful "to isolate the element of consent and collaboration, turning it into a contractual and theatrical staging." John Kenneth Noyes, *The Mastery of Submission: Inventions in Masochism* (Ithaca: Cornell University Press, 1997), 81.

51. Trumbull, *Anthony Comstock*, 30.

52. Donna Dennis, *Licentious Gotham: Erotic Publishing and Its Prosecution in Nineteenth-Century New York* (Cambridge: Harvard University Press, 2009), 1.

53. Patricia Cline Cohen, Timothy J. Gilfoyle, and Helen Lefkowitz Horowitz, *The Flash Press: Sporting Male Weeklies in 1840s New York* (Chicago: University of Chicago Press, 2008), 1. See also Dennis, *Licentious Gotham*, 67, 70; and Stone, *Sex and the Constitution*, 154–156.

54. Although many states, including Connecticut, Vermont, and Massachusetts, wrote their own statutory obscenity laws during the early years of the Republic, New York did not do so until 1868, even though (or perhaps because) they were "responsible for approximately 40 percent of the domestic smut market." Whitney Strub, *Obscenity Rules: Roth v. United States and the Long Struggle Over Sexual Expression* (Lawrence: University Press of Kansas, 2013), 11. See also Dennis, *Licentious Gotham*, 26–35; Cohen, Gilfoyle, and Horowitz, *The Flash Press*, 82; and Stone, *Sex and the Constitution*, 60–61.

55. Dennis, *Licentious Gotham*, 164–166, 255.

56. Ibid., 164. Dennis also provides an excellent overview of antebellum laws regarding obscenity in Donna I. Dennis, "Obscenity Law and the Conditions of Freedom in the Nineteenth-Century United States," *Law & Social Inquiry* 27, no. 2 (spring 2002): 381–385.

57. Dennis, *Licentious Gotham*, 117–118.

58. "Address by Mr. Anthony Comstock," 95.

59. "Manual of the Congregational Church, New Canaan, Conn. 1733–1876" (New York: Livesy Brothers, Steam Job Printers, 1876), 3–4. Confessions of Faith presumably were the same in the South Norwalk Congregational Church.

60. Trumbull, *Anthony Comstock*, 26.

61. Stephen B. Hoyt, "The Library," *Landmarks of New Canaan* (New Canaan, CT: The New Canaan Historical Society, 1951), 9.

62. Fairley, "A History of New Canaan," 176.

63. Alan Trachtenberg, *The Incorporation of America: Culture and Society in the Gilded Age*, Twenty-Fifth Anniversary Edition (New York: Hill and Wang, 2007), 101–102.

64. Trumbull, *Anthony Comstock*, 27.

65. Thomas Day, *The History of Sandford and Merton*, reprint edition (New York: George Routledge and Sons, 1850), 1.

66. Day, *The History of Sandford and Merton*, 295–296.

67. Trumbull, *Anthony Comstock*, 10–12.

68. Homer N. Dunning, *Our National Trial: A Thanksgiving Sermon, Preached at the Union Meeting of the Churches of Gloversville, on Thanksgiving Day, November 28th, 1861* (Gloversville, NY: Geo. W. Heaton, Book & Job Printer, 1861), 3–5. Yale Divinity School Library.

69. W. A. Croffut and John M. Morris, *The Military and Civil History of Connecticut During the War of 1861–1865* (New York: Ledyard Bill, 1869), 229.

70. Bvt. Brig.-Gen. William H. Noble, "History of the Seventeenth Regiment C. V. Infantry" in *Record of Service of Connecticut Men in the Army and Navy of the United States During the War of the Rebellion* (Hartford: Press of The Case, Lockwood, and Brainard Company, 1889), 640.

71. "Muster Roll of Captain Enos Kellogg December 31, 1864 to February 28, 1865," Connecticut State Library.

72. Broun and Leech, *Anthony Comstock*, 32.

73. Trumbull, *Anthony Comstock*, 33.

74. Broun and Leech, *Anthony Comstock*, 32.

75. Edward Marcus, ed., *A New Canaan Private in the Civil War: Letters of Justus M. Silliman, Seventeenth Connecticut Volunteers* (New Canaan, CT: New Canaan Historical Society, 1984), 58.

76. Ibid., 63.

77. Ibid., 79.

78. Ibid., 100.

79. Ibid., 109.

80. Noble, "History of the Seventeenth Regiment C. V. Infantry," 641–642.

81. Broun and Leech, *Anthony Comstock*, 33. Geoffrey Stone notes that for evangelicals, "blasphemy" included "speaking ill of 'sacred matters.'" Stone, *Sex and the Constitution*, 140.

82. Ibid., 47.

83. Ibid., 54. Judith Giesburg details Comstock's sour relations with his campmates and other Civil War experiences in Judith Giesburg, *Sex and the Civil War: Soldiers, Pornography, and the Making of American Morality* (Chapel Hill: University of North Carolina Press, 2017), 67–81.

84. Captain M. G. Tousley was so concerned about the material circulating among the troops that he sent President Abraham Lincoln a long letter of complaint and included a sample catalog as demonstration. Thomas P. Lowry, M.D., *The Story the Soldiers Wouldn't Tell: Sex in the Civil War* (Mechanicsburg, PA: Stackpole Books, 1994), 54–55. See also Dennis, *Licentious Gotham*, 200–202.

85. Giesburg, *Sex and the Civil War*.

86. Broun and Leech, *Anthony Comstock*, 55–56.

87. Ibid., 59–60.

88. Trumbull, *Anthony Comstock*, 45; "Antony Comstock, Suppressor of Vice: Side Lights on a Relentless Veteran in the War Against the Indecent and Obscene," *Belleville News Democrat*, November 9, 1906.

89. Edwin G. Burrows and Mike Wallace, *Gotham: A History of New York City to 1898* (New York: Oxford University Press, 1999), 921.

90. Edward Winslow Martin [James D. McCabe], *The Secrets of the Great City: A Work Descriptive of the Virtues and the Vices, the Mysteries, Miseries and Crimes of New York City* (Philadelphia: Jones, Brothers & Co., 1868), 212–213.

91. Burrows and Wallace, *Gotham*, 921.

92. Martin, *Secrets of the Great City*, Table of Contents and 313.

93. Timothy J. Gilfoyle, *City of Eros: New York City, Prostitution, and the Commercialization of Sex, 1790–1920* (New York: W. W. Norton, 1992), 218. Gilfoyle notes that these conditions persisted throughout the post–Civil War era.

94. *George P. Rowell & Co.'s American Newspaper Directory* (New York: George P. Rowell & Co, 1873), 147–160.

95. "Anthony Comstock, Suppressor of Vice: Side Lights on a Relentless Veteran in the War Against the Indecent and Obscene," *Belleville News Democrat*, November 9, 1906.

96. Trumbull, *Anthony Comstock*, 45–48.

97. A circular advertising the firm's wares in 1875 lists expensive imported and domestic woolen fabrics, including "Northumberland Fancy Cassimeres," "Gilt Edge Doeskins," and "New Orleans Cashmeretts." Collection of the author, purchased October 5, 2016, at MJG Postal History, http://mgjpostalhistory.com/node/153.

98. "The Clerks of New York," *New York Evening Post*, March 3, 1866, Box 377, folder "Clippings," Kautz Family YMCA Collection, University of Minnesota Libraries [hereafter Kautz].

99. Paula Lupkin, *Manhood Factories: YMCA Architecture and the Making of Modern Urban Culture* (Minneapolis: University of Minnesota Press, 2010), 74–75.

100. "The New Building of the Young Men's Christian Association," *New York Times*, November 30, 1869, 5.

101. Martin, *Secrets of the Great City*, 45–46.

102. *Miller's New York As It Is, or Stranger's Guide-Book to the Cities of New York, Brooklyn, and Adjacent Places* (New York: James Miller, 1872), 104, 107.

103. Brian Merlis, *Brooklyn's Historic Clinton Hill and Wallabout* (New York: Israelowitz, 2011), 26.

104. Ibid.

105. "Double Page Plate No. 27: Bounded by Willoughby Avenue, Steuben Street, Lafayette Avenue, Grand Avenue, Atlantic Ave (Jamaica Turnpike), Flatbush Avenue, Fulton Street, (Fort Green) Dekalb Avenue and Washington Park." The New York Public Library, Lionel Pincus and Princess Firyal Map Division, New York Public Library Digital Collections, accessed October 15, 2016, at http://digitalcollections.nypl.org/items/510d47e2-165b-a3d9-e040-e00a18064a99.

106. Broun and Leech, *Anthony Comstock*, 62.

107. Ibid.

2. ONWARD CHRISTIAN SOLDIERS: CREATING THE INDUSTRY AND INFRASTRUCTURE OF AMERICAN VICE SUPPRESSION

1. William Ives Budington, *Responsive Worship: A Discourse, With Notes* (New York and Chicago: A. S. Barnes, 1873).
2. Heywood Broun and Margaret Leech, *Anthony Comstock: Roundsman of the Lord* (New York: A. & C. Boni, 1927), 71. Helen Lefkowitz Horowitz discusses Comstock's relationship with Budington further in *Rereading Sex: Battles Over Sexual Knowledge and Suppression in Nineteenth-Century America* (New York: Vintage, 2003), 367–368.
3. Broun and Leech, *Anthony Comstock*, 69.
4. Charles Gallaudet Trumbull, *Anthony Comstock, Fighter: Some Impressions of a Lifetime of Adventure in Conflict with the Powers of Evil* (New York: Fleming H. Revell, 1913), 51.
5. Ibid., 51–52. For a meticulous account of Comstock's early investigations and arrests, see Donna Dennis, *Licentious Gotham: Erotic Publishing and Its Prosecution in Nineteenth-Century New York* (Cambridge: Harvard University Press, 2009), 238–252.
6. Quoted in Broun and Leech, *Anthony Comstock*, 72.
7. Report of Persons Arrested under the Auspices of the New York Society for the Suppression of Vice, Library of Congress Manuscript Division MSS34587; MMC-3288 [hereafter ROA] I, 1–2.
8. Sven Beckert, *The Monied Metropolis: New York City and the Consolidation of the American Bourgeoisie, 1850–1896* (Cambridge: Cambridge University Press, 2001), 5–6.
9. On this topic, see the excellent research and analysis of Nicola Beisel, *Imperiled Innocents: Anthony Comstock and Family Reproduction in Victorian America* (Princeton: Princeton University Press, 1997).
10. Broun and Leech, *Anthony Comstock*, 88.
11. Minutes of the Board of Directors, New York Young Men's Christian Association, 1865–1873, Box 386, Kautz.
12. This report is discussed in Horowitz, *Rereading Sex*, 359–361; and Dennis, *Licentious Gotham*, 221–222.
13. Minutes of the Board, 1865–1868, 94–95. Box 386.
14. Ibid., 135, 144. Donna Dennis chronicles the legislative debate and proceedings in detail, in *Licentious Gotham*, 221–229. For the most recent history of efforts to limit contraceptives and abortion, with abundant citations, see Geoffrey R. Stone, *Sex and the Constitution: Sex, Religion, and Law from America's Origins to the Twenty-First Century* (New York: Liveright, 2017), 179–202.
15. Minutes of the Board, 1868–1870, 37–38, 43–53; and 1870–1876, 34, 38, 66, 105–106. Box 418. Dennis details cases at this time utilizing district attorney records in *Licentious Gotham*, 230–233.
16. Helen Lefkowitz Horowitz discusses Brainerd's background in detail in *Rereading Sex*, 364–367.
17. Cephas Brainerd to Mr. Bowne, October 22, 1901. John Saxton Sumner Papers, Wisconsin Historical Society. This letter is discussed in Dennis, *Licentious Gotham*, 244; and Horowitz, *Rereading Sex*, 372–373.
18. William Adams Brown, *Morris Ketchum Jesup: A Character Sketch* (New York: Charles Scribner's Sons, 1910), 54.
19. Broun and Leech, *Anthony Comstock*, 83–84.

20. Brown, *Morris Ketchum Jesup*, 2–3, 8.

21. Ibid., 34–36.

22. Jesup's home at 197 Madison Avenue is documented in "Plate 17: Bounded by W. 36th Street, E. 36th Street, Lexington Avenue, E. 25th Street, Madison Avenue, E. 26th Street, Fifth Avenue, W. 25th Street and Eighth Avenue," *The New York Public Library Digital Collections*, 1897, Lionel Pincus and Princess Firyal Map Division, The New York Public Library, http://digitalcollections.nypl.org/items/510d47e2-0ac3-a3d9-e040-e00a18064a99.

23. Brown, *Morris Ketchum Jesup*, 55–59.

24. ROA I, 1–2. Here, Comstock was telling the story of a Trustee of the Congregational Church in Morrisania, New York named Thomas Timpson who profited from investment in obscene book publishing.

25. "Measures for the Suppression of Obscene Literature," *New York Times*, May 10, 1872, 8.

26. Ibid.

27. Helen Lefkowitz Horowitz, "Victoria Woodhull, Anthony Comstock, and Conflict Over Sex in the United States in the 1870s," *Journal of American History* 87, no. 2 (September 2000): 432–433.

28. Comstock detailed his efforts in a letter to Hon. Clinton Merriam, which Merriam entered in the Congressional Record at the time the Comstock Act was passed. Appendix to the *Congressional Globe*, 42nd Cong., 3d Sess., 168 (March 3, 1873).

29. YMCA Committee for the Suppression of Vice, "Private and Confidential: Obscene Books, Etc. Summary Report" (New York, 1872), Box 386, Folder "NYSSV Pamphlets," Kautz. McBurney mailed the report in December 1872.

30. Ibid.

31. "Personal and News Items," *New-York Evangelist*, March 7, 1872, 8.

32. Amanda Frisken, *Victoria Woodhull's Sexual Revolution: Political Theater and the Popular Press in Nineteenth-Century America* (Philadelphia: University of Pennsylvania Press, 2004), 15.

33. For full accounts of the trials of Victoria Woodhull, see ibid., 85–116; Horowitz, *Rereading Sex*, 342–379; and Broun and Leech, *Anthony Comstock*, 90–127.

34. "The Principle of Social Freedom, Involving Free Love, Marriage, Divorce, &c. Lecture by Victoria C. Woodhull," *New York Times*, November 21, 1871, 1.

35. Horowitz, *Rereading Sex*, 349–350.

36. "'The Woodhull's' Debts: She Is Not Worth a Single Dollar," *New York Times*, August 28, 1872, 2.

37. Frisken, *Victoria Woodhull's Sexual Revolution*, 88.

38. Ibid., 111, 91.

39. For a full account of the trial, see Frisken, *Victoria Woodhull's Sexual Revolution*, 94–112.

40. ROA I, 4.

41. Broun and Leech, *Anthony Comstock*, 138.

42. "Washington," *New York Times*, January 31, 1873. On February 7, the *New York Herald* chimed in, noting that Comstock "exhibited to a large number of Senators in the Vice President's room a collection of obscene books and pictures which he has obtained through the mails." "Washington," *New York Herald*, February 7, 1873, 3.

43. At the time, Samuel Clarke Pomeroy, Republican of Kansas, had little to lose in hosting a reception for visitors to view Comstock's obscenity exhibition. He had recently been embroiled in a separate bribery scandal involving Crédit Mobilier of America and had

been defeated in his bid for reelection. "Comstock's Christianity Refused by the Senate," *New York Herald*, February 24, 1873, 3.

44. "Measures for the Suppression of Obscene Literature," *New York Times*, May 10, 1872, 8.

45. Appendix to the *Congressional Globe*, 42nd Cong., 3d Sess., vol. 67, part 2 (March 1, 1873), 2005. For a comprehensive discussion of these legislative maneuvers, see Gaines M. Foster, *Moral Reconstruction: Christian Lobbyists and the Federal Legislation of Morality, 1865–1920* (Chapel Hill: University of North Carolina Press, 2002), 52–53.

46. Broun and Leech, *Anthony Comstock*, 142.

47. Candy Gunther Brown, *The Word in the World: Evangelical Writing, Publishing, and Reading in America, 1789–1880* (Chapel Hill: University of North Carolina Press, 2004), 5.

48. Wayne E. Fuller, *Morality and the Mail in Nineteenth-Century America* (Urbana: University of Illinois Press, 2003), 105.

49. "Amending the Constitution: Organization of the National Convention—The Proposed Religious Amendment," *New York Times*, February 27, 1873.

50. Gaines M. Foster summarizes Rep. Benjamin Butler's persuasive arguments against amending the preamble: "The founders expected the nation 'to be the home of the oppressed of all nations of the earth, whether Christian or Pagan.'" Foster, *Moral Reconstruction*, 30.

51. Fuller, *Morality and the Mail*, 101; see also Judith Giesburg, *Sex and the Civil War: Soldiers, Pornography, and the Making of American Morality* (Chapel Hill: University of North Carolina Press, 2017), 84–87.

52. Clinton Merriam, "Obscene Literature: Speech of Hon. Clinton L. Merriam, of New York, in the House of Representatives, March 1, 1873, on the bill (S. 1572) for the suppression of trade in and circulation of obscene literature and objects of immoral use" (Watertown, NY: Ingalls, Brockway, and Skinner Printers, 1873), 5. Collection, Library of Congress; see also Appendix to the *Congressional Globe*, 42nd Cong., 3d Sess., vol. 67, part 2 (March 1, 1873), 2004–2005. Note that Merriam's speech on March 1, 1873, as printed in pamphlets is substantially longer than the speech recorded in the *Congressional Globe*. The Library of Congress notes: "with the 32nd Congress (1851) . . . the *Globe* began to provide something approaching verbatim transcription." It seems likely that Merriam's lengthy quotation from Anthony Comstock's letter was not transcribed at the time it was read. "Congressional Globe—About," Library of Congress, https://memory.loc.gov/ammem/amlaw/lwcg.html.

53. For a thorough discussion of Comstock's crusade against contraceptives and abortion, see Beisel, *Imperiled Innocents*, 25–48; see also Anna Louise Bates, *Weeder in the Garden of the Lord: Anthony Comstock's Life and Career* (Lanham, MD: University Press of America, 1995), 151–172.

54. ROA I, 11–12. This case is discussed in "Arrests for Malpractice," *New York Times*, August 31, 1872, 5.

55. Andrea Tone, *Devices and Desires: A History of Contraceptives in America* (New York: Hill and Wang, 2001), 15.

56. As Paul Erickson notes, "Sinking the 290" "most likely is a double entendre referring to the sinking of the Confederate warship *Alabama* in 1864." Paul Erickson, "Prints for a Different Parlor," *Past Is Present: The American Antiquarian Society blog*, published December 12, 2011, http://pastispresent.org/2011/good-sources/prints-for-a-different-parlor/. Erickson here is addressing Mme. M. Simmons & Co. (N.Y.), *Price Current of Conjugal Goods*

from Mme. M. Simmons, & Co., Importers of the Best French Manufacture (New York, 1865). Collection, American Antiquarian Society.

57. Horowitz, *Rereading Sex*, 68.
58. ROA I, 3–4, 9–10.
59. Fuller, *Morality and the Mail*, 108.
60. YMCA Committee for the Suppression of Vice, "Obscene Books."
61. Noah Webster et al., *A Dictionary of the English Language* (New York: American Book Company, 1867), 212, 219.
62. Webster et al., *A Dictionary of the English Language*, 245, 250.
63. Wayne C. Bartee and Alice Fleetwood Bartee, *Litigating Morality: American Legal Thought and Its English Roots* (New York: Praeger, 1992), 58–59. Geoffrey R. Stone considers problems with the language of the Comstock Act in *Sex and the Constitution*, 162–163.
64. Appendix to the *Congressional Globe*, 42nd Cong., 3d Sess., vol. 67, part 2 (February 21, 1873), 1571.
65. "United States Commissioners' Court: The Examination in the Case of Woodhull, Claflin and Blood Resumed," *New York Herald*, January 15, 1873, 8.
66. Ibid.
67. Paul Marcus, "The Development of Entrapment Law," *William and Mary Law School Faculty Publications* Paper 572 (1986): 9, http://scholarship.law.wm.edu/facpubs/572.
68. "Woodhull and Claflin Acquitted: A Technicality Under the Old Law," *New-York Tribune*, June 28, 1873, 5.
69. Daniel P. Carpenter discusses McAfee, Comstock, and the postal inspection service in the context of larger executive branch shifts in *The Forging of Bureaucratic Autonomy: Reputations, Networks, and Policy Innovation in Executive Agencies, 1862–1928* (Princeton: Princeton University Press, 2001), 84–88. The Post Office Department became the United States Postal Service in 1971. See also Wayne Fuller's excellent and comprehensive book, *Morality and the Mail*.
70. Fuller, *Morality and the Mail*, 108.
71. YMCA Committee for the Suppression of Vice, "Private and Confidential: Improper Books, Prints, Etc." (New York, 1874), 12. Newberry Library. This final report was mailed to those who had donated funds, with the request that it be destroyed after reading. One other copy of this report survives in the collection of the American Antiquarian Society, preserved with the original cover letter sent with it.
72. AC to C. Cochran, August 21, 1875, Box 23, Folder AC Correspondence 1874–1877, CFI.
73. Clinton Merriam, "Obscene Literature," 7.
74. YMCA Committee for the Suppression of Vice, "Obscene Books," 4–5. Geoffrey Stone notes concern about dildos dating back to the early eleventh century. Stone, *Sex and the Constitution*, 31–32.
75. Tone, *Devices and Desires*, 54.
76. The manufacturer Comstock referred to was Louis Beer. Comstock noted in his arrest blotter that he "first introduced "Dildoes" in America. YMCA Committee for the Suppression of Vice, "Obscene Books," 16; ROA I, 1–2.
77. The ideology of female passionlessness in nineteenth-century America first was articulated in Nancy F. Cott, "Passionlessness: An Interpretation of Victorian Sexual Ideology, 1790–1850," *Signs* 4, no. 2 (winter 1978): 219–236. The significance of the concept and term has since been debated, but the dominance of this ideology among nineteenth century New England evangelicals is not in question.

78. Karen J. Renner, "Seduction, Prostitution, and the Control of Female Desire in Popular Antebellum Fiction," *Nineteenth-Century Literature* 65, no. 2 (September 2010): 166–191. Quotes taken from pages 167, 172, and 169.

79. Horowitz, *Rereading Sex*, 29.

80. Rachel P. Maines, *The Technology of Orgasm* (Baltimore: Johns Hopkins University Press, 2001), 34–35.

81. Ibid., 11.

82. *The Grand Fancy Bijou Catalogue of the Sporting Man's Companion for 1870* (Philadelphia, 1870), 6. Collection, American Antiquarian Society.

83. ROA I, 1–2. Comstock organized the seizure of Ackerman's stock in 1872. See also Dennis, *Licentious Gotham*, 259–261. Ackerman's name is spelled Akarman in some documents.

84. ROA I, 1–2.

85. *Venus' Miscellany* (various issues, 1857), 22, Rare Book Division in the Department of Rare Books and Special Collections, Princeton University Library, http://libweb10.princeton .edu/visual_materials/books/VENUSMISCELLANY9BSIDES.pdf. Dennis also discusses this story in *Licentious Gotham*, 171–172.

86. Donna Dennis recounts Brady's many entanglements with the law, and the materials listed in indictments, including *Mary Ann Temple*, in *Licentious Gotham*, 152–160.

87. *Mary Ann Temple: Being an Authentic and Romantic History of an Amorous and Lively Girl, of Exquisite Beauty, and Strong Natural Love of Pleasure* (New York, n.d.), 8, 9, 84–86. Collection, American Antiquarian Society.

88. Oliver Wendell Holmes, "The Stereoscope and the Stereograph," *Atlantic Monthly* (June 1859); quoted in American Antiquarian Society, "Stereographs," accessed October 13, 2016, http://www.americanantiquarian.org/stereographs.htm.

89. Merriam, "Obscene Literature," 2, 7.

90. Brown, *Morris Ketchum Jesup*, 56; Broun and Leech transcribe Comstock's diaries regarding the Committee's "jealousies" at this time, in *Anthony Comstock*, 151–153.

91. Lyman Beecher, "The Practicability of Suppressing Vice, by Means of Societies Instituted for That Purpose: A Sermon Delivered Before the Moral Society, in East-Hampton (Long-Island), September 21, 1803" (New London, CT: Samuel Green, 1804), 14.

92. "An Address to the Public, from the Society for the Suppression of Vice, Instituted in London, 1802: Part the Second, Containing an Account of the Proceedings of the Society from Its Original Institution" (London: Printed for the Society by T. Woodfall, 1804), 4–5, 8, 26, 15–37. Newberry Library. See also "Society for the Suppression of Vice: Consisting of Members of the Established Church" (London, 1803), 3, *Nineteenth Century Collections Online*, accessed November 2015, http://tinyurl.galegroup.com/tinyurl/qFnn4.

93. Lyman Beecher's *Autobiography* discusses "agitations" in support of these societies chiefly around 1812, but then moves on to other causes, including arguments against Unitarianism. Barbara M. Cross, ed., *The Autobiography of Lyman Beecher*, vol. 1 (Cambridge: Belknap Press of Harvard University, 1961), 185–193. More work is needed to determine the precise fates of these individual societies, many of which produced one or two initial reports that have been preserved in the Jacob Bowne Pamphlet Collection, Kautz.

94. "An Address to the Public, from the Society for the Suppression of Vice," 19–20. For an excellent analysis of the culture of dissent strikingly evident in America during the revolutionary era, see Stephen D. Solomon, *Revolutionary Dissent: How the Founding Generation Created the Freedom of Speech* (New York: St. Martin's Press, 2016).

95. "The Temptations of Young Men: Multiform and Enticing," 2. YMCA collection, Box "Boone Pamphlets 2" folder American Tract Society, Kautz. The pamphlet dates between 1832 and 1848, judging by the criteria meticulously outlined in S. J. Wolfe, "Dating American Tract Society Publications through 1876 from External Evidences: A Series of Tables," American Antiquarian Society, accessed October 15, 2016, http://www.american antiquarian.org/node/6693#10; Geoffrey R. Stone discusses Beecher's efforts in *Sex and the Constitution*, 134–139, including his leadership in later, successful efforts to end Sunday mail service.

96. Beecher, "The Practicability of Suppressing Vice," 25.

97. Catharine Esther Beecher, *A Treatise on Domestic Economy for the Use of Young Ladies at Home, and at School* (New York: Harper & Brothers, 1845), 249–250.

98. NYSSV, *First Annual Report of the NYSSV for 1874* (New York: privately printed, 1875), 1.

99. YMCA Committee, "Improper Books," 1–11.

100. The *Annual Report* of the YMCA for 1873 noted that a Society for the Suppression of Vice had "recently been organized, and is now entirely independent of the Association." *Twenty-First Annual Report of the Young Men's Christian Association of the City of New York* (New York: Published by the Association, 1874), 17. Many YMCA committee members continued on to this new organization with leadership roles, including Charles E. Whitehead, Jacob F. Wyckoff, William H. S. Wood, Robert McBurney, and Morris K. Jesup. "The New York Society for the Suppression of Vice: Officers, Act of Incorporation, and Laws Relating to Obscene Literature, etc.," Box 386, Kautz.

101. NYSSV, *First Annual Report*, 12.

102. Ibid.

103. NYSSV, *Fourth Annual Report for the NYSSV for 1877* (New York: privately printed, 1878), 9.

104. Brown, *Morris Ketchum Jesup*, 56.

105. Beecher, "The Practicability of Suppressing Vice," 8.

106. Beecher, *A Treatise on Domestic Economy*, 250.

107. Broun and Leech, *Anthony Comstock*, 120–121.

108. Beisel, *Imperiled Innocents*, 53.

109. NYSSV, *Fourth Annual Report*, 5–6.

110. NYSSV, *Fifth Annual Report of the NYSSV for 1878* (New York: privately printed, 1879), 25. The report here made reference to the *Kindlifresser* or "Child Eater" sculpture in the Kornhausplatz in Bern, which dates to 1546.

111. "Vice: Meeting of the Society for its Suppression," *Brooklyn Daily Eagle*, December 10, 1875, 4.

112. NYSSV, *First Annual Report*, 12; NYSSV, *Third Annual Report for 1876* (New York: privately printed, 1877), 20; NYSSV, *Fourth Annual Report*, 16; *Fifth Annual Report*, 20–23. Donations rose from $2,844 in 1874 to $6,631 five years later.

113. The *New York Times* reported, for example, that the hall at the annual meeting of the NYSSV was "well filled with men, no ladies being admitted." "The Prevention of Vice," *New York Times*, February 6, 1878, 2.

114. Beisel, *Imperiled Innocents*, 53–57.

115. Remarks by Rev. Dr. Potter, NYSSV, *Sixth Annual Report of the NYSSV for 1879* (New York: privately printed, 1880), 23.

116. "The Temptations of Young Men: Multiform and Enticing," 2.

3. TAMING AMERICA'S "RICH" AND "RACY" UNDERBELLY
(VOLUME I: 1871–1884)

1. Most of the volumes' pages are titled "Report of Persons Arrested under the Auspices of the New York Society for the Suppression of Vice"; they are held in the Library of Congress Manuscript Division, MSS34587, MMC-3288 [hereafter ROA].

2. For analysis and discussion of this literature, see Helen Lefkowitz Horowitz, *Rereading Sex: Battles Over Sexual Knowledge and Suppression in Nineteenth-Century America* (New York: Vintage, 2003). For analysis and discussion of prosecutions of these publishers and their responses, see Donna Dennis, *Licentious Gotham: Erotic Publishing and Its Prosecution in Nineteenth-Century New York* (Cambridge: Harvard University Press, 2009).

3. ROA I, 1–4.

4. NYSSV, *First Annual Report of the NYSSV for 1874* (New York: privately printed, 1875), 6.

5. ROA I, 5–6.

6. "Alleged False Imprisonment," *New York Times*, October 13, 1874, 8; "Vacation of the Order Against Anthony Comstock," *New York Times*, October 15, 1874, 6; "The Assault on Mr. Anthony Comstock," *New York Times*, November 3, 1874, 5.

7. ROA I, 45–46.

8. ROA I, 59–60.

9. The second example is in the Library of Congress, where it was granted copyright and shelved in 1875.

10. See, for example, several cases listed in ROA I, 65–76.

11. NYSSV, *Third Annual Report of the NYSSV for 1876* (New York: privately printed, 1877), 17.

12. Ibid.

13. ROA I, 53–54.

14. AC to P. H. Woodward, April 15, 1876; Box 23, Folder AC Correspondence 1874–1877, CFI.

15. AC to P. H. Woodward, March 11, 1876; Box 23, Folder AC Correspondence 1874–1877, CFI; Benkerts ROA I, 63–64; McIntire ROA I, 65–66. Trumbull narrates these arrests in genteel language in Charles Gallaudet Trumbull, *Anthony Comstock, Fighter: Some Impressions of a Lifetime of Adventure in Conflict with the Powers of Evil* (New York: Fleming H. Revell, 1913), 201–205.

16. For an excellent analysis of the Kinsey Institute's unparalleled photography archive, see Jennifer Pearson Yamashiro, "Sex in the Field: Photography at the Kinsey Institute" (PhD diss., Indiana University, 2001). For a discussion of American prostitution and fashion, see Jennifer Marie Schulle, "Fashion and Fallen Women: The Apparel Industry, the Retail Trade, Fashion, and Prostitution in Late Nineteenth Century St. Louis" (PhD diss., Iowa State University, 2005).

17. Dennis, *Licentious Gotham*, 279–280.

18. NYSSV, *Second Annual Report*, 5.

19. Manches also offered a "womb veil for females to prevent conception . . . in neat, compact paper boxes, accompanied by the full directions for use. . . . This preventive device will last a life time, and the lady can apply it unknown to her husband." Ultimately, Manches was found not guilty. "A Raid Upon Dealers in Obscene Merchandise," *New York Times*, March 16, 1872, 3; *People v. Charles Manches* and *People v. Charles McCabe*, Obscenity Trials Collection, 1872–1877, Schlesinger Library, Radcliffe College.

20. Manches was among those who died within a year of his arrest, at the age of forty, thus avoiding punishment in that oddly common way among Comstock's early prosecutorial targets. ROA I, 5–6.

21. AC to C. Cochran, Jr., October 3, 1874, Box 23, Folder AC Correspondence 1874–1877, CFI. Although Scroggy's stock was not especially unusual, he was rare in still having a store from which he openly sold his goods even into the 1880s, which he boasted about on the front page of the *Grand Fancy Bijou Catalogue*, Collection, American Antiquarian Society.

22. Matt Bloom, "Stanhopes: Hidden Erotica of the Nineteenth Century," *Inside Indiana University Bloomington*, posted April 10, 2014, http://inside.indiana.edu/features/stories /2014-04-10-iniub-feature-kinsey-stanhopes.shtml

23. Yamashiro, "Sex in the Field," 9. As Yamashiro notes, "In spite of the number of Stanhopes, which suggests quite a variety of images, the photographs, in reality, depict only a dozen or so different scenes (all of female nudes)."

24. AC to P. Woodward, July 3, 1876, Box 23, Folder 99 AC Correspondence 1876–1877, CFI.

25. Howard Chudacoff, *The Age of the Bachelor: Creating an American Subculture* (Princeton: Princeton University Press, 1999), 125. Chudacoff notes that "pure cigar stores included tables and chairs where customers could converse and play checkers, dominoes, or cards as well as indulge in a nickel smoke and peruse erotic pictures that occasionally were sold under the counter."

26. AC to David B. Parker, March 21, 1876, Box 23, Folder 104 AC Correspondence 1877–1878, CFI.

27. ROA I, 113–114.

28. ROA I, 233–234.

29. As Catherine Johnson-Roehr notes, objects "that copulate when moved back and forth" are pervasive amongst the vast quantities of "visual data" Dr. Alfred Kinsey and his staff collected to document and research human sexuality from around the world. Catherine Johnson, "The Kinsey Institute Collections," in *Sex and Humor: Selections from the Kinsey Institute*, ed. Catherine Johnson, Betsy Stiratt, and John Bancroft (Bloomington: Indiana University Press, 2002), 1–2.

30. John Bancroft, "Sex and Humor: A Personal View," in *Sex and Humor*, ed. Johnson, Stiratt, and Bancroft, 9.

31. Comstock noted that McGuire was a "prominent Ward Politician. Recently a Republican. He purchased his foul thing in Cincinnati and said it drew trade, that the past Sunday he had put it up & it paid for itself and more. Cost $35." ROA I, 227–228.

32. ROA I, 243–244. Guild's sentence was suspended when he died in January 1884. He was only thirty-three years old.

33. ROA II, 226–227. In July 1892, Comstock recorded that Patrick Grady, a bartender, was fined $100 for the offense of showing the pot.

34. George Chauncey, *Gay New York: Gender, Urban Culture, and the Making of the Gay Male World, 1890–1940* (New York: Basic Books, 1994), 45.

35. "The Religious Press," *New-York Evangelist*, September 3, 1874, 6.

36. "The Society for the Suppression of Vice," *Brooklyn Daily Eagle*, December 11, 1875, 2.

37. "The Suppression of Vice," *New York Observer*, February 3, 1876, 38.

38. Ibid.

39. "The Religious Press," *The New-York Evangelist*, August 10, 1876, 2. The *Evangelist* here reprinted an editorial published in *The Christian Weekly*.

40. ROA I, 79–80.

41. Ibid.

42. "Prevention of Vice," *New York Times*, November 26, 1876, 2. See also "Law Reports. The Immoral Schoolmaster in Court," *New York Times*, November 27, 1876, 3.

43. Geoffrey Stone outlines the Christian prejudice against homosexuality in Geoffrey R. Stone, *Sex and the Constitution: Sex, Religion, and Law from America's Origins to the Twenty-First Century* (New York: Liveright, 2017), 34–43. For an excellent overview of the legal and cultural status of homosexuality in the late nineteenth and early twentieth centuries, see Stone, *Sex and the Constitution*, 211–233.

44. ROA I, 63–64.

45. ROA I, 83–84.

46. Amanda Frisken asserts that Fox responded to the threat of censorship by giving new primacy to stories with racialized stereotypes of black brutality, positioning the "white" status of the *Gazette*'s many German and Irish American readers as superior. Amanda Frisken, "Obscenity, Free Speech, and 'Sporting News' in 1870s America," *Journal of American Studies* 42, no. 3 (2008): 537–577; Guy Reel calculates that stories about sex in the *Police Gazette* dropped from an average of 1.4 pages in 1880 to .13 pages in an 1885 issue, and then was back up to 1.2 pages in 1895. Guy Reel, *The National Police Gazette and the Making of the Modern Man, 1879–1906* (New York: Palgrave Macmillan, 2006), 151.

47. Joshua Brown, "*The Days' Doings*: The Gilded Age in the Profane Pictorial Press," paper presented at the American Studies Association Annual Meeting, Hartford, Connecticut, October 17, 2003, http://joshbrownnyc.com/daysdoings/index.htm.

48. Joshua Brown, "'The Social and Sensational News of the Day': Frank Leslie, the *Days' Doings* and Scandalous Pictorial News in Gilded Age New York," *New-York Journal of American History* 66, no. 2 (fall 2003): 14–15. See also Amanda Frisken, *Victoria Woodhull's Sexual Revolution: Political Theater and the Popular Press in Nineteenth-Century America* (Philadelphia: University of Pennsylvania Press, 2004), 101–102.

49. "Anthony Comstock's Adventure with a Vicious Vendor," *National Police Gazette*, March 8, 1879, 4.

50. "Simpson Arrested Again," *New York Times*, February 18, 1885; see also an attempt to arrest Richard Fox on January 18th, 1898. The case was discharged by the Jury. Records of the Post Office Department. Bureau of the Chief Inspector. Case Files of Investigations, Entry 231, Box No. 150. Date of Arrest January 18, 1898; and "To Destroy Paper and Plates. The Police Gazette Withdraws an Objectionable Edition," *New York Times*, November 13, 1897, 5.

51. Robert Allen, *Horrible Prettiness: Burlesque and American Culture* (Chapel Hill: University of North Carolina Press, 1991), 21.

52. "Columbia Opera House" [advertisement], *New York Herald*, February 16, 1877, 11.

53. ROA I, 83–84. On this case, see also the superb source: Jack W. McCullough, *Living Pictures on the New York Stage* (Ann Arbor: UMI Research Press, 1983), 83–87.

54. ROA I, 95–96. See also "Jake Berry Indicted," *The Sun*, March 27, 1877, 1.

55. The records of the SPC are housed in the Rare Book & Manuscript Library at Columbia University in the City of New York.

56. "Unfinished Programmes," *New York Herald*, February 26, 1878, 10.

57. Berry still promised "the handsomest formed and prettiest Young Ladies in the world appearing in 'THE FEMALE BATHERS,' in real water"; the "SULTAN"S HAREM; or the Secrets of the Seraglio" and "THE ARTIST'S MODELS.'" "Columbia Opera House" [advertisement], *New York Herald*, February 24, 1878, 4.

58. Timothy Gilfoyle discusses prostitution and its relationship to nineteenth-century theater in Timothy J. Gilfoyle, *City of Eros: New York City, Prostitution, and the Commercialization of Sex, 1790–1920* (New York: W. W. Norton, 1992), 128–134.

59. "Columbia Opera House," *New York Herald*, March 8, 1878, 6.

60. ROA I, 59–60.

61. *Jacob Berry Against the People of the State of New York: Error Book* (New York: Cameron & Co., 1878), Collection, U.S. Supreme Court Library.

62. *Jacob Berry*, 34–36.

63. *Jacob Berry*, 8–96, 149.

64. *Jacob Berry*, 43–50.

65. *Jacob Berry*, 29.

66. *Jacob Berry*, 187–192.

67. *Jacob Berry*, 217–218.

68. Alan Trachtenberg, "Preface," in Allen, *Horrible Prettiness*, xii.

69. "Columbia Opera House," *New York Herald*, March 8, 1878, 6.

70. *Jacob Berry*, 246, 251.

71. Ibid., 242–243.

72. Ibid., 252–258; "Summary of Law Cases," *New York Herald*, May 1, 1878, 5.

73. "Jake Berry on the Island," *The Sun*, May 15, 1879, 4.

74. Gilfoyle, *City of Eros*, 186–196. See also Kristen Pullen, *Actresses and Whores: On Stage and in Society* (Cambridge: Cambridge University Press, 2005), 93–133.

75. ROA I, 119–120. For further description of this case and American brothel entertainments before 1920, see Gilfoyle, *City of Eros*, 161–178. In another study, Gilfoyle notes documentation of the household property of an elite brothel shut down in New York City in 1883, including "framed oil paintings and chromolithographs (sometimes as many as four in a room." In Timothy J. Gilfoyle, "Archaeologists in the Brothel: 'Sin City,' Historical Archaeology and Prostitution," *Historical Archaeology* 39, no. 1 (2005): 135.

76. Disappointments such as this demonstrate why Comstock ultimately "conceded he could do little to remove prostitution in its most obvious form from the city." Gilfoyle, *City of Eros*, 162; ROA I, 119–120. The trial was held on September 24 and 25, 1878.

77. "Informers: To the Editor of the Brooklyn Eagle," *Brooklyn Daily Eagle*, February 5, 1878, 1. Donna Dennis discusses similar sentiments, and legal efforts including a failed "Anti-Spy" bill, in *Licentious Gotham*, 300.

78. "Detective Methods," *New-York Tribune*, June 24, 1878, 4. For an expanded discussion of complaints about Comstock's spy methods, see Edward J. Balleisen, *Fraud: An American History from Barnum to Madoff* (Princeton: Princeton University Press, 2017), 209–213.

79. "Miscellaneous City News: Mrs. Dr. Sara B. Chase Arrested," *New York Times*, May 10, 1878, 8; "Anthony Comstock Arrested," *New York Times*, June 26, 1878, 8; "Sharp Practice by Mr. Comstock," *New York Times*, July 11, 1878, 3. Scholarship contextualizing these prosecutions includes Leslie J. Reagan, *When Abortion Was a Crime: Women, Medicine, and Law in the United States, 1867–1973* (Berkeley: University of California Press, 1997).

80. "The News This Morning," *New-York Tribune*, July 11, 1878, 4.

81. "Anthony Comstock," *Christian Advocate*, June 20, 1878, 393.

82. A search of the *Chronicling America Historic American Newspapers* database for "Anthony Comstock" for 1878 yields sixty-one articles: http://chroniclingamerica.loc.gov/search/pages /results/?date1=1878&rows=20&searchType=basic&state=&date2=1878&proxtext =%22anthony+comstock%22&y=14&x=10&dateFilterType=yearRange&page=1&sort=relevance.

83. "Christmas Presents," *Puck*, December 19, 1877, 2.

84. Untitled, *Puck*, January 15, 1879, 13.

85. Frisken, *Victoria Woodhull's Sexual Revolution*, 101–102. Frisken provides excellent summary and detail of the course of Woodhull's case and those who condemned and supported her; see also Horowitz, *Rereading Sex*, 342–357.

86. Susan Jacoby, *Freethinkers: A History of American Secularism* (New York: Henry Holt, 2004), 1, 205–212.

87. The trials of American freethinkers, liberals, free love advocates, etc., have been written about extensively in publications including Jacoby, *Freethinkers*; Roderick Bradford, *D. M. Bennett: The Truth Seeker* (New York: Prometheus Books, 2006); David M. Rabban, *Free Speech in Its Forgotten Years* (Cambridge: Cambridge University Press, 1997), 23–45; Martin Henry Blatt, *Free Love and Anarchism: The Biography of Ezra Heywood* (Urbana: University of Illinois Press, 1989); and Heywood Broun and Margaret Leech, *Anthony Comstock: Roundsman of the Lord* (New York: A. & C. Boni, 1927), 170–193.

88. Janice R. Wood, "The National Defense Association," in *An Indispensable Liberty: The Fight for Free Speech in Nineteenth-Century America*, ed. Mary M. Cronin (Carbondale: Southern Illinois University Press, 2016), 228–249; quote is from page 235.

89. Rabban, *Free Speech in Its Forgotten Years*, 24.

90. Dennis, *Licentious Gotham*, 296. Mary Cronin argues that Heywood, Foote, Bennett, and Harman are responsible for the "formative period of modern First Amendment development." Mary M. Cronin, "The Liberty to Argue Freely: Nineteenth-Century Obscenity Prosecutions and the Emergence of Modern Libertarian Free Speech Discourse," *Journalism and Communications Monographs* 8, no. 3 (fall 2006): 163–219.

91. Quoted in John D'Emilio and Estelle B. Freedman, *Intimate Matters: A History of Sexuality in America*, 3d ed. (Chicago: University of Chicago Press, 2012), 163.

92. John R. Vile, "Ex Parte Jackson," in *Encyclopedia of the Fourth Amendment*, ed. John R. Vile and David L. Hudson, Jr. (Thousand Oaks, CA: CQ Press, 2013), 1:245.

93. For an excellent account of Comstock's pursuit of Heywood, Bennett, etc., see Rabban, *Free Speech in Its Forgotten* Years, 32–41. For Comstock's version of events and issues, see Anthony Comstock, *Frauds Exposed; or, How the People Are Deceived and Robbed, and Youth Corrupted* (New York: J. Howard Brown, 1880), 388–415.

94. In *D. M. Bennett: The Truth Seeker*, Roderick Bradford details Comstock's lengthy and complex pursuit and prosecution of America's foremost nineteenth-century atheist. Bradford, *D. M. Bennett*, 131–139, 151–153, 165–183; see also D. M. Bennett, *From Behind the Bars: A Series of Letters Written in Prison* (New York: D. M. Bennett Liberal and Scientific Publishing House, 1879); and Stone, *Sex and the Constitution*, 160–164.

95. Stone, *Sex and the Constitution*, 161–162.

96. On Blatchford's affiliation, see: Sven Beckert, *The Monied Metropolis: New York City and the Consolidation of the American Bourgeoisie, 1850–1896* (Cambridge: Cambridge University Press, 2001), 309.

97. Katherine Mullin, "Poison More Deadly Than Prussic Acid: Defining Obscenity After the 1857 Obscene Publications Act (1850–1885)," in *Prudes on the Prowl: Fiction and Obscenity in England, 1850 to the Present Day*, ed. David Bradshaw and Rachel Potter (Oxford: Oxford University Press, 2013), 22–23.

98. Stephen Gillers, "A Tendency to Deprave and Corrupt: The Transformation of American Obscenity Law from *Hicklin* to *Ulysses*," *Washington University Law Review* 85, no. 2 (2007): 228–229; Horowitz, *Rereading Sex*, 40.

99. Gillers, "A Tendency," 239.
100. E. H. Heywood, *Cupid's Yokes: or The Binding Forces of Conjugal Life* (Princeton, MA: Co-Operative Publishing, 1876), 8–9.
101. Ibid., 21.
102. Ibid., 9.
103. D'Emilio and Freedman, *Intimate Matters*, 160.
104. For an excellent discussion of the legal issues involved, see Rabban, *Free Speech*, 36–41.
105. NYSSV, *Fifth Annual Report of the NYSSV for 1878* (New York: privately printed, 1879), 15–17.
106. The defendant of whom he was speaking was Newell Campbell. ROA I, 135–136.
107. On *The Decameron*, see Stone, *Sex and the Constitution*, 56–57.
108. In his comparative analysis of obscenity old and new, Twain pointedly left stars in the place of text passages, noting "best to omit." Mark Twain [Samuel Langhorne Clemens], "The Walt Whitman Controversy," ed. Ed Folsom and Jerome Loving, *Virginia Quarterly Review* 83, no. 2 (spring 2007), http://www.vqronline.org/vqr-symposium /walt-whitman-controversy.
109. Jerome Loving, "Osgood's Folly," *Walt Whitman Quarterly Review* 24, no. 2 (2006): 118–125.
110. By 1939, there were forty-four privately printed editions of *1601*. "New Information About an Edition of Mark Twain's *[1601] Conversation as it was by the Social Fireside in the Time of the Tudors*," Rare Books Collection @ Princeton, blog post, October 18, 2012, https://blogs .princeton.edu/rarebooks/2012/10/new-information-about-an-editi/comment-page-1/. For a fascinating discussion of Twain's anti-censorship efforts and beliefs, see Ed Folsom and Jerome Loving, eds., "The Walt Whitman Controversy: A Lost Document," http:// www.vqronline.org/vqr-symposium/walt-whitman-controversy-lost-document.
111. ROA I, 231–232.
112. ROA I, 235–236.
113. NYSSV, *The NYSSV Ninth Annual Report for 1882* (New York: privately printed, 1883), 8.
114. Defendant Brief, Court of Appeals, *The People of the State of New York against August Muller* (New York: C. G. Burgoyne, 1884), Box 4, Folder 9, RGP.
115. Ibid., 12.
116. Ibid., 17, 21.
117. Ibid., 21, 22, 25.
118. Ibid, 34, 36–7.
119. NYSSV, *Tenth Annual Report for 1883* (New York: privately printed, 1884), 11.
120. Beckert, *The Monied Metropolis*, 211.
121. Trumbull, *Anthony Comstock*, 128–140.
122. Anthony Comstock, *Traps for the Young* (New York: Funk & Wagnalls, Co., 1883), 182–183.
123. "During the 1880s and 1890s, the NYSSV's *Arrest Records* record an astonishing 710 arrests for gambling and related offenses." Anna Louise Bates, *Weeder in the Garden of the Lord: Anthony Comstock's Life and Career* (Lanham, MD: University Press of America, 1995), 109.
124. "Anthony Comstock's Cheek: Barber Koechlein Will Shave It with a Two-Pound Razor," *New York Times*, February 13, 1885.
125. "Do Not Like Him: Anthony Comstock Blackballed by Veterans," *Brooklyn Daily Eagle*, April 24, 1889, 6.
126. "Kay Replies to Comstock's Reflections on His Character," *Brooklyn Daily Eagle*, April 26, 1889, 8.

127. Trumbull, *Anthony Comstock*, 141–142.

128. Comstock, *Frauds Exposed*, 5.

129. Ibid., 393. For a review of this text and Comstock's place in the history of efforts to suppress fraud, see Balleisen, *Fraud*, 137–139.

130. Comstock, *Traps for the Young*, x, 7.

131. Ibid., 179.

132. Ibid., 182.

133. Ibid., 168-172

134. Ralph Ginzburg [or assistant], "Notes on the Diary of Samuel Colgate," typed manuscript, 8, Box 1, Folder 27, RGP. The present location of Colgate's diaries is unclear. Ralph Ginzburg (or a research assistant) typed twenty pages of notes on the diaries when they were held in the collection of the library at Colgate University in the 1950s. They have since been mysteriously deaccessioned and may be in the (uncatalogued) collections of the American Baptist Historical Society.

135. Ibid.

136. Anthony Comstock, O. B. Frothingham, and J. M. Buckley, "The Suppression of Vice," *North American Review* 135, no. 312 (November 1882): 495–499.

137. Ibid., 491–492.

138. Andrea Tone, *Devices and Desires: A History of Contraceptives in America* (New York: Hill and Wang, 2001), 28–29. Tone quotes from D. M. Bennett, *An Open Letter to Samuel Colgate* (New York, 1879), 8–9.

139. Ralph Ginzburg [or assistant], "Notes on the Diary of Samuel Colgate," 2.

140. Frederick William Ricord and Sophia B. Ricord, *Biographical and Genealogical History of the City of Newark and Essex County, New Jersey* (New York: The Lewis Publishing Company, 1898), 126.

141. Museum of Fine Arts, Boston, "Artwork: The Colgate Family," accessed October 15, 2016, http://www.mfa.org/collections/object/the-colgate-family-338683.

142. Broun and Leech, *Anthony Comstock*, 254. Thomas died on April 14, 1881. Bertha died there as well in 1892, and both were buried in New Canaan. Johns Adams Comstock, *A History and Genealogy of the Comstock Family in America* (Los Angeles: privately printed, 1949), 99.

143. These comments derive from Ralph Ginzburg's notes, taken during an interview with the son of Comstock's gardener, Box 10, Folder 7, RGP. The Comstocks lived in two houses in Summit, at 25 Franklin Place from 1883 to 1897, and then at 35 Beekman Road. Edmund B. Raftis, *Summit, New Jersey: From Poverty Hill to the Hill City* (Seattle: Great Swamp Press, 1996), 113.

144. These comments are based on Ralph Ginzburg's notes (or an assistant's) taken on "a Book of Inventories, Surrogate's Court, Union County, NJ, Vol. 0 pp. 275-7" at the time of Maggie's death in 1919, Box 10, Folder 7, RGP.

145. ROA I, 213–214.

146. The best research on this question is contained in Ralph Ginzburg's research file, "Comstock—Home Life," Box 10, Folder 7, RGP.

147. Kiliaen Van Rensselaer, "Letter," *New Canaan Messenger*, July 17, 1886, New Canaan Historical Society.

148. Margaret Leech, in Broun and Leech, *Roundsman of the Lord*, 68.

149. Raftis, *Summit, New Jersey*, 109–110.

150. ROA II, 54–55.

151. Broun and Leech, *Anthony Comstock*, 68.

4. ARTISTS, LIBERTARIANS, AND LAWYERS UNITE: THE RISE OF THE RESISTANCE (VOLUME II: 1884–1895)

1. ROA II, 2,3. This testimony is discussed in: NYSSV, *Eleventh Annual Report for 1884* (New York: privately printed, 1885), 11–17.
2. Samuel Colgate writes in his diary on April 11, 1884: "I have spent the whole day at the Metropolitan Hotel at the Roosevelt Committee listening to an examination of C before that Committee." Ralph Ginzburg [or assistant], "Notes on the Diary of Samuel Colgate," typed manuscript, 8, Box 1, Folder 27, RGP. See also Edward P. Kohn, "'A Most Revolting State of Affairs': Theodore Roosevelt's Aldermanic Bill and the New York Assembly City Investigating Committee of 1884," *American Nineteenth Century History* 10, no. 1 (2009): 71–92.
3. "Comstock in Philadelphia: He Arrests a Dealer in Obscene Books and Pictures," *New York Times*, October 4, 1884, 1; ROA II, 10–11.
4. NYSSV, *Eleventh Annual Report*, 10.
5. ROA II, 10–11.
6. "His Fist in Comstock's Face: An Exciting Scene in the Jefferson Market Court," *New York Herald*, November 30, 1884. Clipping located in Box 1, Folder 28, RGP.
7. David S. Shields, "Jose Maria Mora," Broadway Photographs, University of South Carolina, accessed October 10, 2016, http://broadway.cas.sc.edu/content/jose-maria-mora. Shields's website is invaluable for the study of theater photography and early film; see also Susannah Broyles, "Vanderbilt Ball—How a Costume Ball Changed New York Elite Society," Museum of the City of New York, accessed October 10, 2016, https://blog.mcny.org/2013/08/06/vanderbilt-ball-how-a-costume-ball-changed-new-york-elite-society/.
8. "Cross-Examining Mr. Comstock," *Daily Time* (location unrecorded), December 12, 1884. Clipping located in Box 1, Folder 28, RGP.
9. Jane M. Gaines, *Contested Culture: The Image, the Voice, and the Law* (Chapel Hill: University of North Carolina Press, 1991), 51–55.
10. "Comstock Gets Excited: He Protests Against the Lawyers' Way of Putting Questions," (source undocumented), December 12, 1884. Clipping located in Box 1, Folder 28, RGP.
11. "Comstock Gets Excited."
12. Ibid.
13. Chamberlain began his recounting of the trial with the following: "I wish to record the story of one more outrage by the obscenists. An outrage so atrocious and of such far reaching consequences so subversive of order and justice so arbitrary brutal and in human that I cannot permit it to be smothered overlooked or forgotten." This account initially was addressed to Ezra Heywood for publication in *The Truth Seeker*, but that section of the text is crossed out. Box 1, Folder 28, RGP. Chamberlain's account is preserved in the files of the nation's first attorney specializing in obscenity law, Theodore Schroeder. In 1902, Schroeder and Chamberlain worked together to help found the Free Speech League.
14. Ibid.
15. "Evil to Him Who Evil Thinks," *Telegram* (location undocumented, presumably New York), December 27, 1884. Clipping located in Box 1, Folder 28, RGP.
16. *Deposition of Otto Sarony, Sworn to before Edward W. Chamberlain, Notary Public, December 19th, 1884.* Box 1, Folder 28, RGP.

17. "Comstock Gets in a Rage . . . Photographers Give Evidence That the Picture Which Conroy Sold Is Not Indecent," (source unclear), December 28, 1884. Clipping located in Box 1, Folder 28, RGP; "Comstock's Art Censorship," *New York Sun*, December 28, 1884, 1.

18. "Emergence of Advertising in America, 1850–1920—More About Tobacco Advertising and the Tobacco Collections," John W. Hartman Center for Sales, Advertising, and Marketing, Duke University, accessed October 10, 2016, http://library.duke.edu/rubenstein /scriptorium/eaa/tobacco.html; "The Art of American Advertising: National Markets," Baker Library Historical Collections, Harvard Business School, accessed October 10, 2016, http:// www.library.hbs.edu/hc/artadv/national-markets.html. For a fascinating article on early cigarette advertising in Cuba, see Asiel Sepúlveda, "Humor and Social Hygiene in Havana's Nineteenth-Century Cigarette Maquillas," *Nineteenth-Century Art Worldwide* 14, no. 3 (fall 2015), http://www.19thc-artworldwide.org/autumn15/sepulveda-on-havana-19th-century -cigarette-marquillas. Much more work remains to be done on this rich material culture.

19. Many women did smoke before 1910, judging from available evidence, but not in large enough numbers for tobacco companies to market products specifically to them. "Cigarettes: Women," *Harper's Weekly Archives*, accessed September 2, 2016, http://tobacco .harpweek.com/hubpages/CommentaryPage.asp?Commentary=Women

20. ROA II, 112–113.

21. See, for example, Umberto Eco, "The Comic and the Rule," *Faith in Fakes*, trans. William Weaver (New York: Vintage Press, 1998).

22. Susan Fillin-Yeh, for instance, in her study of Georgia O'Keeffe and other early modernists, briefly suggests that "female cross-dressers sometimes functioned as sex symbols for nineteenth-century men who attempted to eroticize and thus possess independent women or who repressed homosexual fantasies." Susan Fillin-Yeh, "Dandies, Marginality and Modernism: Georgia O'Keeffe, Marcel Duchamp and Other Cross-Dressers," *Oxford Art Journal* 18, no. 2 (1995): 36. Kristen Pullen summarizes: "In the eyes of conservative critics, feminists, prostitutes, and burlesquers all wore pants, and thus all were unnatural, masculine monsters." Kristen Pullen, *Actresses and Whores: On Stage and in Society* (Cambridge: Cambridge University Press, 2005), 98.

23. Harry Oosterhuis, *Stepchildren of Nature: Krafft-Ebing, Psychiatry, and the Making of Sexual Identity* (Chicago: University of Chicago Press, 2000), 59.

24. Oosterhuis, *Stepchildren of Nature*, 60, 64. Oosterhuis points out that many of Krafft-Ebing's views are considered incorrect today—for example, his assumption that some amount of sadism in men was natural, as was some masochism in women.

25. Martin Berger surmises that some Gilded Age men made "selective use of manhood's fluid and complex codes to craft more comfortable subject positions." Martin A. Berger, *Man Made: Thomas Eakins and the Constructions of Gilded Age Manhood* (Berkeley: University of California Press, 2000), 123. David Scobey finds in the heart of New York City "a relatively open site of gender experimentation and cultural conflict." David Scobey, "Nymphs and Satyrs: Sex and the Bourgeois Public Sphere in Victorian New York," *Winterthur Portfolio* 37, no. 1 (spring 2002), 61. Laura Horak's extended analysis of silent films before 1915 notes that more than 400 included images of women in men's clothes, which not only were uncontroversial, but actually were praised as "wholesome alternatives to violent and sexualized fare." Laura Horak, *Girls Will Be Boys: Cross-Dressed Women, Lesbians, and American Cinema* (New Brunswick, NJ: Rutgers University Press, 2016), 11.

26. For a brilliant extended essay on the sexual and cultural signification of *Nymphs and Satyr* in the Hoffman House Hotel, see Scobey, "Nymphs and Satyrs."

27. Fronia E. Wissman, "William-Adolphe Bouguereau, Nymphs and Satyr," in *Nineteenth-Century European Paintings at the Sterling and Francine Clark Art Institute*, ed. Sarah Lees (Williamstown, MA: Sterling and Francine Clark Art Institute, 2012), 1:78.

28. NYSSV, *Twelfth Annual Report for 1885* (New York: privately printed, 1886), 9; Anthony Comstock, *Traps for the Young* (New York: Funk & Wagnalls, Co., 1883), 168; William H. Gerdts, *The Great American Nude: A History in Art* (New York: Praeger, 1974), 103. Gerdts's book remains an invaluable classic.

29. Madelon Powers, *Faces Along the Bar: Lore and Order in the Workingman's Saloon, 1870–1920* (Chicago: University of Chicago Press, 1998), 12–13, 65. For an overview of American saloon culture in the late nineteenth century, see also Howard Chudacoff, *The Age of the Bachelor: Creating an American Subculture* (Princeton: Princeton University Press, 1999), 107–115.

30. I am grateful to Joshua Brown for assistance in understanding the neighborhoods of lower Manhattan in the nineteenth century.

31. ROA I, 51–52; see also "Exhibition of Improper Pictures," *New York Times*, March 14, 1875. In December, Comstock also arrested William Reagan, who seemed to be at the center of the saloon pictures ring. After such careful detective work, Comstock was especially bitter when the district attorney failed to subpoena any witnesses and the case was dropped. ROA I, 61–62. Despite this blow, Comstock did not relent, and a grand jury in 1877 "found a true bill of indictment against Clarke for 'selling & having in his possession to sell obscene pictures.' This is in addition to bills already found." AC to C. Cochran, Jr., Chief of Division of Mail Depravations, March 15, 1875; Box 23, Folder AC Correspondence 1874–1877, CFI; AC to P. H. Woodward, Chief Special Agent, Post Office Dept., February 26, 1876, Box 23, Folder AC Correspondence 1874–1877, CFI.

32. Gerdts, *The Great American Nude*, 103–111. Gerdts documents several examples of American artists who painted nudes for this market, but most are later.

33. AC to C. Cochran, August 21, 1875; Box 23, Folder AC Correspondence 1874–1877, CFI; see also ROA I, 57–58.

34. In Comstock's arrest blotters, this case is listed as "called and adjourned" three times. ROA I, 51–52.

35. Tom Miller, "The Lost Hoffman House Hotel—Broadway and 25th Street, *Daytonian in Manhattan*, May 20, 2013, http://daytoninmanhattan.blogspot.com/2013/05/the-lost-hoffman-house-hotel-broadway.html.

36. "Some of the Art Attractions of New York," *National Academy Notes including the Complete Catalogue of the Spring Exhibition, National Academy of Design*, no. 5 (1885), 167.

37. William C. Beecher was the son of Henry Ward Beecher. He served as the attorney for the NYSSV for many years, as well as one of its executive committee members. ROA II, 30–31.

38. F. G. De Fontain, *The Hoffman House, C. H. Read & E. S. Stokes Proprietors: Its Attractions* (New York: The Photo-Engraving Company, 1885), Collection, American Antiquarian Society.

39. "Notes," *The Connoisseur* 1, no. 2 (March 1887), 46–47.

40. Moses King, *King's Handbook of New York City* (Boston: Moses King, 1892), 205–206, accessed October 10, 2016, https://books.google.com/books?id=cKkUAAAAYAAJ&printsec=frontcover&source=gbs_ge_summary_r&cad=0#v=onepage&q&f=false

41. Patrick A. Morris, *A History of Taxidermy: Art, Science, and Bad Taste* (London: MPM, 2010), 302–30.3

42. For a poetic discussion of the multiple meanings of taxidermy, see Rachel Poliquin, *The Breathless Zoo: Taxidermy and the Culture of Longing* (University Park: Pennsylvania State University Press, 2012). The well-known story of the "Teddy" bear dates to 1902 during the presidency of Theodore Roosevelt.

43. George Chauncey, *Gay New York: Gender, Urban Culture, and the Making of the Gay Male World, 1890–1940* (New York: Basic Books, 1994), 45.

44. *Brooklyn Daily Eagle*, April 18, 1886, 4.

45. "Gallery and Studio: The A. T. Stewart Collection of Works of Art," *Brooklyn Daily Eagle*, February 27, 1887, 4.

46. In 1915, Maria Van Antwerp Jesup bequeathed the couple's paintings to the Metropolitan Museum of Art, along with a fund for the future purchase of American art. The collection included no nudes. Bryson Burroughs, "Bequest of Mrs. Morris K. Jesup," *Metropolitan Museum of Art Bulletin* 10, no. 2 (February 1915): 22–23. Both families also eschewed works with overt religious themes, despite the increasing popularity of this genre even among Protestants. Kirstin Schwain, *Signs of Grace: Religion and American Art in the Gilded Age* (Ithaca: Cornell University Press, 2008), 2–3.

47. John Ott, "How New York Stole the Luxury Art Market: Blockbuster Auctions and Bourgeois Identity in Gilded Age America," *Winterthur Portfolio* 42, no. 2/3 (fall 2008), 134. See also Jennifer Hardin, "The Nude in the Era of the New Movement in American Art: Thomas Eakins, Kenyon Cox, and Augustus Saint-Gaudens" (PhD diss., Princeton University, 2000), 76–81.

48. James L. Yarnall, *John La Farge: Watercolors and Drawings* (Yonkers, NY: Hudson River Museum of Westchester, 1990), 39–42. I am deeply indebted to James Yarnall for his gracious generosity in providing me with a copy of the court documents for *George A. Chamberlain v. John La Farge*, which are preserved at the New York City Municipal Archives.

49. For a thorough review of the problems leading up to La Farge's arrest, see James L. Yarnall, *John La Farge, A Biographical and Critical Study* (Burlington, VT: Ashgate, 2012), 118–120. For a description of the window and La Farge's many innovations in stained glass, see Julie L. Sloan and James L. Yarnall, "Art of an Opaline Mind: The Stained Glass of John La Farge," *American Art Journal* 24, no. 1/2 (1992): 4–43.

50. *George A. Chamberlain v. John La Farge*.

51. For a thorough discussion of Leeds and censorship in Philadelphia, see Nicola Beisel, *Imperiled Innocents: Anthony Comstock and Family Reproduction in Victorian America* (Princeton: Princeton University Press, 1997), 128–157.

52. C. M. S. [Charles Montgomery Skinner], "Gallery and Studio: An Artistic Partnership by Two Brooklyn Painters," *Brooklyn Daily Eagle*, July 31, 1887, 12.

53. Circular advertising Eadweard Muybridge, *Animal Locomotion* (Philadelphia, 1886), Eadweard Muybridge Collection, University of Pennsylvania, accessed October 10, 2016, http://www.archives.upenn.edu/primdocs/upt/upt50/upt50m993/upt50m993b62f05.pdf.

54. For an analysis of Eakins's and Muybridge's photographic work during this time, see Amy Werbel, *Thomas Eakins: Art, Medicine, and Sexuality in Nineteenth-Century Philadelphia* (New Haven: Yale University Press, 2007), 86–131.

55. C. M. S. [Charles Montgomery Skinner], "Gallery and Studio: The Vexed Question of the Nude in Art," *Brooklyn Daily Eagle*, December 27, 1885, 7.

56. Werbel, *Thomas Eakins*, 122.

57. Ibid., 127–128. For a thorough review of Muybridge's project, see Sarah Gordon, *Indecent Exposures: Eadweard Muybridge's 'Animal Locomotion' Nudes* (New Haven: Yale University Press, 2015). On photographs of the nude used by artists in Paris and Philadelphia, see an excellent article by Anne McCauley, "'The Most Beautiful of Nature's Works'": Thomas Eakins's Photographic Nudes in Their French and American Contexts," in *Eakins and the Photograph: Works by Thomas Eakins and His Circle in the Collection of the Pennsylvania Academy of the Fine Arts*, ed. Susan Danly and Cheryl Leibold (Washington: Smithsonian Institution Press, 1994), 23–63.

58. AC to William A. West, October 27, 1886, Case File, *New York vs. Frank Hegger and Lance R. Keough* (October 27, 1886), Entry 231, Box 30, CFI.

59. McCauley, "The Most Beautiful of Nature's Works," 26.

60. Thomas Waugh, *Hard to Imagine: Gay Male Eroticism in Photography and Film from their Beginnings to Stonewall* (New York: Columbia University Press, 1996), 61.

61. McCauley, "The Most Beautiful of Nature's Works," 29.

62. "Art Works and Their Photographic Reproduction," Musée d'Orsay, accessed October 10, 2016, http://www.musee-orsay.fr/en/events/exhibitions/in-the-musee-dorsay/exhibitions-in-the-musee-dorsay-more/page/2/article/loeuvre-dart-et-sa-reproduction-photographique-4241.html?tx_ttnews%5BbackPid%5D=252&cHash=709ebb557a

63. AC to William A. West, October 27, 1886.

64. Henry G. Pearson, Postmaster of New York City, to William A. West, Post Office Inspector, November 1, 1886, Case File, *New York vs. Frank Hegger and Lance R. Keough* (October 27, 1886), Entry 231, Box 30, CFI.

65. "Comstock's New Departure," *New York Herald*, December 10, 1886; "Raiding the 'Art Galleries,'" *New York Star*, December 10, 1886; "Comstock on His Rounds" (source unclear), December 21, 1886, Box 17, Folders 5–6, RGP.

66. "Raiding the 'Art Galleries.'"

67. ROA II, 56–57.

68. "Comstock's Big Contract: He Imports the French Art Issue and Arrests Five Picture Dealers," *Philadelphia Press*, November 30, 1886, 3.

69. "Comstock Rebuked," *Philadelphia Press*, January 25, 1888, 3.

70. Janentzky & Weber, *Illustrated Trade Price List of Artists' Materials* (Philadelphia, 1886), Winterthur Museum Library, accessed October 10, 2016, https://archive.org/details/illustratedtradeoojane.

71. "Comstock Rebuked."

72. The sequence and content of the testimony in the Philadelphia cases suggests that Eakins was the customer who had made the initial request to Weber to order *académies* from France in 1881. This was the same year he also started to create his own versions. In its coverage of the testimony, the *Public Ledger* recounted: "The defence [sic] claimed that it was as necessary to have pictures of this character to study the fine arts as it was to have a dead body for the study of anatomy." "What Are 'Art' Pictures: Judge Biddle Tells What Pictures Are Not Indecent," *Public Ledger. Philadelphia*, January 25, 1888, 4. This conflation of artistic and medical approaches to the body was precisely Eakins's argument in his own defense two years earlier. McCauley, "The Most Beautiful of Nature's Works," 38; Werbel, *Thomas Eakins*, 131–132.

73. "Comstock Rebuked."

74. Ibid.

75. Ibid.

76. ROA II, 60–61.

77. For important differences between New York and Philadelphia, see Nicola Beisel, "Upper Class Formation and the Politics of Censorship in Boston, New York, and Philadelphia, 1872–1892" (PhD diss., University of Michigan, 1990).

78. For an excellent and extensive analysis of the Knoedler trial, press coverage, and sociological frameworks for understanding Comstock's censorship campaigns, see Nicola Beisel, "Morals Versus Art: The Politics of Interpretation, and the Victorian Nude," *American Sociological Review* 58, no. 2 (April 1993): 145–162; and Beisel, *Imperiled Innocents*, 168–193.

79. Charles R. Henschel, *A Catalogue of an Exhibition of Paintings and Prints of Every Description on the Occasion of Knoedler: One Hundred Years, 1846–1946* (New York: Knoedler Gallery, 1946), n.p., vertical file "Knoedler," pamphlet collection, Library of the Smithsonian American Art Museum and National Portrait Gallery. John Ott discusses Knoedler's innovations in catering to wealthy clients in Ott, "How New York Stole the Luxury Art Market, 154–155.

80. ROA II, 86–87.

81. Ibid.

82. "Mr. Comstock's Work," *New York Times*, November 13, 1887.

83. *New York Herald*, November 15, 1887, 4. Quoted in Beisel, *Imperiled Innocents*, 170–171.

84. "The Comstock Nuisance," *New York Times*, November 16, 1887.

85. "Gotham Gossip: Comstock Wants the Evening Telegram Indicted," *Times Picayune* (New Orleans), November 22, 1887.

86. Will H. Low, *A Painter's Progress* (New York: Charles Scriber's Sons, 1910), 19.

87. J. B. F. W., "Society of American Artists," *The Aldine* 9, no. 9 (1879): 275–278, 281–282. See also David Sellin, "The First Pose: Howard Roberts, Thomas Eakins, and a Century of Philadelphia Nudes," *Philadelphia Museum of Art Bulletin* 70, no. 311/312 (spring 1975): 44–45; and Jennifer Hardin, "The Nude in the Era of the New Movement," 28–43.

88. "Artists Denounce Comstock," *New York Sun*, November 17, 1887. This document is reproduced and discussed in Sarah Burns and John Davis, eds., *American Art to 1900: A Documentary History* (Berkeley: University of California Press, 2009), 788–789.

89. Kimberly Orcutt, "Buy American? The Debate Over the Art Tariff," *American Art* 16, no. 3 (Autumn 2002): 90.

90. For a detailed chronology of lobbying efforts by artists, collectors, and others, see Robert E. May, "Culture Wars: The U.S. Art Lobby and Congressional Tariff Legislation During the Gilded Age and Progressive Era," *Journal of the Gilded Age and Progressive Era* 9, no. 1 (January 2010): 37–91.

91. J. M. Mancini, *Pre-Modernism: Art-World Change and American Culture from the Civil War to the Armory Show* (Princeton: Princeton University Press, 2005), 46.

92. Sarah Burns, *Inventing the Modern Artist: Art and Culture in Gilded Age America* (New Haven: Yale University Press, 1996), 2, and passim.

93. "Fie, Anthony Comstock!," *New York World*, November 18, 1887, 6.

94. Untitled, *Springfield Daily Republican* (Sprinfield, Ohio), November 16, 1887, 2, and [Untitled], *Chicago Tribune*, November 19, 1887, 4. The *Springfield Daily Republican* credited its quote to the *Toledo Commercial*.

95. Ralph Ginzburg [or assistant], "Notes on the Diary of Samuel Colgate," 12–13.

96. "Review 2—No Title," *New Englander and Yale Review*, March 1888, 12.

97. Here I am summarizing the excellent analysis of Kathleen Pyne. The final quote in this passage specifically refers to the writings of John Fiske regarding the concept of "racio-cultural hierarchy." Kathleen Pyne, *Art and the Higher Life: Painting and Evolutionary Thought in Late Nineteenth-Century America* (Austin: University of Texas Press, 1996), 33–34. Jennifer Greenhill's analysis of Cosmopolitan artists and writers and their satirical jabs at Puritanism provide fascinating examples of the way these cultural debates shaped art and literature in these years. Jennifer A. Greenhill, *Playing It Straight: Art and Humor in the Gilded Age* (Berkeley: University of California Press, 2012), 108–138.

98. Anthony Comstock, *Morals Versus Art* (New York: Ogilvie & Co., 1887), 4.

99. Richard Christian Johnson, "Anthony Comstock: Reform, Vice, and the American Way" (PhD diss., University of Wisconsin, 1973), 190.

100. For a substantive examination of these social and political conditions, see Paul Boyer, *Urban Masses and Moral Order in America* (Cambridge: Harvard University Press, 1978), 121.

101. Greenhill, *Playing It Straight*, 103–107.

102. Comstock, *Morals Versus Art*, 6–7.

103. E., "Mr. Inness on Art Matters," *Art Journal* 5 (1879), 374–375.

104. Quoted in Burns and Davis, eds., *American Art to 1900*, 787.

105. Comstock, *Morals Versus Art*, 30.

106. Ibid., 8–9.

107. "Review 2—No Title," 216.

108. Nicola Beisel aptly summarizes this argument: "A painting might be obscene when viewed by a working class person, but was a work of art when viewed by a wealthy person." Beisel, "Morals Versus Art," 151.

109. *Daily Times* (Richmond, Virginia), December 11, 1886, 2.

110. Writing of the situation in the late twentieth century, Amy Adler notes: "Free speech law governs culture, yet in surprising ways, culture also governs free speech law." That phenomenon was no less true in the late nineteenth century. Amy Adler, "The First Amendment and the Second Commandment," in *Law, Culture, and Visual Studies*, ed. Ann Wagner and Richard K. Sherwin (Dordrecht: Springer, 2014), 177.

111. Beisel, *Imperiled Innocents*, 188–189.

112. Hollis Clayson discusses censorship of Gervex's *Rolla* in France in Hollis Clayson, *Painted Love: Prostitution in French Art of the Impressionist Era* (New Haven: Yale University Press, 1991), 81–90. The second photograph was of a painting entitled *Entre 5 et 6 Heures en Breda Street*, which also depicted prostitution.

113. Knoedler's attorney insisted that court records note that his clients were not admitting to any intentional violation of the law. "City and Suburban News," *New York Times*, March 27, 1888.

114. "Roland F. Knoedler (1856–1932)," The Frick Collection Center for the History of Collecting, accessed October 10, 2016, http://research.frick.org/directoryweb/browserecord.php?-action=browse&-recid=7033

115. Ralph Ginzburg [or assistant], "Notes on the Diary of Samuel Colgate," 14.

116. Comstock, *Morals Versus Art*, 11–12.

117. "Book Notes," *The Sun*, January 8, 1888, 4.

118. Ibid.

119. "Very Nude Art: How the Boston Beauties Are Photographed," *Saint Paul Daily Globe*, June 7, 1887, 1; "Boston Culture: Society Belles Have Their Photographs Taken as 'Nymphs at the Bath,' Etc.," *Weekly Gazette: Fort Worth, Texas*, June 17, 1887, 3; "As Greek Goddesses: More About the Boston Girls Posing in Scanty Costumes Before Photographer Chickering," *Columbus Daily Enquirer*, June 14, 1887.

120. "Very Nude Art."

121. Anthony Comstock, "Vampire Literature," *North American Review* 153, no. 417 (August 1, 1891), 160–161.

122. "New York News," *Wheeling* (West Virginia) *Register*, September 21, 1890. "Sibyl" is spelled in various ways in accounts of the actress.

123. Alexander Dumas, *The Clemenceau Case*, trans. William Fléron (New York: American News Company, 1890), 23–25. For an excellent discussion of fictional accounts of artist's models in the second half of the nineteenth century, see Jane Desmarais, "The Model on the Writers' Block: The Model in Fiction from Balzac to du Maurier," in *Model and Supermodel: The Artist's Model in British Art and Culture*, ed. Jane Desmarais, Martin Postle, and William Vaughan (Manchester: Manchester University Press, 2006), 47–60. See also David S. Shields, "Carnal Glory? Nudity and the Fine and Performing Arts, 1890–1917," Broadway Photographs, University of Southern California, accessed October 10, 2016, http://broadway .cas.sc.edu/content/carnal-glory-nudity-and-fine-and-performing-arts-1890-1917.

124. Alan Dale, "The Clemenceau Case," *New York Evening World*, September 16, 1890, 2.

125. Quoted in *Rock Island* (Illinois) *Daily Argus*, December 29, 1890, 3.

126. "Boston Aldermen Called Hogs," *New York Sun*, October 17, 1890, 7.

127. "The Clemenceau Case," *Helena* (Montana) *Independent*, March 28, 1891, 8.

128. Edgar W. Nye, "Samples of the Bright Little Notes He Has Gathered Concerning the Stage," *Salt Lake Herald*, May 24, 1891, 10.

129. This label may possibly be the one referred to in the NYSSV, *Thirty-First Annual Report for 1904* (New York: privately printed, 1905), 23: "we discovered in certain cigar stores in the lower part of the city, certain pictures displayed upon the inside of cigar boxes, which were placed in the window so that boys and girls passing could see them." After making a phone call to the company, the vice president ordered them removed. "There had been convictions upon this same picture, but this firm did not know of it."

130. Desmarais, "The Model," 54–55. On the influence of *Trilby*, see Burns, *Inventing the Modern Artist*, 255–267.

131. Shields, "Carnal Glory?" See also McCullough, *Living Pictures*, 140–142.

132. "The World for the Summer," *New York Evening World*, August 6, 1890, 2.

133. "Rivals in Vice Crushing," *New York Evening World*, June 21, 1890, 4.

134. The "prosecution" of the American News Company is an excellent example of the scheme. On August 5, 1890, Britton visited the company's offices and procured evidence of "immoral" publications. Among the haul of 1,244 books he brought with three defendants to the police court were 100 copies of *The Clemenceau Case*. Britton argued that the men should be let go if they promised not to distribute "disreputable or immoral" books again. From his perspective (presumably), if the men were scared and set free, he could then collect a monthly fee. But the judge refused to throw out the case, and the grand jury refused unanimously to bring an indictment for obscenity. "Comstock's Competitors: Britton Raids the American News Company's Office," *New York Sun*, August 6, 1890, 5; "The Grand Jury Doesn't Agree With Britton," *New York Sun*, August 13, 1890, 6.

135. "Agent Britton a Plunger," *New York World*, June 13, 1891, 3; see also "Queer Excise Methods," *New-York Tribune*, October 08, 1890, 4.

136. Alison M. Parker, *Purifying America: Women, Cultural Reform, and Pro-Censorship Activism, 1873–1933* (Urbana: University of Illinois Press, 1997), 4–19.

137. NYSSV, *Twenty-Second Annual Report for 1895* (New York: privately printed, 1896), 7.

138. The best sources on these subjects are two excellent recent books: Richard Zacks, *Island of Vice: Theodore Roosevelt's Doomed Quest to Clean Up Sin-Loving New York* (New York: Random House, 2012); and Daniel Czitrom, *New York Exposed: The Gilded Age Police Scandal That Launched the Progressive Era* (New York: Oxford University Press, 2016).

139. Whitney Strub, *Obscenity Rules: Roth v. United States and the Long Struggle Over Sexual Expression* (Lawrence: University Press of Kansas, 2013), 23–24.

140. Edward W. Chamberlain, "In the Midst of Wolves," *Arena*, November 1894, 837.

141. Janice R. Wood, "The National Defense Association," in *An Indispensable Liberty: The Fight for Free Speech in Nineteenth-Century America*, ed. Mary M. Cronin (Carbondale: Southern Illinois University Press, 2016), 242–243.

142. Brodie's story has been told many times. See, for example, R. N. Stephens, *The Life and Adventures of Steve Brodie, B. J., of the Bowery* (New York: Thomas H. Davis, 1894), accessed October 10, 2016, http://pds.lib.harvard.edu/pds/view/4938530?n=1&s=4&print Thumbnails=no; Luc Sante, *Low Life: Lures and Snares of Old New York* (New York: Farrar, Strauss, Giroux, 1991), 122–125; and David McCullough, *The Great Bridge: The Epic Story of the Building of the Brooklyn Bridge* (New York: Simon and Schuster, 1972), 546–547.

143. "Brodie's Path to Wealth," *New York Times*, July 25, 1886.

144. Comstock also wrote in his blotter: "Had a vile card advertising his Saloon, & then had vile cards & pictures framed upon his Saloon walls." ROA II, 208–209.

145. "Tony Makes Brodie Weary," *New York World*, October 15, 1891.

146. "Mr. Brodie's Black Thursday," *Princeton* (Minnesota) *Union*, December 10, 1891, 2.

147. ROA II, 268–269. Comstock came back again the following month and arrested Brodie himself while Reiley was in prison. Offensive pictures once again were back on the walls, but Brodie managed to avoid incarceration a second time, with witnesses testifying that he had not been in the saloon for months. ROA II, 268–269.

148. For a comprehensive study of these shifts, see Lawrence W. Levine, *Highbrow/Lowbrow: The Emergence of Cultural Hierarchy in America* (Cambridge: Harvard University Press, 1988); see also J. M. Mancini's apt critique of the concept of "cultural hierarchy" in *Pre-Modernism*, 9–10.

149. Sante, *Low Life*, 123–124.

150. J. Chris Westgate, *Staging the Slums, Slumming the Stage: Class, Poverty, Ethnicity, and Sexuality in American Theatre, 1890–1916* (New York: Palgrave Macmillian, 2014), 29. See also Chad Heap, *Slumming: Sexual and Racial Encounters in American Nightlife, 1885–1940* (Chicago: University of Chicago Press, 2009), 3, 8.

151. Heap, *Slumming*, 3.

152. As David Scobey notes, women's similar interest in seeing *Nymphs and Satyr* at the Hoffman demonstrates a profound shift in American society at the turn of the twentieth century, as "elite women and men . . . began to forge a new, class-stratified, mixed-sex public sphere. Within it, they replaced earlier ideals of gender segregation and erotic self-discipline with an ethos of heterosexual pleasure and sensuous display." Scobey, "Nymphs and Satyrs," 48. Stokes did, however, hold fast against sex integration. In 1907,

for example, the hotel was sued for refusing to serve three members of the Democratic Women's Club in its rooftop dining room because they were not chaperoned by a man. The complainant in the case was Harriot Stanton Blatch, the daughter of Elizabeth Cady Stanton. While the Age of the 'Bachelor' brought a wealth of places to dine and recreate, women similarly on their own faced a quite different situation. Women were also prohibited from smoking in public facilities until at least 1908. Andrew P. Haley, *Turning the Tables: Restaurants and the Rise of the American Middle Class, 1880–1920* (Chapel Hill: University of North Carolina Press, 2011), 145–148, 162. See also Michael Lesy and Lisa Stoffer, *Repast: Dining Out at the Dawn of the New Century, 1900–1910* (New York: W. W. Norton, 2013).

153.   Donna Dennis, *Licentious Gotham: Erotic Publishing and Its Prosecution in Nineteenth-Century New York* (Cambridge: Harvard University Press, 2009), 301.

154.   As Wayne Fuller points out, "Lewd books . . . were possessed by nearly every large and small dealer in obscene publications in the nation and proved, if proof were needed, the existence of a national network of the pornography trade that the postal system had made possible by the 1890s." Fuller provides an excellent overview of U.S. Post Office Department efforts involving obscenity, in Wayne E. Fuller, *Morality and the Mail in Nineteenth-Century America* (Urbana: University of Illinois Press, 2003), 222–247; quote is from page 227.

155.   Case File, *U.S. v. Oscar Saemann, alias Sunbeam Gallery &c.* (September 13, 1894), Entry 231, Box 111, CFI. The date of indictment was October 2, 1894, in the Southern Circuit of Iowa at Council Bluffs.

156.   *Report of the Population of the United States: Eleventh Census 1890*, vol. 1, part 1 (Washington: Government Printing Office, 1895), 130.

157.   Daniel P. Carpenter, *The Forging of Bureaucratic Autonomy: Reputations, Networks, and Policy Innovation in Executive Agencies, 1862–1928* (Princeton: Princeton University Press, 2001), 85; McAfee's thorough case reports preserved in the National Archives and Records Administration deserve further research.

158.   Frank Teel, ROA II, 262–263; Ambrose Teel, ROA II, 264–265. See also "Mr. Comstock's Raid," *New York World*, September 11, 1894, 8. Evidence described in these cases is included in Robert McAfee's report on the case of Oscar Saemann, Case File, *U.S. v. Oscar Saemann, alias Sunbeam Gallery &c.* (September 13, 1894), Entry 231, Box 111, CFI.

159.   Case File, *U.S. v. George Watts and Ralph Watts* (September 10, 1894), Entry 231, Box 111, CFI. See also "Mr. Comstock's Raid," *New York World*, September 11, 1894, 3. For an excellent overview of fraud and skepticism at the time, see Michael Leja, *Looking Askance: Skepticism and American Art from Eakins to Duchamp* (Berkeley: University of California Press, 2004).

160.   AC to Martin D. Wheeler, Esq., Chief P. O. Inspector, December 4, 1891; Case File, *U.S. v. Carl N. Casper* (December 1, 1891), Entry 231, Box 80, CFI.

161.   At the time of the arrest, Comstock discovered a substantial photography and printing studio in a backyard woodshed, where he seized 400 books, 2,156 photographs, and 183 negatives. Case File, *U.S. v. Frank S. Partridge, alias Elite Art Co., alias Elite Photo Co.* (March 1, 1898), Entry 231, Box 152, CFI.

162.   Case File, *U.S. v. George Watts and Ralph Watts* (September 10, 1894), RG 28 Entry 231, CFI; Case File, *U.S. v. Oscar Saemann, alias Sunbeam Gallery &c.* (September 13, 1894), Entry 231, Box 111, CFI; Case File, *U.S. v. Frank S. Partridge, alias Elite Art Co., alias Elite*

Photo Co. (March 1, 1898), Entry 231, Box 152, CFI. Sentences in federal courts generally were much harsher than in municipal and state cases; Case File, *U.S. v. Eugene LeBeuf, alias Joseph J. Harkins* (August 22, 1894), Entry 231, Box 109, CFI.

163. Gertrude Grace Sill, *John Haberle: American Master of Illusion* (New Britain Museum of Art, 2009), 39.

164. The most comprehensive discussion of this painting is Sill, *John Haberle*, 35–43. For a fascinating extended discussion of Haberle's "proto-modernist" humor, see Greenhill, *Playing It Straight*, 139–163.

165. John D'Emilio and Estelle B. Freedman, *Intimate Matters: A History of Sexuality in America*, 3d ed. (Chicago: University of Chicago Press, 2012), 180.

5. NEW WOMEN, NEW TECHNOLOGY, AND THE DEMISE OF COMSTOCKERY (VOLUME III: 1895–1915)

1. NYSSV, *Twenty-Second Annual Report for 1895* (New York: privately printed, 1896), 9.

2. Alan Trachtenberg, *The Incorporation of America: Culture and Society in the Gilded Age,* Twenty-Fifth Anniversary Edition (New York: Hill and Wang, 2007), 209, 211.

3. "St. Gaudens Defends His Art," *New York World*, January 20, 1894, 1. Saint-Gaudens refused to redesign the reverse and it was completed by Charles Barber, who represented Columbus's ship the *Santa Maria* with "two winged (and ironically bare-breasted) females." John H. Dryfout, *The Work of Augustus Saint-Gaudens* (Hanover, NH: University Press of New England, 1982), 201–202; "Online Collection Record: World's Columbian Exposition Commemorative Presentation Medal," accessed October 15, 2016, http://www.metmuseum.org/art/collection/search/14941.

4. Thayer Tolles, "Augustus Saint-Gaudens in the Metropolitan Museum of Art," *The Metropolitan Museum of Art Bulletin* new series 66, no. 4 (spring 2009): 31–32. For a thorough account of American sculpture during these years, and the rise of the National Sculpture Society, see Michele H. Bogart, *Public Sculpture and the Civic Ideal in New York City, 1890–1930* (Chicago: University of Chicago Press, 1989).

5. Jennifer A. Greenhill, *Playing It Straight: Art and Humor in the Gilded Age* (Berkeley: University of California Press, 2012), 134–135. For an excellent account and analysis of *Diana*, see Elizabeth Lee, "The Electrified Goddess: Augustus Saint-Gaudens, Stanford White and Diana at Madison Square Garden," *Nineteenth Century* 31, no. 1 (spring 2011): 13–22.

6. "To Glorify the Nude: The Great Gotham Art Exhibition Will Have This Object," *Washington Post*, February 25, 1894, 15. Quoted in David S. Shields, "Carnal Glory? Nudity and the Fine and Performing Arts, 1890–1917," Broadway Photographs, University of Southern California, accessed October 10, 2016, http://broadway.cas.sc.edu/content/carnal-glory-nudity-and-fine-and-performing-arts-1890-1917.

7. Kenyon Cox, for example, wrote a lengthy defense of "the nude in art" in *Scribner's Magazine* in December 1902, in which he declared that "the figure should be nude if it is to express great and simple ideas." Quoted in Sarah Burns and John Davis, eds., *American Art to 1900: A Documentary History* (Berkeley: University of California Press, 2009), 788. Artists in London similarly advocated for the nude in art in the early 1890s, including Sir Lawrence Alma-Tadema and Ford Maddox Brown. Jane Clapp, *Art Censorship: A Chronology of Proscribed and Prescribed Art* (Lanham, MD: Rowman & Littlefield, 1972), 165.

8. Michele H. Bogart, *The Politics of Urban Beauty: New York and Its Art Commission* (Chicago: University of Chicago Press, 2006), 16.

9. Case File, *U.S. v. George Watts and Ralph Watts* (September 10, 1894), Entry 231, Box III, CFI.

10. David S. Shields provides further fascinating examples of nudity, and concerns over nudity at the Exposition, in "Carnal Glory?"

11. Trachtenberg, *Incorporation*, 220–221.

12. "Anthony Is Shocked," *Sunday Globe* [Saint Paul, Minnesota], August 13, 1893, 1. This is one example of a newspaper that reprinted, and cited, the article in the *New York Recorder*.

13. Ibid.

14. "Opinions on the Danse du Ventre," *New York World*, August 13, 1893, 1. Clipping located in Box 2, Folder 2, RGP. This file contains several of Craddock's publications that were suppressed, along with some personal correspondence regarding her prosecution.

15. Leigh Eric Schmidt, *Heaven's Bride: The Unprintable Life of Ida C. Craddock, American Mystic, Scholar, Sexologist, Martyr, and Madwoman* (New York: Basic Books, 2010), 195–196.

16. Ida C. Craddock, *The Danse du Ventre* (Philadelphia, 1897), 2, 10, 16–17, Box 2, Folder 2, RGP.

17. For a full examination of Craddock's life and philosophy, see Leigh Eric Schmidt, *Heaven's Bride: The Unprintable Life of Ida C. Craddock, American Mystic, Scholar, Sexologist, Martyr, and Madwoman* (New York: Basic Books, 2010). For a history of the Free Speech League, see David M. Rabban, "The Free Speech League, the ACLU, and Changing Conceptions of Free Speech in American History," *Stanford Law Review* 45, no. 1 (November 1992): 47–114. Quote is from page 81, where Rabban is quoting league organizer Lincoln Steffens. See also Geoffrey R. Stone, *Sex and the Constitution: Sex, Religion, and Law from America's Origins to the Twenty-First Century* (New York: Liveright, 2017), 164–165.

18. For a comprehensive analysis of the ideologies of "new women," see Ellen Wiley Todd, *The New Woman Revised: Painting and Gender Politics on Fourteenth Street* (Berkeley: University of California Press, 1993), 1–38.

19. Quoted in Parker, *Purifying America*, 34.

20. "The Midway Dancers Fined," *New-York Tribune*, December 7, 1893, 3; "Dancing Girls Fined $50," *New York Evening World*, December 6, 1893, 3; ROA II, 248–249. Comstock listed the religion of the women as "heathen." Comstock also noted: "A.C. prepared brief & assisted in prosecution."

21. Although Allen suggests that all of these had to be "morally-unobjectionable," the many protests of the WCTU and Comstock suggest that this was at least a subject of debate. Robert Allen, *Horrible Prettiness: Burlesque and American Culture* (Chapel Hill: University of North Carolina Press, 1991), 186; see also Nancy Mowll Mathews, "Art and Film: Interactions," in *Moving Pictures: American Art and Early Film, 1880–1910*, ed. Nancy Mowll Mathews (Williamstown, MA: Williams College Museum of Art, 2005), 153.

22. In 1890, for example, American artists combined their efforts to put on a Living Pictures Exhibition in Brooklyn Heights as a fundraiser for a men's old age home. "Programme for Living Pictures by American Artists" (1890), Warshaw Collection of Business Americana, National Museum of American History, Collection No. 60, Box 3 See also McCullough, *Living Pictures*.

23. See, for example, the instructions in *Gilbert's Book of Pantomimes* (New York: H. C. Wilkinson & Co., undated), Collection, New York Public Library.

24. "Artist W. M. Chase a Witness: He Thinks the Bronze Statues Are Modest in the Extreme," *New York Times*, March 27, 1895, 8. See also McCullough, *Living Pictures*, 121–124.

25. For a discussion of Chase's work with living pictures, and the relationship of this medium to photography by artists such as Gertrude Käsebier, see Judith Fryer Davidov, *Women's Camera Work: Self/Body/Other in American Visual Culture* (Durham: Duke University Press, 1998), 60–63. See also Erica E. Hirschler, "Old Masters Meet New Women," in *William Merritt Chase: A Modern Master* (Washington: Phillips Collection; New Haven: Yale University Press, 2016), 18–20.

26. *Sarony's Living Pictures: Photographed from Life* seems to have been intended as an ongoing journal, but only vol. 1, no. 1 (1894) was published; see also Shields, "Carnal Glory?"

27. Alison M. Parker discusses WCTU efforts to censor living pictures in depth in *Purifying America*, 124–133.

28. Ibid., 39–40.

29. I am indebted to my former student, Shelby Superneau, for her excellent research in preparation of a senior thesis on the subject of "A Most Cruel and Unwarranted Attack: The Woman's Christian Temperance Union of the State of New York vs. Federal Censor Anthony Comstock" (senior thesis, Saint Michael's College, 2011).

30. Parker, *Purifying America*, 39.

31. NYSSV, *Twenty-Third Annual Report for 1896* (New York: privately printed, 1897), 4, 13.

32. ROA III, 10–11.

33. "Huber's Museum Closes Its Doors," *New York Times*, July 16, 1910. The New-York Historical Society holds the catalogue of Huber's collection, which was sold at auction on August 1, 1910.

34. Janice R. Wood, "The National Defense Association," in *An Indispensable Liberty: The Fight for Free Speech in Nineteenth-Century America*, ed. Mary M. Cronin (Carbondale: Southern Illinois University Press, 2016), 231.

35. As Charles Musser writes, "by June 1891 over a third of the country's 3,200 phonographs were being used as nickel-in-the-slot machines." Charles Musser, *The Emergence of Cinema: The American Screen to 1907* (New York: Charles Scribner's Sons, 1990), 60–61. The defendants, Serafio Artiaga and Charles A. Kramer, each received a fine of fifty dollars. ROA II, 270–271.

36. ROA III, 18–19.

37. Wonderful literature on Coney Island includes John Kasson, *Amusing the Million: Coney Island at the Turn of the Century* (New York: Hill and Wang, 1978); Michele Bogart, "Barking Architecture: The Sculpture of Coney Island," *Smithsonian Studies in American Art* 2, no. 1 (winter 1988): 2–8, 11–17; and Robin Jaffee Frank, ed., *Coney Island: Visions of an American Dreamland, 1861–2008* (Hartford: Wadsworth Atheneum Museum of Art; New Haven: Yale University Press, 2015).

38. ROA III, 26–27; "Arrests by Comstock: Charged with Making Objectionable Phonographs," *Brooklyn Daily Eagle*, June 25, 1896, 1.

39. "Gramophone Record Making," *Brooklyn Daily Eagle*, December 18, 1897, 7.

40. Musser, *Emergence*, 62.

41. NYSSV, *Twenty-Sixth Annual Report for 1899* (New York: privately printed, 1900), 15–16.

42. ROA III, 102–3, 114–115.

43. NYSSV, *Twenty-Ninth Annual Report for 1902* (New York: privately printed, 1903), 32.

44. Howard Chudacoff, *The Age of the Bachelor: Creating an American Subculture* (Princeton: Princeton University Press, 1999), 132.

45. Musser, *Emergence*, 114.

46. Shields, "Carnal Glory?" See also Allen, *Horrible Prettiness*, 265–271.

47. Thomas A. Edison, Inc., *Turkish Dance, Ella Lola*, 1898, Paper Print Collection, Library of Congress, https://www.loc.gov/search/?in=&q=ella+lola+turkish+dance&new=true&st=

48. Mathews, "Art and Film: Interactions," 153–154.

49. For example, in 1900 Comstock appeared before the Assembly Codes Committee of the New York State Assembly "to urge favorable action on Senator Wagner's bill making it a misdemeanor to exhibit any indecent moving picture in slot machines." "To Prohibit Indecent Pictures," *New York Times*, February 28, 1900, 9.

50. For a review of efforts to constrain the increasingly sexual entertainments of the 1890s and early 1900s, see Daniel Czitrom, "The Politics of Performance: From Theater Licensing to Movie Censorship in Turn-of-the-Century New York," *American Quarterly* 44, no. 4 (December 1992): 525–553; Lewis A. Erenberg, *Steppin' Out: New York Nightlife and the Transformation of American Culture* (Chicago: University of Chicago Press, 1981): 60–91; and Andrea Friedman, *Prurient Interests: Gender, Democracy, and Obscenity in New York City, 1909–1945* (New York: Columbia University Press, 2000).

51. ROA III, 58–59.

52. Katherine Manthorne, "John Sloan's Moving-Picture Eye," *American Art* 18, no. 2 (summer 2004): 80–95. For an expansive analysis of Sloan's politics in relation to his aesthetics, see Michael Lobel, *John Sloan: Drawing on Illustration* (New Haven: Yale University Press, 2014).

53. Fred Bassett, "Wish You Were Here!: The Story of the Golden Age of Picture Postcards in the United States," New York State Library, last updated August 16, 2016, http://www.nysl.nysed.gov/msscfa/qc16510ess.htm.

54. NYSSV, *Thirty-Second Annual Report for 1905* (New York: privately printed, 1906), 13–14.

55. Ibid., 14.

56. Leigh Ann Wheeler, *Against Obscenity: Reform and the Politics of Womanhood in America, 1873–1935* (Baltimore: Johns Hopkins University Press, 2004), 19–20.

57. "Raid on 'The Black Rabbit,'" *New York Times*, October 6, 1900, 2.

58. *New York vs. Michael Davis, William Sheldon, Jules Dumont, Edith Myrtle Lynch, John Doe, Richard Roe, and Pauline Sheldon* (November 2, 1900), Case File 32946, New York City Municipal Archives. I am grateful to Dr. Cary Costello for helping me understand and properly describe the testimony regarding Pauline Sheldon's status.

59. Cary Costello writes: "it was a common practice at the time for women in freak shows to give special exhibitions to all-male audiences, in which they would reveal their genitalia . . . the sexual display of 'freaks,' including intersex people, was very popular at the time." Personal communication, August 5, 2016.

60. NYSSV Arrest Blotter III, 100–101. Comstock did not record the sentence for Richard Roe (initially identified as John Doe).

61. William Eskridge, Jr., *Dishonorable Passions: Sodomy Laws in America, 1861–2003* (New York: Viking, 2008), 45–46.

62. George Chauncey, *Gay New York: Gender, Urban Culture, and the Making of the Gay Male World, 1890–1940* (New York: Basic Books, 1994), 36–37.

63. NYSSV, *Twenty-Seventh Annual Report for 1900* (New York: privately printed, 1901), 10.

64. Chauncey, *Gay New York*, 39–42.
65. ROA I, 119–120. The trial was held on September 24 and 25, 1878.
66. *New York vs. Michael Davis*.
67. Lee, "The Electrified Goddess," 13. For a thorough discussion of *Diana* in many contexts, see Hardin, "The Nude," 266–347.
68. Lee, "Electrified Goddess," 18; Emily Kies Folpe, *It Happened on Washington Square* (Baltimore: Johns Hopkins University Press, 2002), 124.
69. Lee, "The Electrified Goddess," 19. Jennifer Greenhill also offers an extended discussion of the jocular and unrestrained relationship between the two men, in: Greenhill, *Playing it Straight*, 130–138.
70. White's murder, and Thaw's trial, have been analyzed in several books and articles, including Paula Uruburu, *American Eve: Evelyn Nesbit, Stanford White, The Birth of the "It" Girl and the Crime of the Century* (New York: Riverhead Books, 2008). The Library of Congress also offers a helpful list of primary sources at: Library of Congress, "Topics in Chronicling America—The first 'trial of the century' the murder of Stanford White," accessed October 15, 2016, http://www.loc.gov/rr/news/topics/stanfordwhite.html.
71. "Comstock Wants to Tell about White and Others," *New York Times*, June 29, 1906, 2. See also an example of how this small story was reprinted outside New York: "Mrs. Thaw will be Chief Witness for her Husband," *Lexington Herald-Leader*, July 1, 1906.
72. "Editorial Comment," *Philadelphia Inquirer*, August 6, 1906.
73. "20,000 in a Crush at the Beauty Show," *New York Times*, October 10, 1905, 10.
74. ROA III, 184–5.
75. Mariah Larsson, "Pornography and Erotica," in Michael Kimmel, Christine Milrod, and Amanda Kennedy, eds., *Cultural Encyclopedia of the Penis* (Lanham, MD: Rowman & Littlefield, 2014), 166.
76. "New Bills," *New-York Tribune*, October 29, 1905, 3.
77. "Daly Cuts Lines and Tones Down Shaw Play," *New York Evening World* (October 30, 1905), 11.
78. "Bernard Shaw Resents Action of Librarian. Calls 'American Comstockery' World's Standing Joke," *New York Times*, September 26, 1905, 1. The NYPL subsequently denied the accusation. "Shaw Not Under the Ban," *New-York Tribune*, September 27, 1905, 7.
79. "Bernard Shaw Resents," 1.
80. NYSSV, *Thirty-Second Annual Report*, 17.
81. William Cowper, in *Twenty-six Letters on Religious Subjects*, by John Newton, 1774.
82. NYSSV, *Thirty-Third Annual Report for 1906* (New York: privately printed, 1907), 33–35.
83. Ibid., 9. The watches were probably imported from a German manufacturer that patented similar designs in 1901 and 1902. Christoph Prignitz, *Erotische Uhren: Zeit für die Liebe* (Ulm: Ebner, 2004), 177.
84. NYSSV, *Thirty-Third Annual Report*, 5.
85. ROA III, 188.
86. "Comstock Hit Thrice; Told, 'Serves You Right,'" *New York Times*, March 10, 1906, 1.
87. "Art Students' League Raided by Comstock," *New York Times*, August 3, 1906, 1.
88. Ibid.
89. Marchal E. Landgren, *Years of Art: The Story of the Art Students League of New York* (New York: Robert M. McBride, 1940), 23.
90. [André Champollion?], "Editorial," *American Student of Art* 1, no. 1 (January 1906): 35–36.

91. "Art Students' League Raided," 2.

92. The clerk's name was originally listed as "Jane Doe" at the time of arrest, and then as Anna Robinson for a time, in both cases to protect her identity. However, during the trial, the presumably real name Anna Reibley was used in court and entered the newspapers against Comstock's wishes. In court and board of trustee documents, the last name appears alternately as Reibling or Riebley.

93. ROA III, 196.

94. "Art Students' League Raided," 1.

95. Many thanks to an anonymous peer reviewer for pointing out that Shinn here was quoting "the Yellow Kid," a popular cartoon character representing a tenement waif, who appeared in a variety of publications including the *New York World* and *New York Evening Journal* around the turn of the century.

96. "Art Students Jeer at Comstock's Raid," *New York Times*, August 4, 1906, 7.

97. "Art Students Jeer," 7.

98. "Pictures Which Comstock Calls Lewd and for Which He Raided Art Students," *New York World*, August 3, 1906; "Caricatures of Anthony Comstock and His Latest Raid, *New York* as Drawn To-Day by Members of the Art Students' League, Whose Home Was Raided," *Evening World*, August 3, 1906, 10.

99. "Mr. Anthony Comstock," *Duluth News*, August 16, 1906.

100. "Sanctum Talks," *Life* 48, no. 1242 (August 16, 1906): 187.

101. "Mr. Comstock and the Nude in Art," *Current Literature* 41, no. 3 (September 1906), 286.

102. Quoted in ibid.

103. "Salon of the Dilettanti: XI. Comstock's Fight for the Fig Leaf," *Brush and Pencil* 18, no. 4 (October 1906): 170–172.

104. Anthony Comstock, "The Crime of the Nude," *Leslie's Weekly*, (August 30, 1906), 206.

105. Ibid.

106. Many thanks are due to Ellen Wiley Todd for this astute observation and her other thoughtful and helpful suggestions.

107. For an extended discussion of this situation in Philadelphia, see Amy Werbel, *Thomas Eakins: Art, Medicine, and Sexuality in Nineteenth-Century Philadelphia* (New Haven: Yale University Press, 2007).

108. On this episode, see Annette Blaugrund, "Introduction," in *Challenging Tradition: Women of the Academy, 1826–2003* (New York: National Academy of Design, 2003–2004), 10; Sarah Burns and John Davis recount a controversy regarding Augustus St. Gaudens's short-lived coeducational modeling class at the League in 1890, after which League artists seem to have shied away from the practice—at least until after 1906. Burns and Davis, eds., *American Art to 1900*, 792–794; Raymond J. Steiner, *The Art Students League of New York: A History* (Saugerties: CSS Publications, 1994), 115–116; and Landgren, *Years of Art*, 49–55.

109. "Comstock Battles with Art," *New York Sun*, October 16, 1906; "Art League Raid Case Heard in Police Court," *New York Times*, October 16, 1906, 5.

110. "Comstock Relents: His Offer Rejected," *New York Times*, October 30, 1906, 6.

111. "Art League Raid Case Heard in Police Court," *New York Times*, October 16, 1906, 5.

112. "Comstock Again Has a Brisk Day in Court," *New York Times*, October 31, 1906, 7.

113. Worldcat lists the publication only at the Whitney Museum of American Art and at the New York Public Library, where I viewed the series. The Art Students League also holds all of the issues.

114. This decision was made by the Board of Control on October 2, 1906. Minutes of the Meetings of the Board of Control (October–December 1906), Archives of the Art Students League of New York.

115. Landgren, *Years of Art*, 87–89.

116. "Comstock in Statuette," *Washington Post*, March 6, 1907, 3; "Annual Fakirs' Stunts," *American Art News* 5, no. 28 (April 27, 1907): 2. For more on the Fakirs, see Ronald G. Pisano and Bruce Weber, *Parodies of the American Masters: Rediscovering the Society of American Fakirs, 1891–1914* (New York: Museums at Stony Brook and the Art Students League, 1993).

117. Richard Meyer uses this phrase to describe the reactions of artists including Paul Cadmus, Andy Warhol, Robert Mapplethorpe, and others to attempted censorship of twentieth-century homoerotic art. He writes: "Like the censorship of dreams, the censorship of visual art functions not simply to erase but also to enable representation; it generates limits, but also reactions to those limits; it imposes silence even as it provokes responses to that silence." Richard Meyer, *Outlaw Representation: Censorship and Homosexuality in Twentieth-Century American Art* (New York: Oxford University Press, 2002), 15, 16–17.

118. John Fagg, "Chamber Pots and Gibson Girls: Clutter and Matter in John Sloan's Graphic Art," *American Art* 29, no. 3 (fall 2015): 46.

119. Sylvia L. Yount, "Consuming Drama: Everett Shinn and the Spectacular City," *American Art* (fall 1992): 88.

120. Leo G. Mazow, "Everett Shinn's Time Warp," in *The Eight and American Modernisms*, ed. Elizabeth Kennedy (Chicago: Terra Foundation for American Art, 2009), 129–130.

121. Quoted in Helen Farr Sloan, *John Sloan's New York Scene* (New York: Harper & Row, 1965), 50.

122. Lobel, *John Sloan*, 121–128.

123. Rebecca Zurier, *Art for the Masses: A Radical Magazine and Its Graphics, 1911–1917* (Philadelphia: Temple University Press, 1988), 96.

124. Marianne Doezema, "Tenement Life: Cliff Dwellers, 1906–1913," in *George Bellows* (Washington: National Gallery of Art, 2012), 48, 52.

125. For a thoughtful discussion of the meanings of "representation" and "realism" for Ashcan artists, see Rebecca Zurier, *Picturing the City: Urban Vision and the Ashcan School* (Berkeley: University of California Press, 2006), 8–10.

126. Ibid., 107.

127. Ibid., 35–36.

128. Allan Antliff, *Anarchist Modernism: Art, Politics, and the First American Avant-Garde* (Chicago: University of Chicago Press, 2001), 25–29. As Charles Brock notes, George Bellows followed Henri's example, teaching at the Ferrer Center, supporting Goldman when she was arrested under the Comstock Act, and caricaturing the censor in *The Masses* in 1915. Charles Brock, "George Bellows: An Unfinished Life," in *George Bellows* (Washington: National Gallery of Art, 2012), 14–15.

129. Emma Goldman, *Anarchism and Other Essays* (New York: Mother Earth Publications, 1911), 176.

130. Allan Antliff credits Henri as "prime instigator" for the development "in which old aesthetic norms and institutional practices were displaced by a new modernism suffused with anarchist principles." Antliff, *Anarchist Modernism*, 11; see also Marian Wardle, "Thoroughly Modern: The 'New Women' Art Students of Robert Henri," in *American Women Modernists: The Legacy of Robert Henri, 1910–1945*, ed. Marian Wardle (Provo, UT: Brigham Young University Museum of Art, 2005).

131. Valerie Ann Leeds discusses this work in "Pictorial Pleasures: Leisure Themes and the Henri Circle," in *Life's Pleasures: The Ashcan Artists' Brush with Leisure, 1895–1925,* ed. James W. Tottis (Detroit: Detroit Institute of Arts, 2007), 32–34.

132. Udo Kultermann, "The 'Dance of the Seven Veils': Salome and Erotic Culture Around 1900," *Artibus et Historiae* 27, no. 53 (2006): 187–215; see also Shields, "Carnal Glory?"

133. For a comprehensive overview of the Armory Show, see Marilyn Kushner, Kimberly Orcutt, and Casey Blake, *The Armory Show at 100: Modernism and Revolution* (New York: New-York Historical Society, 2013).

134. Kimberly Orcutt, "Robert Henri's Manifesto," in *The Armory Show at 100,* 266–273.

135. William Innes Homer, *Robert Henri and His Circle* (Ithaca: Cornell University Press, 1969), 173. See also Kimberly Orcutt, *Painterly Controversy: William Merritt Chase and Robert Henri* (Greenwich, CT: Bruce Museum, 2007), for an excellent review of Henri's many battles in this moment.

136. *The Ethiopian,* Luce Center, Smithsonian American Art Museum online collection label, http://americanart.si.edu/collections/search/artwork/?id=31892. Thanks to Stephanie Cassidy for clarification on Arthur Lee's relationship with the Art Students League.

137. For a meticulous recounting of these events, see Kathleen A. Foster and Cheryl Leibold, eds., *Writing About Eakins: The Manuscripts in Charles Bregler's Thomas Eakins Collection* (Philadelphia: University of Pennsylvania Press, 1990). See also Werbel, *Thomas Eakins.*

138. Jonathan Weinberg, *Male Desire: The Homoerotic in American Art* (New York: Harry N. Abrams, 2004), 19.

139. For a thoughtful and thorough discussion of Eakins's *William Rush* series, see Akela Reason, *Thomas Eakins and the Uses of History* (Philadelphia: University of Pennsylvania Press, 2010). See also Werbel, *Thomas Eakins,* 97–99.

140. "Comstock on the Griddle," *New York Times,* October 18, 1906, 16.

141. "Anthony Comstock Protests," *New York Times,* October 21, 1906, 22.

142. "Comstock's Mileage for Court Cases," *New York Times,* November 25, 1906, 10.

143. Schroeder's *Albany Law Journal* article is reprinted in Theodore Schroeder, *"Obscene" Literature and Constitutional Law: A Forensic Defense of Freedom of the Press* (New York: privately printed, 1911), 13.

144. Ibid.

145. "Comstock Not Removed," *New York Times,* December 30, 1906, 18; "To Fight Comstock," *Fort Worth Star-Telegram,* January 3, 1906.

146. The *Wilkes-Barre Times,* for example, wrote: "Saint Anthony has waged one too many battles with sin." "Comstock Loses Post-Office Inspectorship," *Wilkes-Barre Times,* December 29, 1906.

147. "Editorial Comment," *Philadelphia Inquirer,* December 31, 1906.

148. "Art, Business and Mr. J. P. Morgan," *Life* 49, no. 1284 (June 6, 1907), 767.

149. NYSSV, *Thirty-Fifth Annual Report for 1908* (New York: privately printed, 1909), 16.

150. ROA III, 256–257.

151. Amy Sueyoshi, *Queer Compulsions: Race, Nation, and Sexuality in the Affairs of Yone Noguchi* (Honolulu: University of Hawaii Press, 2012), 83–84.

152. ROA III, 288–289; "Missouri Death Certificates, 1910–1966," *Missouri Digital Heritage,* accessed October 11, 2016, https://s1.sos.mo.gov/Records/Archives/ArchivesMvc/Death Certificates/SearchResults.

153. John R. Corvell, "Comstockery," *Mother Earth* 1, no. 1 (March 1906): 32, 34. See also Candace Falk, ed., *Emma Goldman: A Documentary History of the American Years: Vol. 2. Making Speech Free, 1902–1909* (Urbana: University of Illinois Press, 2008), 557–558.

154. NYSSV, *Thirty-Seventh Annual Report for 1910* (New York: privately printed, 1911), 5.

155. ROA III, 306–307.

156. NYSSV, *Forty-First Annual Report for 1914* (New York: privately printed, 1915), 18.

157. John J. Leary, Jr., "Comstock's Rule in Vice Society Near Overthrow," *New-York Tribune*, June 13, 1915, 1, 3.

158. Christine Stansell, *American Moderns: Bohemian New York and the Creation of a New Century* (Princeton: Princeton University Press, 2009), 235.

159. Ibid.; ROA III, 328–329. Sanger was arrested on January 19, 1915.

160. ROA III, 328–329.

161. "Sanger Prefers Prison to Fine," *New-York Tribune*, September 11, 1915, 14.

162. Ellen Chesler, *Woman of Valor: Margaret Sanger and the Birth Control Movement in America* (New York: Simon and Schuster, 1992), 133; on Sanger's efforts and trial, see also Stone, *Sex and the Constitution*, 194–204.

163. ROA III, 338–339.

164. Chesler, *Woman of Valor*, 140.

165. Ibid., 142–143.

166. Ibid., 151–152.

167. Stansell, *American Moderns*, 76.

168. Sadakichi Hartmann, in *Camera Work* 32 (October 1910): 17–18.

169. NYSSV, *Twenty-Sixth Annual Report*, 14; Luc Sante, *Low Life: Lures and Snares of Old New York* (New York: Farrar, Strauss, Giroux, 1991), 119–121.

170. NYSSV, *Thirty-Ninth Annual Report for 1912* (New York: privately printed, 1913), 11–12.

171. Ralph Ginzburg [or assistant], "A Trip to Vineland in Summer of 1959: From Her dossier," typed ms., Box 10, Folder 7, RGP.

CONCLUSION: POSTMORTEM

1. Some of her solutions, including eugenics, are wholly indefensible today. Angela Franks, *Margaret Sanger's Eugenic Legacy: The Control of Female Fertility* (Jefferson, NC: McFarland, 2005).

2. Walt Whitman, "A Memorandum at a Venture," *North American Review* 134 (June 1882): 547–548. Accessed April 16, 2017, at https://archive.org/stream/jstor-25101059/25101059#page /n3/mode/2up.

3. Geoffrey Stone succinctly chronicles Sumner's difficulties in Geoffrey R. Stone, *Sex and the Constitution: Sex, Religion, and Law from America's Origins to the Twenty-First Century* (New York: Liveright, 2017), 168–171.

4. The NYSSV by that time had been renamed the Society to Maintain Public Decency. NYSSV, *Seventy-Fifth Year Book: 1948 Report* (New York: privately printed, 1948), 13.

5. Andrea Tone, *Devices and Desires: A History of Contraceptives in America* (New York: Hill and Wang, 2001), 26.

6. Quoted in Stone, *Sex and the Constitution*, 202, fn. 61.

7. NYSSV, *Twenty-Seventh Annual Report for 1901* (New York: privately printed, 1902), 9–10.

8. The U.S. Supreme Court did not declaratively reject the *Hicklin* standard until 1957, in *Roth v. United States*. Stone, *Sex and the Constitution*, 166, 275.

9. "Anthony Comstock Dies in His Crusade," *New York Times*, September 22, 1915, 1, 6.

10. Stone, *Sex and the Constitution*, 165.

11. Heywood Broun and Margaret Leech, *Anthony Comstock: Roundsman of the Lord* (New York: A. & C. Boni, 1927), 270.

12. H. L. [Henry Louis] Mencken, *A Book of Prefaces* (New York: Alfred A. Knopf, 1917), 254.

13. Richard Christian Johnson, "Anthony Comstock: Reform, Vice, and the American Way" (PhD diss., University of Wisconsin, 1973), 195. Johnson's data remains the best source for statistical analysis of Comstock's arrest records.

14. A recent Comstock cartoon and three-volume illustrated novel present him as a "Godly hero . . . armed only with faith in God and a desire to protect children from the evils of his generation, Anthony Comstock put himself under the Providential care of the Lord, and lived to see sweeping victories against impossible odds." The materials are beautifully produced, in the cause of promoting a renewed era in which birth control is illegal. *Anthony Comstock: FIGHTER (Origins of a Hero)*, published March 31, 2014, https://www.youtube.com/watch?v=bLE1uCFlFsE.

15. Michael Ravnitzky wisely notes that this amounted to "implicit recognition by the legal participants of rather victim-less crimes" (personal communication, October 2016).

16. Mencken, *A Book of Prefaces*, 250–251.

17. Recent scholarship, thankfully, is renewing interest in this topic. See, for example, David M. Rabban, *Free Speech in Its Forgotten Years* (Cambridge: Cambridge University Press, 1997); Stone, *Sex and the Constitution*; and Stephen D. Solomon, *Revolutionary Dissent: How the Founding Generation Created the Freedom of Speech* (New York: St. Martin's Press, 2016).

18. *Jacobellis v. Ohio* 378 U.S. 184 (1964) in regard to declaring a French film *The Lovers* not obscene.

19. Stone, *Sex and the Constitution*, 278. For an extended essay on this famous phrase, see Paul Gerwitz, "On 'I Know It When I See It,'" *Yale Law School Faculty Scholarship Series*, paper 1706 (1996), accessed October 13, 2016, http://digitalcommons.law.yale.edu /fss_papers/1706.

20. Charles Edward Hopkins, *The Rise of the Social Gospel in American Protestantism, 1865–1915* (New Haven: Yale University Press, 1940), 14, 19.

21. For an analysis of the YMCA's organizational strategies and success, see Mayer N. Zald and Patricia Denton, "From Evangelism to General Service: The Transformation of the YMCA," *Administrative Science Quarterly* 8, no. 2 (September 1963): 214–234.

SELECTED BOOKS, ARTICLES, AND DIGITAL RESOURCES

···

Adler, Amy. "The First Amendment and the Second Commandment." In *Law, Culture, and Visual Studies*, ed. Ann Wagner and Richard K. Sherwin, 161–178. London: Springer, 2014.

Allen, Robert. *Horrible Prettiness: Burlesque and American Culture*. Chapel Hill: University of North Carolina Press, 1991.

Antliff, Allan. *Anarchist Modernism: Art, Politics, and the First American Avant-Garde*. Chicago: University of Chicago Press, 2001.

"The Art of American Advertising: National Markets." Baker Library Historical Collections, Harvard Business School. http://www.library.hbs.edu/hc/artadv/national-markets.html.

Balleisen, Edward J. *Fraud: An American History from Barnum to Madoff*. Princeton: Princeton University Press, 2017.

Bartee, Wayne C., and Alice Fleetwood Bartee. *Litigating Morality: American Legal Thought and Its English Roots*. New York: Praeger, 1992.

Bates, Anna Louise. *Weeder in the Garden of the Lord: Anthony Comstock's Life and Career*. Lanham, MD: University Press of America, 1995.

Beckert, Sven. *The Monied Metropolis: New York City and the Consolidation of the American Bourgeoisie, 1850–1896*. Cambridge: Cambridge University Press, 2001.

Beecher, Catharine E. *A Treatise on Domestic Economy for the Use of Young Ladies at Home, and at School*. New York: Harper & Brothers, 1845.

Beisel, Nicola. *Imperiled Innocents: Anthony Comstock and Family Reproduction in Victorian America*. Princeton: Princeton University Press, 1997.

——. "Morals Versus Art. The Politics of Interpretation, and the Victorian Nude." *American Sociological Review* 58, no. 2 (April 1993): 145–162.

——. "Upper Class Formation and the Politics of Censorship in Boston, New York, and Philadelphia, 1872–1892." PhD diss., University of Michigan, 1990.

Bennett, D. M. *From Behind the Bars: A Series of Letters Written in Prison*. New York: D. M. Bennett Liberal and Scientific Publishing House, 1879.

Berger, Martin A. *Man Made: Thomas Eakins and the Constructions of Gilded Age Manhood.* Berkeley: University of California Press, 2000.

Blatt, Martin Henry. *Free Love and Anarchism: The Biography of Ezra Heywood.* Urbana: University of Illinois Press, 1989.

Blum, Edward J. "The Kingdom of Satan in America: Weaving the Wicked Web of Antebellum Religion and Politics." *Common-Place Journal* 15, no. 3 (spring 2015). http://www.common-place.org/vol-15/no-03/blum/#.VXCGlmRViko.

Bogart, Michele. "Barking Architecture: The Sculpture of Coney Island." *Smithsonian Studies in American Art* 2, no. 1 (winter 1988): 2–8, 11–17.

——. *The Politics of Urban Beauty: New York and Its Art Commission.* Chicago: University of Chicago Press, 2006.

——. *Public Sculpture and the Civic Ideal in New York City, 1890–1930.* Chicago: University of Chicago Press, 1989.

Boyer, Paul. *Urban Masses and Moral Order in America.* Cambridge: Harvard University Press, 1978.

Bradford, Roderick. *D. M. Bennett: The Truth Seeker.* New York: Prometheus Books, 2006.

Bradshaw, David, and Rachel Potter, eds. *Prudes on the Prowl: Fiction and Obscenity in England, 1850 to the Present Day.* Oxford: Oxford University Press, 2013.

Brock, Charles. "George Bellows: An Unfinished Life." In *George Bellows.* Washington: National Gallery of Art, 2012.

Broun, Heywood, and Margaret Leech. *Anthony Comstock: Roundsman of the Lord.* New York: A. & C. Boni, 1927.

Brown, Candy Gunther. *The Word in the World: Evangelical Writing, Publishing, and Reading in America, 1789–1880.* Chapel Hill: University of North Carolina Press, 2004.

Brown, Joshua. "'The Social and Sensational News of the Day': Frank Leslie, *The Days' Doings,* and Scandalous Pictorial News in Gilded Age New York." *New-York Journal of American History* 66, no. 2 (fall 2003): 10–20.

Brown, William Adams. *Morris Ketchum Jesup: A Character Sketch.* New York: Charles Scribner's Sons, 1910.

Buggeln, Gretchen Townsend. *Temples of Grace: The Material Transformation of Connecticut's Churches, 1790–1840.* Hanover, NH: University Press of New England, 2003.

Burns, Sarah. *Inventing the Modern Artist: Art and Culture in Gilded Age America.* New Haven: Yale University Press, 1996.

Burns, Sarah, and John Davis, eds. *American Art to 1900: A Documentary History.* Berkeley: University of California Press, 2009.

Burrows, Edwin G., and Mike Wallace. *Gotham: A History of New York City to 1898.* New York: Oxford University Press, 1999.

Carpenter, Daniel P. *The Forging of Bureaucratic Autonomy: Reputations, Networks, and Policy Innovation in Executive Agencies, 1862–1928.* Princeton: Princeton University Press, 2001.

Chamberlain, Edward W. "In the Midst of Wolves." *Arena,* November 1894, 835–837.

Chauncey, George. *Gay New York: Gender, Urban Culture, and the Making of the Gay Male World, 1890–1940.* New York: Basic Books, 1994.

Chesler, Ellen. *Woman of Valor: Margaret Sanger and the Birth Control Movement in America.* New York: Simon and Schuster, 2007.

Chudacoff, Howard. *The Age of the Bachelor: Creating an American Subculture.* Princeton: Princeton University Press, 1999.

Clapp, Jane. *Art Censorship: A Chronology of Proscribed and Prescribed Art*. Lanham, MD: Rowman & Littlefield, 1972.

Clayson, Hollis. *Painted Love: Prostitution in French Art of the Impressionist Era*. New Haven: Yale University Press, 1991.

Cocks, Catherine. "Rethinking Sexuality in the Progressive Era." *Journal of the Gilded Age and Progressive Era* 5, no. 2 (April 2006): 93–118.

Cohen, Patricia Cline, Timothy J. Gilfoyle, and Helen Lefkowitz Horowitz. *The Flash Press: Sporting Male Weeklies in 1840s New York*. Chicago: University of Chicago Press, 2008.

Comstock, Anthony. *Frauds Exposed; or, How the People Are Deceived and Robbed, and Youth Corrupted*. New York: J. Howard Brown, 1880.

——. *Morals Versus Art*. New York: Ogilvie & Co., 1887.

——. *Traps for the Young*. New York: Funk & Wagnalls, 1883.

——. "Vampire Literature." *North American Review* 153, no. 417 (August 1, 1891): 160–171

Comstock, Anthony, O. B. Frothingham, and J. M. Buckley. "The Suppression of Vice." *North American Review* 135, no. 312 (November 1882): 484–501.

Cott, Nancy F. "Passionlessness: An Interpretation of Victorian Sexual Ideology, 1790–1850." *Signs* 4, no. 2 (winter 1978): 219–236.

Cronin, Mary M. "The Liberty to Argue Freely: Nineteenth-Century Obscenity Prosecutions and the Emergence of Modern Libertarian Free Speech Discourse." *Journalism and Communications Monographs* 8, no. 3 (fall 2006): 163–219.

Cross, Barbara M., ed. *The Autobiography of Lyman Beecher*. Vol. 1. Cambridge: Belknap Press of Harvard University, 1961.

Czitrom, Daniel. *New York Exposed: The Gilded Age Police Scandal That Launched the Progressive Era*. New York: Oxford University Press, 2016.

——. "The Politics of Performance: From Theater Licensing to Movie Censorship in Turn-of-the-Century New York." *American Quarterly* 44, no. 4 (December 1992): 525–553.

Davidov, Judith Fryer. *Women's Camera Work: Self/Body/Other in American Visual Culture*. Durham: Duke University Press, 1998.

D'Emilio, John, and Estelle B. Freedman. *Intimate Matters: A History of Sexuality in America*. 3rd ed. Chicago: University of Chicago Press, 2012.

De Fontain, F. G. *The Hoffman House, C. H. Read & E. S. Stokes, Proprietors: Its Attractions*. New York: Photo-Engraving Company, 1885.

Dennis, Donna. *Licentious Gotham: Erotic Publishing and Its Prosecution in Nineteenth-Century New York*. Cambridge: Harvard University Press, 2009.

Dryfout, John H. *The Work of Augustus Saint-Gaudens*. Hanover, NH: University Press of New England, 1982.

Eco, Umberto. "The Comic and the Rule." In *Faith in Fakes*, trans. William Weaver. New York: Vintage Books, 1998.

"Emergence of Advertising in America, 1850–1920: More About Tobacco Advertising and the Tobacco Collections." John W. Hartman Center for Sales, Advertising, and Marketing, Duke University. http://library.duke.edu/rubenstein/scriptorium/eaa/tobacco.html.

Erenberg, Lewis A. *Steppin' Out: New York Nightlife and the Transformation of American Culture*. Chicago: University of Chicago Press, 1981.

Eskridge, William, Jr. *Dishonorable Passions: Sodomy Laws in America, 1861–2003*. New York: Viking, 2008.

Fagg, John. "Chamber Pots and Gibson Girls: Clutter and Matter in John Sloan's Graphic Art." *American Art* 29, no. 3 (fall 2015): 28–57.

Feldman, Stephen M. *Free Expression and Democracy in America: A History.* Chicago: University of Chicago Press, 2008.

Fillin-Yeh, Susan. "Dandies, Marginality and Modernism: Georgia O'Keeffe, Marcel Duchamp and Other Cross-Dressers." *Oxford Art Journal* 18, no. 2 (1995): 33–44.

Finlay, Nancy, ed. *Picturing Victorian America: Prints by the Kellogg Brothers of Hartford, Connecticut, 1830–1880.* Hartford: Connecticut Historical Society, 2009.

Folsom, Ed, and Jerome Loving. "The Walt Whitman Controversy: A Lost Document." *Virginia Quarterly Review* 82, no. 2 (spring 2007). http://www.vqronline.org/vqr-symposium/walt-whitman-controversy-lost-document.

Foster, Gaines M. *Moral Reconstruction: Christian Lobbyists and the Federal Legislation of Morality, 1865–1920.* Chapel Hill: University of North Carolina Press, 2002.

Foster, Kathleen A., and Cheryl Leibold, eds. *Writing About Eakins: The Manuscripts in Charles Bregler's Thomas Eakins Collection.* Philadelphia: University of Pennsylvania Press, 1990.

Frank, Robin Jaffee, ed. *Coney Island: Visions of an American Dreamland, 1861–2008.* Wadsworth Athenaeum Museum of Art in Association with Yale University Press, 2015.

Franks, Angela. *Margaret Sanger's Eugenic Legacy: The Control of Female Fertility.* Jefferson, NC: McFarland, 2005.

Freshwater, Helen. "Towards a Redefinition of Censorship." In *Censorship and Cultural Regulation in the Modern Age,* ed. Beate Müller, 225–245. Amsterdam: Rodopi, 2003.

Friedman, Andrea. *Prurient Interests: Gender, Democracy, and Obscenity in New York City, 1909–1945.* New York: Columbia University Press, 2000.

Frisken, Amanda. "Obscenity, Free Speech, and 'Sporting News' in 1870s America." *Journal of American Studies* 42, no. 3 (2008): 537–577.

——. *Victoria Woodhull's Sexual Revolution: Political Theater and the Popular Press in Nineteenth-Century America.* Philadelphia: University of Pennsylvania Press, 2004.

Fuller, Wayne E. *Morality and the Mail in Nineteenth-Century America.* Urbana: University of Illinois Press, 2003.

Gaines, Jane M. *Contested Culture: The Image, the Voice, and the Law.* Chapel Hill: University of North Carolina Press, 1991.

Gerdts, William H. *The Great American Nude: A History in Art.* New York: Praeger, 1974.

Gerhard, Frederick. *The Dark Side of New York Life and Its Criminal Classes from Fifth Avenue down to the Five Points.* New York: Frederick Gerhard, Agent, 1873.

Giesburg, Judith. *Sex and the Civil War: Soldiers, Pornography, and the Making of American Morality.* Chapel Hill: University of North Carolina Press, 2017.

Gilfoyle, Timothy J. "Archaeologists in the Brothel: 'Sin City,' Historical Archaeology and Prostitution." *Historical Archaeology* 39, no. 1 (2005): 133–141.

——. *City of Eros: New York City, Prostitution, and the Commercialization of Sex, 1790–1920.* New York: W. W. Norton, 1992.

Gillers, Stephen. "A Tendency to Deprave and Corrupt: The Transformation of American Obscenity Law from *Hicklin* to *Ulysses.*" *Washington University Law Review* 85, no. 2 (2007): 215–296.

Goldman, Emma. *Anarchism and Other Essays.* New York: Mother Earth Publications, 1911.

Gordon, Sarah. *Indecent Exposures: Eadweard Muybridge's 'Animal Locomotion' Nudes.* New Haven: Yale University Press, 2015.

Green, Steven K. *The Second Disestablishment: Church and State in Nineteenth-Century America*. New York: Oxford University Press, 2010.

Greenhill, Jennifer A. *Playing It Straight: Art and Humor in the Gilded Age*. Berkeley: University of California Press, 2012.

Greenhouse, Wendy. "Daniel Huntington and the Ideal of Christian Art." *Winterthur Portfolio* 31, no. 2/3 (summer/fall 1996): 103–140.

Gurstein, Rochelle. *The Repeal of Reticence: America's Cultural and Legal Struggles Over Free Speech, Obscenity, Sexual Liberation, and Modern Art*. New York: Hill and Wang, 1996.

Haley, Andrew P. *Turning the Tables: Restaurants and the Rise of the American Middle Class, 1880–1920*. Chapel Hill: University of North Carolina Press, 2011.

Hardin, Jennifer. "The Nude in the Era of the New Movement in American Art: Thomas Eakins, Kenyon Cox, and Augustus Saint Gaudens." PhD diss., Princeton University, 2000.

Heap, Chad. *Slumming: Sexual and Racial Encounters in American Nightlife, 1885–1940*. Chicago: University of Chicago Press, 2009.

Heywood, E. H. *Cupid's Yokes: or The Binding Forces of Conjugal Life*. Princeton, MA: Co-Operative Publishing, 1876.

Historical Account of the Celebration of the One Hundred and Fiftieth Anniversary of the Organization of the Congregational Church of New Canaan, Conn., June 20, 1883. Stamford, CT: Gillespie Brothers, 1883.

Homer, William Innes. *Robert Henri and His Circle*. Ithaca: Cornell University Press, 1969.

Horak, Laura. *Girls Will Be Boys: Cross-Dressed Women, Lesbians, and American Cinema*. New Brunswick: Rutgers University Press, 2016.

Horowitz, Helen Lefkowitz. *Rereading Sex: Battles Over Sexual Knowledge and Suppression in Nineteenth-Century America*. New York: Vintage Books, 2003.

———. "Victoria Woodhull, Anthony Comstock, and Conflict Over Sex in the United States in the 1870s." *Journal of American History* 87, no. 2 (September 2000): 403–434.

Jacoby, Susan. *Freethinkers: A History of American Secularism*. New York: Henry Holt, 2004.

Jaffee, David. *A New Nation of Goods: The Material Culture of Early America*. Philadelphia: University of Pennsylvania Press, 2010.

Johnson, Catherine, Betsy Stiratt, and John Bancroft, eds. *Sex and Humor: Selections from the Kinsey Institute*. Bloomington: Indiana University Press, 2002.

Johnson, Richard Christian. "Anthony Comstock: Reform, Vice, and the American Way." PhD diss., University of Wisconsin, 1973.

Kasson, John. *Amusing the Million: Coney Island at the Turn of the Century*. New York: Hill and Wang, 1978.

Kimmel, Michael, Christine Milrod, and Amanda Kennedy, eds. *Cultural Encyclopedia of the Penis*. Lanham, MD: Rowman & Littlefield, 2014.

King, Mary Louise. *Portrait of New Canaan: The History of a Connecticut Town*. New Canaan, CT: New Canaan Historical Society, 1981.

Kultermann, Udo. "The 'Dance of the Seven Veils': Salome and Erotic Culture Around 1900." *Artibus et Historiae* 27, no. 53 (2006): 187–215.

Kushner, Marilyn, Kimberly Orcutt, and Casey Blake. *The Armory Show at 100: Modernism and Revolution*. New York: New-York Historical Society, 2013.

Landgren, Marchal E. *Years of Art: The Story of the Art Students League of New York*. New York: Robert M. McBride, 1940.

Lane, Frederick S., III. *The Decency Wars: The Campaign to Cleanse American Culture.* New York: Prometheus Books, 2006.

———. *Obscene Profits: The Entrepreneurs of Pornography in the Cyber Age.* New York: Routledge, 2000.

Lee, Elizabeth. "The Electrified Goddess: Augustus Saint-Gaudens, Stanford White and Diana at Madison Square Garden." *Nineteenth Century* 31, no. 1 (spring 2011): 13–22.

Leja, Michael. *Looking Askance: Skepticism and American Art from Eakins to Duchamp.* Berkeley: University of California Press, 2004.

Levine, Lawrence W. *Highbrow/Lowbrow: The Emergence of Cultural Hierarchy in America.* Cambridge: Harvard University Press, 1988.

Lobel, Michael. *John Sloan: Drawing on Illustration.* New Haven: Yale University Press, 2014.

Loving, Jerome. "Osgood's Folly." *Walt Whitman Quarterly Review* 24, no. 2 (2006): 118–125.

Low, Will H. *A Painter's Progress.* New York: Charles Scriber's Sons, 1910.

Lum, Kathryn Gin. *Damned Nation: Hell in America from the Revolution to Reconstruction.* New York: Oxford University Press, 2014.

Lupkin, Paula. *Manhood Factories: YMCA Architecture and the Making of Modern Urban Culture.* Minneapolis: University of Minnesota Press, 2010.

Maines, Rachel P. *The Technology of Orgasm.* Baltimore: Johns Hopkins University Press, 2001.

Mancini, J. M. *Pre-Modernism: Art-World Change and American Culture from the Civil War to the Armory Show.* Princeton: Princeton University Press, 2005.

Manthorne, Katherine. "John Sloan's Moving-Picture Eye." *American Art* 18, no. 2 (summer 2004): 80–95.

Marcus, Edward, ed. *A New Canaan Private in the Civil War: Letters of Justus M. Silliman, Seventeenth Connecticut Volunteers.* New Canaan, CT: New Canaan Historical Society, 1984.

Marcus, Paul. "The Development of Entrapment Law." *William and Mary Law School Faculty Publications Paper* 572 (1986): 5–37.

Marini, Stephen. "Hymnody as History: Early Evangelical Hymns and the Recovery of American Popular Religion." *Church History* 71, no. 2 (June 2002): 273–306.

Martin, Edward Winslow. *The Secrets of the Great City: A Work Descriptive of the Virtues and the Vices, the Mysteries, Miseries and Crimes of New York City.* Philadelphia: Jones, Brothers & Co., 1868.

Mathews, Nancy Mowll, ed. *Moving Pictures: American Art and Early Film, 1880–1910.* Williamstown, MA: Williams College Museum of Art, 2005.

May, Robert E. "Culture Wars: The U.S. Art Lobby and Congressional Tariff Legislation During the Gilded Age and Progressive Era." *Journal of the Gilded Age and Progressive Era* 9, no. 1 (January 2010): 37–91.

Mazow, Leo G. "Everett Shinn's Time Warp." In *The Eight and American Modernisms,* ed. Elizabeth Kennedy, 129–144. Chicago: Terra Foundation for American Art, 2009.

McCauley, Anne. "'The Most Beautiful of Nature's Works': Thomas Eakins's Photographic Nudes in Their French and American Contexts." In *Eakins and the Photograph: Works by Thomas Eakins and His Circle in the Collection of the Pennsylvania Academy of the Fine Arts,* ed. Susan Danly and Cheryl Leibold, 23–63. Washington: Smithsonian Institution Press, 1994.

McCullough, David. *The Great Bridge: The Epic Story of the Building of the Brooklyn Bridge.* New York: Simon and Schuster, 1972.

McCullough, Jack W., *Living Pictures on the New York Stage.* Ann Arbor: UMI Research Press, 1983.

Mencken, H. L. [Henry Louis]. *A Book of Prefaces*. New York: Alfred A. Knopf, 1917.

Merlis, Brian. *Brooklyn's Historic Clinton Hill and Wallabout*. New York: Israelowitz, 2011.

Meyer, Richard. *Outlaw Representation: Censorship and Homosexuality in Twentieth-Century American Art*. New York: Oxford University Press, 2002.

Miller, Angela. *Empire of the Eye: Landscape Representation and American Cultural Politics*. Ithaca: Cornell University Press, 1993.

Morris, Patrick A. *A History of Taxidermy: Art, Science, and Bad Taste*. London: MPM, 2010.

Müller, Beate, ed. *Censorship and Cultural Regulation in the Modern Age*. Amsterdam: Rodopi, 2004.

Musser, Charles. *The Emergence of Cinema: The American Screen to 1907*. New York: Charles Scribner's Sons, 1990.

Noyes, John Kenneth. *The Mastery of Submission: Inventions in Masochism*. Ithaca: Cornell University Press, 1997.

Nussbaum, Martha. *Upheavals of Thought: The Intelligence of Emotions*. New York: Cambridge University Press, 2010.

Oosterhuis, Harry. *Stepchildren of Nature: Krafft-Ebing, Psychiatry, and the Making of Sexual Identity*. Chicago: University of Chicago Press, 2000.

Orcutt, Kimberly. "Buy American? The Debate Over the Art Tariff." *American Art* 16, no. 3 (fall 2002): 82–91.

———. *Painterly Controversy: William Merritt Chase and Robert Henri*. Greenwich, CT: Bruce Museum, 2007.

Ott, John. "How New York Stole the Luxury Art Market: Blockbuster Auctions and Bourgeois Identity in Gilded Age America." *Winterthur Portfolio* 42, no. 2/3 (fall 2008): 133–158.

Parker, Alison M. *Purifying America: Women, Cultural Reform, and Pro-Censorship Activism, 1873–1933*. Urbana: University of Illinois Press, 1997.

Pisano, Ronald G., and Bruce Weber. *Parodies of the American Masters: Rediscovering the Society of American Fakirs, 1891–1914*. New York: Museums at Stony Brook and the Art Students League, 1993.

Pivar, David J. *Purity Crusade: Sexual Morality and Social Control, 1868–1900*. Westport, CT: Greenwood Press, 1973.

Poliquin, Rachel. *The Breathless Zoo: Taxidermy and the Culture of Longing*. University Park: Penn State University Press, 2012.

Powers, Madelon. *Faces Along the Bar: Lore and Order in the Workingman's Saloon, 1870–1920*. Chicago: University of Chicago Press, 1998.

Pullen, Kristen. *Actresses and Whores: On Stage and in Society*. Cambridge: Cambridge University Press, 2005.

Pyne, Kathleen. *Art and the Higher Life: Painting and Evolutionary Thought in Late Nineteenth-Century America*. Austin: University of Texas Press, 1996.

Rabban, David M. *Free Speech in Its Forgotten Years*. Cambridge: Cambridge University Press, 1997.

———. "The Free Speech League, the ACLU, and Changing Conceptions of Free Speech in American History." *Stanford Law Review* 45, no. 1 (November 1992): 47–114.

Raftis, Edmund B. *Summit, New Jersey: From Poverty Hill to the Hill City*. Seattle: Great Swamp Press, 1996.

Readings in New Canaan History. New Canaan, CT: New Canaan Historical Society, 1949.

Reagan, Leslie J. *When Abortion Was a Crime: Women, Medicine, and Law in the United States, 1867–1973*. Berkeley: University of California Press, 1997.

Reason, Akela. *Thomas Eakins and the Uses of History*. Philadelphia: University of Pennsylvania Press, 2010.

Reel, Guy. *The National Police Gazette and the Making of the Modern Man, 1879–1906*. New York: Palgrave Macmillan, 2006.

Renner, Karen J. "Seduction, Prostitution, and the Control of Female Desire in Popular Antebellum Fiction." *Nineteenth-Century Literature* 65, no. 2 (September 2010): 166–191.

Reynolds, David S. *Walt Whitman's America: A Cultural Biography*. New York: Vintage Books, 1996.

Sante, Luc. *Low Life: Lures and Snares of Old New York*. New York: Farrar, Strauss, Giroux, 1991.

Schmidt, Leigh Eric. *Heaven's Bride: The Unprintable Life of Ida C. Craddock, American Mystic, Scholar, Sexologist, Martyr, and Madwoman*. New York: Basic Books, 2010.

Schroeder, Theodore. *Obscene Literature and Constitutional Law: A Forensic Defense of Freedom of the Press*. New York: privately printed, 1911.

Schulle, Jennifer Marie. "Fashion and Fallen Women: The Apparel Industry, the Retail Trade, Fashion, and Prostitution in Late Nineteenth Century St. Louis." PhD diss., Iowa State University, 2005.

Schwain, Kirstin. *Signs of Grace: Religion and American Art in the Gilded Age*. Ithaca: Cornell University Press, 2008.

Scobey, David. "Nymphs and Satyrs: Sex and the Bourgeois Public Sphere in Victorian New York." *Winterthur Portfolio* 37, no. 1 (spring 2002): 43–66.

Sellin, David. *The First Pose: 1876: Turning Point in American Art: Howard Roberts, Thomas Eakins, and a Century of Philadelphia Nudes*. New York: Norton & Company, 1976.

Sepúlveda, Asiel. "Humor and Social Hygiene in Havana's Nineteenth-Century Cigarette Maquillas." *Nineteenth-Century Art Worldwide* 14, no. 3 (fall 2015). http://www.19thc-artworldwide .org/autumn15/sepulveda-on-havana-19th-century-cigarette-marquillas.

Shields, David S. "Broadway Photographs." University of South Carolina. http://broadway.cas .sc.edu/.

Sill, Gertrude Grace. *John Haberle: American Master of Illusion*. New Britain, CT: New Britain Museum of American Art, 2009.

Sloan, Helen Farr. *John Sloan's New York Scene*. New York: Harper & Row, 1965.

Sloan, Julie L., and James L. Yarnall. "Art of an Opaline Mind: The Stained Glass of John La Farge." *American Art Journal* 24, no. 1/2 (1992): 4–43.

Solomon, Stephen D. *Revolutionary Dissent: How the Founding Generation Created the Freedom of Speech*. New York: St. Martin's Press, 2016.

Stansell, Christine. *American Moderns: Bohemian New York and the Creation of a New Century*. Princeton: Princeton University Press, 2009.

Stone, Geoffrey R. *Sex and the Constitution: Sex, Religion, and Law from America's Origins to the Twenty-First Century*. New York: Liveright, 2017.

Strub, Whitney. *Obscenity Rules: Roth v. United States and the Long Struggle Over Sexual Expression*. Lawrence: University Press of Kansas, 2013.

Sueyoshi, Amy. *Queer Compulsions: Race, Nation, and Sexuality in the Affairs of Yone Noguchi*. Honolulu: University of Hawaii Press, 2012.

Todd, Ellen Wiley. *The "New Woman" Revised: Painting and Gender Politics on Fourteenth Street*. Berkeley: University of California Press, 1993.

Tolles, Thayer. "Augustus Saint-Gaudens in the Metropolitan Museum of Art." *Metropolitan Museum of Art Bulletin* 66 (new series), no. 4 (spring 2009).

Tone, Andrea. *Devices and Desires: A History of Contraceptives in America*. New York: Hill and Wang, 2001.

Tottis, James W., ed. *Life's Pleasures: The Ashcan Artists' Brush with Leisure, 1895–1925*. Detroit: Detroit Institute of Arts, 2007.

Trachtenberg, Alan. *The Incorporation of America: Culture and Society in the Gilded Age*. Twenty-Fifth Anniversary Edition. New York: Hill and Wang, 2007.

Trumbull, Charles Gallaudet. *Anthony Comstock: Fighter: Some Impressions of a Lifetime of Adventure in Conflict with the Powers of Evil*. New York: Fleming H. Revell, 1913.

Twain, Mark [Samuel Langhorne Clemens]. "The Walt Whitman Controversy," ed. Ed Folsom and Jerome Loving. *Virginia Quarterly Review* 83, no. 2 (spring 2007). http://www.vqronline .org/vqr-symposium/walt-whitman-controversy.

Uruburu, Paula. *American Eve: Evelyn Nesbit, Stanford White, the Birth of the "It" Girl, and the Crime of the Century*. New York: Riverhead Books, 2008.

Wardle, Marian, ed. *American Women Modernists: The Legacy of Robert Henri, 1910–1945*. Provo, UT: Brigham Young University Museum of Art, 2005.

Waugh, Thomas. *Hard to Imagine: Gay Male Eroticism in Photography and Film from Their Beginnings to Stonewall*. New York: Columbia University Press, 1996.

Weinberg, Jonathan. *Male Desire: The Homoerotic in American Art*. New York: Harry N. Abrams, 2004.

Werbel, Amy. "Lifting the Lid on Cigar Boxes at Winterthur" *Panorama: Journal of the Association of Historians of American Art* 2.2 (fall, 2016). http://journalpanorama.org/amy-werbel-associate -professor-department-of-the-history-of-art-fashion-institute-of-technology-state-university -of-new-york/.

——. "Tales from the Vault: Searching for Smut," *Common-Place Journal* 11, no. 1 (October, 2010). http://www.common-place-archives.org/vol-11/no-01/tales/.

——. "'The Crime of the Nude:' Anthony Comstock's Raid on the Art Students League of New York and the Origins of Modern American Obscenity" *Winterthur Portfolio* 48, no. 4 (winter, 2014): 249–28.

——. *Thomas Eakins: Art, Medicine, and Sexuality in Nineteenth-Century Philadelphia*. New Haven: Yale University Press, 2007.

Westgate, J. Chris. *Staging the Slums, Slumming the Stage: Class, Poverty, Ethnicity, and Sexuality in American Theatre, 1890–1916*. New York: Palgrave Macmillian, 2014.

Wheeler, Leigh Ann. *Against Obscenity: Reform and the Politics of Womanhood in America, 1873–1935*. Baltimore: Johns Hopkins University Press, 2004.

Whitman, Walt. *The Portable Walt Whitman*, ed. Michael Warner. New York: Penguin Books, 2004.

Wood, Janice R. "The National Defense Association." In *An Indispensable Liberty: The Fight for Free Speech in Nineteenth-Century America*, ed. Mary M. Cronin, 228–249. Carbondale: Southern Illinois University Press, 2016.

Yamashiro, Jennifer Pearson. "Sex in the Field: Photography at the Kinsey Institute." PhD diss., Indiana University, 2001.

Yarnall, James L. *John La Farge, A Biographical and Critical Study*. Burlington, VT: Ashgate, 2012.

——. *John La Farge: Watercolors and Drawings*. Westchester, NY: Hudson River Museum of Westchester, 1990.

Yount, Sylvia L. "Consuming Drama: Everett Shinn and the Spectacular City." *American Art* 6, no. 4 (fall 1992): 86–109.

Zacks, Richard. *Island of Vice: Theodore Roosevelt's Doomed Quest to Clean Up Sin-Loving New York.* New York: Random House, 2012.

Zald, Mayer N., and Patricia Denton, "From Evangelism to General Service: The Transformation of the YMCA" *Administrative Science Quarterly* 8, no. 2 (September 1963): 214–234.

Zurier, Rebecca. *Art for the Masses: A Radical Magazine and Its Graphics, 1911–1917.* Philadelphia: Temple University Press, 1988.

——. *Picturing the City: Urban Vision and the Ashcan School.* Berkeley: University of California Press, 2006.

INDEX

· · · · · · · · · · · ·

Free Speech League, 8, 214, 241, 292, 295, 298,
  309, 341n13, 352n17
Freedman, Estelle, 232
freemasons, 139
French Transatlantic Steam Ship Co., 106
Freshwater, Helen, 322n8, 322n10
Frick, Henry Clay 191, 295
Friedman, Andrea, 354n50
Frisken, Amanda, 60, 329n39, 336n46
Frothingham, Octavius Brooks, 143
Fuller, Loie, 239–240, 241
Fuller, Wayne, 331n69, 350n154

Gaines, Jane, 154
Gaulier, George H., 111–112
George Chamberlain v. John La Farge, 174–177,
  344n48
George Schlegel Lithography Co., 209–210
Gerdts, William H., 164, 343n28, 343n32
Germany, 275
Gérôme, Jean-Léon, 191
Gervex, Henri, 201, 347n112
Gerwitz, Paul, 360n19
Gettysburg, Battle of, 38, 39
Giesberg, Judith, 41
Gilbert, Eliza. *See* Montez, Lola.
Gilbert's Book of Pantomimes, 352n23
Giles, Bertha Edith. *See* Comstock, Bertha.
Gilfoyle, Timothy, 45, 327n93, 337n58, 337n75
Gillers, Stephen, 129
Ginzburg, Ralph, 300, 321n6, 340n134,
  340n143, 340n144, 340n146, 341n2
Gitlow v. New York, 268 U.S. 652 (1925), 34
Glackens, Louis M., 274
Glackens, William, 281
Goldman, Emma, 8, 284, 298, 299, 357n128
Goodyear, Charles, 78
Gordon, Mary, 284
Gordon, Sarah, 345n57
Gould, Jay, 191
Goupil & Cie, 133–134, 191
Grady, Patrick, 335n33
*Grand Fancy Bijou Catalogue of the Sporting
  Man's Emporium*, 80, 103–106, 335n21
Graham, Sylvester, 29
Grant, Ulysses S., 66, 97

Great Awakening, Second, 21
Greek Slave, 28
Greenhill, Jennifer, 236, 347n97, 351n164,
  355n69
Greenwich Village (NY), 257, 297
Grimm v. United States, 156 U.S. 604 (1895),
  213
Gross Clinic, The, 289
Guild, Edward, 110, 335n32
Gunn, Robert, 211

H. A. Thomas & Wylie, 169, 171
Haberle, John, 230–231, 351n164
Hackett, John K., 98, 118, 120–121
Haines, Mary, 52
Haines, William, 52, 97 (as "Haynes")
Haley, Andrew P., 350n152
Hamilton, Jennie (sister-in-law), 50,
  146, 148
Hamilton, Margaret. *See* Comstock,
  Margaret
Hand, Learned, 305–306
Hanse, James, 257
Hapgood, Hutchins, 214
Hardin, Jennifer, 355n67
Harkin, Joseph. *See* Le Beuf, Eugene
Harkness, Herman, 221
Harman, Moses, 126, 338n90
Harper's New Monthly Magazine, 197, 209
Harper's Weekly, 45, 47
Hartford (CT), 22, 26
Hartford Daily Courant, 22
Hartmann, Sadakichi, 299
Havemeyer, Henry Osborne (H.O.), 191
Heap, Chad, 219
Hegger, Frank, 180, 182, 184, 186, 188, 190, 191
Helena Independent, 208
Henri, Robert: 8, 283, 310,130, 357n130; anti-
  censorship attitudes of, 280, 283, 284, 292,
  357nn128; role in the Armory Show, 284, 286
Heptameron, The, 132
Herring, William, 123
Heywood, Angela, 126, 127, 213
Heywood, Ezra: 126, 133, 306, 338n90, 338n93,
  341n13; prosecution for *Cupid's Yokes*,
  128–130